T0332015

Perils of Plenty

Perils of Plenty

Arctic Resource Competition and the Return of the Great Game

JONATHAN N. MARKOWITZ

OXFORD
UNIVERSITY PRESS

Oxford University Press is a department of the University of Oxford. It furthers
the University's objective of excellence in research, scholarship, and education
by publishing worldwide. Oxford is a registered trade mark of Oxford University
Press in the UK and certain other countries.

Published in the United States of America by Oxford University Press
198 Madison Avenue, New York, NY 10016, United States of America.

© Oxford University Press 2020

All rights reserved. No part of this publication may be reproduced, stored in
a retrieval system, or transmitted, in any form or by any means, without the
prior permission in writing of Oxford University Press, or as expressly permitted
by law, by license, or under terms agreed with the appropriate reproduction
rights organization. Inquiries concerning reproduction outside the scope of the
above should be sent to the Rights Department, Oxford University Press, at the
address above.

You must not circulate this work in any other form
and you must impose this same condition on any acquirer.

Library of Congress Cataloging-in-Publication Data
Names: Markowitz, Jonathan N., author.
Title: Perils of plenty : Arctic resource competition and the return of the great game /
Jonathan N. Markowitz.
Other titles: Arctic resource competition and the return of the great game
Description: New York : Oxford University Press, [2020] | Includes
bibliographical references and index.
Identifiers: LCCN 2019052499 (print) | LCCN 2019052500 (ebook) |
ISBN 9780190078249 (hardback) | ISBN 9780190078256 (paperback) |
ISBN 9780190078270 (epub) | ISBN 9780190078287 (online)
Subjects: LCSH: Arctic regions—Strategic aspects. | Arctic regions—Military policy—
Economic aspects. | Energy development—Political aspects—Arctic regions. |
Security, International—Arctic regions. | Geopolitics—Arctic regions.
Classification: LCC UA880 .M38 2020 (print) | LCC UA880 (ebook) |
DDC 333.8/2309113—dc23
LC record available at https://lccn.loc.gov/2019052499
LC ebook record available at https://lccn.loc.gov/2019052500

1 3 5 7 9 8 6 4 2

Paperback printed by LSC Communications, United States of America
Hardback printed by Bridgeport National Bindery, Inc., United States of America

CONTENTS

ACKNOWLEDGMENTS

When I was eighteen, I fell in love with rock climbing. Rock climbing humbled me. I survived only because more skilled people took the time to teach and support me. To the outsider, climbing may look like a solo endeavor, but the reality is no one reaches the summit alone. The more difficult the climb, the more support and skill you need. This project has been my longest and most challenging climb. I would not have reached the summit without mentors who gave me the skills I needed to survive and a team that supported me through every crux and challenge.

This project began nearly a decade ago, when I was a graduate student at the University of California San Diego. In the winter of 2009, I came to my adviser, David Lake, and told him that I had found the mountain I wanted to climb. I wanted to explain why states projected power to secure control over resources, and I wanted to use Arctic climate change as a natural experiment to test my theory. At the time, there were few people working on power projection and even fewer working on the Arctic. Spending years focusing on a region and issue that few people cared about was risky, and many advisers would have stopped me. Instead, David supported my choice, acting as a wise and patient mentor. Erik Gartzke also played a key role in training me, shaping my thinking, and encouraging me to dream big. I was also fortunate to have the generous support and guidance of the other members of my committee—Miles Kahler, Tai Ming Cheung, and Susan Shirk.

Always a careful scholar, David Lake taught me to take the time to get things right. To acquire the specialized knowledge and training my research demanded, I spent two years as a National Science Foundation Integrative Graduate Education and Research Traineeship fellow at Scripps Institution of Oceanography (SIO), training with the world's leading climate scientists. Many conversations with climatologists, oceanographers, and geologists at SIO helped me gain traction on the science underpinning the processes that spurred resource competition in the Arctic. I spent the final two years of my Ph.D. as a predoctoral fellow at the Belfer Center's Geopolitics of Energy Project. Interacting with the scholars and policymakers at Belfer helped shape my thinking about the interactions between environmental change, social science, and public policy. I am particularly grateful to Kelly Greenhill, Sean Lynn Jones, Steve Walt, Steve Miller, Meghan O'Sullivan, and the members of my cohort who provided feedback on the initial stages of this project.

After finishing my dissertation, I arrived at the Dickey Center and the Institute for Arctic Studies at Dartmouth as a postdoc. It felt a little like reaching base camp—the beginning, not the end, of the journey. Given the interdisciplinary nature of my work, it was wonderful to be surrounded by Arctic researchers, historians, economists, and political scientists. I am especially grateful to Jennifer Lind, Daryl Press, Ben Valentino, Bill Wohlforth, Stephen Brooks, Michelle Murray, Michelle Reeves, Benny Miller, Jeff Friedman, and Brian Greenhill, who all provided detailed feedback on what would become the theory chapter of this book.

I departed Dartmouth to start my job at the University of Southern California (USC), eager to begin my ascent. I was well aware that the toughest climbing lay ahead. I knew that my plan of attack was ambitious and that I would need to build an entire research lab to gather the data to make this plan a reality. Shortly after arriving at USC, I began to build my team, cofounding the Security and Political Economy (SPEC) Lab alongside Ben Graham. We were later joined by Megan Becker, as our third principal investigator (PI), and then by Kelly Zvobgo, our lab director. Collaborating with the incredible students in our lab has been the most rewarding part of this project. While there isn't enough space to thank all of them here, a few people in particular who went above and beyond deserve special recognition.

Jacob Tucker and Therese Anders helped to design and write the codebooks for the Arctic military activity event data set, analyzed data, and came up with creative ways to present them visually. Anbar Aizenman, Lauren Cholakian, and Jordan Lee collected and coded thousands of documents. Gavin Michaels, Isabelle Nazha, Srividya Dasaraju, Tyler Gallagher, Shawn Anderson, Nick Tinoco, Johanna Reyes Ortega, Evgeniia Iakhnis, and Stephanie Kang each spent hundreds of hours sifting through documents and gathering qualitative evidence. Lindsay Lauder and Grace Bandeen, a dynamic Canadian duo, troubleshot intractable problems and relentlessly tracked down and double-checked obscure details about Arctic bases, ice-capable ships, and deployments.

The entire lab system would not function without the dedicated efforts of the Arctic team leaders, Alex Bosch and Madison Seeley, who energetically motivated their teammates and managed the massive amount of data they generated. Jocelyn Zhao, Mia Rudd, and Phuong Nguyen kept the lab functioning and preserved my sanity by handling all manner of organizational tasks as lab administrators. Sarah Orsborn wrote, directed, and produced a short trailer and an explainer video for the book, which were both animated and edited by Cameron Kostopoulos. Miriam Barnum helped edit and prepare two revision memos. Douglas Luo, Ryan Barr, and Clara Parkus worked tirelessly to fact-check, copy edit, and prepare the final manuscript. The energy and excitement these students brought to the project was a source of inspiration and motivation. This book is as much theirs as it is mine, and I could not have done it without them. I may be the sole author, but this book is a SPEC Lab product.

This project also benefited from the generosity of my colleagues. First, I am especially grateful to Dave Kang and Pat James, who offered their sage advice and support each step of the way. When I arrived at USC, Pat was assigned to be my faculty mentor. He was always there to help me no matter how big or small the question. Pat read the entire manuscript and provided detailed feedback on each chapter. As someone who works on the Arctic himself and a Canadian with deep expertise on Ottawa's foreign policy, his perspective was particularly valuable. Like a good coach, Dave Kang kept me focused and made sure that I took time off and didn't over-train. Later, when we became co-PIs of the USC US–Asia Grand Strategy Program, Dave selflessly insisted on shouldering the administrative burdens, allowing me to focus on my scholarship. Dave is a role model, both as a researcher and as a leader in building inclusive institutions to train and support young scholars. I am especially grateful to him for organizing my book workshop at the USC Center for International Studies (CIS) and for his focused and insightful feedback.

In addition to Pat and Dave, I have many other wonderful colleagues who, through their kindness, generosity, and insight, left their fingerprints on this manuscript. Brian Rathbun, Saori Katada, Brett Carter, Erin Baggott-Carter, Therese Anders, Xinru Ma, and Andrew Bertoli all read the entire manuscript and attended my book workshop at CIS to provide me with detailed feedback. Brian made many helpful suggestions about framing and, perhaps more importantly, urged me to keep the analogy of addiction and the name Rent-Addiction Theory. Saori suggested a number of helpful works to draw on from International Political Economy and provided especially helpful guidance when it came to choosing between publishers. Andrew Bertoli, James Lo, Nick Weller, and Pablo Barbera all provided helpful suggestions about the research design. The chapter on Russia was improved greatly by the many discussions I had with Bryn Rosenfeld and Rob English. I also benefited in many ways from Steve Lamy's deep Arctic expertise and contacts; in particular, I was able to present my work at a conference that Steve hosted at USC. My work was also enriched by interactions with Lassi Heininen during his frequent trips to USC to visit Steve and Rob. While we often did not agree, I always appreciated Lassi's willingness to engage with my work.

Outside USC, this project was improved tremendously by feedback from a number of scholars. First, I am deeply indebted to those who read my entire book manuscript and attended one of several manuscript review workshops. This project was motivated by these scholars' work, and it was an honor to engage with them about my research. Michael Horowitz and Patrick McDonald attended the first workshop, held at CIS. Mike and Pat operated as a team, carefully working over the manuscript and brainstorming constructive and actionable feedback that helped me to streamline the argument and the presentation of the evidence.

The second workshop was hosted and generously funded by David Lake at UC San Diego and attended by Jeff Frieden, Ben Fordham, Peter Gourevitch, Andrew Coe, and Erik Gartzke. Jeff selflessly read the entire manuscript multiple times and made particularly insightful suggestions about how to clarify the role of path dependency in the theory chapter. Ben leveraged his deep expertise on American foreign policy to improve the chapter on the United States. Peter applied his nearly half-century of wisdom to help frame the project and its wider contribution. Andrew and Erik offered a number of suggestions to clarify the theory and address alternative explanations.

Finally, Steve Brooks and Bill Wohlforth graciously invited me back to Dartmouth for a mini–book workshop, during which they not only gave me detailed notes but also helped me think through how to address the feedback I had received at the previous workshops. Steve and Bill not only read the manuscript but even read certain chapters multiple times. In particular, Bill deserves credit for the book's title, and I am deeply indebted to Steve for his guidance on approaching publishers.

I also want to express gratitude to a number of other people and institutions that provided feedback on this project. Paul Poast, Paul Huth, John Vasquez, Marina Henke, Patricia Sullivan, Eugene Gholz, Steve Oliver, Paul Avey, Michael Beckley, Emily Meierding, Yon Lupu, and Ed Mansfield all provided detailed written comments on the theory. I would also like to thank a number of Arctic experts, including Rob Huebert, Lassi Heininen, Oran Young, Katarzyna Zysk, Jon Rahbek-Clemmensen, and Elana Wilson Rowe, for their detailed feedback, which greatly improved the empirical chapters. I am especially grateful to Elana for organizing a panel at the 2018 Arctic Circle Conference around my research on 2007 as a pivotal year in Arctic politics. Elana also read much of the manuscript and provided especially helpful suggestions regarding the chapter on Russia. Finally, I want to thank the participants in several panels at the annual meetings of the International Studies Association and the American Political Science Association, as well as attendees at seminars at Northwestern, Texas A&M, Dartmouth, Harvard, Yale-NUS, George Washington, and Vanderbilt.

At Oxford University Press, David McBride and Emily Mackenzie were wonderful to work with and helped shepherd the manuscript through the publication process. I owe a debt of gratitude to both David and the reviewers for helping to improve the final manuscript. I would also like to thank John Haslam at Cambridge University Press. Unfortunately, one can only publish a book with one press; and making this choice was difficult, in large part because John was so wonderful to work with. I would also like to thank my copy editor, Vicki Rosenzweig, who meticulously edited and fact-checked every page and footnote twice.

A number of institutions provided generous financial support for my research, including the USC Center for International Studies, the USC Zumberge Research and Innovation Fund, and the Charles Koch Foundation.

Next, I would like to thank my collaborators. Ben Graham, Blake McMahon, Chris Farris, Daniel Enemark, and Megan Becker have been on this journey with me since graduate school. Later, I was lucky enough to find Paul Avey, Rob Reardon, Andrew Coe, Suzy Caldwell, and Therese Anders. No one has endured more arguments or shaped my thinking more than these scholars. These are the people I call when I want to bounce ideas off of someone, and they have been my greatest source of inspiration.

A few especially close friends deserve special recognition for their contribution to this book. Chris, Therese, and Dan spent hundreds of hours helping me think through the research design and measurement strategy. Andrew not only read the entire manuscript but good-naturedly endured countless revisions and conversations aimed at refining and clarifying the theory. But no one has sacrificed more or put more of their own sweat into this book than Ben and Megan. They read, edited, and helped me to revise every chapter through three full drafts. I consulted them on every step of this project, and their insights can be found all over the manuscript. Too many times, they prioritized this book over their own work and put my well-being ahead of their own. I will be forever grateful for their sacrifices and support.

Finally, and most importantly, I would like to thank my family, whose love and warmth sustained me on the darkest, coldest days, when it felt like I might never reach the summit. My sister Sarah and brother-in-law Joe were endlessly understanding when I had to work through the holidays and were there to cheer me on every step of the way. My aunt Celia read early drafts of several chapters and offered much needed encouragement, along with my uncle Doug. And I will never forget that my uncle Alan was the one who taught me how to write.

My greatest debt is to my parents, who have spent thirty-five years caring for, supporting, and inspiring me. My father, Michell, has been my closest counselor; and I have relied on his wisdom to guide and reassure me through each harrowing pitch of the climb. My mom, Minh, has been my great inspiration; and her experiences gave my life and work purpose. In many ways, I made the climb for her. In 1975, my mother's home country of South Vietnam was conquered, and her family was ripped away from her through the ruthless projection of military power. It is because of her experiences that I study the causes of coercion and conquest.

This book is dedicated to my mother and father, who inspired me to climb the mountain, and to my best friend, Ben, and my wife, Megan, who, more than anyone, helped me reach the top.

Introduction

1.1 Introduction

In 1900, the world's population was approximately 1.6 billion. Today, it has exploded to more than 7 billion and is projected to grow to over 10 billion.[1] This has led to fears of a vicious cycle in which increased demand and consumption causes the supply of many resources to dwindle, while also exacerbating climate change. Some warn of a return to the Great Game, in which states scrambled for resources.[2] Resource competition has been intense in the past, often fueling conflict between states. What will the future hold? Are we entering a new era of the Great Game?

In this book, I find that the pessimists who predict a future full of "resource wars," such as Klare, and the optimists who think the era of territorial conquest is behind us, such as Rosecrance and Brooks, are both wrong.[3] Some states will compete over territory and resources, but others will not. This book's thesis turns conventional wisdom on its head, arguing that variation in states' willingness to project military force is driven not by resource *scarcity* but by *abundance*. More specifically, it is states with abundant resources, which become economically *dependent* on the rents these resources generate, that have the strongest preference for controlling additional resources.

This book's core argument is that what states make influences what they *want* to take. More precisely, the source of a state's wealth conditions its foreign policy preferences. I argue that production-oriented states that generate income primarily

[1] United Nations, Department of Economic and Social Affairs, Population Division, *World Population Prospects: The 2015 Revision, Key Findings and Advance Tables* (New York: United Nations Department of Economic and Social Affairs, Population Division, 2015).

[2] Michael Klare, *Rising Powers, Shrinking Planet: The New Geopolitics of Energy* (London: Metropolitan Books, 2008), 87–115.

[3] Stephen Brooks, *Producing Security: Multinational Corporations, Globalization, and the Changing Calculus of Conflict* (Princeton, NJ: Princeton University Press, 2005); Richard N. Rosecrance, *The Rise of the Trading State: Commerce and Conquest in the Modern World* (New York, NY: Basic Books, 1986); Klare, *Rising Powers, Shrinking Planet.*

Perils of Plenty. Jonathan N. Markowitz, Oxford University Press (2020). © Oxford University Press.
DOI: 10.1093/oso/9780190078249.001.0001

by *making* goods and services have less interest in *taking* territory and resources. In contrast, land-oriented states that extract their income from the control of territory and resources have a stronger preference to secure control over territory. For a given state, democratic institutions reduce the value of the political benefits associated with resource rents, but land-oriented democracies still want territory more than production-oriented democracies. This book's key proposition is that *the more resource-dependent a state is, the stronger its preference for projecting power to seek control over resource rents*.

To evaluate this proposition, I use a novel natural experiment in which a sudden exogenous shock driven by climate change resulted in rapidly melting ice and the revelation of resources on the bottom of the Arctic Ocean floor. This shock emerged as a modern version of the "discovery" of the New World by Spanish explorers in the late fifteenth century. This "discovery" opened vast riches to Europeans who had the financial backing, technology, and will to project power across the ocean and extract wealth from the "virgin" territory.

Today, we face another New World: the Arctic and its ocean floor. In the summer of 2007, a shocking sight greeted North Pole observers: where for hundreds of years there had been thick sheets of solid ice, there was now pristine open ocean. It was the largest Arctic ice loss in human history and was not predicted by even the most aggressive climate models.[4] Earlier that year, the Intergovernmental Panel on Climate Change predicted the Arctic would not be ice-free until 2100, igniting a debate among scientists over whether existing models had been too conservative.[5] As scientists and governments argued, nature acted. Climate change rapidly uncovered a vast stock of energy resources with the potential to shift the global distribution of wealth and power.

A perfect storm of exogenous factors beyond the control of individual states—climate change and quantum leaps in energy exploration and deep-sea drilling technology—dramatically increased both the value and the accessibility of Arctic seabed resources. The United States Geological Survey estimates that 30% of the world's natural gas reserves are in the

---

[4] For more on the relationship between climate change and Arctic sea ice change, see Christophe Kinnard et al., "Reconstructed Changes in Arctic Sea Ice over the Past 1,450 Years," *Nature* 479, no. 7374 (2011): 357.

[5] Intergovernmental Panel on Climate Change, ed., *Climate Change 2007: The Physical Science Basis. Contribution of Working Group I to the Fourth Assessment Report of the Intergovernmental Panel on Climate Change* (Cambridge: Cambridge University Press, 2007); Muyin Wang and James E. Overland, "A Sea Ice Free Summer Arctic within 30 Years?," *Geophysical Research Letters* 36, no. 7 (2009): L07502, https://doi.org/10.1029/2009GL037820; Julienne Stroeve et al., "Arctic Sea Ice Decline: Faster than Forecast," *Geophysical Research Letters* 34, no. 9 (2007): L09501; Muyin Wang and James E. Overland, "A Sea Ice Free Summer Arctic within 30 Years: An Update from CMIP5 Models: SUMMER ARCTIC SEA ICE," *Geophysical Research Letters* 39, no. 18 (2012): L18501, https://doi.org/10.1029/2012GL052868.

Arctic.[6] Nearly 80% of these resources are offshore in or beyond states' exclusive economic zones (EEZs), where states have competing claims of ownership. As in the 1500s, the possibility of vast riches drove governments to contemplate investing in projecting power to the ends of the earth. The competition for Arctic resources represents a microcosm of a much larger phenomenon that has driven politics since the Agrarian Revolution: the competition to control land and extract wealth from it.

Five states border the Arctic Ocean and can legally make claims over these newly exposed offshore resources: the United States, Canada, Denmark, Russia, and Norway. How did these states react to this opportunity? Did they, like the empires of the past, rush to project power into this new world? Contrary to sensationalist news accounts, most Arctic states chose *not* to "scramble for Arctic resources." The United States, Canada, and Denmark have been relatively reluctant to project power into the Arctic or build the Arctic ships, bases, and specialized military units that would be required to do so in the future. The United States' response was so tepid, in fact, that it was dubbed "the reluctant Arctic power."[7] In contrast, Russia invested more than any other state in increasing its Arctic military presence recently, deploying bombers, submarines, and surface ships to the Arctic for the first time since the end of the Cold War. Moscow also poured billions of dollars into upgrading its Arctic force structure, acquiring nuclear-powered icebreakers and specialized Arctic military units, and refurbishing long-abandoned Arctic bases. Similarly, Norway, one of the least powerful and most democratic Arctic states, made the Arctic its top foreign policy priority, investing more in building and projecting power into the High North than any other state except Russia.

Thus, variation in the willingness of Arctic states to project power cannot be explained solely by relative power, regime type, or geographic factors, such as the size of each state's Arctic coastline or EEZ or its relative distance from Arctic resources. Conventional wisdom and previous research suggest that resource insecurity or scarcity, both within and between states, drives states to use their militaries to gain direct control over stocks of resources.[8] However, the exposure of Arctic resources resulted in greater resource abundance, not scarcity; and states that were among the most resource-rich and resource-secure were the most willing to deploy military force to bargain over Arctic oil and gas.

---

[6] US Geological Survey, "90 Billion Barrels of Oil and 1,670 Trillion Cubic Feet of National Gas Assessed in the Arctic," podcast, produced by Jessica Robertson, July 23, 2008, https://archive.usgs.gov/archive/sites/www.usgs.gov/newsroom/article.asp-ID=1980.html; Donald L. Gautier et al., "Assessment of Undiscovered Oil and Gas in the Arctic," *Science* 324, no. 5931 (2009): 1175–79, https://doi.org/10.1126/science.1169467.

[7] Rob Huebert, *United States Arctic Policy: The Reluctant Arctic Power,* University of Calgary, School of Public Policy, University of Calgary Publications Series 2, no. 2 (May 2009).

[8] Thomas F. Homer-Dixon, "Environmental Scarcities and Violent Conflict: Evidence from Cases," *International Security* 19, no. 1 (1994): 5–40; John Orme, "The Utility of Force in a World of Scarcity," *International Security* 22, no. 3 (1997): 138–67.

This empirical pattern suggests a puzzle that cannot be explained by existing theories: why are certain states more willing than others to project power to secure control over territory and resources? This puzzle motivates the primary research question: why do some states have a stronger preference than others to project power to secure control over territory and resources as a source of rents and wealth?

Consistent with my theoretical predictions, I find that the most resource-dependent states are also the most likely to project power to secure control over Arctic energy resources. These findings directly contradict sensationalist accounts which suggested that all Arctic nations are scrambling to secure control over resources. My findings also offer a correction to those who suggest Arctic resources have played no role in motivating states to invest in projecting power to the region. The truth is that only some states have chosen to back their claims by projecting military force and that those most willing to do so were the most economically dependent on resource rents.

1.2 Theory in a Nutshell

The purpose of this book is to develop and test a theory that explains why some states have a stronger preference for projecting military power to seek territory as a source of wealth and rents. For this purpose, I develop Rent-Addiction Theory, which deductively identifies states' interests ex ante, allowing me to explain and generate predictions about which states will have revisionist or greedy preferences over territory and resources. My core dependent variable, or outcome of interest, is the degree to which a state invests in pursuing an *exclusionary foreign policy*, defined as the projection of power to seek the economic benefits associated with the control of territory. *Power projection* is defined as the deployment of military force beyond a state's borders.

My core proposition is *the more a state depends economically on extracting income from land, the more it will invest in projecting power to secure territory and resources.* This proposition rests on two core claims. First, states are governed by regimes that seek income in order to remain in power, and there are two sources of income for the regime and its governing coalition (i.e., the group of individuals a regime relies on to stay in power): profits from producing goods and services and rents extracted from the control of territory. States whose economies are largely structured to extract rents from resources have *land-oriented* economies. States that rely on producing goods and services have *production-oriented* economies. Second, the more land-oriented a state is, the higher the regime's returns from securing resources and, subsequently, the stronger its preference for doing so. This effect is moderated by democratic political institutions, which reduce the political benefits a regime gains from resource rents. However, land-oriented democratic states have a stronger preference for territory than production-oriented democracies.

Thus, a regime's preference for resources is influenced by two key independent variables: the state's *economic structure* and its *domestic political institutions*. The economic structure of the state, and more specifically the degree to which the economy is structured to generate income from resources, affects the government's preferences through two causal pathways. First, economic structure conditions the state's source of income and the rate of return from investing in securing resources versus producing goods and services. Second, economic structure influences the degree to which the state's governing coalition is composed of and captured by individuals or organizations from the resource sector of the economy. Each of these pathways is briefly outlined in this section.

The first is a *path-dependent* economic effect that results from factor endowments and prior investment choices that determine the degree to which the economy is land- or production-oriented (i.e., the degree to which the economy is structured to generate income from land as opposed to producing goods and services). Each dollar spent on structuring the economy to extract resources by investing in oil and gas wells, refineries, and pipelines is a dollar not spent on production sector–specific assets, such as schools, research and development, manufacturing facilities, and institutions to enforce property rights. These policies lead to an underdeveloped production sector that lacks the assets necessary to be competitive in global markets. This drives up the cost of substitution as the regime must first pay high switching costs associated with investing in the infrastructure, education, and subsidies necessary to make the production sector competitive. This delays the time until profits are generated by years or even decades. The higher the switching costs and the longer the time until returns can be generated from production, the stronger the regime's preference to continue investing in generating income by extracting rent from territory.

The second is a political effect that results from prior choices that influence the *composition* of the state's governing coalition. The more a state's economy is structured to generate income from land, the more likely its governing coalition is to be composed of and captured by those who depend economically on the land-oriented sector. The governing coalition creates rules that shift political power and economic benefits toward themselves and away from their political opponents. They reinvest income from land into consolidating political power, restricting the power and economic productivity of the political opposition, thus solidifying their control over the state.[9] The more the governing coalition is composed of and captured by individuals with land-oriented economic interests, the stronger the regime's preference for investing in securing territory to serve its interests.

---

[9] Kenneth L. Sokoloff and Stanley L. Engerman, "History Lessons: Institutions, Factors Endowments, and Paths of Development in the New World," *Journal of Economic Perspectives* 14, no. 3 (2000): 217–32.

Domestic political institutions influence the regime's preference for territory through a third causal pathway: they condition the regime's value for the political benefits associated with land rents. Compared to the profits from producing goods and services, land rents are easier for a regime to monopolize control over and deny to the political opposition. All regimes should value these political benefits, but autocrats should value them more. Autocratic political institutions generate stronger incentives for the ruler to monopolize control over the country's income in order to monopolize political power. The more a regime values these benefits, the less willing it will be to move investment away from land. Doing so would reduce its control over the state's income and, thus, increase its risk of losing power. In short, the more autocratic a state's domestic institutions, the stronger the value to the regime of the political benefits associated with land rents and, thus, the stronger its preference for territory.

To sum up, state preferences are a function of regime preferences. These are, in turn, influenced by the state's economic structure and domestic political institutions. The more land-oriented a state's economy, the higher the rate of return from investing in securing territory relative to producing goods and, thus, the stronger the regime's preferences for territory. This effect is conditioned by the domestic political institutions of the state. The less autocratic a state is, the less it should value the political benefits of land rents. However, even democratic land-oriented states should have a stronger preference for territory than production-oriented democracies. In sum, a state's economic structure and domestic political institutions have both a conditional and an independent effect on the regime's preference for territory. The stronger the regime's preference for territory, the more it should invest in securing control over territory.

1.2.1 Theoretical and Empirical Contribution

My theory and findings contribute to three research areas which are central to international relations scholarship and policy. First, international relations, as a field, lacks a comprehensive theory that explains why some states have a stronger preference for territory than others. Although most scholars agree that states seek to survive, there is intense debate over why some have more revisionist, greedy, or aggressive foreign policy preferences, especially with regard to territory.[10] By incorporating insights from theories of the rent-seeking state and the resource curse, I develop a theory that explains the formation of a state's preference for territory. In doing so, I shed new light on how states' economic interests condition their foreign

---

[10] See Charles L. Glaser, *Rational Theory of International Politics* (Princeton, NJ: Princeton University Press, 2010); James D. Fearon, "Two States, Two Types, Two Actions," *Security Studies* 20, no. 3 (2011): 437–38.

policy preferences in terms of territory and resources and why this interest endures even after revolutions and changes in the state's leadership and domestic political institutions.[11]

Second, my theory has implications for two related debates, namely whether conquest still pays and why territorial conflict has declined. Each of these debates has important real-world ramifications: whether peace is here to stay or whether states are likely to compete over territory and resources in the future.[12] Research suggests that economic development and globalization have decreased the gains from securing control over territory, which explains why conquest no longer pays. While the gains from territorial control are generally decreasing, these explanations cannot account for why some states have a stronger preference to capture these gains than others. Rent-Addiction Theory, as put forward in this book, offers such an explanation and challenges the conventional wisdom that economic development and trade generally reduce a state's incentive to engage in territorial conquest.[13] Critically, under certain conditions, increased development and trade may *increase* a state's interest in conquest. My theory implies that the relationship between trade, development, and peace is conditioned by the source of that trade and development. Specifically, if a state's economic development is driven by resource extraction and export, then increased development and trade may increase, rather than decrease, the state's desire to secure control over territory. This suggests that certain states, such as Russia, Iraq, and Iran, which pursued development paths that made them more economically dependent on territory, also have a stronger preference to secure territory than states whose economies are based on the production of goods and services.

My theory also provides an explanation for why large-scale territorial conquest has declined.[14] I contend that the majority of the world's most powerful states are

[11] Jeffry A. Frieden, "International Investment and Colonial Control: A New Interpretation," *International Organization* 48, no. 4 (1994): 559–93; Benjamin O. Fordham, "Economic Interests, Party, and Ideology in Early Cold War Era US Foreign Policy," *International Organization* 52, no. 2 (1998): 359–96; Patrick J. McDonald, *The Invisible Hand of Peace: Capitalism, The War Machine, and International Relations Theory* (New York: Cambridge University Press, 2009); Stephen G. Brooks, "Economic Actors' Lobbying Influence on the Prospects for War and Peace," *International Organization* 67, no. 4 (2013): 863–88, https://doi.org/10.1017/S0020818313000283.

[12] Peter Liberman, *Does Conquest Pay?: The Exploitation of Occupied Industrial Societies* (Princeton, NJ: Princeton University Press, 1996); Stephen Brooks, "The Globalization of Production and the Changing Benefits of Conquest," *Journal of Conflict Resolution* 43, no. 5 (1999): 646–70; Eugene Gholz, "Globalization, Systems Integration, and the Future of Great Power War," *Security Studies* 16, no. 4 (2007): 615–36.

[13] Rosecrance, *Rise of the Trading State*; Carl Kaysen, "Is War Obsolete?: A Review Essay," *International Security* 14, no. 4 (1990): 42–64; Brooks, *Producing Security*.

[14] Note that scholars such as Altman have found that while large-scale territorial conquest has declined, small-scale conquest is still alive and well. See Dan Altman, "By Fait Accompli, Not Coercion: How States Wrest Territory from Their Adversaries," *International Studies Quarterly* 61, no. 4 (2017): 881–91; and "The Evolution of Territorial Conquest after 1945 and the Limits of the

no longer interested in investing in and acquiring wealth through conquest because they are no longer economically dependent on territory. Because these states have little interest in conquest themselves and have much to lose if others engage in conquest, they have coordinated in enforcing a norm against territorial aggrandizement.[15] This has largely deterred states that are still economically dependent on territory from acting on their preferences. Thus, if the United States decides to pull back and no longer enforce this norm, the level of territorial conflict may increase, especially in regions populated by resource-dependent states, such as the Middle East, central Asia, and Africa.

Third, my theory informs the prospects for militarized territorial and resource competition in the future. Rent-Addiction Theory provides an explanation for why, even in an era in which states can obtain resources by simply buying them on open markets, some states may still prefer to conquer them. If we treat resources as a source of rents, rather than as inputs to economic growth or military power, we are better able to explain why states choose to take resources rather than buy them. Viewed through the lens of rent-seeking, conquest is a competition over *resource rents*—economic benefits derived from the control of territory—that can be controlled and extracted using military force. Liberals are right that, during peacetime, capturing resources to ensure access makes little sense as it will nearly always be cheaper to buy rather than take. However, if states are not seeking access but control, open markets will not deliver those benefits. This casts resource competition as not just a struggle over inputs but also one over the control of future revenue. The problem for these states is not that they have too few resources but that their dependency on natural resources drives them to invest in seeking more resources, rather than pursuing other means of generating wealth. The same logic applies to agrarian empires of the past. Their challenge was not that they lacked agrarian land but rather that their economy depended on extracting land rents, making conquest a more attractive way to secure more wealth.

My theory challenges the conventional wisdom that increased development and trade necessarily decrease a state's interest in conquest.[16] I distinguish economic

---

Norm of Territorial Integrity," September 24, 2019, http://www.danielwaltman.com/uploads/3/2/3/1/32312379/evolution_of_territorial_conquest.pdf. Wallensteen and Pettersson find that, while the number of interstate conflicts has dramatically declined in the twenty-first century, there are still a significant number of active intrastate conflicts, many of which are motivated by control over territory. See Thérése Pettersson and Peter Wallensteen, "Armed Conflicts, 1946–2014," *Journal of Peace Research* 52, no. 4 (2015): 537. My theory has implications for some of these conflicts, such as those in Sudan and South Sudan that are discussed in the concluding chapter.

[15] For a related argument that examines how increasing economic productivity has decreased incentives for conquest and increased states' willingness to enforce the norms against territorial conquest, see Andrew J. Coe and Jonathan N. Markowitz, "Crude Calculations: When Does Conquest Pay?" (paper presented at the 76th Annual MPSA Conference, Chicago, April 5–8, 2018).

[16] On this point, see Jeff Colgan, "Fueling the Fire: Pathways from Oil to War," *International Security*, 38, no. 2 (2013a): 147–80; Erik Gartzke and Dominic Rohner, "Prosperous Pacifists: The Effects of

structure from economic development. *Economic structure* captures a country's source of wealth and its dependence on that source, while *economic development* captures the accumulation of wealth. My theory suggests that the degree to which trade and development reduce a state's interest in conquest hinges on the source of that trade and development. If development is driven by extracting and exporting primary commodities (i.e., agricultural products and natural resources), increased development and trade may result in states having more, rather than less, interest in securing control over territory.

Critically, my theory suggests that, so long as states derive their income primarily from extracting commodities from land, they will continue to have a stronger preference to seek territory, even if they are economically developed and trade-oriented. Thus, in states where the extraction of resource rents is the principal source of income, economic development has the potential to escalate geopolitical and military competition both within and between states.[17] However, in regions where states are largely democratic and do not depend on land rents, economic development should not be associated with increased military competition. This suggests that the potential for resource competition is real but limited and that such competition is most likely when states are economically dependent on extracting wealth from territory.

These theoretically guided insights into how states' economic interests shape their foreign policy goals have implications for understanding the link between climate change and international security. As climate change makes resources in regions like the Arctic accessible for extraction, it is critical for policymakers to anticipate whether states will only use international law to bargain over these resources or will also back their claims with military force. My theory suggests that while the prospects for militarized resource competition are real, they will be limited to autocratic states that are more economically dependent on resource rents, such as Russia, and, to a lesser extent, democratic states with resource-based economies, such as Norway. Beyond the Arctic, resource competition will be most likely in regions where states are more dependent on resource rents, such as the Middle East and sub-Saharan Africa. The implications for conflict in these regions are discussed in the concluding chapter.

1.3 Three Sets of Prior Explanations

Having summarized my own theory and its contribution to international relations scholarship and policy, I now briefly outline three sets of prior explanations. I discuss how my theory is different and why it offers a more compelling explanation of

Development on Initiators and Targets of Territorial Conflict" (IEW Working Papers 500, Institute for Empirical Research in Economics, University of Zurich, Zurich, Switzerland, 2011a).

[17] On this point, see Colgan, "Fueling the Fire"; Gartzke and Rohner, "Prosperous Pacifists."

why some states invest more in projecting power to secure control over resources and territory by looking specifically at the Arctic. In addition to these general international relations theories, there are a number of Arctic-specific alternative explanations; I address these in the research design chapter and in my cases.

1.3.1 Power, Plenty, and Profits

The first set of explanations of why and when states compete over resources focuses on three independent variables—power, plenty, and profits.[18] Power is used as a supply-side and demand-side explanation for state resource competition. Supply-side explanations suggest that the most powerful states should be the most likely to project power to secure access to or control over resources.[19] In contrast, demand-side explanations contend that states fight over control of resources because the resources enhance their ability to generate power[20]; states may also work to keep resources out of the hands of other states in order to prevent a shift in the distribution of power.[21] This is closely tied to the concept of plenty: if resources are plentiful, states will have less incentive to fight. However, if resources are scarce globally or if individual states are resource-insecure, they will have stronger incentives to fight over control.[22] Finally, profits-based explanations suggest that states fight over resources because they seek profits or rents.

Collectively, these supply- and demand-side explanations determine the payoff that states expect from competing over resources. By informing our understanding of the factors that influence the expected gains from resource competition, these theories make predictions about when states should be more or less likely to compete over resources.

However, these theories are incomplete as they cannot explain why some states have stronger or weaker preferences to capture resource gains. Climate change has dramatically increased the expected gains associated with gaining control over Arctic resources. Yet, as Table 1.1 demonstrates, these prior theories alone cannot explain why some states invested in projecting power to compete over these gains while others did not.

---

[18] For an excellent literature review, see Jeff Colgan, "Oil and Revolutionary Governments: Fuel for International Conflict," *International Organization* 64, no. 4 (2010): 661–94, https://doi.org/10.1017/S002081831000024X.

[19] Hans J. Morgenthau, *Politics among Nations: The Struggle for Power and Peace* (New York: Knopf, 1948), 133.

[20] John Mearsheimer, *The Tragedy of Great Power Politics* (New York: W. W. Norton & Company, 2001), 150.

[21] See Daryl G. Press, *Calculating Credibility: How Leaders Assess Military Threats* (Ithaca, NY: Cornell University Press, 2005), 27; Morgenthau, *Politics among Nations*, 133.

[22] Michael Klare, *Resource Wars: The New Landscape of Global Conflict* (New York: Henry Holt, 2001).

Table 1.1 **Prior Theories of Resource Competition**

Independent Variable	Condition	Expected Arctic Outcome	Can It Explain Arctic Resource Competition?
Power — Supply side	The more powerful the state, the more willing it will be to project power.	The United States projects the most power relative to ability.	No; the United States projects the least power.
Power — Demand side	If resources shift the distribution of power, states will have stronger incentives to compete.	The United States projects the most power relative to ability.	No; the United States projects the least power.
Plenty	The more resources a state has, the weaker its incentive to compete over resources.	Russia and Norway project the least power relative to ability.	No; Russia and Norway project the most power.
Profits	The larger the profits, the stronger states' incentives to compete over their control.	All states invest heavily in projecting power.	No; only some states invest heavily in projecting power.
My theory	The more resource-dependent the state, the stronger its preference to compete over resources.	Norway and Russia project the most relative to ability; Canada, Denmark, and the United States project the least.	Yes.

1.3.2 Resource-Dependent States and Foreign Policy Aggression

While this first set of prior explanations focuses on resources as a source of competition, other scholars, such as Colgan, consider resource dependence as a driver of conflict. Colgan suggests that resource-dependent states and, specifically, petrostates have a stronger preference for aggression and therefore tend to be more violent but only if they are revolutionary states.[23] One might reasonably conclude that my theory and Colgan's are similar in that both focus on the degree to which the

---

[23] Jeff Colgan, *Petro-Aggression: When Oil Causes War* (Cambridge: Cambridge University Press, 2013b).

state is economically dependent on resources and both are interested in explaining variation in states' foreign policy preferences.

However, our theories differ in two crucial aspects, which have important implications for their explanatory power. First, Colgan's theory is designed to explain why states have "aggressive foreign policy preferences" more broadly, where aggression is a means rather than an end. Thus, Colgan's theory may explain why some states use more or less aggression but does not explain the objectives they will pursue. Given that I am interested in explaining why states project power to pursue certain objectives, I focus on explaining why some states have a stronger preference for certain foreign policy objectives, such as the acquisition of territory.

Second, Colgan's theory is unable to explain why nonrevolutionary petro-states, such as Russia and Norway, have pursued more aggressive foreign policies and invested heavily in securing control over resource-rich territory. In contrast, my theory suggests that it is not whether a state is governed by revolutionary leaders but rather whether it is economically dependent on territory that matters. If states remain economically dependent on territory, they will continue to have a strong preference for territory, regardless of their leadership. Thus, my theory explains not only why some Arctic states have a stronger preference for territory than others but also why petro-states in the Middle East have invested so heavily in projecting power and competing over territory even when they were not governed by revolutionary leaders.

1.3.3 The Trading State and the Decline of Territorial Conquest

The third set of prior explanations relates to work on the commercial peace. Rosecrance and other scholars who contributed to the commercial peace research agenda suggest that trade and development cause states to become less dependent on territory and therefore less interested in fighting over it.[24] According to Rosecrance, trading states seek wealth from trade, not land, and are therefore no longer interested in territory. Thus, one might think that Rosecrance has already explained why states are no longer interested in territory and, by extension, why most states do not scramble for Arctic resources.

However, Rosecrance's argument is incomplete, both for explaining the decline in territorial competition generally and for the Arctic case more specifically. First, he argues that trade and development make states less economically dependent on and interested in territory; but, as previously discussed, in some cases it is trade

---

[24] Rosecrance, *Rise of the Trading State*; Kaysen, "Is War Obsolete?"; Brooks, *Producing Security*. Due to space constraints, I focus mainly on Rosecrance here, but there are many other scholars who have contributed to the commercial peace research agenda. For a helpful literature review, see Kenneth A. Schultz, "Borders, Conflict, and Trade," *Annual Review of Political Science* 18, no. 1 (2015): 125–45.

that causes states to remain or even become more economically dependent on territory. In the Arctic, both Norway and Russia are highly trade-oriented; but because they primarily export resources extracted from territory, their economies are still highly dependent on land, so both states are still interested in securing control over territory.

Second, it is difficult to apply Rosecrance's theory to ex ante identify whether a given country is a trading state (i.e., before it chooses a strategy of either trade or conquest). This is because Rosecrance largely identifies trading states ex post based on whether they adopt a strategy of "internal economic development sustained by a world market for their goods and services" instead of "trying to conquer and assimilate large tracts of land."[25] Without identifying whether a given country is a trading state ex ante, we cannot generate theoretical predictions about a country's behavior before we observe its choice of strategy (i.e., the degree to which it chooses to seek territory), which is the very thing we seek to explain. This is a problem for both applying the theory to explain a given outcome and testing its predictions.

To illustrate why this is a problem, consider this question: is Norway a trading state? Using Rosecrance's criteria, the answer is unclear, and this ambiguity makes it hard to falsify his theory. On the one hand, Norway has pursued a policy of internal economic development sustained by trade, and it is a western European state, which he collectively categorizes as trading states. This seems to imply that Norway is a trading state and should not be interested in securing control of territory. If Norway is a trading state but still adopts a strategy of projecting power to secure control over Arctic resources, then Rosecrance's theory cannot explain its behavior. On the other hand, after observing Norway's behavior, one could use Rosecrance's criteria to claim that because Norway adopted a strategy of seeking to secure control over Arctic territory and resources, it is not a trading state, given that trading states do not pursue territory. This explanation is a tautology and cannot be falsified. Either way, Rosecrance does not offer a compelling explanation for why some Arctic states, such as Norway, still seek territory, while others, such as Canada, the United States, and Denmark, do not.

In sum, prior international relations theories either cannot be applied or are unable to explain why some states have a stronger preference to seek control over territory and resources. In contrast, my theory offers clear theoretical predictions that can be tested and applied both generally and in the Arctic specifically.

1.4 Road Map

I close this chapter by providing a brief overview of the book. Chapter 2 develops the Rent-Addiction Theory of foreign policy preferences and derives propositions

---

[25] Rosecrance, *Rise of the Trading State*, 25.

about states' willingness to compete over resource rents. Chapter 3 lays out the research design that is employed to test these propositions. Chapter 4 employs data from three new data sets that allow a systematic comparison of each state's Arctic military forces and deployments before and after the shock of Arctic climate change. The descriptive statistical comparisons reveal that states that were most economically dependent on resource rents were the most willing to back their claims by projecting military force to disputed areas and to invest in Arctic bases, ice-hardened warships, and icebreakers. Chapters 5 through 8 supplement this quantitative data with more detailed qualitative evidence that is used to both illustrate the theory's causal mechanisms and provide a more nuanced accounting of each state's Arctic claims, commitments, and military investment and activity. Each chapter tests a distinct hypothesis about how each country should respond to the shock, given the structure of its economy. These cases are the empirical heart of the book.

Chapter 5 evaluates the case of Russia, the most land-oriented state in the Arctic. The theory predicts that Russia should invest more in projecting power to seek control over Arctic resources, despite being less wealthy per capita than any other Arctic state and having a smaller economy than Canada or the United States. This chapter reveals that Russia's ruling elite are utterly economically dependent on resource rents and that this drove them to invest more heavily in projecting power to secure control over Arctic resources than any other state.

Chapter 6 assesses the United States, the most powerful production-oriented state. If capabilities drive intentions, the United States should project the most power to the Arctic. However, if economic structure strongly influences states' preferences, as this book argues, then Washington should be more interested in securing markets and less interested in seeking control over Arctic resources.

Chapter 7 considers Canada, which is more resource-dependent than the United States but still relatively production-oriented. My theory predicts that Canada should invest more in seeking control over Arctic resources than the United States but less than land-oriented states like Russia and Norway. It also helps explain why Canada made major Arctic commitments but consistently cut funding.

Chapter 8 leverages a natural experiment by comparing the behavior of two small, wealthy, and democratic Nordic countries. The first, Norway, by random luck discovered vast North Sea oil resources in the 1960s, making it one of the most land-oriented states; the second, Denmark, did not have such luck and was forced to generate income by producing goods, making it one of the most production-oriented states in the Arctic. The theory predicts that Norway should invest much more in seeking control over Arctic resources than Denmark, Canada, or the United States.

Chapter 9 concludes with a discussion of my core findings and their implications for the future of resource competition and territorial conflict. I demonstrate the generalizability of the theory by applying it broadly to explain the decline in territorial conflict and the prospects for resource competition in regions beyond the Arctic, such as the Middle East and Africa, as well as other maritime regions, such as the North Sea and the South China Sea. The core findings support the book's thesis that *what states make influences what they want to take*. The theory and findings contribute to burgeoning research on the link between economic development and conflict, suggesting that if development is driven by resource extraction, it may make states more conflict-prone rather than less. These findings will also be relevant for policymakers who seek to anticipate how states will respond to global forces, such as climate change and technological innovation, which are rapidly revealing maritime seabed resources. Finally, it provides a stronger microfoundational explanation for why, despite a general decline in territorial conflict, some states still have strong interests in seeking territory as a source of rents.

A Theory of State Preferences and Resource Competition

The revenue of the state is the state.

Edmund Burke, *Reflection on the Revolution in France*[1]

Whether states are predatory or developmental depends in large part on the origins of their chief revenues.

Terry Karl, *Paradox of Plenty*[2]

You can learn a lot watching things eat.

Frank Costello, *The Departed*

2.1 Introduction

The benefits from controlling territory have been decreasing over time. Yet, as ongoing militarized territorial disputes from the deserts of Africa to the frozen Arctic make clear, some states are still willing to invest in projecting power to secure control over territory. Given that projecting power is costly and that the gains associated with doing so are falling, why are some states still investing in projecting power to capture these gains while others have stopped? This puzzle motivates my research question: why do some states have a stronger preference to invest in projecting power to secure control over territory than others?[3]

In this chapter, I develop Rent-Addiction Theory to answer this question. My core argument is this: what states make influences what they *want* to take. More precisely, the more economically dependent a state is on land and the greater the

---

[1] Edmund Burke, *Reflections on the Revolution in France*, reprint, ed. Conor O'Brien (London: Penguin Classics, 1982). Terry Lynn Karl, *The Paradox of Plenty: Oil Booms and Petro-States* (Berkeley: University of California Press, 1997), 222.

[2] Karl, *Paradox of Plenty*, 237.

[3] Investing in power projection includes both the investments made in power projection capabilities and those made in deploying force beyond the state's borders. Power projection capabilities are defined as the force structure necessary to deploy forces over distance (such as bases and ships).

Perils of Plenty. Jonathan N. Markowitz, Oxford University Press (2020). © Oxford University Press.
DOI: 10.1093/oso/9780190078249.001.0001

value of land rents to the regime, the stronger its preference for territory. This argument rests on three core claims that I will defend in detail. First, all states are governed by rulers who seek income, and there are two sources of income for a state and its constituents: profits from producing goods and services and land rents extracted from the control of territory.[4] Second, path dependency leads some states to become economically dependent on, and addicted to, income from land rents. The further states proceed down this path, the more their economies become structured to generate income from territory. The more land-oriented their economic structure, the more rent-addicted they become, and the harder it is to kick the addiction by transitioning off land rents to generate profits from production. Third, the effect of economic structure on the ruler's preference for territory is endogenous to, and conditioned by, the domestic political institutions of the state. The more autocratic a state's political institutions are, the less representative its governing coalition and the more the ruler will value the political benefits associated with land rents.

In sum, a ruler's preference for territory is influenced by two key independent variables: the state's *economic structure* and its *domestic political institutions*. The more land-oriented a state's economy and the more autocratic its institutions, the stronger the ruler's preference for territory. While we cannot directly observe a ruler's preferences, we can observe the actions that ruler takes to realize those preferences. This leads to my core observable implication: *the more land-oriented the economy and the more autocratic the regime, the more the state will invest in projecting power to secure control over territory and resources.*

Rent-Addiction Theory is developed in universal terms and is designed to be applied generally, even though the empirical application of the theory in this book focuses on how five Arctic littoral states responded to the opportunity to compete over Arctic territory and resources. The theory can be applied broadly over time and

---

[4] The primary source of economic benefits associated with controlling territory is land rents, and investment in seeking these rents is called *rent-seeking*. Rent-seeking is defined as investing in seeking income by redistributing or preventing the redistribution of wealth, rather than by creating it. Rent-seeking is the pursuit of supernormal profits by limiting economic competition rather than by producing a superior product or service, as defined in Gordon Tullock, "Rent Seeking as a Zero-Sum Game," in *Toward a Theory of the Rent-Seeking Society*, ed. James M. Buchanan, Robert D. Tollison, and Gordon Tullock, 16–38 (College Station: Texas A&M University Press, 1980). Rents are returns greater than what is necessary to sustain the factors of production in their current use. Put simply, they are the returns from producing a good that are greater than the cost of producing that good. Under perfect market competition, there are no rents as competitive market forces drive the price of goods down until it equals the cost of producing those goods. Thus, an actor's ability to earn rents (i.e., charge prices above the cost of production) depends on the degree to which economic competition is limited. Efforts or investments in limiting competition are known as rent-seeking. Unlike normal profit-seeking, in which producers create value for consumers by creating a better or cheaper product, rent-seeking directly redistributes wealth from consumers to producers.

across a much larger and more representative sample of states to explain changes in states' preferences to project power in order to secure control over territory.[5]

The rest of this chapter unfolds as follows. I begin by defining my terms and concepts of interest. I then explain my theoretical foundations and defend the core assumptions underpinning the logic of Rent-Addiction Theory. Next, I illuminate the causal pathways through which the cause, the state's economic structure and domestic political institutions, influences the effect, the regime's preferences for resource rents and ultimately its willingness to invest in projecting power to secure resource-rich territory. I subsequently derive my core theoretical predictions, before defining the scope and limitations of my theory—illustrating why and where it is most useful.

2.2 The Dependent Variable: Foreign Policy Pursued versus Conflict Initiation

Existing theories of territorial aggrandizement and resource competition have used bargaining outcomes, such as aggrandizement or initiation of conflict, as their dependent variables. The focus on *conflict initiation* rather than *foreign policy pursued* may have misled scholars and caused them to draw incorrect inferences about the role of resources in motivating conflict. Bargaining failure can be thought of as one end point of a causal process that begins with actors having incompatible preferences. States do not move immediately from a desire to control resources to starting a war; rather, they first decide whether to employ military coercion when bargaining. If a state employs coercion when bargaining over resources but bargaining succeeds, we will not observe conflict.

By focusing on conflict as the dependent variable, scholars have, in some instances, incorrectly inferred that states are not engaging in coercive competition over resources. For example, some scholars have observed no war in the Arctic and concluded that it is a peaceful region where little resource competition is occurring.[6] Just because coercive bargaining over resources rarely ends in war does not mean that resources are not a motivation for coercive bargaining.

To avoid drawing incorrect inferences, we begin with the actors, their preferences, and the policies they choose to adopt. I propose changing the dependent variable

---

[5] For a more general empirical test of the theory, see Jonathan N. Markowitz, Christopher J. Fariss, and Blake McMahon, "Producing Goods and Projecting Power: How What You Make Influences What You Take," *Journal of Conflict Resolution*, 63, no. 6 (2018): 1368–1402; Jonathan N. Markowitz et al., "Productive Pacifists: The Rise of Production-Oriented States and Decline of Territorial Conquest," APSA Working Paper, 2019, https://ssrn.com/abstract=3382506.

[6] Oran R. Young, "A Peaceful Arctic," *Nature* 478, no. 7368 (2011): 180–81, https://doi.org/10.1038/478180a.

from *conflict initiation* to *foreign policy pursued*. I focus on the goals of a state's foreign policy and, more precisely, how much a state invests in an *exclusionary foreign policy*, defined as investing in projecting power to seek rents from control of territory.[7]

I seek to explain a state's choice of how much to invest in projecting military power to control resource rents. I concentrate on power projection because it is an observable and costly signal of a state's choice to bargain coercively. The stronger a state's preference to seek resource rents, the more willing it should be to invest in building and projecting military power to secure control over those resources.

Connecting a state's foreign policy preferences to the means used to pursue its objectives has three advantages over approaches focused solely on either means or bargaining outcomes. First, it illuminates *why* states employ coercion to pursue certain objectives, rather than just *whether* they used coercion. Second, it allows us to develop the theoretical conditions under which states will be more likely to seek particular foreign policy objectives. Third, building such theories enhances our ability to predict the interests these states will compete over and how they will react to global trends that affect their interests.

States' foreign policy preferences are complex and multifaceted, so no theory can parsimoniously explain the full range of variation in these preferences. I focus on the preference to pursue an exclusionary foreign policy (i.e., seek land rents) because control over territory is among the most prevalent issues over which states have bargained coercively and fought in recent centuries.[8] Broadly defined, states choose a foreign policy along a continuum between two ideal types—open or exclusionary. *Open* foreign policies are designed to generate economic benefits by facilitating trade by securing sea lanes and access to markets. *Exclusionary* foreign policies are designed to seek land rents by securing control over territory.[9]

---

[7] By focusing on why some states are more likely to seek control over territory, my research builds on previous work, such as Snyder's *Myths of Empire*, that sought to explain why some coalitions are more likely to engage in expansion than others. However, this book seeks to solve a key problem associated with Snyder's approach. Specifically, Snyder's choice of dependent variable, the likelihood of a state engaging in overexpansion, cannot be operationalized ex ante because Snyder never defines the optimal level of expansion. We cannot know what overexpansion is until we observe it. In practice, this results in overexpansion being identified based on whether a state's expansion was deemed a success or failure after the fact. Shifting the dependent variable from overexpansion to foreign policy pursued avoids the problem of defining the optimal level of expansion. See Jack L. Snyder, *Myths of Empire: Domestic Politics and International Ambition* (Ithaca, NY: Cornell University Press, 1991).

[8] Kalevi J. Holsti, *Peace and War: Armed Conflicts and International Order, 1648–1989* (Cambridge: Cambridge University Press, 1991).

[9] Tullock, "Rent Seeking as a Zero-Sum Game."

2.2.1 Defining Preferences for Territory

A state's preference for territory can be defined as how strongly it prefers a unit of territory relative to a unit of some other good. While states' interest in territory can be driven by nonmaterial factors, for my purposes, a state's preference for territory is defined as its preference for the profits associated with territorial control.[10] I am interested in states' preferences or interests because I seek to explain why states adopt certain foreign policy goals rather than others and why they choose to invest more or less in realizing a given goal.

Virtually all of international politics involves states employing both competitive and cooperative tools or policies to realize their goals. My theory suggests that if states have a stronger preference to realize a given goal, such as control over resources, they will be incentivized to invest in whatever tools will allow them to realize that goal. This includes cooperative policies, such as working within international institutions and using international law to pursue claims, as well as competitive tools, such as projecting military power to back their claims. Thus, for my theory, coercive and cooperative tools are complements rather than substitutes. The stronger the state's preference for a given goal, the more it will invest in both cooperative and competitive tools to realize that goal.

Given that cooperative policies—such as making territorial claims using international law—are relatively inexpensive, my theory suggests that all states will make at least a minimal investment in such policies even if they have only a relatively weak interest in their claims. In contrast, given that competitive or coercive tools, such as power projection, are typically costly to employ, the degree to which states are willing to invest in those tools is a useful measure of the strength of their interest in realizing a given goal. The stronger their interest, the more willing they will be to pay the costs associated with projecting power to realize that goal. The degree to which states are willing to complement relatively inexpensive cooperative tools with more costly competitive tools is a function of the strength of their interest in realizing their claims. Given this, while the empirical chapters in the book also consider the degree to which states invest in cooperative policies, they focus primarily on whether states chose to complement these efforts with investment in power projection.

The stronger a state's preference for territory, the more willing it should be to invest in securing control over both the territory it already controls and additional territory. Although it is certainly the case that most states will fiercely defend against attempts to appropriate resources they already control, there is variation in their

---

[10] It is important to note that my theory does not preclude states having preferences for territory for reasons other than the profits associated with its control. It only claims that, all else being equal, states with land-oriented economies and autocratic political institutions should have a stronger preference for territory.

willingness to do so. For example, some states were willing to fight harder than others to hold onto resource-rich colonial possessions.[11] Additionally, there is variation in how much states invest in the capabilities to secure territory that is nominally under their control. For illustration, we see variation in the willingness of states to secure the economically valuable territory at the bottom of the sea that is within their exclusive economic zones (EEZs), and therefore at least nominally under their control. Some states, such as Vietnam, invest heavily in defending the resources in their EEZs, while others, such as the Philippines, invest less in the capabilities required to do so. My theory suggests that the stronger a state's preference for territory, the more willing it will be to invest in military capabilities to both protect the resources within its territorial boundaries and EEZ and seek control over additional resources beyond these boundaries.

2.3 Theoretical Foundations: Core Assumptions

Developing a theory of foreign policy interests from first principles requires starting with strong microfoundations. States themselves are constructed and controlled by individuals to pursue various ends.[12] Thus, I must begin with those individuals and their incentives.

This book's core argument follows from two key propositions. First, the more a state's economy depends on territory and the more autocratic its political institutions, the stronger its preference for territory. Second, the stronger this preference, the more a state should invest in projecting power to secure control over territory.

These two core theoretical propositions, in turn, rest on five assumptions. First, state preferences are a function of the ruler who controls and governs the state. Rulers govern with the backing of a governing coalition (i.e., the group of citizens whose political support a ruler relies upon to stay in power). Second, the ruler's highest priority is to maintain the support of their governing coalition, and the ruler attempt to do this by securing the goods those people want (such as security and prosperity). Third, rulers view foreign and domestic policy as important tools and investment opportunities for securing the income needed to provide those goods. Fourth, there are two sources of income: profits from producing goods and services and land rents extracted from the control of territory. Fifth, the ruler's expected payoff from seeking income from territory is conditioned by the structure of the state's economy and its domestic political institutions. I will now defend these assumptions.

---

[11] Frieden, "International Investment and Colonial Control."
[12] Fearon, "Two States, Two Types, Two Actions."

My first three assumptions are self-evident and need little defense. States have always been ruled by individuals, and no ruler can stay in power without the support of at least some citizens.[13] It is important that the ruler is defined broadly as the individual or set of individuals who controls the government. (Note that in this book I use the terms *ruler, regime,* and *government* interchangeably. I do this to reduce the amount of repetition the reader must endure.)

The second assumption is one commonly adopted by scholars of both comparative and American politics: that officeholders seek to remain in power, and the citizens whose support they rely on seek to maximize their consumption of goods.[14] Thus, rulers have but one core interest—to secure some set of goods for their governing coalition—and one set of tools to pursue it—policy. This leads to my third assumption: rulers view policy strategically as a set of tools to secure and redistribute goods. Foreign policy, and military force in particular, is one of the most important tools that can be deployed to secure goods for the members of the state's governing coalition. Military force is useful not only for providing security from violent attack but also for securing critical inputs, such as resources and income, that are needed to realize the coalition's other objectives, be they material, ideological, or religious in nature.

My fourth assumption is that there are two sources of income that states can invest in securing: land rents extracted from the control of territory and profits from producing goods and services. Thus, states can seek income by investing in securing control over territory and extracting land rents, or they can seek to earn profits by producing goods and services. For the purposes of my argument, land rents have two attributes that make them distinct from the profits from production. First, land rents are *appropriable* because they are income earned from fixed assets, which are tied to territory that can be conquered. Second, once the territory is conquered, a government can forcibly extract income because it can calculate how much wheat an acre should yield or how many barrels of oil a well should produce per day. This allows them to coercively extract income from a population and punish shirking.

[13] Philip G. Roeder, *Red Sunset: The Failure of Soviet Politics* (Princeton, NJ: Princeton University Press, 1993); Susan L. Shirk, *The Political Logic of Economic Reform in China* (Berkeley: University of California Press, 1993).

[14] These might be basic goods, such as food, water, and security; more expansive goods, such as providing education, healthcare, and public transportation for the citizens; or particularistic goods, such as building palaces for themselves. These goods may be material—income and housing—or non-material, such as the rights of certain religious groups to engage in certain practices or occupy certain holy locations. As long as providing these goods requires revenue, the state will have an interest in securing income. For more information, see John R. Zaller, "Monica Lewinsky's Contribution to Political Science," *PS: Political Science and Politics* 31, no. 2 (1998): 182–89; Gary W. Cox and Mathew D. McCubbins, "Electoral Politics as a Redistributive Game," *Journal of Politics* 48, no. 2 (1986): 370–89; Arthur Lupia et al., "Were Bush Tax Cut Supporters 'Simply Ignorant?' A Second Look at Conservatives and Liberals in 'Homer Gets a Tax Cut,'" *Perspectives on Politics* 5, no. 4 (2007): 773–84.

Thus, critically for my theory, securing economically valuable territory allows states to extract land rents. In contrast, as previous work has demonstrated, acquiring the profits from producing goods through conquest is much harder.[15] A key reason for this is that the efficient production of goods generally requires people to be incentivized because the output is difficult to monitor, thus making it harder for the government to detect and punish shirking. Critically, this makes territorial control much more useful for extracting land rents than for capturing the profits associated with production.[16]

Rulers are sensitive to the costs and benefits associated with choosing one source of income over another. Investing in projecting power to control territory means that those forces cannot be used to secure sea lanes and maintain access to markets. It also means that funds spent on building and projecting military power cannot be spent on alternative strategies for producing goods, such as investing in the state's human and intellectual capital by spending more on education or research. This is the trade-off that states must confront when pondering two interrelated choices: (1) what goods to pursue and (2) how much to invest in seeking those goods.

The trade-offs associated with the investment of scarce resources in different income-generation strategies are governed by the payoffs associated with each strategy. The higher the payoff associated with a good, the more likely states will be to seek that good and the more they will invest in securing it. The *ruler's preference for territory* depends on the degree to which securing territory generates the economic and political benefits they need to remain in power, relative to investing in producing goods and services.

This leads to my fifth and final assumption: the ruler's expected payoff from seeking income from territory is conditioned by the structure of the state's economy and its domestic political institutions. Recall that a state's economic structure and its regime type are my two independent variables. As I will explain in greater detail, these variables condition the ruler's preferences for territory by influencing the size of the payoffs from either extracting land rents or production. From these five assumptions, I deduce the following proposition: *the larger a ruler's expected payoff*

---

[15] For more on why this is the case, see Rosecrance, *Rise of the Trading State*; Kaysen, "Is War Obsolete?"; Brooks, *Producing Security*; Frieden, "International Investment and Colonial Control."

[16] In a world of relatively open markets, states do not need to conquer territory in order to gain access to markets. But, even in an open market, capturing the lion's share of the profits from extracting natural resources does require securing control over territory. While a state or firm can make direct foreign investments and earn some of the rents from natural resource extraction in territory that it does not control, in general, the host government will capture the rents. Over time, host governments have generally extracted the majority of the income earned from natural resource extraction when foreign firms have provided nearly all the capital and labor. In many cases, host governments have chosen to nationalize and appropriate the foreign firm's investments. In short, a government that seeks to maximize its share of the income extracted from natural resources must control the territory under which the resources lie.

from securing land rents, the stronger the ruler's preference for territory and the more they
should invest in securing control of territory. Next, I explain how the economic structure and domestic political institutions of the state condition the ruler's payoff from
pursuing territory as opposed to production.

2.4 The Cause: The Economic Structure and Domestic Political Institutions of the State

My first and most important independent variable is the economic structure
of the state. A state's economy can be crudely divided into two sectors: land
and production. The economic *structure* of the state is the degree to which the
economy is organized to generate income either from land rents or from production. Land-oriented economies are structured to extract income from rents generated by territory. Production-oriented economies are structured to generate
income from the sale of goods and services produced by people living in the
state. The relative size of each sector is defined by the share of *national income*
generated by that sector.[17] The comparative size of these sectors, in turn, serves
as a proxy for the state's economic structure (on a continuum from land-oriented
to production-oriented).

The economic structure of a state conditions the source of income for the ruler
and their governing coalition through several causal mechanisms. The more land-
oriented the economic structure of the state, the greater the returns from investing
in securing and extracting land rents and the more economically dependent the
governing coalition will be on land. Thus, the more land-oriented the economic
structure of the state is, the stronger the ruler's preference to invest in securing control over territory will be.

The ruler's preference for territory is also influenced by my second independent
variable, the state's domestic political institutions, which are endogenous to its economic structure.

Domestic political institutions condition the degree to which a ruler is representative of and accountable to the state's citizens. The more autocratic these
institutions are, the less representative the governing coalition. The less representative the governing coalition, the greater the benefits of holding office but the more
the ruler will need to rely on coercion to maintain power. As will be explained in
greater detail, both these factors should give autocratic rulers a stronger value for
the political benefits associated with land rents.

---

[17] Following standard usage, *national income* is defined as net domestic output plus net income
from abroad. For more on this definition, see Thomas Piketty, *Capital in the Twenty-First Century*
(Cambridge, MA: Harvard University Press, 2014), 45.

Land rents generate specific political benefits, making them more valuable than profits of a similar size derived from production. All rulers should value these political benefits but, as I will explain in section 2.4.4, there are several reasons why autocrats should value them more highly. Land rents are particularly valuable because they are sources of income that can be forcibly *appropriated* and *extracted*. As a result, they are easier to directly control and to deny to the political opposition, making them a more secure set of assets from which to generate the income that rulers need to remain in power. Monopolizing control over the country's source of wealth helps the ruler to monopolize power. Thus, the more autocratic a state's political institutions, the stronger the ruler's value for the political benefits associated with land rents and, as a result, the stronger the ruler's preference for territory.

The economic structure and domestic political institutions of a state are at least partially endogenous to one another. As previous work on the resource curse makes clear, the greater the share of the state's income that is derived from land rents, the stronger the incentive for elites to gain control over those rents and to concentrate political influence among a narrow coalition in order to concentrate their distribution.[18] This creates incentives among the ruling elite to adopt autocratic institutions and results in a governing coalition that is representative of narrow interests. A burgeoning literature on the relationship between resource rents and regime type suggests that the incidences of autocracies and petro-states are highly correlated. Scholars of the resource curse have suggested that oil retards the transition to democracy.[19] Others have argued for the opposite causal relationship: rather than resource wealth fostering autocracy, autocracies have a stronger preference for pursuing resource wealth.[20] If it is true that autocratic rulers are more likely to restructure an economy to extract income from territory, autocratic political institutions may cause states to adopt a more land-oriented economic structure. While interesting, for the purposes of my theory the direction of this endogenous relationship is unimportant. What does matter is that states with autocratic political institutions should have greater value for the political benefits associated with land rents.

2.4.1 The Addiction Analogy

A ruler's preference for territory is a function of the state's economic structure and political institutions. To understand how these variables condition the source of

---

[18] Michael Ross, "The Political Economy of the Resource Curse," *World Politics* 51, no. 2 (1999): 297–332; Thad Dunning, *Crude Democracy: Natural Resource Wealth and Political Regimes* (Cambridge, MA: Cambridge University Press, 2008).

[19] Ross, "Political Economy of the Resource Curse"; Cullen S. Hendrix, "Cold War Geopolitics and the Making of the Oil Curse," *Journal of Global Security Studies* 3, no. 1 (2018): 2–22.

[20] Menaldo, Victor. *The Institutions Curse: Natural Resources, Politics, and Development* (Cambridge: Cambridge University Press, 2016).

income for the governing coalition and influence the ruler's preference for territory, it is helpful to start with the analogy of addiction. I draw on Becker and Murphy's (1988) rational theory of addiction, in which addiction is defined as past consumption influencing current consumption.[21] States seek income just as addicts seek drugs to get their fix. All states seek income, and historically their drug of choice was land rents earned by controlling agrarian land. Prior to the Industrial Revolution, agrarian land was the largest source of wealth, giving states a strong incentive to secure control over territory.[22] Thus, just as becoming addicted to opium drives addicts to seek opium, becoming addicted to land rents drives states to seek land.

States never stop being addicted to rents—once an addict, always an addict. In the same way that an addict's brain never stops seeking drugs to get high, rulers never stop seeking rents to generate income. But just as some addicts can replace their drug habits with alternative rewards, some states can find substitutes for the income they used to generate from land rents. Many former addicts find extreme sports such as ultramarathons to be an alternative reward that motivates them to chase endorphins instead of opiates. Reward-seeking still drives the behavior, but as the source of the reward changes, so does an individual's behavior. Similarly, states that shift their source of income also shift their behavior. States that can substitute income from producing goods rather than land rents will be less interested in securing territory and more interested in producing goods and securing markets for those goods.

The technologies associated with the Industrial Revolution allowed states to manufacture goods much more efficiently, which gave agrarian states a far more attractive investment opportunity. By substituting manufacturing for agriculture, this alternative source of income allowed many states to break their addictions to land rents. Put another way, the technologies associated with the Industrial Revolution dramatically increased the productivity of all factors of production, but they disproportionately increased the productivity of capital and labor, relative to agrarian land. As a result, nations that adopted those technologies could generate higher returns from investing capital and labor in manufactured goods and services. Thus, agriculture's relative share of national income fell despite an increase in agricultural production in absolute terms.[23]

---

[21] See Gary S. Becker and Kevin M. Murphy, "A Theory of Rational Addiction," *Journal of Political Economy* 96, no. 4 (1988): 675–700. Addiction is not necessarily the result of some psychological disorder or bias but rather is defined as a result of past consumption influencing current consumption. Critically, I am not implying that addiction is necessarily irrational, only that the past consumption of a good influences actors' preferences regarding their current consumption of that good.

[22] Piketty, Capital in the Twenty-First Century, 117–18.

[23] D. Gale Johnson, "The Declining Importance of Natural Resources: Lessons from Agricultural Land," *Resource and Energy Economics* 24, no. 1–2 (2002): 170–71.

However, the Industrial Revolution also led to an explosion in the consumption of natural resources and the creation of a new and highly addictive source of land rents, natural resource rents derived from resources such as oil. For certain states with large endowments of natural resources, the temptation presented by the tidal wave of income generated by resource rents was too strong to resist. Not all states with large natural resource endowments chose to follow a path of resource-driven economic development, but those that did became economically dependent on those resources. The citizens of these states became accustomed and addicted to the enormous income hit generated by these resource rents. Just as fentanyl is a new, concentrated opiate that delivers a more powerful and more addictive hit, the income from natural resource rents delivers a much larger and more addictive revenue hit than does agriculture. In short, the bigger the hit, the harder to quit.

The rents generated by extracting natural resources tend to be much larger in absolute terms than the rents from agrarian surplus. While productivity in both agriculture and petroleum has increased over time, the gap between the costs of production and the market price (i.e., the profitability of the sector) has remained consistently higher for oil than for agricultural products. Persistently higher profits in the natural resource sector provide an explanation for why many agrarian states have successfully transitioned to a production-oriented economy, while petro-states have been less willing or able to do so. The revenue hit from oil has historically been much larger than that from agrarian surplus.

The problem that addicts and governments face is that while they might be better off quitting, they need the hit today; and if they do not get it, they will suffer the consequences. Rulers who fail to provide the goods their citizens expect to consume in the short run are more likely to be removed from office. Thus, a government's ability to transition off land rents depends in part on its ability to generate an alternative source of income to maintain the political support of its governing coalition. The bigger the revenue hit that the governing coalition enjoys from resource rents, the larger the alternative source of income must be.

The upshot is that the further down the path of resource extraction–driven development a state goes and the more land-oriented the structure of its economy becomes, the harder it becomes to break the addiction. Following this path creates path-dependent sources of positive feedback that raise the switching costs associated with shifting to a production-oriented economy.[24] The higher these switching costs, the more a state will be locked into a land-oriented economic structure and continue to depend on income extracted from land. I argue that the economic structure of the state, and more specifically the degree to which it is structured to

---

[24] I build on Pierson's work on path dependency and positive feedback loops. See chapters 1 and 2 in Paul Pierson, *Politics in Time: History, Institutions, and Social Analysis* (Princeton, NJ: Princeton University Press, 2004).

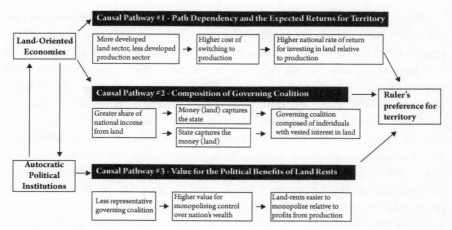

Figure 2.1 Causal Pathways Diagrammed

generate income from territory, influences its preference for territory through three causal pathways: First, path dependency affects the national rate of return associated with investing in land relative to production. Second, economic structure influences the degree to which the governing coalition is composed of individuals whose economic interests are tied to land. Third, economic structure is endogenous to the domestic political institutions of the state, which condition the ruler's value for the political benefits associated with land rents. Each of these pathways is previewed in Figure 2.1 and explained in greater detail in the following sections.

2.4.2 Causal Pathway One: Path Dependency and the Expected Returns from Territory

Factor endowments and prior investment choices determine the degree to which an economy is structured to generate income from land. Some states are endowed with more highly productive land (such as fertile, highly productive agrarian land or large deposits of natural resources) than others. Not all states that are endowed with natural resources choose a path of development that makes them economically dependent on income extracted from land. However, those that do choose this path are affected by several path-dependent sources of positive feedback that increase the switching costs associated with shifting to a production-oriented economy.

First, agrarian and, to an even greater extent, resource-driven development involves sinking investment into assets with high fixed costs, such as clearing land and building irrigation systems in the case of agriculture and digging mines, drilling oil wells, and building refineries in the case of natural resources. Once these large investments have been made, they create economies of scale that dramatically improve the productivity of the land-oriented sector. This generates positive feedback by increasing the returns from each dollar invested in generating income from land relative to production. Critically, once these investments have been sunk into assets that improve the efficiency with which profits can be generated from land, they cannot be unsunk and invested instead in assets that improve the ability of the economy to produce goods.

Second, following a land-oriented economic development path generates learning effects; the longer a state's citizens farm or mine, the more they learn and the more efficient they become at generating return in agriculture or mining.[25] This generates a positive feedback loop as the higher return encourages more citizens to invest in learning to farm or mine. Every hour people spend learning to farm and mine is an hour they do not spend learning to manufacture goods or produce services. Thus, just as infrastructure investments in the land-oriented sector cannot be completely unsunk, neither can investments in sector-specific skills or training.

Third, the further states proceed down a path of land-oriented development, the more their exports tend to be dominated by natural resource–based commodities. Trade and the forces of globalization tend to reward specialization, which increases the returns of the land-oriented sector relative to production-oriented sectors. As previous scholarship on the Dutch disease suggests, this generates a positive feedback loop leading to more capital and labor being invested in land-oriented sectors at the expense of the production-oriented sector.[26] Additionally, as foreign currency earned from commodity exports flows into the economy, it drives up the value of the local currency, inflating the prices of labor and other domestic inputs, making it more costly to produce goods. This, in turn, makes the production-oriented sector less competitive globally. The further behind the production-oriented sector falls, the harder it is to catch up. Over time, land's share of exports grows as production's share of exports shrinks, and the state becomes more economically dependent on income from exporting commodities.[27]

These three interrelated sources of positive feedback generate lock-in effects that make economic structure "sticky" or hard to change even if rulers believe that greater profits could be earned in the future by shifting to a production-oriented economy. These effects are compounded by the fact that rulers face the constant need to generate income in order to remain in power, but the returns from shifting investment to production-oriented sectors may be decades or more away. As evidence, one need look no further than Russia's recent difficulties in building its own Silicon Valley.[28] Having spent years underinvesting in education and basic research

[25] Pierson, *Politics in Time*, 24.

[26] Warner Max Corden, "Booming Sector and Dutch Disease Economics: Survey and Consolidation," *Oxford Economic Papers* 36, no. 3 (1984): 359–80.

[27] Karl, *Paradox of Plenty*.

[28] *Economist*, "Can Russia Create a New Silicon Valley?," July 14, 2012, http://www.economist.com/node/21558602.

and development, Russian companies cannot simply flip a switch and begin creating wealth from innovation in science and technology. For further illustration, Saudi Arabia's first economic diversification strategy went on the books in 1970.[29] Nearly half a century later, the kingdom is still trying to diversify its economy and remains highly dependent on resource rents; 90% of government revenue still comes from oil and gas.[30]

In summary, path dependency leads some states to become economically dependent on and addicted to income from land rents. Resource-driven development causes path-dependent effects that increase the switching costs associated with shifting from extracting land rents to producing goods and services. Just as an addict's previous consumption influences current consumption, a state's prior economic and political investments influence its current investment preferences. The further states proceed down a development path that results in a more land-oriented and rent-addicted economy, the harder it is to kick this addiction by transitioning off land rents to profits from production. This also lowers their expected returns from investing in production, which increases the comparative attractiveness of investing in seeking land rents. Critically, the more rent-addicted states are, the stronger their preferences for territory. In contrast, regimes with production-oriented economies should be less interested in controlling territory and more interested in securing inputs, such as human capital, to produce products and access markets to sell those products.

2.4.3   Causal Pathway Two: The Composition of the Governing Coalition

Addicts generally have the opportunity to kick their habit but often lack the will to do so. Why do some rulers have the political will to kick their addiction to land rents while others do not? The answer lies in the economic interests of the regime's governing coalition. The degree to which a regime has the political will to break its addiction to land rents is a function of the individuals in the governing coalition whose interests it represents. The more these interests rely on land rents, the less willing the ruler will be to invest in shifting away from those rents.

Changes in the structure of the economy can alter a state's foreign policy preferences through two related causal pathways: first, by changing the degree to which a given sector's interests are represented in the state's governing coalition and, second, by shifting the preferences of the individuals in the governing coalition. Put

---

[29] Robert E. Looney and P. C. Frederiksen, "The Evolution and Evaluation of Saudi Arabian Economic Planning," *Journal of South Asian and Middle Eastern Studies* 9, no. 2 (1985): 3.

[30] Tom Lippman, "Saudi Arabian Oil and U.S. Interests," accessed April 19, 2017, https://www.academia.edu/26575022/Chapter_4_Saudi_Arabian_Oil_and_U.S._Interests.

another way, either money captures the state or the state captures the money (see Figure 2.1). Each will now be explained in greater detail.

Money captures the state—or, more precisely, money captures the governing coalition—when the individuals in a given sector invest their financial resources in exchange for greater political representation in the governing coalition.[31] The larger a sector's share of the state's income and assets, the more the individuals in that sector will be able to invest in activities such as lobbying, campaign donations, or bribery. This enhances their capacity to buy their way into the governing coalition, capture the state, and entrench their interests within the halls of government.

The further a country proceeds down a resource-driven development path, the larger the share of the nation's income that will flow to land-oriented interests and the more those interests will be able to invest in capturing the state. This generates positive feedback that further enhances the land-oriented sector's influence. The greater that sector's capacity to invest in securing political influence, the more those interests can become entrenched and create rules and institutions that shift political power and economic benefits to themselves and away from their political opponents. This source of positive feedback generates a lock-in effect. Specifically, the land-oriented faction is able to reinvest economic gains into securing additional political influence. This allows it to further restrict the power and economic productivity of the political opposition, thus solidifying its control over the state. In sum, the more the governing coalition is controlled by land-oriented interests, the stronger the ruler's incentives to pursue policies that benefit that sector, and thus the stronger the ruler's preferences for securing territory should be.

Alternatively, the state captures the money—or, more precisely, the governing coalition captures and becomes dependent on the income from a given sector— through two pathways: first, when the state becomes reliant on revenues generated from nationalizing or taxing that sector and, second, when individuals in the governing coalition capture and become dependent on private flows of income from that sector. These pathways are not mutually exclusive as the state can become reliant on the revenue generated by a sector while individuals in the governing coalition depend on the same sector for their private incomes. In either case, the governing coalition develops a vested interest in a sector because it generates flows of income from which they benefit. The more income a sector generates for the members of the governing coalition, the stronger the coalition's interest in enhancing the sector's size and profitability.

[31] It is important to note that my use of the term *state capture* differs from previous works, which have used it to describe situations in which a narrow interest group captures the state at society's expense. My usage of the term does not preclude this possibility but is only meant to reflect a pathway by which economic sectors or groups gain political influence over the state. I do not assume that the groups are necessarily narrow or that they will use their influence to pursue policies at society's expense, although both outcomes are possibilities.

Thus, if the people who govern the state capture and come to depend on flows of income from raw commodities such as agricultural products or natural resources, they should have a stronger interest in the profitability of the land-oriented sector. This creates a source of positive feedback as the more the governing coalition depends on income from land, the greater its incentives to invest in both policies that increase the returns generated by land and the apparatus to tax that income.

The more private income the land-oriented sector generates for members of the governing coalition and the more revenue the state is able to extract and redistribute to the coalition, the more goods the coalition can consume. As people consume more goods, they generally get used to and come to expect the benefits—such as a higher standard of living—provided by this consumption. This expectation makes them loath to shift off a given source of income if doing so would require them to consume fewer goods and accept a lower standard of living. This incentivizes the government to continue investing in extracting land rents unless it can quickly find an alternative source of income. The more that the ability of the governing coalition to generate income from land rents depends on securing control over resource-rich territory or highly productive agrarian land, the stronger the regime's preference for territory will be.

The important take-away is this: the source of a nation's income will find a way into politics, or politicians will find a way to capture this income. Why does this matter? If we want to understand the source of a state's interests, we should look to the source of its money. The right place to start is the source of the *nation's* income, not just the source of the *government's* revenue. This is because, over time, the source of the nation's income will become the source of the governing coalition's income. Why? Because individuals from that sector will capture the governing coalition, or the governing coalition will capture the income from that sector. In either case this income flows into the pockets of individuals in the governing coalition, giving them a vested economic interest in that sector.

The logic of my argument applies both to states with land-oriented economies and to states, such as the United States, with production-oriented economies. For illustration, at the height of the economic crisis in 2008, the US government injected several trillion dollars into US banks to prevent their failure.[32] This move was deeply unpopular with the American public. Even some of the banks' chief executive officers declined to accept the cash infusion until they were threatened with nationalization.[33] Some have argued that this is an example of how the financial sector has captured the US government. At the very least, few would question that the

[32] *New York Times*, "Adding Up the Government's Total Bailout Tab," accessed April 13, 2017, http://www.nytimes.com/interactive/2009/02/04/business/20090205-bailout-totals-graphic.html?_r=2&.

[33] Mark Landler and Eric Dash, "Drama Behind a $250 Billion Banking Deal," *New York Times*, October 14, 2008, http://www.nytimes.com/2008/10/15/business/economy/15bailout.html.

financial sector has enormous political influence in Washington. However, the US government had also come to depend on revenue generated directly from the financial sector, as well as from other sectors whose economic health and profitability depended on the stability of the financial sector. The state had captured the money and had become dependent on this revenue. In addition, the members of the US governing coalition (i.e., both political and economic elites, as well as the voters who could remove the government from power) depended on private income from the financial sector and closely connected sectors. In short, whether money had captured the state or the state had captured the money, the size of the bailout demonstrates the strength of the government's interest in the economic health of the financial services sector.

In sum, the domestic balance of power or influence within a state's governing coalition will be, in part, a function of the balance of national income. Thus, a group or sector's relative share of national income should generally covary with its relative share of political representation and influence within the state's governing coalition. Governing coalitions that are more economically dependent on the production and trade of manufactured goods and services will naturally have economic interests that differ from those of coalitions that rely primarily on the extraction of wealth—such as oil, gas, coal, minerals, timber, and agricultural commodities—from land. Coalitions that depend on the extraction of wealth from territory have land-oriented economic interests. Coalitions that rely on the production of manufactured goods and services have production-oriented economic interests. Both types of coalitions seek rents in some form, but land-oriented coalitions are much more dependent on land rents to generate income. Coalitions that rely on revenue derived from the control of land should be more likely to project power to pursue territory and the resources it contains. In contrast, coalitions that rely on producing manufactured goods and services should be less interested in the pursuit of territory and resources and more interested in pursuing access to markets.

2.4.4 Causal Pathway Three: Value for the Political Benefits of Land Rents

The political benefits of land rents are the third causal pathway through which the state's economic structure and domestic political institutions condition the ruler's preference for territory. A dollar of income from extracting land rents has the same economic value to a ruler as a dollar of income from producing goods, but it does not have the same political value. Recall that land rents have two attributes, *appropriability* and *extractability*, which generate political benefits that make them more valuable than profits of similar magnitude derived from producing goods. I first discuss these attributes and the benefits they provide. I then explain why autocratic rulers should value these benefits more than democratic rulers.

First, land rents derive from assets that are more appropriable than the assets needed to produce goods. Small-scale, subsistence agriculture is labor-intensive to tax; but, like mining and oil, it is relatively difficult to hide agricultural production, and the physical location of production is fixed.

Second, the income from these assets is easier to forcibly extract, and it declines less in response to the assertion of state control. A ruler can coerce people to farm or mine and estimate how much grain each acre will yield or how much coal should be extracted per day. It is harder to force someone to be innovative as it is extremely difficult to estimate how much innovation a person should produce per day. Thus, efficiently generating profits from production generally requires that the people producing the goods are positively incentivized to produce and innovate. If they are not incentivized, production will decrease.[34] Individuals have less incentive to produce if they do not have secure property rights that guarantee that they get to keep the profits from production. Indeed, innovation may not occur at all without both secure property rights and an open environment for information-sharing.[35] This makes the development of high-end manufacturing, services, and knowledge-based industries more sensitive to the establishment of secure physical and intellectual property rights.

The appropriability and extractability of land rents generate two primary political benefits: *monopoly* and *control*. More precisely, land rents are a source of wealth that is easier for the ruler to monopolize and a stream of income that is less sensitive to being controlled by the ruler. Monopolizing control over the country's source of wealth allows the regime to solidify its hold on power. The more the ruler is able to monopolize control over the state's wealth, the more the ruler is able to deny income to individuals who are not in their governing coalition. This not only incentivizes individuals in the governing coalition to remain loyal; it makes those who are not in the coalition poorer and less powerful. This in turn reduces the opposition's ability to challenge the ruler. In addition, because land rents represent a stream of income that is less sensitive to being appropriated and controlled by the ruler, the

---

[34] For evidence, one need look no further than the command economies of the twentieth century, which struggled to efficiently produce goods and services whose quality or price was competitive on global markets.

[35] Nathan M. Jensen, *Nation-States and the Multinational Corporation: A Political Economy of Foreign Direct Investment* (Princeton, NJ: Princeton University Press, 2006); Michael A. Peters, "Three Forms of the Knowledge Economy: Learning, Creativity and Openness," *British Journal of Educational Studies* 58, no. 1 (2010): 67–88; Ernest J. Wilson III and Adam Segal, "Trends in China's Transition Toward a Knowledge Economy," *Asian Survey* 45, no. 6 (2005): 886–906; Brooks, *Producing Security*; Rosecrance, *Rise of the Trading State*. Making matters worse, the highly educated people essential to these industries can emigrate if they lack the political freedoms they desire. It is no coincidence that Russian emigres like Google cofounder Sergei Brin have been critical to the development of Silicon Valley, while Russia's efforts to create a domestic tech industry, including concentrated investment in a technology cluster known as Akadempark, have largely failed.

government has less need to grant political rights and freedoms that could be used by the political opposition to threaten its hold on power. Thus, because these assets are easier to expropriate and extract, they are a more secure source of the income the ruler needs to remain in power.

2.4.4.1 Why Autocrats Value These Political Benefits More Than Democrats

While incumbent rulers in democracies also value the political benefits associated with land rents, autocratic rulers should value them more. This is because their ability to maintain power depends more on their ability to monopolize control over the state's wealth and restrict the political rights of its citizens. In addition, because autocratic leaders tend to both enjoy greater benefits from maintaining power and suffer greater costs from losing power, they should value these political benefits more. I will explain each of the three reasons in greater detail.

First, relative to democracies, autocracies tend to rely less on popular support and more on coercion to stay in power. The more the government relies on the threat of coercive violence to maintain power, the greater its need to maintain monopoly control over the means to generate that violence. Put simply, we can think of two ideal types of rulers: those who rely on popular support and those who rely on tanks. Rulers who rely on tanks need to make sure that they have the money to buy tanks and that potential challengers do not have the money to buy them (or, perhaps more importantly, the money to buy the loyalty of those who drive the tanks). Recall that money is power, and thus, the more the ruler can monopolize control over the source of money, the more that ruler can monopolize control over the source of power.

Second, the less the ruler relies on popular support to maintain political power and the more they rely on coercion, the more that ruler will need to restrict citizens' political freedoms. Indeed, autocratic governments are often only in power *because* they restrict their citizens' political freedoms. Thus, they face far greater uncertainty about whether they will be able to maintain power if they relax these restrictions. In contrast, democratic rulers tend to come to power with their citizens already having greater political freedoms, giving them greater confidence that they will not suddenly be removed from power if they continue to grant their citizens these freedoms. This makes it less costly for democracies to allow their citizens the freedom necessary for them to reap the profits from producing goods.

Third, I expect autocratic leaders to have a stronger preference for maintaining power. This is because both the benefits of holding office and the costs of losing power tend to be greater for autocrats. The benefits are greater because autocratic institutions allow rulers to concentrate the benefits from holding office among themselves and the members of their narrowly representative governing coalition.[36]

---

[36] Roeder, *Red Sunset*; Shirk, *Political Logic of Economic Reform*; Bruce Bueno de Mesquita et al., *The Logic of Political Survival* (Cambridge, MA: MIT Press, 2005).

In contrast, democratic leaders are accountable to governing coalitions that are more representative of societal interests, and thus must distribute these benefits more broadly. The cost of being removed from power is also higher for autocrats because it generally involves losing access to these benefits and entails a greater risk of violent punishment for the regime and its governing coalition.[37] In contrast, democratic rulers have less to lose if they are removed from power, and they and their families are less likely to suffer violent punishment. Because I expect autocratic leaders to have a stronger preference for maintaining political power, I expect they should also value the political benefits associated with land rents more highly.

In summary, the domestic political institutions and structure of a state's economy influence the government's preference for territory through three causal pathways. First, factor endowments and prior investment choices lead some states to have land-oriented economies. Following a land-oriented economic development path generates path-dependent effects that increase the rate of return for investment in extracting land rents relative to producing goods. The higher the relative rate of return, the stronger the ruler's value for territory. Second, economic structure influences the economic interests of the members of the governing coalition in either of two ways: money captures the state or the state captures the money. Either way, the structure of the economy conditions the source of income for those who govern the state, which in turn determines its economic interests. If the governing coalition is dominated by individuals whose economic interests are tied to land rents, the ruler will have a stronger preference for securing territory. Third, domestic political institutions condition the ruler's value for the political benefits associated with land rents. The more the ruler values these benefits, the stronger his or her preference for territory.

2.5 Theoretical Predictions

Rent-Addiction Theory produces a set of predictions about how economic structure influences states' preferences and behavior, as well as predicting several process outcomes related to the causal pathways by which states' economic interests influence their foreign policy preferences. The present section lays out my theoretical predictions about how a state's domestic political institutions and economic structure influence its tendency to pursue an exclusionary foreign policy. These theoretical predictions are represented by a set of comparative statics that assume that all else is equal.

---

[37] Alexander Debs and Hein Goemans, "Regime Type, the Fate of Leaders, and War," *American Political Science Review* 104, no. 3 (2010): 430–45

This book focuses primarily on explaining the origin of a state's preference for an exclusionary foreign policy:

1) The more autocratic the state's domestic political institutions and the more economically dependent it is on land rents, the stronger its preference for an exclusionary foreign policy will be.

Unfortunately, foreign policy preferences are unobservable, but under certain conditions (described in the following section), they drive foreign policy investments that are observable.

2) The stronger a state's preference for an exclusionary foreign policy, the more it should invest in an exclusionary foreign policy.

Combining predictions 1 and 2 leads us to conclude that, all else being equal, the more autocratic a state's domestic political institutions and the more economically dependent it is on land rents, the more it should invest in an exclusionary foreign policy. Chapter 3 describes how Arctic climate change provides an opportunity to test this prediction. The theory also generates several process-oriented outcomes that are described in greater detail in the case studies.

These observable implications were stated in continuous terms but can also be expressed as binary ideal types. Figure 2.2 expresses my theory using ideal types and previews my theoretical predictions about the degree to which each of the Arctic states should invest in projecting power to secure control over territory and resources. My theory predicts that production-oriented democratic states (such

		Representativeness of Domestic Political Institutions	
		Broad	Narrow
Economic Structure	Land-oriented	More (Norway)	Most (Russia)
	Production-oriented	Least (United States, Canada, Denmark)	More (China[1])

Figure 2.2 Ideal State Type Predictions

[1] Note that China is not an Arctic littoral state and cannot make claims on Arctic resources; therefore, it is not included in the Arctic cases. However, my theory does generate predictions about China's preference for territory given that it is a production-oriented autocratic state. I discuss the implications of these predictions in the conclusion (chapter 9)

as Denmark, the United States, and Canada) should have the weakest preference for territory and should invest the least in pursuing an exclusionary foreign policy. Land-oriented democratic states (e.g., Norway) and production-oriented autocratic states (e.g., China) should have a stronger preference for territory and invest more in pursuing an exclusionary foreign policy than production-oriented democracies. Finally, land-oriented autocratic states (such as Russia) should have the strongest preference for territory and should invest the most in pursuing an exclusionary foreign policy.

2.6 Scope Conditions and Limitations

The scope of Rent-Addiction Theory is broad, and its theoretical foundation is developed in universal terms to explain how variation in states' domestic political institutions and economic structure influences their foreign policies. The foundations of the theory can be applied generally to all states and tailored with additional variables to explain states' foreign policy preferences across a wide range of goods, outcomes, and grand strategy objectives. In this book, I have tailored the theory to focus specifically on how states' preferences for land rents influence their preferences to secure control over resource-rich territory.

It is important to separate a theory's scope, which determines the set of units and phenomena to which the theory applies, from the conditions under which we should be most likely to observe the theory's predictions. The issue is especially relevant for my theory, given that it is a theory of preferences, and preferences cannot be observed directly.[38] Therefore, we must observe the degree to which states behave *as if* they have a given set of preferences. The difficulty here is that the influence of preferences on state behavior is contingent on the state's strategic environment. Thus, even if states with land-oriented economies have a stronger preference to secure control over territory, we will only be able to observe the effect of these preferences on a state's foreign policy actions under a limited set of conditions. In the present section, I outline these conditions and, conversely, the phenomena that the theory is not designed to explain.

First, my theory only explains the preferences and behavior of states that have secure access to natural resources, either through markets or through domestic production. If access is not secure, even states that are not economically dependent on resource rents may have strong incentives to seek control over stocks of resources in order to secure access to those resources. Existing explanations have already demonstrated that because all modern economies and militaries run on energy, all

[38] Jeffry A. Frieden, "Actors and Preferences in International Relations," in *Strategic Choice and International Relations*, ed. David A. Lake and Bob Powell, 39–76 (Princeton, NJ: Princeton University Press, 1999).

states will have a strong preference to secure access to resources.[39] However, some states that have already secured access to resources invest in securing *control* over resources. This is puzzling because once states have secured access to resources, there is nothing in existing explanations to suggest why some states have a stronger preference than others for securing control over resources. Rent-Addiction Theory solves this puzzle by explaining why certain states seek control over resources even if they already have secure access. Thus, the theory developed here is not designed to explain variation in states' willingness to seek access to resources as a source of inputs. My theory concerns states that already have access to resources through markets or their own supply. By shifting the focus from *access to inputs* to *control over rents*, resource competition can be thought of as a subcategory of territorial competition, in which to the victor go the spoils. Put simply, some states want more than access to resources; they want the revenue derived from controlling stocks of resources and are willing to project military force to get it. This theory is designed to explain why.

Second, my theory only applies if there is a stock of resources that states can control, with some expected gains from controlling those resource rents. If there are no resources that a state could protect or take, its preference for rents will do little to explain its behavior.

Third, I can only explain the behavior of states that have the capacity to invest in securing control over resources. Some states are too weak to secure control over resources even within their own territorial borders. Some states are so weak that they cannot project force beyond the capital city. States might have a strong preference to secure control over resources, but if they are relatively weak, we will be less likely to observe this preference reflected in their behavior. Additionally, some states might have a stronger preference to seek control over additional resources but be deterred by other actors from attempting to do so. In both cases, we will be less likely to observe an impact of these preferences on a state's actions.

Fourth, and finally, Rent-Addiction Theory does not purport to explain when states will necessarily fight over resources, only when they will have a stronger preference to secure control over those resources. Although the strength of states' preferences for a given good influences their willingness to fight over it and, hence, the probability of bargaining failure, the theory is not designed to explain deterministically when resource competition will lead to bargaining failure. Rather, I seek to explain why states have a stronger preference for investment in projecting power to engage in coercive bargaining in the first place.

Future work could build on this theoretical framework to explain how the sources of a state's income interact with additional variables to condition state interests. Subsequent work might incorporate additional factors into this framework, such as

---

[39] Daniel Yergin, *The Quest: Energy, Security, and the Remaking of the Modern World* (New York: Penguin, 2011).

the characteristics of individual leaders and the ideological or religious preferences of those who govern a state or society.

2.7 Why Is This Framework Useful?

This framework makes three primary contributions: First, it explains the origins of a state's preferences for territory and how they influence the state's economic structure and political institutions. Second, my theory can be applied to deduce and identify different types of states and their corresponding interests ex ante. Third, it permits scholars and policymakers to identify states with stronger interests in seeking rents through taking territory before they act on those interests. I will explain each of these contributions in greater detail.

First, this book develops a theory of the origins of states' foreign policy preferences and, more specifically, why some states have a stronger preference for territory. Developing such a theory in the realm of international security has been the holy grail of international relations theorists for over two decades. Major strides have been made by scholars in international political economy in terms of explaining variation in states' preferences related to foreign economic policy. However, despite a few notable exceptions, there are few deductively valid theories that are capable of predicting variation in preferences with regard to interests over which states coercively bargain and fight. This book develops such a theory and suggests that the origin of states' foreign policy preferences can be deduced from the structures of their economies and political institutions. In doing so, this work builds on previous research that claims a state's appetite for territory and empire is a function of its regime type.[40] My theory contributes to research on the democratic and capitalist peace by providing a more nuanced explanation of how a state's economic structure and political institutions interact to influence its foreign policy preferences.

My theory suggests that the relationship between regime type and economic development is more complicated than theories of the democratic or capitalist peace have suggested. Two propositions can be derived from my theory that provide a more nuanced explanation of the effects of regime type and economic development on states' preferences for territory. The first proposition is that democratic institutions reduce the incentive for states to seek rents, but even democracies will have a strong preference to take territory if they are economically dependent on land rents. In making this argument, I follow previous work which suggests that the effect of democracy on conflict is conditioned by the structure of a state's economy. These explanations have focused on stocks of public property (McDonald 2009) and the

---

[40] David A. Lake, "Powerful Pacifists: Democratic States and War," *American Political Science Review* 86, no. 1 (1992): 24–37; Bueno de Mesquita et al., *Logic of Political Survival*; Frieden, "International Investment and Colonial Control"; Gartzke and Rohner, "Prosperous Pacifists."

lack of contract-intensive economies (Mousseau 2005) to explain why the relationship between peace and democracy was weaker prior to World War I.[41] In contrast, my theory suggests that the weak relationship between democracy and peace prior to World War I can best be explained by the fact that nearly all states were economically dependent on territory and, thus, even democracies had strong incentives to compete for territory.

The second proposition is that the effect of economic development on a state's appetite for territory is conditioned by the *nature* of the state's economic development. Research suggests that economic development[42] and energy modernity[43] dampen a state's preference to seek territory. However, my theory suggests that the strength of this effect is conditioned by the degree to which economic development coincides with a state's economy shifting from deriving income from land to producing goods and services. Critically, my theory suggests that states which develop economically as a result of extracting resources from territory should have a stronger preference to seek territory than states that develop as a result of producing goods and services. This is where Rent-Addiction Theory differs from the work of Gartzke and Rohner (2011) and Colgan (2015). My theory provides an explanation for why land-oriented states like Russia still project power to seek territory, even though they are economically developed, advanced, and energy-modern. Furthermore, it explains why production-oriented rising powers, such as China, are less interested in seeking territory and more interested in projecting power to secure access to markets and sea lanes.

Finally, my theory allows us to operationalize and identify states' foreign policy interests ex ante from their economic structure and domestic political institutions. Although my work is far from the first to suggest that a state's "type" or interests matter in terms of explaining its foreign policy preferences, it is one of the first that can identify the strength of states' interests in territory ex ante. This is an improvement because it allows us to make more precise predictions of how states' economic structure and domestic political institutions will shape their foreign policy goals and behavior.[44] Previous research, such as Schweller's work on revisionist states, utilizes differences in ideal types to explain foreign policy behavior.[45] Schweller made an

[41] Michael Mousseau, "Comparing New Theory with Prior Beliefs: Market Civilization and the Democratic Peace," *Conflict Management and Peace Science* 22, no. 1 (2005): 63–77; McDonald, *Invisible Hand of Peace.*

[42] Gartzke and Rohner, "Prosperous Pacifists."

[43] Jeff Colgan, "Modern Energy and the Political Economy of Peace," APSA, 2015.

[44] In doing so, my book seeks to build on previous work on how states' domestic political coalitions shape their foreign policy interests and behavior. See Snyder, *Myths of Empire*; Etel Solingen, *Regional Orders at Century's Dawn: Global and Domestic Influences on Grand Strategy* (Princeton, NJ: Princeton University Press, 1998).

[45] Randall L. Schweller, "Bandwagoning for Profit: Bringing the Revisionist State Back in," *International Security* 19, no. 1 (1994): 72–107.

important contribution by refocusing attention to variation in state preferences. The shortcoming of this approach is that the state's type cannot be identified ex ante and, thus, is of limited value for predicting behavior. For example, we only know a state is revisionist if it has behaved in a revisionist manner. This is a problem both for theory-testing and for policymakers who must anticipate how states are likely to behave and do not have the luxury of waiting until after they have acted on their preferences.

2.8 Conclusion

This chapter has sought to develop a theory of states' interests to explain why some states have a stronger preference to seek control over territory and resources as a source of rents. I have argued that what states make influences what they take. More precisely, the more dependent states are on land rents, the stronger their preference will be to secure economic control over territory. This theoretical framework suggests that if we want to predict whether rising powers are likely to project power to secure territory, we need to look not only at their political institutions but also at the economic interests of the governing coalition. The United States has been considered a democracy since the late eighteenth century, but its appetite for territorial aggrandizement has varied tremendously over time. This example suggests the importance of looking beyond regime type when explaining variation in states' foreign policy interests.

I have provided an explanation for why states project military power that incorporates insights from research on domestic political institutions, the *rentier* state, and the resource curse. This theory's primary contribution is that it allows us to make ex ante theoretical predictions about which states will have a stronger preference to secure control over resources. Using an exogenous shock that rapidly exposed resources, the following chapters test my theoretical predictions.

Research Design—The Arctic as a Natural Laboratory

3.1 Introduction

This chapter describes the research design used to evaluate the theoretical predictions developed in Chapter 2. It begins with a discussion of the core challenges associated with testing my theory against its competitors. Specifically, I explain why the exogenous shock of Arctic climate change presents a rare opportunity to tackle these challenges, allowing me to test my theoretical claim that states with land-oriented economies have a stronger preference to seek control over resource rents than other states.

I also discuss the limitations and trade-offs associated with this design. I save the discussion of how I measure my key theoretical construct for the following empirical chapter. In the first part of that chapter, I introduce three novel data sets, each of which operationalizes the degree to which states invested in projecting power to the Arctic. The second part of Chapter 4 uses these novel variables to provide a descriptive statistical comparison of how each state responded to the shock of climate change.

3.2 Research Design: Why the Arctic Shock?

Some powerful states invest in projecting power to seek control over resources, while others do not. Why is this? My answer is that the more economically dependent a state is on extracting wealth from the control of territory, the stronger its preference will be to seek land rents; and the stronger this preference is, the more the state will invest in projecting power to secure control over territory.[1] Put simply,

---

[1] This effect is conditioned by the domestic political institutions of the state as autocratic institutions enhance the ruler's value for the political benefits associated with land rents. However, this research design focuses on assessing the influence of my core independent variable, the economic structure of the state, for reasons discussed in greater detail in section 3.3, *Research Design Limitations and Trade-offs*.

Perils of Plenty. Jonathan N. Markowitz, Oxford University Press (2020). © Oxford University Press.
DOI: 10.1093/oso/9780190078249.001.0001

this research design focuses on assessing whether a land-oriented economy creates a preference for exclusionary foreign policy and whether this preference drives the decision to project power. Does A cause B, and does B cause C?

My theory is parsimonious and has the potential to explain a large part of international competition over territory and resources, but it is difficult to test. The core problem in gauging the extent to which a state's desire for resources drives its foreign policy choices is that these choices are generally tangled up with other factors. After all, when countries formulate their foreign policy toward any given region, they take several considerations into account. For example, they might be motivated by the strategic importance of the region, other economic opportunities the region offers, and/or historical and ethnic ties. Thus, even if a country projects force into a particular area, it is difficult to know the extent to which it was motivated by natural resources rather than other factors.

To conduct an ideal test, first we would need to procure an Earth-sized laboratory. Then we would drop a massive stock of natural resources between half a dozen states with varying economic structures. If some states' economic structures gave them a stronger preference to compete over resources, we should expect them to respond to this shock by investing more in projecting power to secure control over resources.

While this kind of controlled experiment is impossible, nature has provided us with a surprisingly similar natural experiment: the sudden and unexpected melting of a significant portion of the Arctic ice cap in 2007. Only five states (Canada, Denmark, Norway, Russia, and the United States) border the Arctic Ocean, and under the United Nations Convention on the Law of the Sea (UNCLOS), only those states can make territorial claims in the region. According to a 2008 estimate from the US Geological Survey (USGS), between 13% and 30% of the world's undiscovered oil and natural gas is located north of the Arctic Circle. Approximately 80% of these reserves are believed to be offshore in the Arctic Ocean, which until recently has largely been covered by ice.[2] Thus, the rapid melting of this ice represents a tremendous shock in resource availability.

To test the impact of this shock on the behavior of Arctic states, I use an interrupted time series design.[3] I present a simplified version of the design visually in Figure 3.1.[4]

---

[2] US Geological Survey, "Circum-Arctic Resource Appraisal: Estimates of Undiscovered Oil and Gas North of the Arctic Circle," USGS Fact Sheet 2008-3049, 2008, accessed July 8, 2017, https://pubs.usgs.gov/fs/2008/3049/fs2008-3049.pdf.

[3] This quasi-experimental design is similar to the design employed by Campbell and Ross (1968), in which they compare the number of traffic fatalities before and after an intervention, specifically, a crackdown on speeding. The design I employ, however, allows for stronger causal inference than the design employed by Campbell and Ross because the "intervention" is driven by a climatological shock that is exogenous to the outcome of interest. For more on this design, see Donald T. Campbell and H. Laurence Ross, "The Connecticut Crackdown on Speeding: Time-Series Data in Quasi-Experimental Analysis," *Law & Society Review* 3, no. 1 (August 1968): 33, https://doi.org/10.2307/3052794.

[4] This figure presents both the independent and dependent variables as binary, but in the actual design these variables are continuous ratio- and ordinal-level measurements, respectively.

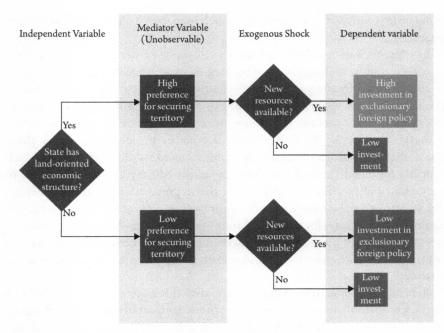

Figure 3.1 Theoretical Prediction and Research Design

To understand this design, consider an analogy. Say you want to know whether being fed a high-sugar diet at home causes children to develop a preference for candy and other unhealthy treats. You can measure the sugar content of the food kids eat at home, but you cannot directly measure their preference for candy. So, you throw a party and present a group of children with a piñata. When the piñata explodes, the kids with strong preferences for candy will make the most effort to seize the candy. If the children whose parents feed them more sugary diets make the most effort to get candy, we can confirm that sugary diets create a strong preference for candy.

A similar problem confronts researchers who want to know whether being economically dependent on income from natural resources causes states to develop a stronger preference for securing resource-rich territory. The problem is this: we can measure the degree to which states have a land-oriented economy and are economically dependent on resource rents, but we cannot directly measure their preference for territory. Because the 2007 climate shock is a recent event, there are no memoirs or declassified documents that would allow us to observe the degree to which the shock drove policymakers' individual decisions. But we can observe what happens when climate change suddenly and exogenously presents states with a stock of natural resources over which they can compete, just as we could see what happens when a piñata suddenly explodes and presents children with the opportunity to compete for candy. We can observe states' behavior, even if we cannot observe their reasoning.

In sum, because we cannot observe policymakers' preference for territory directly, we must instead focus on the degree to which they behaved *as if* they were motivated by the sudden opportunity to secure control over resources. For this reason, I focus on the amount of change in states' observed level of interest and investment in projecting power to the Arctic immediately before and after the shock. More specifically, I examine the degree to which there was a change in official rhetoric and commitments and the degree to which officials followed through on those commitments by actually investing in projecting military force. I also assess the degree to which officials explicitly mentioned the desire for control over the region's resources in statements and official strategic documents. If states with more land-oriented economic structures project more military power in pursuit of those resources, we can confirm that a land-oriented economy creates a strong preference for securing territory.

Before proceeding, it is important to clarify that I am not claiming that this shock was the only important event that these Arctic states experienced during the period of analysis. I am only claiming that this particular climate shock was unique in that it was the only event that resulted in a rapid increase in the resources available for states to compete over. Thus, this is the appropriate event to focus on, given that I am seeking to test my theoretical predictions about why some states have a stronger preference than others to secure control over resources.

3.3 Why the Arctic Shock Represents an Ideal Setting for an Interrupted Time Series

The revelation of new Arctic resources is an ideal setting for an interrupted time series, for five reasons. First, the shock is clearly exogenous with respect to the independent and dependent variables of interest (the economic structure, policy preferences, and power projection of the affected states), which simplifies causal inference. Second, the shock happened rapidly, so we can rule out slower-moving confounds, such as changes in relative power, global status, cultural identity, and nationalism. Third, I am interested in whether states pursued their claims to Arctic resources within the confines of international law or whether they were also willing to back their claims by projecting military force. International law gives only five states the right to make claims on Arctic seabed territory, making a detailed analysis of the entire universe of cases possible. Fourth, these five cases allow for several paired cross-national comparisons of most-similar cases that control for alternative variables. Fifth, climate change has increased the geopolitical importance of the Arctic, so understanding how states are responding to rapid environmental change is substantively important for both scholars and policymakers. These five reasons are described in greater detail below, in subsections 3.3.1–3.3.5.

3.3.1 Reason 1: The Arctic Shock Is Exogenous, Facilitating Estimation of the Impact of Preferences

The exogenous shock of Arctic climate change is a unique and rare opportunity to measure the impact of preferences on states' behavior. This design solves a fundamental problem that has plagued previous efforts to discern the relationship between states' behavior and their preferences. In June of 2007, rising temperatures caused a rapid and unexpected decline in Arctic sea ice, exposing vast stocks of resources on the ocean floor. This was an exogenous shock, a climate event outside of human control that no one, not even the world's best climate scientists, expected.[5] The impact of this shock was further enhanced by two additional exogenous forces—increasing global energy prices and a revolution in deep-sea exploration and drilling technology—which allowed states to find and extract resources that were previously inaccessible.

Using the analogy of an experiment, the "treatment" is the shock or revelation of resources. This treatment was assigned as if randomly and thus allows us to evaluate the interaction between the treatment (the exposure of resources) and each state's preferences to seek control over resources.

I will now provide brief background on the Arctic and justify the use of the June 2007 ice loss as an exogenous shock.

The ideal natural experiment would take place in a region where states had few interests prior to the exposure of resources. Prior to the shock, the Arctic Ocean approximated these conditions. This pre-shock period stands in stark contrast to the Cold War, during which the Arctic was a hotbed of geopolitical competition. American bombers circled the North Pole awaiting orders to hit their targets deep inside Soviet Russia, while nuclear-powered submarines played cat and mouse underneath the Arctic ice. However, as the Cold War ended, states withdrew their military forces from the Arctic. Bombers stopped patrolling, bases were abandoned, and submarines rusted. For two decades, the Arctic was a desolate frozen wasteland where few people lived and little trade occurred. Although

---

[5] Wang and Overland, "A Sea Ice Free Summer Arctic within 30 Years?"

states' military force structure in the Arctic varied, military activity was relatively low prior to the shock.

The ideal natural experiment would randomly and rapidly drop a large stock of resources in between a set of similar states. If some states have a stronger preference to seek resource rents, those preferences should be activated in the post-shock period. The random assignment of states to the post-shock period allows us to estimate the causal impact of states' preferences to seek rents by comparing their behavior in the pre-shock and post-shock periods. The exogenous shock of Arctic climate change approximates these conditions. At the beginning of the summer of 2007, none of the Arctic states could anticipate what was about to happen. Even the most dire climate models, which forecasted that the Arctic would be ice-free during the summer in the 2030s, were too conservative.[6] However, by June of 2007, the amount of Arctic ice cover was already on a trajectory to fall well below the previous record set in the summer of 2005. The ice receded so far and fast that the Northwest Passage (a northern sea route between the Atlantic and Pacific Oceans) became navigable for the first time in recorded history. The exposure of energy resources alone had massive potential, with the USGS estimating that the Arctic holds 30% of the world's natural gas reserves.[7]

This event forced climate scientists to re-evaluate their models and produce new predictions, suggesting that the Arctic might be completely ice-free much sooner than previously predicted.[8] The shock exposed vast swaths of the Arctic Ocean that had been locked under ice for centuries and, more importantly, unlocked the potential for developing previously inaccessible natural resources. Moreover, the Arctic ice surrounding each state's shores was rapidly melting away, allowing them to drill farther offshore. The geopolitical implication of this was that Arctic seabed territory, previously believed to be nearly worthless because it was buried under thick layers of ice, was rapidly uncovered and increased rapidly in value. This dramatic increase in the accessibility and expected value of Arctic seabed territory provides the rare opportunity to test competing theories that try to explain states' resource rent–seeking preferences in a powerful way.

---

[6] For more on the climate models that severely underestimated the rate at which Arctic ice would melt, see Wang and Overland, "A Sea Ice Free Summer Arctic within 30 Years?" For more on the relationship between climate change and Arctic sea ice change, see Kinnard et al., "Reconstructed Changes in Arctic Sea Ice."

[7] US Geological Survey, "90 Billion Barrels of Oil." See also Gautier et al., "Assessment of Undiscovered Oil and Gas in the Arctic."

[8] Wang and Overland, "A Sea Ice Free Summer Arctic within 30 Years?"; Stroeve et al., "Arctic Sea Ice Decline."

3.3.2   Reason 2: The Arctic Shock Happened Quickly, Eliminating Slow-Moving Potential Confounds

I identify the shock as beginning in June of 2007, when data revealed that the area of Arctic sea ice was already on track to decrease below the previous record set in 2005. While 2005 had been a record-setting year, the ice level recovered in 2006, making it difficult for scientists to discern whether 2005 was an outlier or part of a broader shift in the speed at which the ice was melting. Furthermore, the record low set in 2007 was *much* lower than the record set two years earlier. In 2005, the low was 2.05 million square miles of ice cover, compared to 1.59 million square miles in 2007. To provide some context, from 1979 to 2005 the average minimum ice cover was 2.60 million square miles. In 2007, the ice cover was 40% below this average, exposing an additional 1 million square miles of ocean, an area larger than Texas and California combined.[9]

Because actors could have made inferences about the trajectory of Arctic ice disappearance after June of 2007, I code the post-shock period as beginning on July 1, 2007. The shock is the revelation of information that the Arctic might be melting much faster than previously anticipated and that vast stocks of resources might be available much sooner. Therefore, any activity after July 1, 2007, is coded as post-shock. One might argue that the shock period should not begin until September 2007, when Arctic ice hit record lows. This would be a mistake as it assumes that actors were not forward-looking and were not making decisions based on the expectation that the Arctic ice cover would reach record lows.

To provide context, the cases in Chapters 5–8 cover each Arctic state's foreign policy from the end of the Cold War to the present era. Assessing policy before the shock is important because it allows me to assess the baseline level of each state's Arctic interests, claims, military activity, and force structure. However, the years directly before and after the shock will be most informative for comparison. This is because, as time elapses, we can be less certain that changes in state behavior were driven by the exogenous shock of the exposure of resources, as opposed to some other potentially confounding factor. For this reason, I focus more intensely on assessing changes in each state's foreign policy behavior and military activity in the Arctic in the immediate pre- and post-shock periods.

I define the pre-shock period as running from January 1, 2005, to June 30, 2007, and the post-shock period from July 1, 2007, to December 31, 2009. I adopt a two and a half–year instead of a two-year cutoff because the shock occurred in June, approximately the middle of 2007. This helps guard against the possibility that the levels of state interest, investment, and activity were usually high or low in a single year. Additionally, to guard against the possibility that a change in a state's foreign

---

[9] National Snow & Ice Data Center, "Arctic Sea Ice News Fall 2007," accessed April 25, 2017, http://nsidc.org/arcticseaicenews/2007/10/589/.

policy was temporary or driven by anomalous events, I extend the qualitative analyses and, where possible, the quantitative indicators ten years before and after the shock, from January 1, 1997, to December 31, 2017. This approach has the additional advantage of allowing us to assess the continuation in each state's Arctic foreign policy and whether its renewed interest in the Arctic was temporary or whether it followed through on its commitments to build bases, ice-hardened warships, and icebreakers.

The speed of the Arctic shock allows me to distinguish states' response to the shock from their response to other, slower-moving factors. In order for some factor other than the shock itself to explain a change in state behavior from pre-shock to post-shock, the other factor would also have to have changed rapidly right around the summer of 2007. The most powerful alternative explanations rely on variables that shift slowly, such as relative power or concerns over status; these variables can effectively be held constant in the years directly before and after the shock. This allows me to cleanly isolate the effect of the exposure of Arctic resources on foreign policy behavior. The suddenness of the shock means that I can attribute the sharp change in some states' behavior following the shock to the factors I identify, such as the exposure of resources, rather than other long-term factors, such as concerns over status or power.

Alternative explanations propose that states' motivations to project power in the Arctic are driven not by resource exposure but, rather, by geographic nationalism, a desire for status, shifting power, or other confounding factors. It is important to clarify that I am not claiming that factors such as geostrategic concerns, nationalism, a desire for status, or shifting power do not matter or that they cannot explain variation in the baseline level of each state's Arctic interests and military presence. For example, Russia's unique history and geography likely explain why Russia had a higher level of Arctic military activity and more Arctic bases and ice-capable ships before the shock than other states. However, because these factors did not change rapidly around 2007, they cannot explain the rapid and dramatic increase in Russia's Arctic military activity and new investment in its Arctic force structure immediately after the shock.

3.3.3 Reason 3: The Arctic Shock Uniquely Affects the Five States That Are Legally Able to Make Claims, Allowing In-Depth Data Collection for the Full Universe of Cases

I am interested in whether states pursued their claims over Arctic resources purely within the confines of international law or whether they also backed their claims by projecting military force. While all states have the option of pursuing claims by force, if only some states have the option of making claims through international law, this could bias my findings. To deal with this potential source of bias, I select the

Table 3.1 **Cases Match on a Wide Range of Covariates**

	Borders Arctic Ocean	Experienced Shock in 2007	Contestable Resources	Developed Economy	Trade-Oriented	Revolutionary Government
Canada	Yes	Yes	Yes	Yes	Yes	No
Denmark	Yes	Yes	Yes	Yes	Yes	No
Norway	Yes	Yes	Yes	Yes	Yes	No
Russia	Yes	Yes	Yes	Yes	Yes	No
United States	Yes	Yes	Yes	Yes	Yes	No

universe of states that have the option of making international legal claims on Arctic resources under UNCLOS: Russia, Norway, Canada, Denmark, and the United States.[10] The small number of cases has the added benefit of allowing more in-depth data collection for the full universe of cases.

3.3.4 Reason 4: The Arctic Shock Affects States That Are Similar in Ways That Facilitate a Most-Similar-Cases Design

The Arctic shock affected Canada, Denmark, Norway, Russia, and the United States. This set of cases allows me to apply the logic of Mill's method of difference to potential confounding factors, such as geography and time: all five states are approximately equidistant from the Arctic, and all experienced the same shock at the same time (see Table 3.1). This aspect of the research design allows me to control for temporal factors when comparing each state's response. This helps me rule out the possibility that different governments' responses were driven by factors associated with the timing of the shock. Also, at the time of the shock, all the states maintained formal or informal contested claims over Arctic resources, eliminating the possibility that some governments showed less interest because they lacked contestable claims.

The selection of the five Arctic cases allows me to control for potential confounding factors associated with several prior explanations, as discussed in Chapter 1. First, all the states are relatively developed and trade-oriented. Therefore, if Rosecrance and others who privilege the role of development and trade are correct, these states should all have a weaker preference to seek territory.[11] Second, none of the states are governed by revolutionary governments. This is especially

---

[10] It is important to note that while the United States has the option to ratify UNCLOS and make international legal claims, it has not chosen to do so.

[11] Rosecrance, *Rise of the Trading State*.

informative for evaluating the behavior of Norway and Russia, which, according to Colgan, should not behave more aggressively despite being petro-states because they do not have revolutionary governments.[12] In contrast, my theory suggests that Norway and Russia should have a strong preference for territory and resources and should invest in projecting power to secure their control.

Selecting this set of states also facilitates several paired cross-national comparisons that allow me to control for additional potentially confounding variables. These comparisons are discussed in greater detail in the following empirical chapters.

3.3.5 Reason 5: States' Responses to Arctic Climate Change Are Substantively Significant for Scholars and Policymakers

Understanding how states responded to the Arctic shock—and why—is important for understanding the future of global affairs. Climate change is rapidly transforming the Arctic; the poles are warming twice as fast as the rest of the planet, and the impact of this change has profound environmental, economic, and political impacts that ripple far beyond the Arctic, including rising sea levels, changing weather patterns, and changes in the accessibility of resources and sea lanes. Focusing on the Arctic allows me to investigate the geopolitical implications of climate change: how it is altering the relative abundance and scarcity of resources and what impact it is likely to have on international politics.

Also, the revolution in deep-sea drilling and exploration technology has thrust maritime resource competition to the forefront of international politics in places such as the South and East China Seas, the eastern Mediterranean, and the Caspian Sea. Exploring maritime resource competition in the Arctic allows me to test a theory of resource competition that can then be applied to explain other cases of maritime resource competition. Understanding when and why states should be more likely to compete for resources requires research that is grounded in theory and tested rigorously. The Arctic case is far more amenable to testing theories of resource competition because the exposure of resources occurred rapidly and in an area where states had not been militarily active in recent years.

3.4 Research Design Limitations and Trade-offs

As outlined in this chapter, the research design I employ in this book has several advantages that allow me to perform a rigorous test of my theory against competing theories. However, all research designs involve trade-offs and limitations. The five biggest challenges for my research design are (1) the limited number of cases,

---

[12] Colgan, "Oil and Revolutionary Governments."

(2) the limited historical information about those cases, (3) the lack of a control group, (4) the possibility that intervening variables could explain states' behavior, and (5) the lack of a production-oriented autocratic comparison group. I next discuss these challenges and the steps I have taken to address them.

First, investigating a shock that impacts a small number of states allowed in-depth data collection for the full universe of states that can legally make claims on Arctic resources. However, one might reasonably be concerned that the small number of cases presents an obstacle for the generalizability of my findings to non-Arctic states. However, prior coauthored work has already demonstrated the generalizability of my findings by testing the theory on a larger and more representative group of states.[13] Using a sample of all states from 1816 to 2001, the prior work demonstrates that as states become less economically dependent on territory, they become less likely to engage in territorial conflict. The cases developed in this book complement the previous work by providing a more detailed, nuanced measure of the key theoretical constructs and by illustrating the causal pathways through which economic structure should influence a regime's preference for territory and its willingness to compete for control of territory. Also, I demonstrate the generalizability of my theory by demonstrating that it can be applied broadly to explain existing cases of resource competition outside the Arctic.

Second, dealing with a recent shock allows assessment of how well my theory explains variation in states' preferences and behavior today and in the future. With contemporary cases, however, there are fewer rich histories and publicly available archives to illuminate how rulers thought about their response to Arctic climate change. The lack of such evidence limits my ability to assess which individuals were in the governing coalition and how much they influenced the state's view of the Arctic as a source of potential resources or rents. To help deal with this issue, I drew from secondary sources on each of the states' Arctic foreign policies and, when possible, conducted interviews with government officials and Arctic experts. However, even if archival sources and rich histories were available, they might not reveal the true intentions of the governing coalitions, given that people might have strong incentives to conceal their motivations. Fortunately, my theory allows me to focus on measuring observable behavior. Thus, I can show that the states which my theory suggests should have a strong preference to secure control over resources responded *as if* they did, in fact, have that preference.

Third, all states received the treatment of the shock at the same time. This allows me to compare each of their responses, but the trade-off is that there is no control group that did not receive the treatment. Thus, we must rely on the pre-shock period as the control and assume that the timing of each state's assignment to the

---

[13] Markowitz, Fariss, and McMahon, "Producing Goods and Projecting Power"; Markowitz et al., "Productive Pacifists."

post-treatment period is "as if random." Consequently, this design cannot rule out the possibility that the shock caused or covaried with a change in some other variable that might be driving state behavior.[14]

Fourth, state behavior may be driven by factors that covary with the shock. For example, receding ice exposes both resources and sea lanes. This may alter states' incentives to project power to the Arctic as they seek to govern those sea lanes and to protect their newly exposed northern flanks. However, as I demonstrate in the cases, while climate change is altering the accessibility of Arctic sea lanes, this is unlikely to be driving states' responses to the shock, for several reasons. The Arctic is unlikely to be a major thoroughfare for global trade for many decades because it is full of dangerous and unpredictable icebergs. As a result, shipping companies refuse to insure Arctic shipping, making it unprofitable. The Arctic also lacks basic shipping infrastructure, such as deep-water ports, robust communications systems, and search-and-rescue assets. These same factors mitigate concerns over an exposed northern flank as they would hinder invasion from the sea. Any potential invader would have to navigate a minefield of icebergs and risk being a sitting duck for enemy aircraft and antiship missiles. Even after landing, the invading forces would be operating in hostile, remote conditions where they could easily be cut off from resupply. (This may explain why most states have done relatively little planning and war gaming related to executing or repelling an Arctic amphibious assault.) These factors may change in several decades if the Arctic becomes ice-free during the summer, but the prospect of open sea lanes is unlikely to have driven states' immediate response to the shock that occurred in 2007.

Fifth, ideally, there would be an equivalent comparison group of states that were autocratic, production-oriented, and able to make claims to Arctic resources. This would allow me to isolate the impact of regime type by comparing this group to the production-oriented democracies and the effect of economic structure by comparing this group to land-oriented autocracies. Unfortunately, no such group exists. I deal with this in five ways. First, I point to existing research which has already demonstrated that autocracies tend to have a stronger interest in seeking rents and engaging in territorial expansion.[15] Second, in other coauthored work I employed a large-n test with a larger sample of states to demonstrate that both regime type and economic structure have an independent and conditional effect on a state's

---

[14] An ideal method of dealing with these issues might be to employ a factorial design that compared the pre- and post-treatment behavior of four groups of states: one exposed only to new resources, one exposed only to a change in economic structure, one exposed to both, and one exposed to neither. Since that design is not an option, I employ a less ideal but feasible design. In order to address the trade-off associated with my design, future research should look for cases in which the economic structure of the state and the source of income for the state's governing coalition shift due to exogenous forces, such as technology, an increase in the global demand for certain commodities, or the discovery of resources.

[15] Lake, "Powerful Pacifists"; Bueno de Mesquita et al., *Logic of Political Survival.*

propensity to seek territory.[16] Third, as discussed in greater detail in Chapters 4 and 8, I test the impact of economic structure while holding regime type constant by comparing land-oriented, democratic Norway to the three production-oriented democracies. Fourth, I examine the influence of regime type by assessing whether Russia's autocratic political institutions led its rulers to have a stronger value for the political benefits associated with land rents and to narrowly concentrate those rents among the ruling elite. Fifth, in the conclusion I briefly apply my theory to illustrate how China's production-oriented economy and autocratic political institutions should condition its foreign policy preferences in the South China Sea and beyond.

3.5 Conclusion

This chapter introduced a novel research design that uses the exogenous shock of Arctic climate change to measure the influence of variation in states' preferences on their foreign policy behavior.

Having defended my research design, the stage is now set to test my theoretical predictions against those of my competitors. The empirical analysis in this book begins in Chapter 4 by explaining my measurement of the independent variable of interest, namely the economic structure of the state, and the dependent variable, investment in an exclusionary foreign policy. Chapter 4 provides these definitions, presents quantitative data that group the five Arctic states by economic structure, and compares their foreign policy choices before and after the 2007 shock. My theory makes predictions about the change in foreign policy choices that should occur in resource-dependent states following the shock, and these quantitative data provide a clean test of those predictions. In Chapters 5 through 8, I conduct a more detailed qualitative analysis of each of the five cases, allowing me to bring to bear a more complete and diverse set of evidence regarding how each state responded to the shock. This evidence complements and serves as a robustness check on the findings from the quantitative analysis. The cases also illustrate the causal pathways through which my theory suggests that the economic structure should influence the foreign policy preferences of those who govern the state.

---

[16] Markowitz et al., "Productive Pacifists."

4

Descriptive Statistics and Cross-National Comparisons of Arctic Power Projection

4.1 Introduction

Take the theory to the data; doing so, of course, requires data. However, until now there was little systematic data on Arctic power projection and states' power projection capabilities. This chapter remedies this lack by unveiling three new data sets created for this project that capture variations in each state's Arctic power projection capabilities and military deployments before and after the shock. The data are the product of extensive, detailed research into the military assets and procurement activity of each of these five states and the military exercises they conducted. Collecting these data took the better part of a decade, and one data set, the Arctic Military Activity Events Data Set, required sifting through and hand-coding more than 5,000 news articles. These data sets are the first to measure not only changes in states' power projection capabilities but also the actual projection of power as measured by regional military deployments. This allows for a more systematic comparison of these states' regional military activity.

I compare the changes in each state's level of investment in its Arctic military activity force structure after the shock. The data decisively confirm my theoretical predictions by demonstrating that resource-dependent states, such as Russia, not only invested more in enhancing their ability to project power in the Arctic but also projected power more frequently and intensely in disputed areas of the Arctic.

This chapter makes three principal contributions. First, I develop a clear definition of power projection, locating it within a network of related constructs, and provide a novel strategy for operationalizing this construct. Power projection is a critical concept in the study of international relations, but its measurement has proven elusive. Second, I introduce three original data sets that are used to operationalize my dependent variable, the degree to which states invested in projecting power in the Arctic. These data will be of broad interest to scholars whose work is

Perils of Plenty. Jonathan N. Markowitz, Oxford University Press (2020). © Oxford University Press.
DOI: 10.1093/oso/9780190078249.001.0001

related to power projection but who have struggled to measure this concept.[1] Third, the descriptive statistics generated from these data offer the most comprehensive and systematic comparison to date of how each state's Arctic military presence and capabilities changed over time. These data have been presented to officials from the US military, State Department, Coast Guard, and intelligence community as well as to policymakers from other nations. According to both scholars and officials, these are the first ever data sets that systematically measure changes in each state's Arctic force structure and military activity with this level of detail and over this period.

4.1.1 Road Map

The remainder of this chapter proceeds as follows. The first step is to introduce my strategy for measuring states' economic structure (my key independent variable) and their investments in exclusionary foreign policy (my dependent variable). I provide precise definitions of the variables used in this study and explain how they are measured. The chapter then proceeds to present paired cross-national comparisons that test the core predictions of my theory. I examine pairs of states that are similar on a number of dimensions but differ in their level of resource dependence, to see how they responded to the 2007 shock in terms of the degree to which they invested in projecting power to the Arctic. While many factors may explain differences in states' baseline levels of power projection in the Arctic, only the desire to secure control over resources should explain *changes* in state behavior that occurred immediately after the 2007 shock.

For readers who wish to skim the following section, Table 4.1 provides a summary of the following: (1) my theoretical constructs, (2) the variables used to measure these constructs, (3) the variables' role in the theory and test, and (4) the indicators used to operationalize these variables.

4.2 Measuring the Independent Variable: The Economic Structure of the State

Before conducting the analysis, we must describe the data upon which it is based. I begin with the independent variable of interest, the economic structure of the state. When past research has sought to incorporate the characteristics of a state's governing coalition to explain its foreign policy preferences, scholars have struggled

---

[1] Until now there have been no data sets that directly measured power projection regarding military deployments. The Military Activity Events Data Set is also the first data set to code attributes of states' military deployments, such as whether the states deployed forces to areas under dispute. The methods developed here can be applied and expanded in future work to measure changes in the frequency with which states project power to other regions, such as the South China Sea.

Table 4.1 Relation of Theoretical Constructs to Empirical Measures

Construct	Role in Theory	Variable Used to Measure Construct	Variable Definition	Role of Variable in Test	Operationalization of Variable
Economic Structure of the State	Cause Construct	Land Orientation	Degree to which a state's economy is oriented toward the extraction of land rents vs. the production of goods and services	Independent Variable	Resource rents as % of GDP (from World Bank) Robustness checks: fuel exports as % of GDP; oil exports as % of government revenue
Preference for Securing Territory	Effect of Cause and Mediator of Observable Implication	Preference for Territory	Degree to which a state prefers to secure control over territory	Mediator Variable	[Unobservable]
Exogenous Exposure of Contestable Resources	Opportunity to Observe Observable Implication	Arctic Shock	A rapid exposure of contestable resources unrelated to states' economic structures or levels of investment in exclusionary foreign policy	Exogenous Shock	The post-shock period begins July 1, 2007. (This is approximately the time when a coming rapid drop in the level of Arctic ice became common knowledge.)
Foreign Policy Choice	Observable Implication	Exclusionary Foreign Policy	The degree to which a state invests in projecting power to seek rents.	Dependent Variable	(1) Commitments to the Arctic. (2) Arctic force posture (where and how they deploy) (3) Arctic force structure (ice-hardened ships, Arctic bases)

to identify coalition types ex ante. Identifying the economic interests of the individuals in the coalition is difficult, in that we cannot directly observe ex ante who is in or out of the coalition. The measurement strategy I employ here solves this problem by allowing us to identify the economic interest of the individuals in a state's governing coalition by looking at the source of their income.

The income source of a state's governing coalition is conditioned by the economic structure of the state. My theory focuses on a single dimension of that economic structure—the degree to which the economy is organized to generate income from land, as opposed to producing goods and services. I call states on either extreme of this dimension *land-oriented* and *production-oriented*, respectively. Measures that indicate the share of a state's economy generated by these two sectors are employed as proxy measures for the economic interest of the state's governing coalition. The key assumption here is that there is a relatively tight relationship between the means by which wealth and income are generated and political representation in a state's governing coalition. The more a society derives income from land, the more political representation the land-oriented sector will have in the state's governing coalition. This assumption is plausible because money generally finds its way into politics. As explained in Chapter 2, either money captures the state or the state captures money.[2]

To operationalize how land-oriented a state's economy is and how dependent the regime is on resources, I follow research on the resource curse and adopt several indicators, including resource rents, oil exports, and fuel exports as a percentage of gross domestic product (GDP; see Table 4.2).[3] Where possible, I also include government data on oil and natural gas as a percentage of GDP and government revenues. The greater the share of a state's economy that is derived from resources, the more land-oriented that economy and the more resource-dependent the regime. Thus, I expect that the more land-oriented a state's economic structure, the stronger its preference for territory will be.

4.3 Measuring the Dependent Variable: Investment in Exclusionary Foreign Policy

Recall that pursuing an exclusionary foreign policy is defined as investing in the projection of power to seek land rents.[4] There are three ways to conceptualize variation

---

[2] For additional details on my measurement strategy, see section A of the Appendix.

[3] There are two primary sources of income that can be derived from territory: agrarian surplus and natural resource rents. Historically, agriculture represented the majority of economic output; but today agriculture is only a few percent of the GDP of developed states, and resource rents are the largest source of income derived from territory. For more on this, see section A of the Appendix.

[4] Despite numerous attempts to measure the concept of power, there are relatively few studies that have sought to measure power projection in a systematic way. For previous attempts to systematically

Table 4.2 **Operationalizing Land-Oriented Economic Structure**

Country	Oil Exports % of GDP[*a]	Fuel Exports % of GDP[**b]	Resource Rents % of GDP[**c]
United States	0.325	0.171	1.01
Canada	1.04	4.88	3.75
Denmark	0.766	2.04	1.15
Norway	9.72	19.1	8.38
Russia	9.44	16.5	15.5

[*] Data only available through 2001 (average 1991–2001).

[**] Average 1997–2007.

[a]Note that in some cases, such as the United States, oil exports as a percentage of GDP will appear to be larger than fuel exports as a percentage of GDP. This occurs because the data on oil exports as a percentage of GDP are from Ashford, who uses data from the World Bank as well several different sources including the BP Statistical Index and the Energy Information Administration, while the data on fuel exports as a percentage of GDP come only from the World Bank. For more on this, see Emma Ashford, "Oil and Violence: The Foreign Policy of Resource-Rich States" (ISA-ISSS Conference, 2013), 21.

[b]Calculated based on World Bank data on fuel exports as a percentage of merchandise exports. World Bank staff estimates are via the WITS platform from the Comtrade database maintained by the United Nations Statistics Division. World Bank, "Fuel Exports (% of Merchandise Exports)," 2005, http://data.worldbank.org/indicator/TX.VAL.FUEL.ZS.UN.

[c]World Bank, "Total Natural Resources Rents (% of GDP)," World Development Indicators, June 25, 2018, https://data.worldbank.org/indicator/NY.GDP.TOTL.RT.ZS.

in the adoption of an exclusionary foreign policy, the third of which I employ in this book. First, it could be treated as a binary outcome: states either adopt an exclusionary foreign policy or don't. In this approach, the exclusionary foreign policy is an outcome, and we are comparing the probability of that outcome occurring in different states.[5] Second, the dependent variable could be expressed as foreign policies varying in their degree of exclusion. This approach would be similar to Lake's continuum of economic hierarchy, which has free market exchange at one end and economic dependency at the other.[6] Third, and most relevant for this book, the dependent variable can be expressed as the relative level of *investment* that states make

measure power projection, see Douglas Lemke, *Regions of War and Peace* (Cambridge: Cambridge University Press, 2002); Benjamin O. Fordham, "Who Wants to Be a Major Power? Explaining the Expansion of Foreign Policy Ambition," *Journal of Peace Research* 48, no. 5 (2011): 587–603, https://doi.org/10.1177/0022343311411959.

[5] This approach is used in a series of papers by Markowitz, McMahon, and Fariss that assess the probability of states engaging in territorial militarized interstate disputes as a proxy measure for a state's choice to pursue an exclusionary foreign policy.

[6] David A. Lake, "Anarchy, Hierarchy, and the Variety of International Relations," *International Organization* 50, no. 1 (1996): 1–33.

in pursuing an exclusionary foreign policy. I use this third approach because the data available on states' foreign policy behavior are most informative and appropriate for coding the level of investment in exclusion.

My goal is to observe how states responded to the Arctic shock by investing in seeking control over Arctic resources. This strategy builds on previous efforts to operationalize rent-seeking by measuring the investments made by actors to obtain rent.[7] Since I am interested in states' investments in projecting power to seek rents, I assess a set of observable state behaviors that indicate such investment.

I operationalize my dependent variable using several observable indicators that should covary with a state's choice to invest in projecting military power into the Arctic. Specifically, I assess changes in a state's Arctic commitments, military activity, and force structure.[8] To operationalize changes in commitments, I gathered qualitative evidence from government documents, showing officials' claims over resources and commitments to defend those claims by investing in projecting military force. The more a state invests in making expansive territorial claims and building and projecting military force to areas under dispute, the stronger the evidence that it is pursuing an exclusionary foreign policy.

To assess whether officials followed through on these commitments, I created three original data sets that measure variation in states' Arctic military activity (deployments) and force structure (i.e., Arctic-specific forces, icebreakers, ice-hardened ships, and bases).[9] These data sets allow me to demonstrate that the shock caused a change in states' behavior immediately following the shock. More specifically, they allow me to assess how each state responded to the shock by comparing its pre- and post-shock levels of Arctic military activity. The data sets also allow me to assess the change in states' investment in projecting military power after the shock. If my theory is correct, then, all else being equal, we should observe the greatest change in the most resource-dependent states.

First, I consider changes in states' Arctic military activity using my Arctic Military Activity Events Data Set, which codes data on Arctic military deployments. In order to gather data on Arctic military activity, a sample of over 5,000 news articles that reported on states' Arctic military deployments from January 1, 2005, to December 31, 2009, was coded.[10] The data allow for comparison of the frequency and intensity

---

[7] For an excellent review of the rent-seeking literature, see Roger D. Congleton, Arye L. Hillman, and Kai A. Konrad, "Forty Years of Research on Rent Seeking: An Overview," June 16, 2008, http://www.tax.mpg.de/fileadmin/TAX/pdf1/2008-introduction_rent_seeking_june_16_2008.pdf.

[8] Additional details on the theory of measurement that informed the collection of the data and the details of its coding are available in sections B and C of the Appendix.

[9] The full code books that describe how these data were coded and the data sets themselves are available upon request.

[10] For more detail on how the data was coded, see the Arctic Bases and Ice-Capable Ships Codebook which is available upon request.

of each state's Arctic military activity for approximately two years before and after the shock. For each event, three main characteristics were coded: whether a state deployed forces (1) within its borders, (2) beyond its borders (power projection), and (3) to areas under dispute or to the Arctic borders or airspace of other states with which it had disputes.

The first category, "within borders," involves the deployment of a state's forces within its borders. This includes any event in which a state's forces—military (such as troops), nonmilitary, or paramilitary (including the US Coast Guard and Canadian Arctic Rangers)—are deployed above the Arctic Circle. The second type of event, "power projection," involves deployments of state forces beyond the state's borders. For example, if Canadian Rangers engaged in exercises on Canadian soil, this would count as a state activity, not power projection, because they did not deploy beyond the state's borders. In contrast, if Canada deployed a warship to the Arctic, this would be coded as power projection because it projected force outside Canada. The third type of event, "to disputed area/other state's borders," involves incidents in which a state projected power to a claimed or disputed area or to the border of a state with which it had a dispute. For illustration, this type of event would be coded "yes" if Canada deployed a ship to a disputed area such as the North Pole (over which it disputes ownership with Russia) or to the borders of Russia. The purpose of these categories is to allow us to assess not just whether there was a change in each state's Arctic military activity but whether there was a change in states' willingness to project power beyond their borders and engage in gunboat diplomacy by deploying forces to back their resource claims. All else being equal, the more frequently a state deploys force, the stronger its preference to project power into a given region.

Next, I assess the change in each state's investment in Arctic-specific assets before and after the shock. Following the shock, many leaders promised to back their states' claims by increasing their Arctic presence and enhancing the capabilities needed to do so. Maintaining a presence in this harsh environment demands specialized equipment such as icebreakers, ice-hardened patrol ships, and Arctic bases equipped with specialized facilities that can keep people alive in temperatures that dip below −58°F. Information on these Arctic-specific forces will be the most informative about states' intentions to project power into the Arctic, given their limited utility outside the Arctic.

States can and do employ dual-use assets such as submarines and aircraft to project power to the Arctic. However, without Arctic-specific assets, such as bases equipped with deep-water ports or runways and refueling and maintenance facilities, aircraft have no place to land and ships have nowhere to dock and refuel. This would severely limit the amount of time that aircraft and ships could spend on station patrolling, demonstrating presence, and showing the flag. As expressed in the Norwegian government's Arctic white paper,

Showing a presence is a goal in itself. Norway promotes stability by having a clear military presence and operating in a consistent and predictable way. Today, the Armed Forces' presence in North Norway is a permanent part of the status quo. Norway must also have the capacity to prevent difficult situations arising, and to handle any situations that do arise adequately, using appropriate means.[11]

Ice-hardened submarines can patrol Arctic waters, but without icebreakers and ice-capable patrol ships, it is impossible to maintain a continuous presence above the surface for most of the year. Maintaining a presence is critical for executing many missions related to furthering a state's claims, upholding its sovereignty over the areas it claims, and managing and developing the offshore resources there. These missions require specialized capabilities to clear sea lanes of ice, conduct search-and-rescue operations, and survey the ocean floor both to gather data to further the state's claims and to discover and develop the resources there. Maintaining a presence also allows states to monitor other actors and prevent them from exploiting the maritime resources in the state's exclusive economic zone (EEZ) without permission. Thus, the more a state is interested in securing control over and developing Arctic resources, the more we should observe it investing in the capabilities needed to do so.

Variation in states' investments in Arctic power projection capabilities is measured with two additional original data sets, the Icebreaker and Ice-Hardened Warships Data Set and the Arctic Bases Data Set. The Icebreaker and Ice-Hardened Warships Data Set records the number of icebreakers and ice-hardened patrol ships and warships that each state owns, orders, and commissions. The data set includes all icebreakers that are owned directly by the state or owned by state-controlled firms. This data set also records the attributes of each ship, such as its length and tonnage.

The Arctic Bases Data Set records the location and attributes of all bases located above the Arctic Circle. I include attributes such as whether a base closed, reopened, or was upgraded.[12] I adopt the commonly used definition of the Arctic Circle as 66.3°N. I include all bases above the Arctic Circle for two main reasons. First, because I am interested in the degree to which states invested in projecting power to the Arctic, my goal was to include bases whose primary purpose was to maintain a military presence in the Arctic. If a base is located above the Arctic Circle, by definition it is evidence of a military presence in the Arctic. While bases below the Arctic Circle can be used to project power into the Arctic, it is more difficult to discern

---

[11] Norwegian Ministry of Foreign Affairs, *The High North: Visions and Strategies*, Meld. St. 7 (2011-2012) Report to the Storting (White Paper) (Oslo: Norwegian Ministry of Foreign Affairs, 2012), 69.

[12] For more detail on this, see the Arctic Bases and Ice-Capable Ships Codebook which is available upon request.

whether this is their primary purpose. Thus, including only bases above the Arctic Circle provides a clear basis for deciding whether to include or exclude a base. In the qualitative case studies, I included a discussion of potentially important bases located near but below the Arctic Circle to guard against the possibility that excluding them might bias the results in my favor.

As it turns out, limiting my data to bases above the Arctic Circle actually makes it more difficult for me to find support for my theory. Norway and Russia, the two states I predicted would invest the most in Arctic power projection, each have many bases located near but below the Arctic Circle. Excluding those bases from the analysis tilts the results against my theoretical prediction. The fact that even excluding these bases I still find that Norway and Russia made a larger investment in their Arctic force structure than other states represents especially strong evidence for my theory.

Governments often announce plans to acquire military units that never materialize due to lack of funds. This failure to follow through on announced acquisitions is informative about the strength of their preferences. Because talk is cheap (states often promise to build a warship but don't deliver), the most salient indicators are the actual construction of military forces, units, and bases. For this reason, I extended the data for these indicators over a long period, from January 1, 1997, to December 31, 2017, allowing me to ascertain which of the announced acquisitions and upgrades were actually completed. Note that ships that were commissioned or bases that were built or upgraded after December 31, 2017, are not included in the data set. However, in the qualitative cases, I discuss a small number of ships that were commissioned and bases that were built or upgraded after this date to help reassure the reader that excluding them does not bias my findings. The pre-shock period runs from January 1, 1997, to May 31, 2007, and the post-shock period runs from June 1, 2007, to December 31, 2017. This provides us with approximately ten years before and after the shock. Recall that extending the data back further in time helps avoid incorrectly counting ships or bases ordered before the shock as part of a state's response to the shock. Extending the data to longer after the shock allows us to assess whether states followed through on their commitments to build additional forces.[13]

In the following chapters, the data are supplemented with qualitative evidence that serves three purposes. First, the qualitative evidence serves as a robustness check on the quantitative data. Second, it allows me to discuss individual military deployments in great detail and in relation to other contextual factors, such as whether the deployments coincided with statements by officials regarding their

---

[13] Where data permit, the data set also includes information on when officials announced the construction of the base or ship, when funding was allocated, when construction actually began, and when the asset was commissioned. For a more in-depth discussion of this data set, see the code book in the supplementary materials.

state's claims over resources and territory. Third, while my quantitative data on military activity events end on December 31, 2009, the qualitative evidence allows me to consider military deployments that occurred after this date. This enables me to assess whether the land-oriented, resource-dependent states, namely Russia and Norway, continued to regularly deploy military force to the Arctic after the end of 2009, and thus whether they continued to follow through on their commitments.

In sum, the most informative behaviors are those that cost the most. Investments in site-specific force structure and force posture are the costliest behaviors and are therefore the most informative about a state's willingness to invest in pursuing one type of foreign policy rather than another. Thus, the greater a state's investment in its geographically specific force structure and force posture, the stronger the signal that it has invested in projecting power to a specific geographic area. Conversely, the less a state invests in such capabilities, the less willing it is to invest in projecting location-specific military force. Many states have promised to invest in their Arctic force structures but have not followed through on their commitments. Therefore, the empirical section focuses on whether or not states actually invested in altering their Arctic military presence.

4.4 Summary of Empirical Predictions

Before discussing the empirical patterns in the data, I will briefly summarize my theoretical predictions for those reading this as a stand-alone chapter. The more economically dependent a state is on resource rents, the stronger its preference should be to secure Arctic resources. Thus, the more resource-dependent a state is, the greater the change we should observe in its willingness to invest in projecting power to the Arctic after the shock.

The United States and Denmark are the least economically dependent on resource rents, and Canada is the next least dependent. Given this, all else being equal, Rent-Addiction Theory suggests that the United States and Denmark should invest the least and Canada should invest the second least. In contrast, Norway is more economically dependent on resource rents than any of the Arctic states except Russia. Thus, I expect Russia to invest the most and Norway to invest the next most. A summary of these theoretical predictions can be seen in Table 4.3.

As this chapter will demonstrate, the data decisively confirm my theoretical predictions. I demonstrate that resource-dependent states, such as Norway and Russia, not only invested more in enhancing their Arctic power projection capabilities but also projected power more frequently and intensely to Arctic areas under dispute than other states with a similar or even greater capacity to do so. The qualitative evidence presented in the following chapters will show that this shift in investment was no accident but rather part of a broader shift in foreign policy to prioritize the Arctic and secure control over the resources there.

Table 4.3 **Summary of Theoretical Predictions for All Arctic States**

	Predicted Change in Investment	Observed Change in Investment	Rank among Arctic States
United States	Small	Small	Least
Denmark	Small	Small	Least
Canada	Small	Small	Second least
Norway	Moderate	Moderate	Second most
Russia	Very large	Large	Most

4.5 Denmark versus Norway

In comparing how states responded to the shock, it is important to compare states that are as similar as possible in terms of their capacity to respond. This helps to control for the possibility that some states invested in projecting power simply because they had more capacity to invest. Following standard practice, I use GDP as a proxy for economic capacity. I begin by comparing how Norway and Denmark responded to the shock because they have similar economic capacities. They are also both small and relatively weak states whose Arctic claims are contested by more powerful states such as Russia. Comparing these two states is useful for two other reasons. First, in the late 1960s Norway struck it rich with the discovery of oil in the North Sea, while Denmark's share of the North Sea is much smaller, with far fewer resources. As a result, Norway became highly economically dependent on oil, while Denmark did not. Norway's discovery of North Sea oil represents a natural experiment that randomly assigns Norway to the treatment (by altering its economic structure to make it more land-oriented) while assigning Denmark as the control.[14] This enhances the internal validity of my research design by randomly and exogenously manipulating my core independent variable, the economic structure of the state.

Second, the two nations are similar in a number of other ways that allow me to control for potentially confounding factors. This similarity increases our confidence that differences in how they responded to the shock are driven by the treatment and not by other preexisting differences between them. Both countries are ethnically homogenous Nordic nations with a similar history and cultural norms, given that

---

[14] I provide an in-depth defense of my claim that Norway's discovery of North Sea oil represents a "natural experiment" in Chapter 8. For another paper that uses this as a natural experiment to examine the effect of oil on the Norwegian economy relative to other Nordic states, see Erling Røed Larsen, "Escaping the Resource Curse and the Dutch Disease?" *American Journal of Economics and Sociology,* 65, no. 3 (2006), 605–40, http://onlinelibrary.wiley.com/doi/10.1111/j.1536-7150.2006.00476.x/abstract.

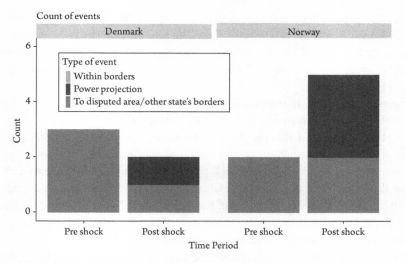

Figure 4.1 Danish versus Norwegian Arctic Military Activity

Norway used to be part of Denmark. Additionally, both states have highly developed and advanced economies, democratic political institutions, and a strong commitment to liberal norms.

Virtually all prior theories that focus on regime type, liberal norms, or a state's type of economy predict that Norway, like Denmark, should have a weak preference to secure control over territory.[15] In contrast, my theory suggests that Norway should have a much stronger preference to secure control over resources than Denmark. This provides us with an opportunity to test my prediction against competing theories. For example, if regime type alone determines a state's preference for territory, then we should observe no difference between Denmark and Norway's willingness to invest in securing control over Arctic resources. If my theory is correct, following the shock we should observe a larger increase in Norway's Arctic military presence than in Denmark's. My theory suggests that Norway should have a strong preference for securing territory and resources despite its democratic political institutions. Additionally, comparing Norway to Denmark allows me to hold regime type constant and assess my claim that land-oriented democracies should have a stronger preference for territory than production-oriented democracies.

As Figures 4.1–4.3 show, the data generally support my theoretical predictions. First, as Figure 4.1 shows, the two states had a similar level of Arctic military activity before the shock. However, after the shock there was a substantial increase in Norway's post-shock military activity, while there was actually a small decrease in Denmark's Arctic military activity and its willingness to project power to disputed

---

[15] For a summary of these competing theories, see Chapter 7.

areas. This pattern is further supported by the qualitative evidence in Chapter 8, where we see that after the shock Norway ramped up its Arctic military exercises, frequently intercepted Russian bombers, and deployed forces more frequently to disputed areas such as Svalbard. We see no similar evidence that Denmark engaged in this type of activity.

Second, I assess the change in each state's level of investment in its Arctic-specific force structure by comparing each state's investment in its ice-capable fleet and Arctic bases before and after the shock. I specifically compare the number and tonnage of new ships commissioned and the number of new, upgraded, or reopened bases in the pre-shock and post-shock periods.[16] I focus on new investments because they most accurately measure states' willingness to invest in their Arctic capabilities.[17] If my theory is correct, after the shock there should be a greater increase in the number of commissioned ice-capable ships and new or upgraded bases among resource-dependent than production-oriented states.

Norway and Denmark both started with ice-capable fleets that were similar in tonnage before the shock, although Denmark had many more ships and slightly more tonnage. Denmark started with four ice-hardened frigates, three offshore patrol vessels (OPVs), and three icebreakers, for a total of ten ships. Today, Denmark has only eight operational ships, two fewer than a decade ago, because it has been less willing to invest in its ice-capable fleet. As Figure 4.2 reveals, Denmark did not commission any new ships in the decade before the shock. In the decade after the shock, Denmark did commission three new OPVs, which were larger and more capable than the ships it replaced.[18] However, these ships were not enough to replace the five ships—two patrol ships and three older icebreakers—that Denmark decommissioned after the shock. As a result, a decade after the shock, Denmark has only eight ice-capable ships that can operate in the Arctic, none of which are dedicated icebreakers.

In contrast, at the time of the shock, Norway had one large armed OPV that also functioned as an icebreaker, the *Svalbard*, and four smaller ice-hardened

---

[16] Recall that for the Arctic Bases and Arctic Icebreakers and Ice-Hardened Warships Data Set, the pre-shock period extends back ten years prior to the shock—from January 1, 1997, to June 30, 2007—and the post-shock period extends ten years after the shock, from July 1, 2007, to December 31, 2017.

[17] Comparing states' existing forces rather than new forces would both be inappropriate and strongly bias the analysis in favor of my theory given that Russia and Norway have a much greater number of bases left over from the Cold War and, as a result, would have more bases than other states even if they did not make any new investments. Additionally, because of geographic and historic factors, Russia has a much larger ice-capable fleet than other states before the shock. Thus, focusing on the change in new investments in the decades before and after the shock helps to eliminate this potential source of bias. However, interested readers can see that my results are robust for measuring the change in the number of operational or existing bases and ships in section D of the Appendix.

[18] Note that two of these were ordered pre-shock, while the third was ordered and built after the shock.

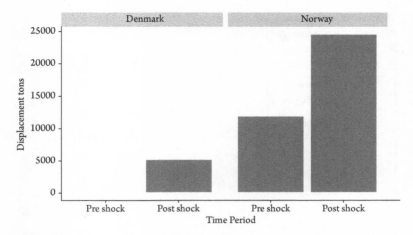

Figure 4.2 New Investment in Ice-Capable Ships: Denmark versus Norway

armed OPVs, for a total of five operational ships. In Figure 4.2, we see that Norway responded to the shock with a much larger investment in new ice-capable ships (which includes both ice-hardened ships and icebreakers). Since the shock, oil-dependent Oslo has completed the construction of six additional ice-capable ships that were announced pre-shock. It is important to note that five of these six ice-hardened OPVs were ordered before the shock and therefore count in the pre-shock period, but it is also informative that Norway chose to follow through on building all of them. This stands in contrast to Canada, which announced plans to build six to eight icebreakers before the shock but did not follow through on this commitment, repeatedly delaying the start of construction and cutting funding.

After the shock Norway also ordered and built a new, more powerful icebreaker, which is capable of breaking ice up to one meter thick. This gives Norway a total of eleven ice-hardened warships, more than double the number that it had before the shock. Moreover, Norway not only built more ships but also built larger ships as measured by tonnage.[19] Larger ships are more capable but are also a larger investment. As a result, the total tonnage of Norway's ice-hardened fleet more than doubled after the shock. In contrast, the total tonnage of the Danish ice-capable fleet fell. This change is even more pronounced considering that before the shock the Danish fleet was larger in terms of both the number of ships and absolute tonnage and that its ships were, on average, bigger than Norway's.[20] As predicted by

[19] Note that, in accordance with standard practice, we use displacement to measure tonnage (see the Arctic Icebreakers and Ice-Hardened Warships Data Set). For more on this, see Brian Benjamin Crisher and Mark Souva, "Power at Sea: A Naval Power Data Set, 1865–2011," *International Interactions* 40, no. 4 (2014): 608, https://doi.org/10.1080/03050629.2014.918039.

[20] To see this relationship graphically, see Figures A.2 and A.3 in section D of the Appendix.

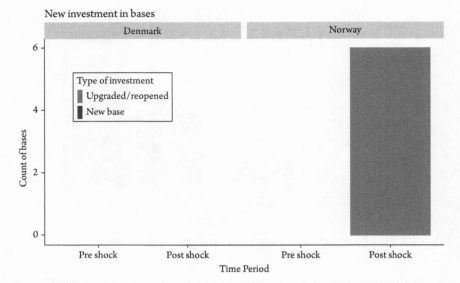

Figure 4.3 New Investment in Arctic Military Bases: Denmark versus Norway

my theory, oil-dependent Norway has invested more than production-oriented Denmark in building a more capable ice-hardened fleet.

Finally, Figure 4.3 shows that only Norway invested in upgrading its bases north of the Arctic Circle after the shock. Before the shock, Norway had seventeen bases above the Arctic Circle and Denmark had only three. Neither state made upgrades or built any new bases in the decade prior to the shock. However, despite Norway's lead in 2007, Denmark did not establish any new Arctic bases post-shock; it didn't even upgrade its existing small outposts above the Arctic Circle. In contrast, Norway closed two obsolete Cold War–era bases, upgraded six bases, and moved its military headquarters above the Arctic Circle (the only state to do so). In the comparative case studies in Chapter 8, I present more detailed qualitative evidence about the scale and significance of these upgrades in the context of a larger shift in Norwegian foreign policy toward the Arctic. Denmark did make minor upgrades to one base at Nuuk, on the southern end of Greenland; but this base is south of the Arctic Circle and nearly 1,800 miles from the North Pole. This base is not included in the quantitative data, which only include bases above the Arctic Circle.[21] In sum, we can see that following the shock, Norway invested more than Denmark in enhancing its Arctic military activity, icebreakers, ice-hardened warships, and bases. Moreover, we shall see in Chapter 8 how Norway's Arctic military presence increased as it

---

[21] Recall that the data set only includes bases located above the Arctic Circle, which tends to bias the results against my theory.

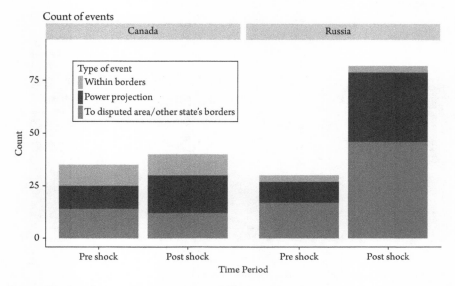

Figure 4.4 Canadian versus Russian Arctic Military Activity

stationed more forces in the Arctic and increased the frequency of Arctic military exercises.

4.6 Canada versus Russia

Comparing Canada and Russia is useful because they have comparably sized Arctic EEZs and economies and similar levels of Arctic military activity, which allows me to compare their behavior while holding these factors roughly constant.[22] Thus, if the size of states' economies or Arctic EEZs or their prior military presence is driving their behavior, we should observe Canada projecting as much power as Russia. However, if preferences for territory matter more than those factors, land-oriented Russia should respond to the resource shock by investing more in boosting its Arctic military presence than production-oriented Canada.

First, comparing their Arctic military activity in Figure 4.4, we can see that the two states had a similar level of activity prior to the shock. However, after the shock Canada's military activity increased only slightly, mostly driven by an increase in

---

[22] Sea Around US Project, "Exclusive Economic Zones" (PEW Charitable Trust, September 24, 2013), http://www.seaaroundus.org/eez/. At the time of the shock, Russia's GDP was approximately 1.3 trillion and Canada's approximately 1.5 trillion in nominal dollars. World Bank, "GDP (Current US$) | Data," 2017, https://data.worldbank.org/indicator/NY.GDP.MKTP.CD.

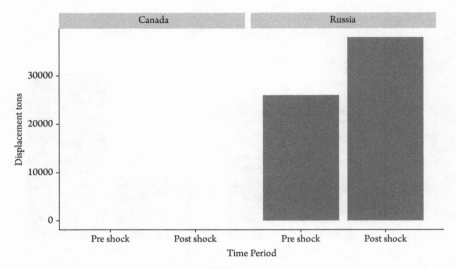

Figure 4.5 New Canadian and Russian Investment in Ice-Capable Ships

its willingness to project power beyond its borders. However, the frequency with which Ottawa projected power to disputed areas actually decreased slightly.

The qualitative evidence in Chapter 5 confirms that Canada has been reluctant to deploy force to back its resource claims. When Canada did deploy military force beyond its borders, it was often to intercept Russian bombers approaching Canada over the Arctic Ocean or to participate in Arctic exercises. Moreover, when Ottawa deployed to disputed areas it generally sent unarmed icebreakers to map the Arctic Ocean floor rather than warships or military aircraft to uphold its claims. In contrast, Russia boosted its Arctic military activity more than any other state, and nearly all of the increase was driven by a major increase in the frequency of power projection. More importantly, Moscow more than tripled the frequency with which it deployed forces to disputed areas and to the borders of the states with which it shared disputes after the shock. These data are consistent with the qualitative evidence presented in Chapter 5, which shows that Moscow was much more willing to back its claims via gunboat diplomacy after the shock. These findings strongly support my theoretical predictions.

Figure 4.5 tells a similar story when comparing ice-capable fleets: only Russia has commissioned new icebreakers since the shock. Russia already had a much larger icebreaker fleet than Canada before the shock. In the summer of 2007, Canada had fifteen ships, all of which were commissioned between 1968 and 1988. Only six of those ships were designated as medium or heavy icebreakers by the Canadian government.[23] In contrast, in June of 2007, Russia had fifty-five ice-capable ships,

---

[23] Canadian Coast Guard, "Icebreaking Operations Services," accessed June 5, 2018, http://www. ccg-gcc.gc.ca/icebreaking/home.

including six massive nuclear-powered icebreakers with a displacement of well over 20,000 tons each.

Despite its aging fleet, Canada did not commission a single icebreaker in the decade before the shock. As we shall see in Chapter 7, Canadian prime minister Stephen Harper promised six to eight ice-hardened patrol ships before the shock, but his government repeatedly delayed funding them. A decade after the shock, Canada has yet to commission a single ship. Four of the patrol ships are still under construction, and work has not even begun on the fifth. Similarly, construction has yet to start on the *John D. Diefenbaker*, the icebreaker Harper promised to build in 2008.

Unlike Canada, which made major commitments but repeatedly delayed or canceled funding for more ice-capable ships, the Russians have actually followed through on their promises. Like Canada, Russia had an aging fleet, having commissioned a number of ships in the early 1990s. However, Russia has made greater investments than Canada in building and commissioning new ships, as we can see from Figure 4.5. Since the shock, Russia has built six ships and started construction on an additional ten, including the gigantic *Arktika*, the first LK-60Ya-class nuclear-powered icebreaker, which launched in 2016 and will be commissioned in 2019. The *Arktika*, weighing in at 33,540 tons, is currently the largest icebreaker in the world.[24] Each of these new nuclear-powered icebreakers is budgeted at $1.1 billion US dollars, representing a substantial investment.[25]

Russia now has a fleet of sixty-one commissioned ships, with another ten under construction, including two more massive LK-60Ya-class nuclear icebreakers. To put this building frenzy in perspective, Russia commissioned a single icebreaker, the *50 Let Pobedy*, which had been under construction since 1989, in the ten years before the shock. In addition, Moscow recently announced plans to build two more nuclear-powered icebreakers, including an unprecedented, gargantuan 55,600-ton icebreaker.[26] Russia is the only state in the world that operates nuclear-powered icebreakers. This unique capability allows Russia to project power year-round in the Arctic Ocean, even under conditions of thick winter ice.

Thus, despite having by far the largest fleet before the shock in terms of both ships and tonnage, resource-dependent Russia has started building and has built

---

[24] We do not have individual data on when these ships were announced, but, as discussed in Chapter 5, immediately following the shock, Russia made a number of promises to build additional icebreakers. Since their construction did not begin until 2010, it is likely they were ordered after the shock.

[25] Eve Conant, "Breaking the Ice: Russian Nuclear-Powered Ice-Breakers," *Scientific American* (guest blog), September 8, 2012, https://blogs.scientificamerican.com/guest-blog/breaking-the-ice/.

[26] GlobalSecurity.org, "Project 10510 Lider LK-100ya—Atomic Icebreaker," accessed August 20, 2017, https://www.globalsecurity.org/military/world/russia/lk-100ya.htm.

New investment in bases

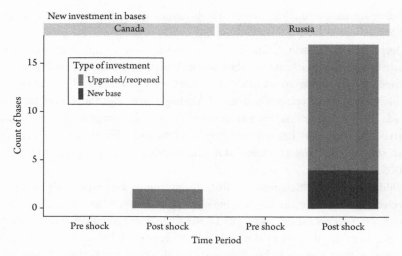

Figure 4.6 New Investment in Arctic Military Bases: Canada versus Russia

more icebreakers since the shock than any other state. The data on each state's tonnage indicate that Russia is not just building more ships; it is also building much
larger ships than before the shock. The ships Russia has built, and started building,
since the shock are approximately twice the size of the ships built before the shock,
measured by mean and median tonnage. Russia's post-shock ships are also much
bigger than those of any other state. To provide some perspective, the ships Canada
ordered (but has yet to finish) after the shock are the second largest of any state,
measured by average tonnage. However, Russia's post-shock ships are on average
more than twice the size of the ships that Canada is building. In sum, since the
shock, Russia has made the largest investment in enhancing its ice-capable fleet.

Finally, we compare Russia and Canada in terms of their Arctic bases (see Figure
4.6). Again, consistent with my theory, Russia dwarfs Canada with its post-shock
investments. Before the shock, Canada had three bases, while Russia had fourteen.
Despite Russia's lead, after the shock Canada not only failed to catch up but actually
fell further behind as it repeatedly delayed funding. Again, the Canadians talked a big
game, promising to build several bases after the shock; but as Chapter 7 will show,
severe delays and reductions in funding forced them to scale back their ambitions.
For example, Ottawa pledged $160 million in 2007 to turn Nanisivik into a per-
manent naval base with a paved runway. However, by 2012, when construction finally started, the plans for Nanisivik had been downscaled to a $60 million summer
refueling station.[27] While Canada did upgrade two existing bases, Resolute Bay and

CFS Alert, a decade after the shock, it still has no new operational bases. In contrast, Russia chose to make much larger investments in upgrading and reopening existing bases and building new ones, despite starting with larger and more capable Arctic bases than any other state. Since the shock, Russia has built four new bases and reopened and/or upgraded an additional thirteen. Ten years after the shock, Russia has a staggering twenty-seven bases above the Arctic Circle. If we include bases south of the Arctic Circle, this number would be even higher. Moreover, as we shall see in Chapter 5, Russia also invested more in its bases, building infrastructure and facilities that allow it to station more troops, supplies, and advanced weapons systems.

In sum, we can see that, as my theory predicts, Russia invested more in boosting its Arctic military activity and building ice-capable ships and Arctic bases than Canada despite having less economic capacity. In the next section, I compare the United States to the other four states.

4.7   The United States versus All Other States

Recall that, on virtually every dimension, the United States is by far the most powerful actor in the Arctic. Thus, the United States is the most likely case for power-based explanations, which suggest that the most powerful states should project the most power. In contrast, my theory suggests that the production-oriented United States should be less interested in securing control over resources and, therefore, less willing to project power to the Arctic than resource-dependent states. Thus, if the United States responded to the shock by projecting less power than other, far weaker states, this would be strong evidence against power-based explanations and suggest that, consistent with my theory, preferences play an important role in explaining US restraint.

Figure 4.7 compares US Arctic military activity to that of the other four states, and we can see that the United States had one of the smallest increases in Arctic military activity. The United States engages in less military activity in the Arctic than Canada or Russia despite being much more powerful. Although American willingness to deploy forces to claimed or disputed areas increased slightly after the shock, these events generally involved sending research missions to map the Arctic Ocean floor, rather than gunboats to uphold US claims. The lack of American military activity in the Arctic is particularly striking given how militarily active the United States is virtually everywhere else in the world. It is reasonable to infer that if the United States did not project power to the Arctic, it was not because it lacked the economic or military capacity but rather because it was not interested in doing so. While the United States does appear to have a higher level of Arctic military activity than Norway, it is much more powerful; and at the time of the shock, its GDP was over thirty times that of Norway. Moreover, as I will discuss in Chapter 8, there are

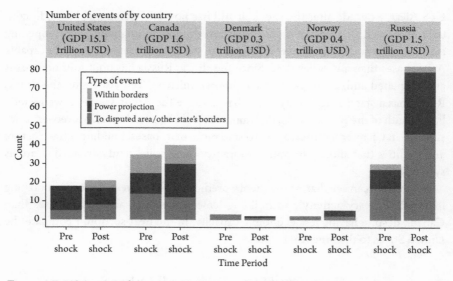

Figure 4.7 US Arctic Military Activity Compared to All Other States

a number of reasons specific to how Norway has chosen to project power in the Arctic that lead me to suspect that the publicly available data are almost certainly severely underreporting Oslo's Arctic military activity.

Figure 4.8 compares the Arctic states' willingness to invest in new icebreaker capacity. Confirming my theoretical predictions, the data show that the United States has been less willing than other far-less-wealthy states to invest in building new icebreakers. At the time of the shock, the United States had two operational icebreakers, the *Polar Sea* and the USCG *Healy*, which were commissioned in the pre-shock period. A third, the *Polar Star*, was out of service for repairs and returned to service in 2012.[28] Today, the United States has only two operational icebreakers (the *Polar Star* and the *Healy*) because the *Polar Sea* suffered massive engine failure and was taken out of service in 2010. The United States did not announce plans to replace it until 2016—nearly a decade after the shock—and has yet to begin construction or even fully fund the project. Thus, the United States has fewer icebreakers now than it did at the time of the shock, and it is unclear if, or when, it will build more ships. Comparing the United States to the other Arctic states, in Figure 4.8, we can see that it is the only state besides Canada that did not commission any ships in the post-shock period, although Canada has a number of ships currently under

[28] It should be noted that the United States National Science Foundation operates a small research icebreaker called the *Nathaniel B. Palmer*, which was delivered in 1992. This is a privately owned ship contracted by the National Science Foundation and is not controlled by either the Coast Guard or the Navy. It is generally not included in discussions of US ice-breaking capacity.

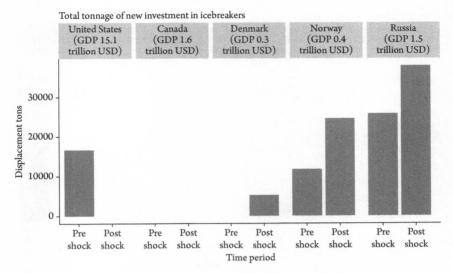

Figure 4.8 New US Investments in Ice-Capable Ships Compared to All Other Arctic States

construction. According to the Government Accountability Office, the result of this lack of investment is that the US Coast Guard is only able to fulfill US government agency icebreaking requests 78% of the time.[29] Admiral Paul Zukunft, US Coast Guard commandant, succinctly summed up the lack of will to invest in the Arctic, saying, "Our GDP is at least eight times that of Russia. And yet we say we can't afford an icebreaker. We just need to make it a priority."[30]

I compare American investments in upgrading Arctic bases to those of the other Arctic nations. The data in Figure 4.9 also confirm my theoretical predictions. As with icebreakers, the data reveal that the United States has not built new bases and still has only one Cold War–era base above the Arctic Circle: a radar station at Thule, Greenland. The United States has two other bases that are included here, both in southern Alaska, well below the Arctic Circle and nearly a thousand miles south of the northern tip of Alaska, which borders the Arctic Ocean. Washington made only minor investments, upgrading the radar at Thule twice, once before the shock, in 2005, and once after, in 2009. As Figure 4.9 shows, the United States has invested less in upgrading and building new bases than any state, except Denmark.

[29] US Government Accountability Office, *Coast Guard: Status of Polar Icebreaking Fleet Capability and Recapitalization Plan*, GAO-17-698R (Washington, DC: US Government Accountability Office, 2017), 2–4, 9, https://www.gao.gov/products/GAO-17-698R.

[30] Jackie Northam, "As the Arctic Opens Up, the U.S. is Down to a Single Icebreaker," NPR.org, June 1, 2015, 17, http://www.npr.org/sections/parallels/2015/06/01/411199853/as-the-arctic-opens-up-the-u-s-is-down-to-a-single-icebreaker.

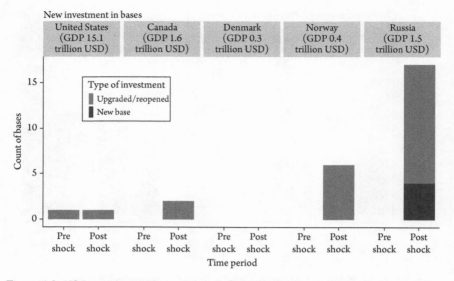

Figure 4.9 US Investment in Bases Compared to All Other Arctic Nations

4.8 Conclusion

The patterns in the data clearly demonstrate that, while some states had a much higher level of military activity and more icebreakers and bases after the shock, there has been only a small change in these indicators for others. These findings offer a corrective to ongoing debates about the degree to which there is a regional arms race and whether the Arctic is being militarized. My findings challenge both sensationalist media accounts that depict the Arctic as a future hotbed of militarized resource competition and many academic accounts that have overcorrected for this mistake by underplaying real shifts in the Arctic military presence of certain states.[31] The data suggest that while the majority of states are not investing heavily in projecting power to the Arctic, there has been an increase in the willingness of states to boost their Arctic military presence, particularly among the states that are more economically dependent on oil and gas to generate income.

The quantitative data match both my theoretical predictions well. Following the shock, the land-oriented Russia and Norway invested much more in projecting power to secure control over Arctic resources than the production-oriented United States, Canada, and Denmark. Moreover, this was not because the land-oriented states had more capacity to invest. On the contrary, Russia had less capacity than

---

[31] For a discussion of the need for a more nuanced perspective on Arctic force, see Oran R. Young, "The Future of the Arctic: Cauldron of Conflict or Zone of Peace?" *International Affairs* 87, no. 1 (2011): 185–93.

Canada and much less than the United States. One might argue that variation in the degree to which states project power to the Arctic can be explained by regime type, given that autocracies should have a stronger preference for territory and land rents. However, democratic, land-oriented Norway invested much more in its Arctic-specific military capabilities than any of the democratic production-oriented states, despite having a similar economic capacity to Denmark, and much less than Canada or the United States. This suggests that regime type and relative power alone cannot explain variations in how much states will invest in securing control over territory and resources. What can explain this variation is the degree to which states are economically dependent on territory and resources.

In sum, I have demonstrated a strong correlation between my core independent variable, the economic structure of a state, and my dependent variable, the degree to which the state invests in pursuing an exclusionary foreign policy, as operationalized by the quantitative indicators discussed here. The following chapters augment the data with case studies that utilize a more diverse set of evidence, which allows me to illustrate both the causal pathways through which the economic structure of a state influences the regime's preference for territory and the Arctic states' response to the shock. These cases also employ more detailed evidence, such as policy documents and official statements that reveal whether securing control over resources was a central motive in driving leaders to boost their Arctic military presence.

5

Russia, the Rent-Seeking Revisionist

5.1 Introduction

In July of 2007, two nuclear-powered Russian icebreakers set off on a scientific expedition to map the ocean floor at the North Pole. On board were two small Finnish-made research submarines, *Mir 1* and *Mir 2*, each just big enough to hold three people. Upon reaching the pole, the expedition team drilled a hole in the ice to deploy the subs. *Mir 2* was occupied by Yevgeny Chernyaev, the Russian pilot who drove the sub; Mike McDowell, an Australian adventurer; and Frederik Paulsen, Jr., an eccentric pharmaceutical billionaire who paid $2 million for the private mission.[1] At first glance, this scientific mission partially funded by an eccentric billionaire looked more like the inspiration for a Wes Anderson film than a major geopolitical event that would elicit condemnation from other Arctic nations. However, the people aboard the other submarine, *Mir 1*, were interested in more than adventure and discovery. Their goal was to make a political statement on behalf of their government that would be seen by the entire world. *Mir 1* carried Vladimir Gruzdev and Artur Chilingarov, both members of the Russian State Duma and the ruling party, and Russian scientist Anatoly Sagalevich. On August 2, the two subs slowly descended through the dark, icy depths to the Arctic Ocean floor, more than 13,000 feet below. When they reached the bottom, *Mir 1*'s crew extended its robotic arm to plant a Russian flag affixed to a titanium pole. Video and photos of the flag planting were beamed around the world.

The move generated a storm of press attention, but most experts viewed it as a publicity stunt, given that planting the flag did not give Russia any international legal rights over the territory and was not used to make a formal legal claim.[2] What many failed to recognize at the time was that this action signaled

[1] Bruce Upbin, "Meet Frederik Paulsen, the Swedish Pharma Billionaire without Fear," *Forbes*, March 23, 2013, https://www.forbes.com/sites/bruceupbin/2013/03/23/meet-frederik-paulsen-the-swedish-pharma-billionaire-without-fear/#4cb3a5eb57eb.

[2] Klaus Dodds, "Flag Planting and Finger Pointing: The Law of the Sea, the Arctic and the Political Geographies of the Outer Continental Shelf," *Political Geography* 29, no. 2 (2010): 63–73.

Perils of Plenty. Jonathan N. Markowitz, Oxford University Press (2020). © Oxford University Press.
DOI: 10.1093/oso/9780190078249.001.0001

a fundamental shift in Russia's foreign policy in the Arctic. We now know that Chilingarov was acting on orders from the ruling United Russia party.[3] Chilingarov, Sagalevich, and Chernyaev were later awarded the title of Hero of the Russian Federation for their mission. This largely symbolic act was orchestrated by the Russian government as part of a broader strategy of laying claim to Arctic resources through symbolic gestures, physical presence, and military power projection.[4] Days after the flag-planting, on order from Russian president Vladimir Putin, Russian bombers began patrolling the Arctic regularly for the first time since the end of the Cold War. Rather than being just a publicity stunt, these events marked the beginning of a major shift in Russia's willingness to invest in its Arctic military presence and its ability to project power in the Arctic.[5] Russia has now invested more in Arctic power projection than any other state, pouring resources into creating a new Arctic command and four new Arctic brigade combat teams and building a string of new Arctic bases, including fourteen new operational airfields.[6]

Russia's actions caught scholars and policymakers off guard. Given Russia's acrimonious relationship with the West today, it is hard to remember that after 9/11 Russia was considered by some to be an ally of the United States in the war on terror. At that time, competition with Russia had largely dropped off the Pentagon's radar; US attention was primarily divided between counterinsurgency in Iraq and Afghanistan and preparation for a potential conflict with China. This is not to argue that there were no signs of Russia's conflicting interests with the West or that Putin was not seeking to reassert Russia's status as a great power.[7] It is only to claim that there was not yet a consensus in the West that Russia was a revisionist power. On the contrary, many in the West viewed Russia not as an expansionist geopolitical threat but as a globalizing emerging market and a promising location for foreign investment.

---

[3] American Embassy Copenhagen, "Second Cable," August 27, 2009.

[4] Russia has continued to back its claims with a combination of military power projection and symbolic gestures. In the fall of 2012, a Russian Orthodox bishop traveled to the North Pole with the nuclear-powered icebreaker *Rossiya* and held a consecration, lowering a metal capsule into the sea carrying the blessing of the church's leader with the inscription, "With the blessing of Patriarch Kirill of Moscow and All Russia, the consecration of the North Pole marks 1150 years of Russian Statehood." See Bruce Jones and Tom Parfitt, "Russia Reasserts Ownership over the North Pole," *Business Insider*, September 28, 2012.

[5] For those reading this as a stand-alone chapter, I define *power projection* as the deployment of military force beyond a state's borders.

[6] Robbie Gramer, "Here's What Russia's Military Build-Up in the Arctic Looks Like," *Foreign Policy* (blog), January 25, 2017, https://foreignpolicy.com/2017/01/25/heres-what-russias-military-build-up-in-the-arctic-looks-like-trump-oil-military-high-north-infographic-map/.

[7] For illustration, see Putin's Munich speech: Andrei Yakovlev, "What Is Russia Trying to Defend?," BOFIT Policy Brief 2016 (Helsinki: Bank of Finland, January 21, 2016).

Given these trends, few scholars would have predicted that Russia would project more military power into the Arctic than any other state. Structural realist explanations that focus on relative power to explain military expansion would predict that the United States, not Russia, would project the most force to the Arctic, given that it is the most powerful state by far.[8] If scarcity increases the incentives for states to project power to secure control over resources, while abundance decreases those incentives, resource-rich Russia should be among the least interested in projecting power to secure control over resources.[9] Even theories of petro-aggression, such as Colgan's, would posit that Russia should have a relatively weak preference for pursuing an aggressive foreign policy because, despite being a petro-state, Russia was not governed by a revolutionary leader.[10] In short, existing explanations cannot explain the sudden change in Russia's willingness to invest in projecting power into the Arctic because they miss how the structure of Russia's economy and domestic political institutions affects the foreign policy preferences of its leaders.

Russia's exclusionary foreign policy in the Arctic is consistent with my theoretical expectation that Russia should have a stronger preference to seek control over resources than any of the other Arctic states. Rent-Addiction Theory contends that a state like Russia invests in projecting power to secure control of resources because it is governed by an autocratic, heavily land-oriented coalition that is economically dependent on resource rents. The members of Russia's governing coalition viewed the Arctic as an opportunity to secure vast stocks of resources that would provide future rents and revenue. These rents would not only enrich the members of the coalition but allow them to remain in power. My theory explains why Russia chose to invest heavily in projecting military force to the Arctic and, counterintuitively, why it chose to double down on this investment despite falling energy prices. I discuss the implications of my theory for the future of Russia's Arctic foreign policy, and the geopolitics of the region more generally, in the conclusion of this chapter.

5.1.1 Overview of the Argument and Evidence

Russia's activity in the Arctic gave rise to sensationalist media accounts warning that this might be the start of a new Cold War in the Arctic. Many scholars have pushed back against this narrative, downplaying Russia's military activity and highlighting its efforts to cooperate.[11] These scholars point out that Russia cooperates actively with other Arctic nations via international institutions such as the Arctic Council.

---

[8] Mearsheimer, *Tragedy of Great Power Politics*.

[9] Klare, *Resource Wars*.

[10] Colgan, *Petro-Aggression*.

[11] Pavel Devyatkin, "Russia's Arctic Strategy: Aimed at Conflict or Cooperation? (Part I)," Arctic Institute, February 6, 2018, https://www.thearcticinstitute.org/russias-arctic-strategy-aimed-conflict-cooperation-part-one/.

Russia also joined the four other Arctic littoral states in backing the Ilulissat Declaration in 2008, which stated that existing international law was a "necessary and sufficient framework" for resolving their territorial disputes.[12] Moreover, Russia has pursued its claims using international law and resolved its disputes with Norway about overlapping exclusive economic zone (EEZ) claims in the Barents Sea. Some scholars have inferred from those efforts to cooperate that Russia has no interest in using military force to bargain coercively for control over Arctic resources.[13]

Neither of these narratives is quite right. While Russia dramatically increased its Arctic military activity following the shock, it is still nowhere near Cold War levels.[14] However, while Russia has pursued its claims via international law, it has also backed them militarily by enhancing its Arctic military presence, projecting force to disputed areas, and deploying forces to the borders of nations with which it has overlapping claims. My theory provides a framework for understanding why Russia has invested in both cooperative and coercive polices and why it has been more willing to pay the costs of building and employing coercive tools, such as power projection, than other Arctic nations.

If my theory is correct, we should observe Russia investing more in realizing its goals (i.e., securing control over Arctic resources) through both cooperative policies, such as making claims via international legal institutions, and coercive policies, such as backing its claims by projecting force to secure control over Arctic resources. Recall that my theory treats coercive policies as complements, rather than substitutes, for cooperative policies. However, coercive tools are typically costly to employ and thus more informative about the strength of a state's interest in a given foreign policy objective. While I provide some discussion of Russia's pursuit of its interests through cooperative channels, this chapter focuses primarily on how Russia has complemented these cooperative policies by projecting military power.

If Rent-Addiction Theory is correct, we should observe a large change in Russia's willingness to invest in projecting power into the Arctic after the shock. Table 5.1 summarizes my theoretical expectations and findings. This table compares the predicted change to the observed change by comparing the pre- and post-shock levels of commitment and investment. As the following sections demonstrate, before the shock, Russia's commitment to the Arctic and its willingness to invest in Arctic military activity and project force to disputed areas were low. Immediately

---

[12] Ernie Regehr, "Arctic Security Briefing Papers" (Vancouver, Canada: Simons Foundation, May 14, 2018).

[13] Alyson J. K. Bailes and Lassi Heininen, *Strategy Papers on the Arctic or High North: A Comparative Study and Analysis* (Reykjavik: University of Iceland, Institute of International Affairs, Centre for Small State Studies, 2012), 42–49.

[14] For a review of this scholarship, see Stephanie Pezard et al., *Maintaining Arctic Cooperation with Russia: Planning for Regional Change in the Far North* (Santa Monica, CA: RAND Corporation, 2017).

Table 5.1 **Russia Predicted and Observed Change in the Level of Investment[a]**

	Predicted Change in Investment	Observed Pre-shock Investment (Scale 1–5)	Observed Post-shock Investment (Scale 1–5)	Observed Change in Investment (Scale 0–4)
Arctic commitments	Large	Low (2)	Very high (5)	Large (3)
Arctic military activity	Large	Low (2)	Very high (5)	Large (3)
Deploying force to claimed or disputed areas	Large	Low (2)	Very high (5)	Large (3)
Icebreakers and ice-hardened warships	Large	Medium (3)	Very high (5)	Moderate (2)
Arctic bases	Large	Low (2)	Very high (5)	Large (3)
Overall investment in exclusionary foreign policy	Large	Low (2)	Very high (5)	Large (3)

[a]For more on how the change in the level of investment was operationalized, see the Appendix, sections B and C.

following the shock, Russia dramatically increased its commitments and invest-ment in Arctic military activity—projecting force to disputed areas and upgrading its Arctic bases, icebreakers, and special Arctic military units. Even though Russia was not the most economically or militarily powerful state in the region, it invested more in projecting power into the Arctic than any other state.

Having foreshadowed my theoretical predictions and evidence, I next provide the details of my coding of the structure of Russia's economy and domestic polit-ical institutions. I then illustrate and evaluate my theoretical expectations about several process outcomes that are connected to my hypothesized causal pathways, which link a state's economic structure and its domestic political institutions to the ruler's preference for territory. My expectations about each outcome are outlined here.

First, if my theory is correct, Russia's decision to proceed down a path of resource-driven development should result in its economy being structured to generate income from land, rather than production. The switching costs should then lower the expected returns associated with investing in production and thus increase the expected rate of return on investments in land relative to investments in production. Thus, we should observe Russia continuing to invest in land rather than production.

Second, the greater the share of Russia's wealth and income that is derived from land, the more the ruler's governing coalition should be dominated by individuals with land-oriented economic interests. We should observe this process in two ways. First, money captures the state when Russians with land-oriented interests invest in securing influence within the governing coalition. Alternatively, the state captures money when the government nationalizes firms in the land-oriented sector, which gives the ruling coalition a vested stake in land and the rents it generates. Either way, as long as the governing coalition is dominated by land-oriented economic interests, we should see the state adopting polices that benefit land at the expense of production. It will invest in the oil and gas sector, rather than in human capital, research and development, and the intellectual property rights needed to produce goods and services.

Third, because Russia has autocratic political institutions, we should observe the ruler adopting a less representative governing coalition and narrowly concentrating the distribution of rents to the ruling elites within the coalition. Autocratic institutions should also lead to stronger preferences for the political benefits associated with land rents. These rents are a source of wealth and patronage that can be directly controlled by the regime and denied to the political opposition. If this is the case, the ruler should seek to ensure that these resources are directly controlled and managed by people loyal to the regime.

5.2 Autocratic and Highly Land-Oriented: Putin's Predatory State

Russia is ruled by a small group of oligarchs and former KGB officials who tightly control both economic and political competition within the state.[15] It is an archetypal

---

[15] Political competition in Russia has long been suppressed. Elections are not generally considered fair and free, and corruption is rampant. Hence, it should not be surprising that Russia is not considered a very democratic state. Looking at a number of quantitative indicators confirms this conclusion. Russia placed 131st out of 176 countries (with the 176th being the most corrupt) on Transparency International's Corruption Perceptions Index and is also rated "Not Free" by Freedom House. During the period 1990–2010, Russia scored between a 3 and a 6 on the POLITY scale, never achieving the score of 7 that is generally used as the cutoff for democracy. Additionally, Cheibub, Ghandi, and Vreeland (2010) code Russia as an autocracy. Based on these indicators, I code Russia as possessing autocratic political institutions that are governed by a narrow coalition. Country experts relying on

predatory state, whose regime is principally concerned with two mutually reinforcing goals: maximizing rents and concentrating power within a small ruling elite.[16] For Russia's ruling elite, the extraction of land rents, principally gleaned from the profits generated by state-owned energy companies, allows them to buy political support and maximize their own consumption of private goods.[17] An excerpt from Fiona Hill and Clifford Gaddy's book *Mr. Putin: Operative in the Kremlin* nicely illustrates this dynamic:

> A small number of trusted figures around Mr. Putin, perhaps twenty to thirty people, make the key decisions. At the very top is an even tighter inner circle of about half a dozen individuals, all with close ties to Putin, who have worked together for twenty years, beginning in St. Petersburg and continuing in Moscow. Real decision-making power resides inside the inner circle, while Russia's formal political institutions have, to varying degrees, been emasculated.[18]

North and his coauthors describe Russia as exemplifying a limited access order, in which the central purpose of the regime is to preserve the stability and order needed for survival, which it achieves by distributing rents to those connected to the regime.[19] Russia's political institutions are often described as an oligarchy, autocracy, or pseudodemocracy in which a small elite uses the façade of elections to maintain power and suppress opposition.[20] Andrew Wilson writes, "As in much of the Third World, political power has become increasingly commodified, valuable not as a means of promoting social change, but as a gateway for a particular group to seize control of a static or dwindling stock of state assets."[21] As we will see, these rents are generally derived from the physical control of territory.

more in-depth and nuanced qualitative evidence confirm this coding of Russia's autocratic political institutions and the narrow nature of its governing coalition. See Antonio Jose Cheibub, Jennifer Gandhi, and James Raymond Vreeland, "Democracy and Dictatorship Revisited," *Public Choice* 143, no. 2–1 (2010): 67–101.

[16] Peter J. Stavrakis, "Russia's Evolution as a Predatory State," in *Russia's Uncertain Economic Future*, ed. John Pearce Hardt (Armonk, NY: M. E. Sharpe, 2003), xxii, 481.

[17] Steve Coll, *Private Empire: ExxonMobil and American Power* (New York: Penguin Press, 2012), 277.

[18] Fiona Hill and Clifford G. Gaddy, *Mr. Putin: Operative in the Kremlin* (new exp. ed.) (Washington, DC: Brookings Institution Press, 2015), 5.

[19] Douglass C. North et al., *Limited Access Orders: Rethinking the Problems of Development and Violence* (Stanford, CA: Stanford University, 2011), 2.

[20] Andrew Wilson, *Virtual Politics: Faking Democracy in the Post-Soviet World* (New Haven, CT: Yale University Press, 2005).

[21] Wilson, *Virtual Politics*, 76.

Table 5.2 **Indicators of Russia's Economic Dependence on Resource Rents**

Country	Oil Exports % of GDP*ᵃ	Fuel Exports % of GDP**ᵇ	Resource Rents % of GDP**ᶜ
United States	0.325	0.171	1.01
Canada	1.04	4.88	3.75
Denmark	0.766	2.04	1.15
Norway	9.72	19.1	8.38
Russia	9.44	16.5	15.5

*Data only available through 2001 (average 1991–2001).

**Average 1997–2007.

ᵃEmma Ashford, "Oil and Violence: The Foreign Policy of Resource-Rich States" (ISA-ISSS Conference, 2013); Benjamin A.T. Graham and Jacob R. Tucker, "International Political Economy Data Resource Version 2.0," July 10, 2017.

ᵇCalculated based on fuel exports as a percentage of merchandise exports data from the World Bank, "Fuel Exports."

ᶜEstimates based on sources and methods described in "The Changing Wealth of Nations: Measuring Sustainable Development in the New World Millennium" (World Bank, 2011), http://data.worldbank.org/indicator/NY.GDP.TOTL.RT.ZS.

5.2.1 Russia's Land-Oriented Economy

The United States and Russia are among the largest producers of oil and natural gas in the world.[22] However, while both countries have abundant resources, only Russia is resource-dependent. While Russia is certainly less resource-dependent than many countries in the Middle East and Africa, it is still highly economically dependent on income from natural resources. Of the five states bordering the Arctic, none relies more heavily on oil and gas for revenue, exports, and economic growth than Russia.[23] Table 5.2 shows several indicators that are generally used to quantify a state's dependency on resource rents, including oil exports, fuel exports, and resource rents as a percentage of GDP. Figure 5.1 reveals that Russia is much more economically dependent on resource rents than any of the other Arctic states. Estimates suggest roughly 40% to 50% of Russia's central government revenue and 60% to 70% of its export earnings derive from the extraction, production, and export of energy.[24] Given this, Russia is coded as having the most land-oriented economy of the Arctic states.

[22] Central Intelligence Agency, "Russia," in *World Factbook*, n.d., https://www.cia.gov/library/publications/the-world-factbook/geos/rs.html.

[23] Charles Emmerson, *The Future History of the Arctic* (New York: PublicAffairs, 2010).

[24] Harvard Kennedy School Belfer Center for Science and International Affairs, "Claim in 2018: Russia Relies Heavily on Energy Exports for Close to Three-Quarters of Its Export Earnings

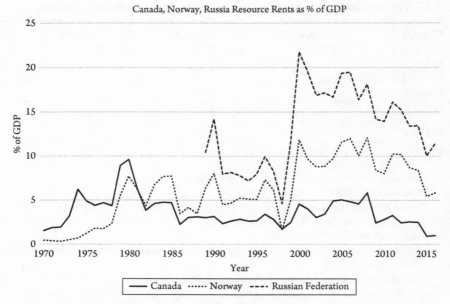

Figure 5.1 Comparing Canadian, Norwegian, and Russian Resource Rents as a Percentage of GDP

5.2.2 Causal Pathway One: Path Dependency and the Expected Returns from Territory

How did Russia become dependent on oil and gas to generate income? Its rulers emerged from the Cold War presiding over a dramatically weaker state with extractive political institutions that made foreign companies reluctant to invest in the country.[25] Russia was in a poor position to compete against countries like China in terms of cheap manufacturing, but it did have a relatively educated population that was able to produce and export some high-end manufactured goods. Russia also had one thing that many other states did not—bountiful natural resources. Political and economic turmoil resulted in a lack of economic opportunities, which led many well-educated Russians to migrate to the West, where they could earn higher wages. Partly as a result of this, Russia lost much of its capacity to generate income by exporting high-end goods and services. Its economy thus became more dependent on resource rents, and natural resources became a greater fraction of its total exports.

and over Half of Its Budget," Russia Matters, July 2018, https://www.belfercenter.org/russia-matters/russia-matters-overview.

[25] Alexei Izyumov and John Vahaly, "Old Capital vs. New Investment in Post-Soviet Economies: Conceptual Issues and Estimates," *Comparative Economic Studies* 50, no. 1 (2008): 79–110.

For illustration, fuel exports increased from 43% of total merchandise exports in 1996 to over 71% in 2013.[26]

Recall that, if my theory is correct, once Russia went down the path of resource-driven development, it should have developed an economic structure that generates income from land instead of production. This should, in turn, increase the switching costs by lowering the expected returns from investing in production. The implication is that Moscow should continue to favor investment in land instead of production. This is exactly what we observe. Moscow continued investing in extractive industries and in building and maintaining oil and gas refineries and pipelines to transport oil and gas to markets in Europe.[27] These investments created economies of scale, which, in turn, created positive feedback loops by allowing Russia to more efficiently extract, refine, and export fuel. This further increased the returns on investments in extracting land rents.

Russia's heavy investment in extractive industries occurred despite the fact that Russian officials were well aware of the risks associated with continuing to proceed down this development path. German Gref, Russia's former minister of economic development and trade, warned in 2003, "At the beginning of the 1990s, high-technology products accounted for over 25% of total Russian exports. In a decade, by 2002, this share fell to 12%. In other words, we lost half of our high-technology exports."[28] Gref's proposed solution was to increase taxes on energy exports and to invest in research and development and high-tech innovations in areas such as nanotechnology and aviation.[29] By 2006, he ominously warned that, "Without decisive measures, without diversification, the economy's development trajectory will go along a path of inertia."[30] Gref clearly understood that the further Russia proceeded down this path, the harder it would be for high-value manufacturing to catch up and that eventually Russia would be locked into relying on land rents for income. These lock-in effects would make Russia's economic structure "sticky" and hard to change in the future. However, Russia's rulers ignored Gref's advice and continued down a path of resource-driven development, underinvesting in human capital, intellectual property rights, and research and development.

The result of these policies was to increase the switching costs associated with moving from land rents to a production-oriented economy. For evidence of this,

[26] World Bank, "Fuel Exports."

[27] Hill and Gaddy, *Mr. Putin*, 226–28.

[28] Quoted in Anna Smolchenko, "Gref Urges Diversity to Preserve Growth," *Moscow Times*, July 11, 2006, http://themoscowtimes.com/business/article/gref-urges-diversity-to-preserve-growth/203864.html.

[29] See Simeon Djankov, "Why Has Russia Failed to Diversify Exports?" Peterson Institute for International Economics, September 28, 2015, https://piie.com/blogs/trade-investment-policy-watch/why-has-russia-failed-diversify-exports.

[30] See Djankov, "Why Has Russia Failed?".

one can simply visit Innopolis, the smallest town in Russia, located approximately 510 miles east of Moscow. In 2012, Innopolis was founded as an information technology park that would serve as Russia's own Silicon Valley. This project was considered to be a model for then-president Dmitry Medvedev's vision for diversifying the Russian economy by investing in technological innovation. Despite building an "innovation city" complete with its own university, Russia has been unable to fill this city with enough well-educated and highly motivated citizens for the project to succeed. Nearly four years after Innopolis opened, barely half of its offices were occupied.[31] This is because Russia lacks both the human capital, due to decades of underinvesting in education, and the motivation to innovate, given the lack of the intellectual property rights that allow Western tech companies to thrive.

Russia cannot simply push a button and build a Silicon Valley capable of producing innovation. Vladimir Gritskikh, a former physicist who ran the program, claimed that "oil is our new human capital."[32] The problem was, while Russia had oil, it lacked human capital. While Moscow invested massive sums in developing its oil fields, it did not invest enough in cultivating the human capital of its citizens.

In the years before the shock, Russia's average annual spending on education, research and development, and healthcare was the lowest of the five Arctic states, even when holding the size of each state's economy constant by comparing spending as a percentage of GDP (see Table 5.3). Even if Russia had begun to make substantial investments in education, research and development, and intellectual property rights in 2007, it would have been many years until it could generate benefits that outweighed the costs of those investments. Thus, because Russia spent years overinvesting in the land-oriented sector of the economy and underinvesting in the production-oriented sector, it would face higher costs in order to shift to a production-oriented economy. These dynamics illustrate how Russia's decision to proceed down a resource-driven development path led to path-dependent effects that influenced the expected rate of returns associated with investing in production relative to land.

5.2.3 Causal Pathway Two: Composition of the Governing Coalition

If Russia could have enjoyed long-run economic benefits from investing in producing goods, why didn't it do so? Why didn't Russia tax energy exports more heavily

---

[31] Ashlee Vance, "Inside Russia's Creepy, Innovative Internet," Bloomberg, November 30, 2016, http://www.bloomberg.com/features/2016-hello-world-russia/.

[32] "Milk without the Cow," Economist, October 22, 2016b, https://www.economist.com/news/special-report/21708876-political-reform-essential-prerequisite-flourishing-economy-milk-without; ITMO.News, "Exploring Innopolis: Russia's Silicon Valley," August 5, 2016, http://news.ifmo.ru/en/archive/news/5887/.

Table 5.3 **Arctic State Production-Oriented Indicators[a]**

	Education Spending (Total % of GDP)*[b]	R & D (% of GDP)**[c]	Health (% of GDP)
United States	5.23	2.55	14.2
Canada	5.16	1.90	9.23
Denmark	8.02	2.30	9.21
Norway	6.99	1.57	8.93
Russia	3.54	1.11	5.75

*Canada data missing: 1997, 2003–2004, 2006; Denmark data missing: 1997; Russia data missing: 1997–1999, 2007; US data missing: 1997, 2000.

** Denmark data missing: 2000; Norway data missing 1998, 2000.

[a]Note that the data are averaged from 1997 to 2007, the ten years prior to the shock. Data for all three indicators from World Bank, "World Development Indicators," July 1, 2017, accessed August 15, 2017, http://data.worldbank.org/data-catalog/world-development-indicators.

[b]World Bank, "World Development Indicators"; note that Canada has data missing for the following years: 1997, 2003, 2004, and 2006.

[c]World Bank, "World Development Indicators"; note that data are missing for Denmark for the year 2000 and for Norway for 1998 and 2000.

in the 1990s or later, in the 2000s? Part of the reason is that Russia's governing coalition had land-oriented economic interests. My theory suggests that the greater the share of Russia's wealth and income that is derived from land, the more the governing coalition should be dominated by individuals with land-oriented economic interests: either money captures the state or the state captures the money.

5.2.3.1 Russia in the 1990s: Money Captures the State

My theoretical predictions are strongly supported by the empirical record. In the 1990s Russian oligarchs and Soviet-era industrial managers used their financial and political capital to capture the state.[33] This allowed them to privatize Russia's natural resources in a blatantly self-serving manner: they used the power of the state to transfer resources that had belonged to society at large to themselves.[34] Because the privatization of Russia's land was determined by small coalitions in which there were few checks on the power of the state, resources were redistributed narrowly

[33] Daniel Yergin and Joseph Stanislaw, *The Commanding Heights: The Battle for the World Economy* (rev. and updated) (New York: Simon & Schuster, 2002).

[34] Tom Bower, *The Squeeze: Oil, Money and Greed in the Twenty-First Century* (London: HarperCollins UK, 2009). See also Daniel Treisman, "'Loans for Shares' Revisited," *Post-Soviet Affairs* 26, no. 3 (2013): 207–27.

to the oligarchs instead of more broadly to society.[35] These events illustrate a key causal mechanism by which a state's economic structure (i.e., its source of income) influences the preferences and policies of the governing coalition. Specifically, my theory suggests that money captures the state or the state captures the money. The privatization of Russia's oil wealth is an example of money capturing the state. Oligarchs and Soviet-era industrial managers invested the money derived partly from their control of oil and gas companies to gain additional political influence, effectively becoming entrenched interests within the state. They then used this influence to bend state policy to favor themselves and their economic interests by ensuring that privatization gave them control over Russia's oil, gas, and mineral assets.

The oligarchs leveraged their influence to ensure that Russia adopted policies that benefited the land-oriented sector of the economy at the expense of the production-oriented sector. For example, in order to transition to a production-oriented economy, Russia would need to invest in intellectual property rights, research and development, and the human and health capital of its citizens. However, rather than taxing the profits from oil and gas to make these investments, the Russian government adopted policies that allowed the oligarchs to keep much of the revenue.

5.2.3.2 The 2000s: The State Captures the Money

Putin came to power with a plan that staked both his own political survival and Russia's economic future on resource-driven development. The strategy worked, at least in the short and medium term. Unusually high energy prices in the first decade of the twenty-first century allowed the Russian economy to recover from the decade of economic hardship that followed the dissolution of the Soviet Union. When Putin came to power in 2000, public anger at the privatization of Russian assets allowed him to coerce the oligarchs into accepting higher taxes in exchange for permission to keep their assets for the time being.[36] However, Putin made sure to incorporate these oligarchs in his governing coalition. Vladislav Surkov, a key aide to Putin, who would eventually rise to deputy prime minister, explained the strategy to a Russian journalist: "The oil men are no less important than the oil; the state has to make the most of both of them."[37] That said, over time, Putin began to reassert and consolidate direct state control over Russia's vast resource wealth. A useful illustration of this dynamic is reported in the *Economist*:

> In 2009, Sistema bought a controlling stake in Bashneft, a medium-sized oil firm, from a local authority for $2.5 billion. It had been given explicit

---

[35] Bower, *The Squeeze*, 91–126.
[36] Bower, *The Squeeze*.
[37] Bower, *The Squeeze*, 209.

approval by Dmitry Medvedev, who was president at the time. But in September 2014, Mr. Yevtushenkov was arrested and charged with buying stolen goods. His real crime was reportedly to refuse to sell Bashneft, which had become one of the world's fastest-growing oil firms, to Rosneft, at a price below its market value. After three months under house arrest, Mr. Yevtushenkov was released and cleared of all charges—but not before giving up Bashneft, a controlling stake in which has now been sold to Rosneft for $5.2 billion. The day after he was released, Mr. Yevtushenkov (who still owns MTS, Russia's largest mobile-phone company) went to a drinks party at the Kremlin and spoke to Mr. Putin. "I thanked him for his wise decision . . . to release me," Mr. Yevtushenkov recently told Dozhd, an independent internet television channel. He continued: "If [you] like any of my other companies—[you are] welcome."[38]

The share of the GDP controlled by state-owned firms and the government doubled, rising from 35% in 2005 to 70% in 2015.[39] Just as money had captured the state, the state recaptured the money (i.e., the natural resource sector). This gave the individuals in the governing coalition a strong interest in the natural resource sector, explaining why Russia has continued to pursue policies that benefit it at the expense of the production-oriented sector. As predicted by my theory, these entrenched interests bent policy in their favor, such that the Russian economy became even more land-oriented as resource rents became an even greater share of GDP through the first decade of the 2000s. As we shall see, my theory also explains why Russia's rulers have such a strong preference for territory and why they are more willing to invest in projecting power to secure control of territory in the Arctic.

5.2.4 Causal Pathway Three: Value for the Political Benefits of Land Rents

If my theory is correct, Russia's autocratic political institutions should incentivize and allow its rulers to concentrate political and economic power among a narrow elite. This should give the regime a stronger value for the political benefits associated with land rents as they are a source of wealth and patronage that is easier for the regime to control directly and deny to the political opposition. If this is true, the ruler should pursue policies that ensure that these resources and the rents they generate are controlled, managed, and enjoyed by members of the governing coalition.

---

[38] *Economist*, "Milk without the Cow," 7.

[39] *Economist*, "In Russia, Privatisation Can Mean Selling One State-Owned Company to Another," October 20, 2016a, 39, http://www.economist.com/news/europe/21709065-government-sells-bashneft-rosneft-and-books-profit-russia-privatisation-can-mean.

As the previous section demonstrated, Putin's regime has done exactly this. Piontkovsky describes Putin's system as a form of feudalism, with the only difference being that "the things Putin is distributing and taking away are not parcels of land, but gas and oil companies."[40] Recall, from my theory, that just like parcels of agrarian land, oil and gas are sources of wealth that are easier for the regime to appropriate and extract, in comparison to the profits from production, which tend to be highly sensitive to the violation of physical and intellectual property rights. Thus, just like feudal Russia's czars before him, Putin chose to sacrifice secure property rights, which might have motivated Russia's citizens to produce more wealth in the long run, in order to monopolize control over a greater share of the nation's wealth today. This gives Putin and his regime a larger slice of what is ultimately a smaller pie. However, it also allows them to directly control the source of the nation's wealth, redistributing rents to the governing coalition and denying them to the political opposition.

For the purposes of my theory, it matters little whether the assets generating rents are in private or public hands, as long as the rents flow to the state's governing coalition. This is because the ruler's main objective is to remain in power by ensuring that benefits flow to the individuals in his coalition and that the source of wealth and patronage is controlled by individuals loyal to the regime. As Hill and Gaddy write, "[W]hether the companies are private or not is not the key issue for Putin. It is rather whether the structures give him the ability to interact with those who head the companies."[41] Just ten oil companies account for 90% of Russia's oil output. The small number of companies allows Putin to maintain a relationship with their leaders, regardless of whether they are public or private.[42]

For example, Putin installed Igor Sechin, a key member of his inner circle, to run the massive state energy firm Rosneft.[43] Rosneft, as a state company, is given privileged access to offshore Arctic energy resources, which allows it to extract monopoly rents.[44] Rosneft and Gazprom have also received generous subsidies and tax incentives with which to develop Arctic offshore resources.[45] Rosneft recently purchased BP's shares of the Russian oil company TNK, making it one of the world's largest oil companies. To provide some perspective on the massive scale of this new joint venture, Rosneft alone will pump 4 million barrels of oil per day, the

[40] Andrei Piontkovsky, "The Dying Mutant," *Journal of Democracy* 20, no. 2 (2009): 52–55.

[41] Hill and Gaddy, *Mr. Putin*, 228.

[42] Hill and Gaddy, *Mr. Putin*, 202.

[43] Hill and Gaddy, *Mr. Putin*.

[44] Andrew E. Kramer and Stanley Reed, "BP Will Switch Russian Partners through a Deal with Rosneft," *New York Times*, October 22, 2012.

[45] Lassi Heininen, Alexander Sergunin, and Gleb Yarovoy, *Russian Strategies in the Arctic: Avoiding a New Cold War* (Valdai Discussion Club, September 2014), 78, http://www.uarctic.org/media/857300/arctic_eng.pdf. See also Eurasia Group, "Opportunities and Challenges for Arctic Oil and Gas Development" (Washington, DC: Wilson Center, n.d.), 18.

equivalent of 40% of Saudi Arabia's total output.[46] The profits from these 4 million barrels of oil are directly under the control of the state and a few Russian oligarchs. It is worth noting that, collectively, Gazprom and Rosneft are estimated to control 80% of Russia's offshore Arctic territory.[47] Foreign companies are barred from negotiating independent access rights. If they want to access these reserves, they must do so through a partnership with either Gazprom or Rosneft.[48] By forcing outside firms to partner with Russian state-backed companies, the Kremlin can extract rents and maintain political control over access to Russian energy reserves.

The link between the Russian energy companies and the Russian state is considered so tight that it is often hard to detect where the corporation ends and the state begins. State energy companies, like Gazprom and Rosneft, exemplify land-oriented interests inside the governing coalition. These energy companies, along with other land-oriented interests like Norisk Nickel, a mining giant, exercise monopoly or near-monopoly control over the production and sale of natural resource commodities. Companies that derive their wealth from the control of territory work in close symbiosis with the Russian political elite, facilitating their near-monopoly control over the state's resources.[49]

For example, Gazprom controls 87% of gas production in Russia.[50] Just as in the case of Rosneft, Putin put members of his inner circle in charge of Gazprom, which was run by Dmitry Medvedev before he became president and later by Viktor Zubkov. Both men are key Putin allies and considered among the closest members of his inner circle.[51] This near-monopoly on production allows both Gazprom and the associated political elite to extract monopoly rents. The regime also forces Gazprom to produce higher volumes of gas than it otherwise would and to sell this gas at below-market rates to Russian citizens as a means of buying off the general public and limiting dissent.[52] However, the largest and most obvious rent is the profits—billions of dollars from the sale of energy that can be siphoned off and redistributed to the ruling elite. These profits would not exist if state companies like Gazprom did not have an effective monopoly, sanctioned by the state. Gazprom's profits are so staggering that it alone provides 25% of Russia's federal tax revenue.[53]

---

[46] Heininen, Sergunin, and Yarovoy, *Russian Strategies in the Arctic.*

[47] Steve Marshall, "Arctic Blocks 'in the Bag' for Rosneft," Upstream, February 4, 2013, http://www.upstreamonline.com/live/article1316019.ece.

[48] Marshall, "Arctic Blocks."

[49] Andy Home, "Will the Real Norilsk Owner Please Stand Up?," Reuters, 2012, http://www.reuters.com/article/2012/12/07/column-home-norilsk-nickel-idUSL5E8N790C20121207.

[50] Arild Moe and Elana Wilson Rowe, "Northern Offshore and Oil and Gas Resources," in *Russia and the North,* ed. Elana Wilson Rowe (Ottawa, Canada: University of Ottawa, 2009).

[51] Hill and Gaddy, *Mr. Putin,* 83.

[52] It is worth noting that this is a broadly redistributed private good, rather than a public good.

[53] Rob Huebert et al., *Climate Change and International Security: The Arctic as a Bellwether* (Arlington, VA: Center for Climate and Energy Solutions, 2012).

Putin did not just reassert control over Russia's energy assets; he also ensured that the rents benefited people in his governing coalition. For illustration, the Panama Papers showed that "between 2007 and 2013, nearly $2 billion had been funneled through offshore accounts linked to Putin associates."[54] Political control over energy companies produces a number of private goods that the ruling elite can redistribute to members of the governing coalition. Gazprom and Rosneft board members are often appointed by the Kremlin. This serves as a means of exercising political control over the activities of the corporations and as a source of patronage that the Russian regime can dole out to its supporters. To illustrate how sitting on a board can generate rents, consider the 2010 appointment of Vladimir Litvinenko to the board of PhosAgro, one of the world's largest producers of phosphate fertilizers. Litvinenko supervised Putin's dissertation and publicly defended him against charges of plagiarism. He also served as Putin's campaign chair for the presidential elections in 2000, 2004, and 2012. The rewards for his loyalty were great—Litvinenko's holdings in PhosAgro are worth half a billion dollars.[55]

The story of the Rotenberg brothers, Arkady and Boris, childhood friends of Putin, is another illustrative example of how Russia's ruler has sought to benefit those in his governing coalition. The brothers are widely known to be members of Putin's coalition and were among those sanctioned by the West after the Russian invasion of Crimea, along with Dmitry Rogozin and Victor Zhukov. In 2001, shortly after Putin replaced Gazprom's executives with his own officials, the Rotenberg brothers began investing in companies that provided services to Gazprom. Gazprom routinely overpaid for these services, which benefited the Rotenbergs. For example, in 2007 Gazprom spent $44 billion, or three times the normal amount, for a 1,500-mile pipeline connecting to an oil field above the Arctic Circle.[56] As a result of their political connections, the brothers have grown exceptionally wealthy, earning approximately $2.5 billion. Arkady, Putin's judo sparring partner, won $9 billion worth of government contracts in 2015 alone, more than anyone else in Russia.[57]

These anecdotes describe not just isolated incidents but rather events illustrative of a broader strategy by which the regime monopolizes control over the nation's wealth (primarily oil and gas rents) and concentrates control over that wealth in the hands of a narrow ruling elite. According to a report by Crédit Suisse in 2013, Russia has one of the highest levels of wealth inequality in the world. The report concludes that wealth inequality in the rest of the world is also high, with the world's 613 billionaires owning 1% to 2% of household wealth globally. However,

[54] Joshua Yaffa, "Putin's Shadow Cabinet and the Bridge to Crimea," New Yorker, May 22, 2017, https://www.newyorker.com/magazine/2017/05/29/putins-shadow-cabinet-and-the-bridge-to-crimea.

[55] Hill and Gaddy, Mr. Putin, 198.

[56] Yaffa, "Putin's Shadow Cabinet and the Bridge to Crimea."

[57] Yaffa, "Putin's Shadow Cabinet and the Bridge to Crimea."

as of 2013, 110 billionaires owned a staggering 35% of Russia's household wealth.[58] These billionaires are closely tied to the state, and their wealth has been generated mostly by their control of Russia's natural resources.[59]

The Russian political elite is utterly dependent upon the production of energy for its political survival. Putin and his party use the revenue to buy off members of the political opposition and to keep factions, such as the military, loyal. For example, the dramatic increase in salary that Russian soldiers were promised in 2012 is directly tied to the regime's ability to keep oil revenues high.[60] Oil and gas revenues allow the Russian elite to literally buy off those whose political support they need for political survival. At the same time, because natural resources are the only game in town and are monopolized by the regime, there are few significant alternative sources of wealth to fund a political opposition, limiting challenges to the current ruling elite.

5.2.5 Summary of the Process Evidence

Russia has a highly land-oriented economy and is ruled by a narrow governing coalition that has a strong interest in controlling and seeking land rents. The previous section provides strong evidence for the three causal pathways through which my theory suggests that Russia's economic structure and domestic political institutions should influence the ruler's preference for territory and then their foreign policy decisions. First, Russia followed a path of resource-driven economic development, with path-dependent effects that increased the switching costs associated with shifting to a production-oriented economy. These switching costs lowered the expected returns from investing in production and thus increased the expected relative rate of return from investing in land. Second, Russia followed this path in part because money captured the state as the oligarchs manipulated policy to benefit their land-oriented interests. Later on, the state captured the money, as the government took control of the natural resource sector, giving the regime a vested interest in that sector. As long as the governing coalition is dominated by individuals with land-oriented interests, Russia's rulers should have a stronger preference for territory. Third, as predicted by my theory, Russia's autocratic political institutions incentivized its rulers to adopt a narrow governing coalition and concentrate resource rents within this coalition. The rulers also demonstrated a strong preference for the political benefits associated with land rents and carefully ensured that the resource sectors were directly controlled by individuals loyal to the regime. The more

[58] Giles Keating et al., *Global Wealth Report 2013* (Zurich, Switzerland: Credit Suisse, 2013), 53.

[59] Karen Dawisha, *Putin's Kleptocracy: Who Owns Russia?* (New York: Simon & Schuster, 2015), 331–50.

[60] Andrew E. Kramer, "Putin Needs Higher Oil Prices to Pay for Campaign Promises," *New York Times*, March 16, 2012.

a ruler values the political benefits associated with land rents, the stronger is that ruler's preference for territory.

Each of these causal pathways should lead Russia's rulers to have a strong preference for territory and a greater interest in investing in securing control over territory via an exclusionary foreign policy. I now move on to assessing how Russia's preference for territory and resources influenced its foreign policy choices in response to the exogenous shock of Arctic climate change. In order to assess how Moscow responded, I must first establish a baseline regarding Russia's level of commitment and investment in the Arctic prior to the shock.

5.3 Establishing a Baseline: Russia's Arctic Foreign Policy Prior to the Shock

5.3.1 Russia's Pre-shock Level of Military Activity

As the Cold War ended and relations with the West improved, Russia dramatically decreased its commitments and military activity in the Arctic. Russian military aircraft, which at the height of the Cold War flew up to five hundred sorties a year, largely stopped patrolling the Arctic.[61] The Russian Northern Fleet also dramatically decreased its Arctic patrols; forward operating bases were closed, and troops were sent home. Whereas during the Cold War military incidents might involve close calls with American nuclear submarines, the most contentious incidents during this period involved disputes over fishing rights. In 2001, a Norwegian Coast Guard cutter arrested a Russian fishing trawler in the disputed fishery protection zone around the Svalbard archipelago. The Russians reacted by deploying a warship, the *Severomorsk*, to the disputed zone.[62] In 2005, Norway attempted to seize a Russian fishing trawler, whose crew then held two Norwegian Coast Guard officers hostage; but the incident ended without violence.

5.3.2 Russia's Pre-shock Force Structure

While geopolitical competition decreased substantially after the Cold War, Moscow still maintained a number of bases above the Arctic Circle. The most substantial base is Murmansk, where Russia has long stationed the Northern Fleet and the majority of its naval forces.[63] Due to geography, Russia has historically lacked access

---

[61] Newsday, "US Is Phasing out Attack Sub Patrols under Arctic Ice Cat-and-Mouse Game with Russians Is Ending," *Baltimore Sun*, November 16, 1997, http://articles.baltimoresun.com/1997-11-16/news/1997320037_1_subs-arctic-russian.

[62] Oystein Jensen and Svein Vigeland Rottem, "The Politics of Security and International Law in Norway's Arctic Waters," *Polar Record* 46, no. 1 (2010): 75–83.

[63] Alexander Golts, "The Arctic: A Clash of Interests or Clash of Ambitions," in *Russia in the Arctic*, ed. Stephen J. Blank (Carlisle, PA: Strategic Studies Institute, 2011), 54.

to warm water ports and thus has been forced to maintain most of its naval forces, including its nuclear submarines, above the Arctic Circle. Therefore, Russia periodically conducted Arctic submarine operations and missile drills, for example, in October of 2006, when Russian ballistic missile submarines conducted a set of drills near the North Pole.[64] The fact that Russia maintains much of its naval forces above the Arctic Circle explains, in part, why it had more Arctic bases and military activity than other Arctic states before the shock. The Northern Fleet ships also need icebreakers, which are sent out to sea during the nonsummer months. This fact, along with Russia's historical interest in developing the Northern Sea Route for cargo shipping, explains why Russia had a far larger and more capable icebreaking fleet than any of the other Arctic states before the shock.

5.3.3 Pre-shock Commitments and Claims

Russia has the largest Arctic territory and the largest absolute number of citizens living above the Arctic Circle. That said, less than 1% of Russia's population lives above the Arctic Circle, compared to 10% of Norwegians.[65] For most Russians, the Arctic is a remote area where few citizens live and is valuable primarily for its commodities, such as minerals, oil, and natural gas. However, the Russian state has long made efforts to construct an Arctic identity, in part to convince its citizens to view the Arctic as fundamentally Russian and an extension of mainland Russia. These efforts are interwoven with Russia's efforts to realize its Arctic claims.

Before the shock, Russia had a number of outstanding claims in the Arctic, including two disputes with Norway. First, Moscow and Oslo had a forty-year-long dispute about overlapping EEZ claims in the Barents Sea. Second, Russia disputed Norway's claim to a fishery protection zone around Svalbard. Third, Russia had a dispute with the United States and many other nations about the status of the Northern Sea Route, which Russia considers to be part of its internal waters.[66] Moreover, the Russian government reserves the right to deny ships access to the route unless they pay a toll to Russian icebreakers to clear a path. Recently, the Russian government passed legislation to restrict the shipping of hydrocarbons along the Northern Sea Route by foreign firms.[67] The United States and other

---

[64] Nuclear Threat Initiative, "Russia Nuclear Chronology," July 2010, http://www.nti.org/media/pdfs/russia_nuclear.pdf?_=1316466791.

[65] For Russia's population, see Mia Bennett, "Arctic Population Map from Russia," Foreign Policy Association, May 25, 2010, https://foreignpolicyblogs.com/2010/05/25/arctic-population-map-from-russia/. For Norway's population, see Statistics Norway, "Population at Population Censuses in 2001 and 2011 by County and Municipality," Oslo: Statistics Norway, 2011.

[66] Viatcheslav V. Gavrilov, "Legal Status of the Northern Sea Route and Legislation of the Russian Federation: A Note," *Ocean Development & International Law* 46, no. 3 (2015): 257.

[67] Pavel Devyatkin, "Russia's Arctic Strategy: Maritime Shipping (Part IV)," Arctic Institute, February 27, 2018, https://www.thearcticinstitute.org/russias-arctic-strategy-maritime-shipping-part-iv/.

nations object to this as international law gives all ships the right to freedom of navigation (i.e., the right to peacefully sail through without being denied access or charged a toll).

Fourth, in 1997, Russia ratified the United Nations Convention on the Law of the Sea (UNCLOS), allowing it to make legal claims to the maritime territory in its EEZ (200 nautical miles out from its shores). UNCLOS allows Russia to do this so long as it can prove that its continental shelf extends beyond its EEZ. Four years later, Russia submitted a massive extended continental shelf (ECS) claim to the United Nations Commission on the Limits of the Continental Shelf, claiming an additional 1.2 million square miles, including the North Pole. Subsequently, both Canada and Denmark have also claimed the North Pole as part of their ECS claims.[68] These Russian claims were rejected due to lack of evidence, and Russia was invited to collect additional information and resubmit its claims. Moscow invested in further research to support its claims and resubmitted new claims in 2015 (see Figure 5.2 for a map of Russia's claims). While substantially smaller than its original 2001 claim, at 463,000 square miles, Russia's 2015 claim was still larger than California and Texas combined.[69] Moscow's submission of its claims to UNCLOS demonstrate how, like the other Arctic states, it has chosen to pursue its claims via existing international legal institutions. However, as we shall see in the following section, unlike most other Arctic states, since the shock Russia has complemented this strategy by substantially increasing its Arctic military presence and projecting power to areas under dispute.

In summary, in the period before the shock the Arctic had faded from the front lines of the Cold War to become a region of secondary interest for Moscow. Even as Russia recovered from its economic doldrums in the early 2000s, it did not make any major new commitments to the Arctic and regressed to the mean in terms of its prior levels of military activity. That said, because of Russia's unique geographic position and its lack of warm-water ports, it maintained a higher baseline level of military forces, bases, and icebreakers than any other Arctic state. Many of these bases were not well maintained, and Russia did not regularly deploy its air force and navy to patrol the Arctic as it had done during the Cold War. What no one knew in the spring of 2007 was that this was all about to change.

---

[68] For news on Canada's claim, see Associated Press, "Canada to Claim North Pole as Its Own," *The Guardian*, December 9, 2013, http://www.theguardian.com/world/2013/dec/10/canada-north-pole-claim. For news on Denmark's claim, see National Public Radio, "Denmark Claims Part of the Arctic, Including the North Pole," December 15, 2014, http://www.npr.org/sections/thetwo-way/2014/12/15/370980109/denmark-claims-part-of-the-arctic-including-the-north-pole.

[69] Sally Deboer, "Yours, Mine, and Moscow's: Breaking Down Russia's Latest Arctic Claims," Center for International Maritime Security, November 27, 2015, http://cimsec.org/mine-moscows-breaking-russias-latest-arctic-claims/18252.

Maritime jurisdiction and boundaries in the Arctic region
Russian Claims

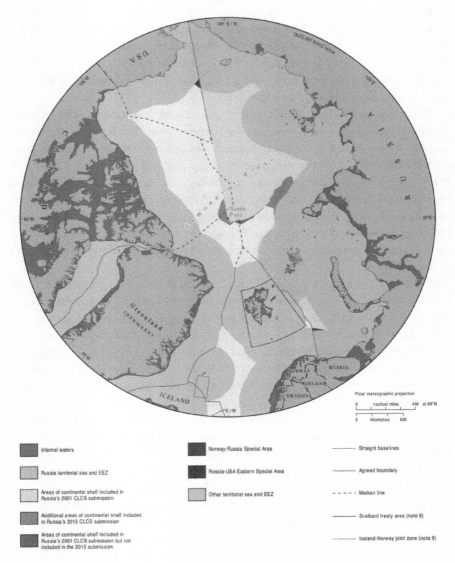

Figure 5.2 Map of Russia's Claims

Source: I thank the IBRU, Durham University, UK for permission to use this map. The full-color version can be found at https://www.dur.ac.uk/resources/ibru/resources/ArcticmapRussianonlycla ims05_08_15.pdf Accessed on May 27, 2018.

5.4 Russia's Response to the Shock

In the summer of 2007, the level of Arctic ice fell to an unprecedented low. The Arctic had not been ice-free for at least 5,400 years and perhaps as many as 125,000 years.[70] What the rapid and unanticipated drop signaled to scientists and policymakers was that the return of an ice-free Arctic was years, not centuries, away. An ice-free Arctic would suddenly make resources lying at the bottom of the ocean and previously locked under thick sheets of ice accessible.

Russia seized the opportunity to assert its military presence and claims in the region. Within days of deploying a submarine to plant the Russian flag on the seafloor at the North Pole, Putin ordered Russian bombers to resume regular patrols of the Arctic for the first time since the end of the Cold War. Despite already having more Arctic bases and icebreakers and maintaining a higher level of Arctic military activity than other states, Moscow responded to the shock by making even greater investments in enhancing its Arctic military capabilities and boosting its Arctic military presence. Russia's resumption of Arctic power projection shattered a period of calm in which little force had been projected into the Arctic by anyone.

Russia reacted to the exposure of Arctic resources by investing heavily in an exclusionary foreign policy. This exclusionary policy was designed to generate rents in two ways: first, by projecting military power to deter what Russia viewed as threats to its claims and to increase its bargaining power over maritime seabed resources (land rents) and, second, by maintaining its ability to control access by charging a toll to ships traveling via the Northern Sea Route.[71] The construction and projection of military power in the Arctic serves as the foundation of this exclusionary foreign policy.

Russia has increased its Arctic military presence as part of a broader strategy aimed at increasing its regional influence and securing the Arctic as a future resource base through a combination of coercive and cooperative polices. By complementing its cooperative diplomatic efforts with an enhanced Arctic military presence, Russia seeks to improve its bargaining position vis-à-vis other powers in the Arctic and to signal the strength of its interest. Unlike other powers, the Kremlin has chosen not just to construct Arctic forces but also to deploy those forces with far greater frequency and intensity and in a more assertive manner. The Russian government has demonstrated a willingness to project military force as part of a wider strategy

---

[70] National Snow & Ice Data Center, "Frequently Asked Questions on Arctic Sea Ice," Arctic Sea Ice News and Analysis (blog), n.d., http://nsidc.org/arcticseaicenews/faq/.

[71] For more on generating a rent by increasing protection costs of competitors, see Frederic C. Lane, *Profits from Power: Readings in Protection Rent and Violence-Controlling Enterprises* (Albany: State University of New York Press, 1979).

of bargaining over the control of Arctic resources. For example, following the shock Moscow opened up negotiations with Oslo over a long-standing dispute about control over resource-rich seabed territory in the Barents Sea. At the same time Russia increased the frequency with which it deployed its military forces and conducted military exercises in Norway's EEZ and along the edge of its airspace. Moreover, while Russia continued to adhere to international legal procedures by gathering evidence to support its ECS claims, Moscow also dramatically enhanced its regional military presence and deployed forces to areas it claimed. The following sections detail these activities.

5.4.1 Arctic Commitments

Why did Moscow respond with so much interest and investment? The answer, as clearly revealed in policy documents and statements by government officials, is that Russia views the Arctic as a strategic source of resources, rents, and revenue that will spur future economic development and assure Russia's return as a great power.[72] As a highly resource-dependent state, Russia's political elite face the long-term problem faced by all petro-states: the resource rents that are the source of their political and economic power are a nonrenewable resource that will eventually dry up. State energy companies are rapidly depleting the country's reserves of oil and natural gas. Despite being one of the world's largest producers of oil, Russia has only the world's eighth largest conventional reserves. This is especially problematic for the stock prices of Russian energy companies. A large part of an energy company's net worth is derived from its bookable reserves (i.e., the reserves of oil or natural gas that it controls).[73] Thus, the long-term problem Russia faces is that it must find more reserves on its own territory, diversify its economy, or acquire additional reserves elsewhere.[74]

The desire to safeguard future offshore energy reserves incentivized Russia to pursue Arctic resources. Securing additional gas reserves allows the Russian political elite to secure future energy rents, wealth, and political power. As Jon

---

[72] Marlene Laruelle, "Resource, State Reassertion and International Recognition: Locating the Drivers of Russia's Arctic Policy," *Polar Journal* 4, no. 2 (2014): 259.

[73] Coll, *Private Empire*.

[74] The Russians may be able to alleviate this problem by importing technologies that will allow them to take advantage of the boom in shale gas. A June 2013 report commissioned by the US Government Energy Information Agency suggests that Russia may have the largest shale gas reserves in the world. See Advanced Resource International, *EIA/ARI World Shale Gas and Shale Oil Resource Assessment* (Arlington, VA: Advanced Resources International, 2013), http://www.adv-res.com/pdf/A_EIA_ARI_2013%20World%20Shale%20Gas%20and%20Shale%20Oil%20Resource%20Assessment.pdf. However, in 2007 no one knew that these reserves existed.

Rahbek-Clemmensen has written, "Oil and gas dwarf all other Russian economic interests in the region, including minerals, fisheries, and the new sea-route through the North-East Passage."[75] The Russian government has indicated in public statements, strategic documents, and private comments behind closed doors that it views its claims to Arctic resources as contested by other states.

In a speech in 2008, Medvedev laid out Russia's Arctic interests, asserting

> This region is literally of strategic importance to our country. Its development is directly linked to the solution of long-term tasks of the state's development and its competitiveness on global markets. According to the data that we have, some 20 percent of Russia's GDP and 22 percent of Russia's exports are produced in this region. Rare and precious metals are extracted in the Arctic region. Major oil and gas provinces, such as Western Siberian, Timano-Pechorskaya and Eastern Siberian, are located there.[76]

Medvedev indicated that the Russian government has prioritized the Arctic because of its centrality to Russia's economic future. He also indicated that he viewed other states as threatening Russia's Arctic resource claims. "Regrettably, we have seen attempts to limit Russia's access to the exploration and development of the Arctic mineral resources. . . . That is absolutely inadmissible from the legal viewpoint and unfair given our nation's geographical location and history."[77] These statements were made not just in public but also in private by high-level Russian officials. For example, a Wikileaks cable revealed that in 2010 Dmitry Rogozin, Russia's ambassador to NATO, remarked that, "The twenty-first century will see a fight for resources" and that, "Russia should not be defeated in this fight."[78] These documents provide evidence that the Russian leadership believed there was a tight link between military competition and the allocation of Arctic resources.

Public statements also reveal that Russian leaders saw Arctic resources as highly valuable. In August of 2010, Putin remarked on the massive potential value of those resources, saying that, "According to rough estimates, the reserves discovered to date are worth approximately $5 trillion, including oil, natural gas, coal, gold and

[75] Jon Rahbek-Clemmensen, "Carving up the Arctic: The Continental Shelf Process between International Law and Geopolitics," *Arctic Yearbook* 2015 (2015): 333.

[76] BBC Monitoring, "Arctic Strategically Important for Russia," September 17, 2008.

[77] Climate Change.ru, "Sovet Bezopasnoti RF Provel Zasedanie Po Problem Izmeneniia Klimata [RF Security Council holds session on the problem of climate change]," March 17, 2010, http://www.climatechange.ru/node/423.

[78] Dmitriy Rogozin, "Third Cable," May 21, 2011, http://news.bbc.co.uk/2/shared/bsp/hi/pdfs/12_05_11_wikicables_artic.pdf.

diamonds."[79] More recently, in April of 2014, at a meeting of the Russian Arctic Security Council, he remarked,

> This region has traditionally been a sphere of our special interest. It is a concentration of practically all aspects of national security—military, political, economic, technological, environmental and that of resources. . . . I would like to stress that we will continue to invest heavily in the Arctic, to resolve issues dealing with this area's socioeconomic development, and strengthen security.[80]

The emphasis on securing resources and enhancing Russia's Arctic military capabilities is reflected in official documents. On September 18, 2008, Russian president Dmitry Medvedev officially adopted a Russian Arctic strategy entitled "The Foundations of the Russian Federation's State Policy in the Arctic until 2020 and Beyond."[81] The policy document unveiled Russia's Arctic interests, which included transforming the Arctic into a "premier strategic resources base" for Russia and the creation of Arctic military forces "capable of ensuring military security under various military–political scenarios."[82] This strategy also emphasized the importance of maintaining Russia's position as the leading Arctic power and revealed plans to create special Arctic military units to defend Russia's Arctic interests. A 2013 update to Russia's Arctic strategy also emphasized the importance of making the Arctic a strategic resource base due to its vast natural resources and reiterated the necessity of investing in increased military capabilities to protect Russian interests.[83] The potential for resource competition in the Arctic is also emphasized in the national security strategy of the Russian Federation up to 2020.[84] This document warns that

---

[79] Quoted in Pavel K. Baev, *Russia's Arctic Policy* (Helsinki: Finnish Institute of International Affairs, 2010), 4.

[80] To read more of Putin's remarks, see Vladimir Putin, "Meeting of the Security Council on State Policy in the Arctic," April 22, 2014, http://en.special.kremlin.ru/events/security-council/20845.

[81] Betsy Baker, "Law, Science, and the Continental Shelf: The Russian Federation and the Promise of Arctic Cooperation," *American University International Law Review* 25, no. 2 (2010): 10–38.

[82] Philip Burgess, "Foundations of the Russian Federation's State Policy in the Arctic until 2020 and Beyond," International Polar Year, December 1, 2010, http://icr.arcticportal.org/index.php?option=com_content&view=article&id=1791:foundations-of-the-russian-federations-state-policy-in-the-arctic-until-2020-and-beyond&catid=45:news-2007&Itemid=111&lang=sa.

[83] See International Expert Council on Cooperation in the Arctic, "The Development Strategy of the Arctic Zone of the Russian Federation," April 14, 2013, accessed July 8, 2017, http://www.iecca.ru/en/legislation/strategies/item/99-the-development-strategy-of-the-arctic-zone-of-the-russian-federation. For analysis of this strategy, see Alexander Sergunin and Valery Konyshev, "Russia in Search of Its Arctic Strategy: Between Hard and Soft Power?" *Polar Journal* 4, no. 1 (2014): 70.

[84] Russian Security Council, *National Security Strategy of the Russian Federation up to 2020* (Moscow: Russian Security Council, 2009), 12.

Russia must be prepared for conflict over access to Arctic resources and suggests that the use of military force to resolve "emerging problems" cannot be ruled out.[85]

Russia also has an interest in developing the Northern Sea Route. Russian leaders understand that in order to profit from Arctic resources, it is critical to develop and secure the transportation infrastructure and sea lanes needed to bring these resources to market. Thus, Russia's strategic documents describe the need for developing the Northern Sea Route by investing in ports, search-and-rescue capabilities, and the military and police capabilities needed to control these sea lanes.[86] The hope is that development of the Northern Sea Route will greatly reduce the cost of transporting Arctic resources.

As my theory would predict, Russia also views the Northern Sea Route as a potential source of rents. In 2009, the Russian Federal Assembly passed a law declaring that the Northern Sea Route is in Russian territorial waters and therefore subject to Russian law. The legislation provided the legal justification for Russia to board vessels, regulate vessel specifications, and set environmental standards.[87] The Russian government sought profits by charging a transit fee of $100,000 per ship, far in excess of what it costs to keep the sea lanes open.[88] In 2014, Russia increased its Arctic ship fee; estimates suggest that the fee will now be closer to $677,000 to $904,000 per ship, depending on the size of the ship and the time of year.[89] This is an example of rent-seeking by the Russian government and is exactly the type of exclusionary behavior that Rent-Addiction Theory would predict. In essence, the opening of the Northern Sea Route allows Russia to ship gas and raw materials to markets in Asia, while also serving as an opportunity to extract rents from shipping.

However, it is important not to overstate the viability of the Northern Sea Route in the near term, especially as an alternative shipping route or source of rents. First, very few ships use the Northern Sea Route. The number of ships making the trip peaked at seventy-one in 2013[90] and has declined substantially since: only eighteen

[85] Kari Roberts, "Jets, Flags, and a New Cold War? Demystifying Russia's Arctic Intentions," *International Journal* 65, no. 4 (2010).

[86] Katarzyna Zysk, "Military Aspects of Russia's Arctic Policy: Hard Power and Natural Resources," in *Arctic Security in an Age of Climate Change*, ed. James Kraska (New York: Cambridge University Press, 2011).

[87] Shelagh D. Grant, *Polar Imperative: A History of Arctic Sovereignty in North America* (Vancouver, Canada: Douglas & McIntyre, 2010).

[88] James Kraska, ed., *Arctic Security in an Age of Climate Change* (New York: Cambridge University Press, 2011).

[89] Carsten Ørts Hansen et al., *Arctic Shipping—Commercial Opportunities and Challenges* (Copenhagen, Denmark: CBS Maritime, 2016), 45, accessed July 18, 2017, https://services-webdav. cbs.dk/doc/CBS.dk/Arctic%20Shipping%20-%20Commercial%20Opportunities%20and%20 Challenges.pdf.

[90] CHNL Information Office, "Transit Statistics," accessed July 9, 2017, http://www.arctic-lio. com/nsr_transits.

ships made the trip in 2015 and nineteen in 2016.[91] Second, the majority of the ships using the route have been Russian, suggesting that international shipping companies and other nations do not yet view the route as viable. Shipping experts have concluded that this is unlikely to change in the near future as no company is currently willing to insure Arctic shipping, given the enormous risks of sailing through the remote, iceberg-filled waters.[92] Thus, while the Northern Sea Route is important to Russia, especially as a means of bringing resources to markets, its potential value as a source of rents and revenue pales in comparison to the value of the Arctic's seabed resources.

5.4.2 Russia's Post-shock Military Activity

Immediately after the shock, Russia began to regularly deploy military aircraft to patrol the Arctic for the first time since the end of the Cold War.[93] In July of 2007, Russia deployed Tupolev Tu-95 bombers into the Arctic. Tu-95s are heavy strategic bombers capable of delivering a large payload of bombs and long-range cruise missiles. This was not the deployment of a coast guard ship or surveillance plane. These bombers were powerful military assets capable of projecting a substantial amount of firepower. These flights would serve as the warm-up for a massive set of exercises in August of 2007, involving 30–50 bomber flights per day and the use of far-north bases that had rarely been used.[94] Later that August, the Kremlin announced that the twelve Tu-95 strategic bombers stationed in the Arctic would fire cruise missiles at targets, in an exercise designed to demonstrate Russia's reach in the region.[95] The decision to resume Arctic bomber flights represented a major departure in Russia's foreign policy in the region.

Following the successful completion of these exercises, President Putin announced that Russia would resume patrolling the Arctic regularly. In addition to the turboprop Tu-95 bombers, the Russian military has deployed supersonic

---

[91] Atle Staalesen, "Moscow Boasts Potential, but Arctic Transit Shipments between Europe–Asia Remain Poor," *Barents Observer*, March 2, 2017, https://thebarentsobserver.com/en/arctic/2017/03/moscow-boasts-potential-arctic-transit-shipments-between-europe-asia-remain-poor. See also Av Malte Humpert, "Shipping Traffic on Northern Sea Route Grows by 40 Percent," *High North News*, December 19, 2017, http://www.highnorthnews.com/shipping-traffic-on-northern-sea-route-grows-by-40-percent/.

[92] Jeroen F. J. Pruyn, "Will the Northern Sea Route Ever Be a Viable Alternative?" *Maritime Policy & Management* 43, no. 6 (2016): 661–75.

[93] Siemon T. Wezeman, "Military Capabilities in the Arctic," SIPRI Background Paper (Stockholm: Stockholm International Peace Research Institute, 2012), 9.

[94] Pavel K. Baev, *Russia's Race for the Arctic and the New Geopolitics of the North Pole* (Washington, DC: Jamestown Foundation, 2007).

[95] Roger Howard, *The Arctic Gold Rush: The New Race for Tomorrow's Natural Resources* (New York: Continuum, 2009).

bombers such as the Tu-160 (Black Jack) and Tu-22M3 (Backfire). The Tu-160 is the most powerful aircraft in the Russian air force; it is capable of flying at a maximum speed of more than 1,300 miles per hour and of carrying 80,000 pounds of bombs or missiles (which is 10,000 pounds more than the already massive B-52).[96] The deployment of these bombers shows Russia's willingness to deploy one of its most expensive and powerful weapons systems in the Arctic.[97]

Rather than a one-off incident, these bomber patrols were the beginning of a shift in Russia's Arctic force posture. In the second half of 2007, Moscow flew more strategic bomber flights into the Arctic than it had in the entire period from 1991 to 2006.[98] Russia also began deploying its forces close to the states with which it had Arctic disputes. As part of this general shift in policy, Russia began provocatively flying its bombers right up to the borders of Canada, Norway, and the United States, in some cases violating the twelve-mile air defense identification zone. Recall that Russia had overlapping maritime claims with Norway, a potential overlapping ECS claim with Canada, and a dispute with the United States over the status of the Northern Sea Route. In 2007 alone, Russian bombers violated the twelve-mile air defense zone around Alaska eighteen separate times.[99]

Russia also ramped up its Arctic naval deployments. In late November 2007, a Russian aircraft carrier, the *Admiral Kuznetsov*, along with the Russian Northern Fleet, conducted military exercises close to the Norwegian Troll oil platform.[100] This effectively shut down Norwegian airspace around the platform as the sky was filled with too many Russian military jets for the platform to safely transport personnel via helicopter to the mainland.[101] In 2008, the Russian Ministry of Defense announced that the Northern Fleet would resume an active presence in the Arctic.[102] By February 2010, Russian Navy Commander Admiral Vladimir Vysotsky claimed

[96] Air Force Technology, "Tu-160 Blackjack Strategic Bomber, Russian Federation," n.d., http://www.airforce-technology.com/projects/tu160/.

[97] Because of limitations in the data, it is not always possible to determine the exact location in the Arctic where the Russian military has deployed its forces. When possible, I state the precise location. However, the sharp increase in military deployment to the Arctic region generally is informative in that it signals Russia's prioritization of the region after the exposure of resources in 2007.

[98] Rolf Tammes, "Arctic Security and Norway," in *Arctic Security in an Age of Climate Change*, ed. James Kraska (New York: Cambridge University Press, 2011), 52.

[99] Ariel Cohen, "Russia in the Arctic: Challenges to U.S. Energy and Geopolitics in the High North," in *Russia in the Arctic*, ed. Stephen J. Blank (Carlisle, PA: Strategic Studies Institute, 2011).

[100] *Barents Observer*, "Russian Aircraft Carrier Training Next to Norwegian Oil Platform," November 12, 2007, http://www.barentsobserver.com/russian-aircraft-carrier-training-next-to-norwegian-oil-platform.4442850.html.

[101] Thomas Nilsen, "'Admiral Kuznetsov' Ready for Winter Migration to the South," *Barents Observer*, September 29, 2011, http://barentsobserver.com/en/news/admiral-kuznetsov-ready-winter-migration-south.

[102] Tammes, "Arctic Security and Norway," 87.

Table 5.4 **Incidents of Norwegian F-16s Being Scrambled**

	2008	2009	2010	2011	2012	2013	2014
Scrambles	32	38	36	34	41	41	43
Identifications	87	77	39	48	71	71	69

that Russian submarines and ships had already conducted ten military patrols in the Arctic.[103]

5.4.3 Russia Projects Power to Disputed Areas and Against States with Which It Has Disputes

Of the disputes discussed in this book, Russia's disputes with Norway involved the largest set of potential oil and gas reserves. Recall that Russia has two disputes with Norway, one about an overlapping EEZ claim in the resource-rich Barents Sea and one about the right to exploit resources in the waters around Svalbard. Extensive Russian power projection toward Norway reveals that resources were an important motivation for Russia's foreign policy actions after the shock.

In 2007, Russia reopened negotiations over its forty-year-long dispute with Norway about overlapping claims in the Barents Sea. At the same time, the number of Russian bomber flights patrolling the Norwegian coast increased dramatically, from fourteen in 2006 to eighty-eight in 2007, a more than 500% increase and more flights than in the previous fifteen years combined.[104] These deployments were also much more assertive as Russia buzzed Norwegian air defenses and conducted mock bombing runs on Bodø, Norway's northernmost command center.[105]

The increase in deployments of Russian aircraft against Norway in 2007 marked the beginning of a far more assertive force posture. Table 5.4 shows data collected by the Norwegian Air Force on the number of missions flown and identifications of foreign aircraft. The numbers represent incidents in which Norwegian F-16s were scrambled to intercept foreign aircraft at Bodø airbase.[106]

---

[103] Vasiliy Batanov, "Russia Increases Combat Capabilities in Arctic," *Sputnik*, February 10, 2010, http://en.rian.ru/russia/20101002/160804543.html.

[104] Zysk, "Military Aspects of Russia's Arctic Policy," 86.

[105] Charles M. Perry and Bobby Andersen, *New Strategic Dynamics in the Arctic Region* (Cambridge, MA: Institute for Foreign Policy Analysis, 2012), 36.

[106] Norwegian Armed Forces, "På Vingene 41 Ganger (English Translation on Wings 41 Times)," n.d., http://forsvaret.no/om-forsvaret/fakta-om-forsvaret/publikasjoner/rapport2012/Sider/qra.aspx. For data on 2013 and 2014, see Trude Pettersen, "Stable Russian Air Activity in the North," *Barents Observer*, December 19, 2014, http://barentsobserver.com/en/security/2014/12/stable-russian-air-activity-north-19-12.

In April 2010, Russia and Norway settled their dispute over the Barents Sea; the agreement was ratified in June of 2011.[107] Russia had originally claimed an enormous area of 67,000 square miles more than it would have received under the equidistance principle recommended by the UNCLOS treaty. Russia received half of its original demand, or approximately 33,500 square miles of maritime seabed territory (an area more than three times the size of Crimea) that would have gone to Norway under the equidistance rule.

However, this did not end Russia's other dispute with Norway or its willingness to deploy military force in close proximity to Norway and the disputed areas. As previously mentioned, the Russians have refused to acknowledge Norway's claimed EEZ or fishery protection zone around Svalbard and demand the right to exploit the maritime resources there. High-level Russian government officials, such as Gennadii Oleinik, chair of a committee of the Council of the Federation that is responsible for northern issues, asserted that, "continued Russian presence at Spitsbergen is perceived as necessary to secure the country's economic and military interests in this 'most promising part of the world.'"[108] In 2012, Russia deployed an antisubmarine destroyer to the waters around Svalbard, followed by a guided missile cruiser armed with sixteen long-range cruise missiles.[109]

In April 2015, Russia's deputy prime minister, Dmitry Rogozin, and representatives of the Russian defense industry suddenly appeared in Svalbard without warning and tweeted photos of themselves at the Svalbard airport.[110] Rogozin is considered one of the chief architects of Russia's Crimea strategy. He was on the European Union's sanction list at the time and therefore banned from visiting EU countries, including Norway. After leaving Svalbard, Rogozin visited the North Pole, another area claimed by Russia. Following the visit, Rogozin said, "Last year, we had the historical reunification of Sevastopol and the Crimea. This year, we present a new view and new powerful stress on the development of the Arctic. Basically, [it] is all about the same . . . [Russia is now] starting to get more conscious about territory, its interests and borders."[111] The Russians returned to Svalbard in April of 2016, when the Russian military used the island as a staging area for paratrooper

107   Perry and Andersen, New Strategic Dynamics in the Arctic Region, 14.

108   Quoted in Katarzyna Zysk, "Russian Military Power and the Arctic," EU-Russia Centre Review no. 8 (2008):   81,   http://kms2.isn.ethz.ch/serviceengine/Files/RESSpecNet/99789/ichaptersection_ singledocument/F3C8FB3B-0DA9-473A-8814-19CB883B6F11/en/Pages+from+review_viii_ final_13_10-9.pdf.

109   Cohen, "Russia in the Arctic," 22. See also Perry and Andersen, New Strategic Dynamics in the Arctic Region.

110   Thomas Nilsen, "Strong Norwegian Reaction to Rogozin's Svalbard Tour," Barents Observer, April 18, 2015, http://barentsobserver.com/en/politics/2015/04/strong-norwegian-reaction-rogozins-svalbard-tour-18-04.

111   Atle Staalesen, "Expansionist Rogozin Looks to Arctic," Barents Observer, April 21, 2015, https:// barentsobserver.com/en/arctic/2015/04/expansionist-rogozin-looks-arctic-21-04.

deployments to the North Pole. This incident may have been in violation of the Svalbard Treaty, which prohibits military forces on the island, and clearly violated Norwegian law, which prohibits any foreign military activity on the island.

Russia has also focused on projecting power to other areas it claims, including the North Pole. Before the shock, Russia occasionally deployed submarines to the North Pole, such as a submarine-launched missile test in October of 2006, but generally did not deploy military force there. Since the shock, the frequency and size of deployments have increased. Just days after the infamous flag-planting, Russia's strategic bomber command deployed aircraft to fly over the North Pole, in a maneuver clearly aimed at backing Russian claims with a show of force. Russia has also deployed nuclear-powered icebreakers, nuclear ballistic missile and attack subs, and even hundreds of paratroopers to land at the North Pole. In July of 2009, the Russian navy sent a fleet of nuclear attack submarines to an area near the North Pole and tested submarine-launched ballistic missiles.[112] On June 30, 2011, just days before Russia deployed a nuclear-powered icebreaker to the North Pole, Putin announced that, "Russia intends without a doubt to expand its presence in the Arctic."[113] In the fall of 2012, a Russian Orthodox bishop traveled to the North Pole with the nuclear-powered icebreaker *Rossilya* and held a consecration, lowering a metal capsule into the sea carrying the blessing of the church's leader, with the inscription, "With the blessing of Patriarch Kirill of Moscow and All Russia, the consecration of the North Pole marks 1150 years of Russian Statehood."[114] In December of 2013, immediately after a Canadian announcement of plans to submit a continental shelf claim that included the North Pole, Putin ordered the Russian military to increase its Arctic presence.[115] Several months later, in April 2014, the Kremlin sent ninety paratroopers to land at the North Pole.[116,117] Since then, Russia has continued to regularly deploy paratroopers and, as of January 2017, claims to have landed a total of 350 troops at the North Pole.[118]

---

[112] It should be noted that Russia had conducted a similar test in 2006. This was the first test at the North Pole in eleven years. See *Defense Update*, "Russian Submarine-Launched Ballistic Missiles Tested," July 24, 2009, http://defense-update.com/20090724_russian_sub_test.html.

[113] Simon Shuster, "As Russia Stakes a Claim, the Race to Control the Arctic Heats Up," July 8, 2011, http://www.time.com/time/world/article/0,8599,2082207,00.html.

[114] See Jones and Parfitt, "Russia Reasserts Ownership over the North Pole."

[115] BBC News, "Putin Orders Russian Military to Boost Arctic Presence," December 11, 2013, http://www.bbc.com/news/world-europe-25331156.

[116] Trude Pettersen, "Russian Military Instructors Plan to Land on Svalbard," *Barents Observer*, April 7, 2016, https://thebarentsobserver.com/en/security/2016/04/russian-military-instructors-plan-land-svalbard.

[117] Atle Staalesen, "More than 300 Russian Paratroopers Have Been on North Pole," *Barents Observer*, January 5, 2017, https://thebarentsobserver.com/en/security/2017/01/more-300-russian-paratroopers-have-been-north-pole.

[118] Staalesen, "More than 300 Russian Paratroopers."

5.4.4 Russia's Post-shock Investment in Its Arctic Force Structure and Force Posture

As Russia increased its Arctic military deployments, military officials publicly drew a link between investing in Arctic military capabilities and resource competition. In June of 2008, Lt. Gen. Vladimir Shamanov, head of the Defense Ministry's combat training directorate, stated that, "After several countries contested Russia's rights for the resource-rich continental shelf in the Arctic, we have immediately started the revision of our combat training programs for military units that may be deployed in the Arctic in case of a potential conflict."[119] In 2009, the Russian government released a document calling for the creation of military bases along the Arctic coast. The document, approved by Medvedev, called the Arctic "the most important area for international and military strategy."[120] As part of this strategy, Russia planned to build twenty frontier posts on Arctic islands and along the Northern Sea Route.[121] Russia stated its intention to establish a comprehensive coastal defense infrastructure that would include forward-deployed air bases in the Arctic.[122] In August of 2009, the Russian military announced that it would upgrade its northernmost border post, on the Franz Josef Land archipelago. The Russian Air Force also recently upgraded airfields on Novaya Zemlya; Graham Bell Island, part of Franz Josef Land, received a 7,000-foot year-round runway.[123] These upgrades will allow the airfields to serve as strategic bomber stations and facilitate Russian power projection throughout the Arctic.

Unlike Canada, Russia has invested in reactivating bases, many of which are now operational. In October of 2013, Russia renovated the Temp Air Base (a.k.a. Northern Clover) on Kotelny Island, where the 99th Arctic Tactical Group is permanently stationed.[124] By Arctic standards, this is a massive base, capable of permanently housing 150 troops. In 2014, additional weapons systems were delivered to Temp, including the Pantsir-S1 missile (an advanced antiaircraft weapon system) and artillery systems.[125] By the end of 2014, military bases on Wrangel Island and Cape Schmidt had also reopened, housing newly stationed troops and hosting

---

[119] Kristian Åtland, "Interstate Relations in the Arctic: An Emerging Security Dilemma?" *Comparative Strategy* 33, no. 2 (2014): 152, https://doi.org/10.1080/01495933.2014.897121.

[120] Tony Halpin, "Russian Bases Stake Claim to Arctic Wealth," *The Australian*, March 30, 2009.

[121] Ilya Kramnik, "NATO, Russia Stage Arctic War Games," April 19, 2012, http://english.ruvr.ru/2012_04_19/72301024/.

[122] Zysk, "Military Aspects of Russia's Arctic Policy," 103.

[123] Jones and Parfitt, "Russia Reasserts Ownership over the North Pole."

[124] Trude Pettersen, "Russia Re-Opens Arctic Cold War Era Air Base," *Barents Observer*, October 30, 2013, http://barentsobserver.com/en/security/2013/10/russia-re-opens-arctic-cold-war-era-air-base-30-10.

[125] Heather A. Conley, *The New Ice Curtain: Russia's Strategic Reach to the Arctic* (Washington, DC: Center for Strategic and International Studies, 2015), 94.

exercises by tactical airborne teams.[126] Also, in 2015, Deputy Defense Minister Dmitry Bulgakov announced that ten Arctic military airfields would be reopened by the end of 2015, which would reportedly give the Russian military fourteen operational airfields in the Arctic.[127] In April of 2017, Russia unveiled pictures of another major base on Alexandra Land called "Trefoil," a 150,000–square foot facility capable of hosting at least 150 troops, complete with a gym, billiard room, and cinema.[128] In March of 2017, Putin visited the base and said, "Natural resources, which are of paramount importance for the Russian economy, are concentrated in this region; reports estimate the value of these resources at $30 trillion."[129]

Many of Russia's new and upgraded Arctic bases and border posts are spread along the country's long Arctic seacoast, allowing the Russians to control traffic along the Northern Sea Route and sustain a military presence near the disputed areas. These bases allow forces to be forward-deployed, host military exercises, and provide the logistical support needed to maintain air and naval operations in the Arctic.

In addition to bases, Russia invested heavily in other Arctic-specific force structure, such as icebreakers, which are necessary for year-round presence and power projection in the region.[130] It is important to note that at the time of the shock Russia already had the largest icebreaker fleet in the world, with fifty-five state-owned icebreakers and ice-hardened patrol ships.[131] While other states, such as Canada and the United States, have been reluctant to invest in additional icebreaking capacity, Russia has sought to increase its lead by ordering additional icebreakers.[132] In 2010, Putin announced the construction of three heavy nuclear-powered icebreakers. Russia is the only country in the world that operates nuclear-powered icebreakers, which are far more powerful and capable than other heavy icebreakers.[133] Each of these icebreakers is a multibillion-dollar platform that represents a major

[126]   Conley, *New Ice Curtain*, 94.

[127]   Conley, *New Ice Curtain*, 94.

[128]   BBC News, "Russia's New Arctic Trefoil Military Base Unveiled with Virtual Tour," April 18, 2017, http://www.bbc.com/news/world-europe-39629819.

[129]   Tom Parfitt, "Russia Unveils Its Giant New Arctic Base," *The Times*, April 18, 2017, https://www.thetimes.co.uk/article/russia-unveils-its-giant-new-arctic-base-p0qjg3jl6.

[130]   Charles K. Ebinger and Evie Zambetakis, "The Geopolitics of Arctic Melt," *International Affairs* 85, no. 6 (2009): 1220.

[131]   This estimate is based on the Arctic Icebreakers and Ice-Hardened Warship Data, an original data set made for this project. For other estimates, see Caitlyn L. Antrim, "The Russian Arctic in the Twenty-First Century," in *Arctic Security in an Age of Climate Change*, ed. James Kraska (New York: Cambridge University Press, 2011), 117; see also National Research Council, *National Security Implications of Climate Change for US Naval Forces* (Washington DC: National Academies Press, 2011).

[132]   National Research Council, *National Security Implications*.

[133]   Milosz Reterski, "Breaking the Ice," *Foreign Affairs*, December 11, 2014, https://www.foreignaffairs.com/articles/united-states/2014-12-11/breaking-ice.

investment. Estimates suggest that Russia could have as many as four to six new nuclear-powered icebreakers by 2020.[134]

Moreover, unlike Canada, which promised to build six to eight ice-hardened ships in 2007 but as of 2017 had completed none, Russia has followed through on its commitments. Since the shock, Russia has built five new icebreakers, bringing it to a total of sixty, with an additional ten under construction.[135] These include the world's most powerful nuclear-powered icebreaker, the *Arktika*, which was ordered in 2009 and launched in 2016 at a cost of $1.9 billion.[136] The 33,500-ton *Arktika* is the length of two football fields.[137] By comparison, the United States' most powerful icebreakers are less than half the tonnage and have significantly less horsepower.[138] Russia's larger and more capable icebreaker fleet gives it the ability to sustain a conventional surface presence in Arctic waters year-round. Russia has also ordered new icebreakers that are to be armed with a 76-millimeter deck gun, antiship cruise missiles, and helicopter pads.[139] Although icebreakers are occasionally armed with deck guns, they do not generally carry antiship cruise missiles, which indicate either an intent or an expectation that these ships will not simply be breaking ice.

Russia has also invested in a number of other Arctic-specific assets, such as special Arctic military units, regionally specific logistical support organizations, and the Arctic Unified Command to coordinate military operations in that theater. Recall that Russia's Arctic strategy, released shortly after the shock, included plans to create special military formations. In June of 2008, the minister of defense asserted that the military must train in the Arctic in order to uphold Russia's Arctic claims.[140] Moscow has followed through on these commitments. Since 2008, Russia has established two Arctic warfare brigades, consisting of approximately 9,000 troops, for

---

[134] Thomas R. Fedyszyn, "Renaissance of the Russian Navy," *Proceedings* 138, no. 3 (March 2012); see also Huebert et al., *Climate Change and International Security*.

[135] J. N. Markowitz, Arctic Icebreakers and Ice-Hardened Warships Data Set, University of Southern California, unpublished data set, 2017.

[136] See Joseph V. Micallef, "Polar Politics: The Competition to Control the Arctic Heats Up," *Huffington Post* (blog), September 11, 2016, http://www.huffingtonpost.com/joseph-v-micallef/polar-politics-the-compet_b_11920192.html.

[137] Mary Louise Kelly, "Russia Aims to Profit Big from *Arktika*, World's Largest Icebreaker Ship," *Weekend Edition Saturday*, NPR.org, June 18, 2016, http://www.npr.org/2016/06/18/482594632/russia-aims-to-profit-big-from-arktika-world-s-largest-icebreaker-ship.

[138] National Research Council, "The U.S. Coast Guard Icebreaker Fleet," in *Polar Icebreaker Roles and U.S. Future Needs: A Preliminary Assessment* (Washington, DC: National Academies Press, 2005), 3, https://doi.org/10.17226/11525.

[139] Robert Beckhusen, "Russia's New Arctic Ice Breaker Has One Very Special Feature: Anti-Ship Missiles and Naval Guns," *The National Interest*, May 14, 2017.

[140] Zysk, "Russian Military Power and the Arctic," 84.

the purpose of defending its natural reserves in the Arctic.[141] In 2012, Russia created the Arctic Center for Material and Technical Support to provide logistical support to the Northern Fleet, which is reportedly staffed by more than 15,000 people.[142] Russia also created the Arctic Unified Command, which has been operational since December of 2014.[143]

The Kremlin has also followed through on its commitment to train its Arctic forces by increasing the frequency and size of its Arctic military exercises.[144] These exercises serve the dual purpose of training Russian forces and simultaneously demonstrating Russia's ability to project power and sustain a military presence under harsh Arctic conditions. Russia has also equipped and tested these forces with specialized Arctic military equipment, such as the DT-210 Vityaz, an off-road vehicle with six-foot-wide wheels that can carry ten tons of equipment across rugged frozen terrain.[145] Finally, Russia has enhanced its Arctic reconnaissance and situational awareness capabilities by building specialized Arctic drones[146] and enhancing its satellite capabilities to improve GLONASS (the Russian version of GPS) coverage of the Arctic.[147]

5.4.5 Summary of Findings

Russia did not just make major commitments to increase its Arctic military presence. It backed those commitments by investing heavily in building new and refurbishing old Arctic military bases and building more nuclear-powered icebreakers. Additionally, Russia not only increased its Arctic military activity immediately after the shock but also increased the frequency of deployments to disputed areas and adopted a more assertive force posture against states with which it has disputes. This was not a temporary shift in policy: Russia has sustained this high

---

[141] Juha Jokela, *Arctic Security Matters* (Paris: EU Institute for Security Studies, 2015); Annika Bergman Rosamond, *Perspectives on Security in the Arctic Area*, DIIS Report 2011:09 (Copenhagen, Denmark: Danish Institute for International Studies, 2011).

[142] Valery Konyshev and Alexander Sergunin, "Is Russia a Revisionist Military Power in the Arctic?" *Defense & Security Analysis* 30, no. 4 (2014): 331, https://doi.org/10.1080/14751798.2014.948276.

[143] Osman Askin, "The High North: Challenges and Opportunities," NATO Parliamentary Assembly, n.d., 6. https://www.nato-pa.int/sites/default/files/documents/2015%20-%20135%20STC%2015%20E%20%20-%20Summary%20Budapest.doc.

[144] Conley, *New Ice Curtain*, 11.

[145] Alexander Vershinin, "Cold Combat: No Fighting in Arctic but Russia to Show Specialized Weapons," *Russia Beyond the Headlines*, April 19, 2017, https://www.rbth.com/defence/2017/04/19/cold-combat-no-fighting-in-arctic-but-russia-to-show-specialized-weapons_746193.

[146] Brian Merchant, "Russia Is Swarming the Arctic With Military Drones," Motherboard, September 14, 2015, https://motherboard.vice.com/en_us/article/8qxzd5/russia-is-swarming-the-arctic-with-military-drones.

[147] Perry and Andersen, *New Strategic Dynamics in the Arctic Region*, 54.

level of military activity in the Arctic since the shock. In the next section, I briefly address counterarguments before discussing my findings and their implications.

5.5 Addressing Counterarguments

Many other explanations of Russia's Arctic foreign policy behavior have been offered. Given space constraints, I will address only the arguments that might threaten the validity of my findings. I begin by laying out a set of alternative explanations which suggest that Russia's renewed Arctic military presence is caused by factors other than the desire to secure control over resources. I then demonstrate that, while these factors might be able to explain why Russia had a high commitment to investing in projecting force into the Arctic before the shock, they cannot explain the change in Russia's level of commitment and investment after the shock. I then address potential confounds either that covaried with the shock or that the shock does not directly address.

5.5.1 Alternative Explanations Addressed by the Speed of the Shock: Geography, Shifting Power, and Status-Seeking

It is undeniable that Russia cares deeply about asserting its great power status, and it would be naive to suggest that history, geography, and geopolitical considerations do not matter for Russia's Arctic foreign policy. Russia has more Arctic territory and a longer Arctic coastline than any other state and historically has lacked warm-water ports, forcing it to base the Northern Fleet above the Arctic Circle. These factors influence Russia's commitment to the Arctic and its investment in its Arctic force posture and force structure. To deal with this, I established the baseline level of Arctic military activity and force structure before the shock and then focused on the size of the change after the shock. This allows me to demonstrate that, although a number of geographic and historical factors resulted in Russia having a much higher baseline activity than other states before the shock, it still invested so much after the shock that the size of the change was larger than that in any other state under study.

In short, these alternative factors are important but are not enough to explain the dramatic change in Russia's Arctic military activity, force structure, and presence immediately after the shock. This is because these factors either did not change or changed too slowly to explain the rapid change in Russia's level of commitment and investment. For example, one might argue that Russia's renewed Arctic military presence was driven by its rising economic power. Russia's economic recovery did give Moscow more income to invest in its military capabilities. However, economic power shifted slowly as Russia's economic recovery, which began in 2000, unfolded over a decade. Thus, this slow shift cannot explain the timing or speed of the shift in Russia's Arctic foreign policy. Moreover, shifting economic power cannot explain why Russia continued to invest in enhancing its Arctic military presence even after its economy contracted after 2009 and from 2014 to 2017. If Russia is only interested in asserting its status or if shifting power is the key factor, why did Moscow dramatically increase its Arctic military presence only after the rapid exposure of resources in the summer of 2007? These alternative explanations offer no answer.

5.5.2 Alternative Explanations Addressed by the Timing of the Shock

5.5.2.1 *Russian Assertiveness and Increased Geopolitical Competition with NATO*

A related alternative argument is that Russia is simply an aggressive or expansionary power, and its actions in eastern Europe and elsewhere have resulted in countermoves by NATO. Russia responded by modernizing its military and beefing up its military activity and forces in the Arctic. There are several reasons why these alternative arguments are unsatisfying and cannot explain the change in Russia's behavior. First and foremost, Russia returned to the Arctic in the summer of 2007, before it adopted a more assertive foreign policy in Georgia in 2008, Crimea in 2014, or Syria in 2015. Recall that at the time of the shock in 2007, there was no consensus that Russia was an adversary of the West; NATO was focused on Afghanistan and on finding new missions to justify its existence, and Moscow was considered by some to be an ally in the war on terror. Second, the claim risks tautology and smacks of circular logic: Russia behaves aggressively because it is an aggressive power, which we know because we observed it engaging in aggressive actions. Third, this does not provide an explanation for why Russia chose to project more power, especially when seeking to secure territory and rents, whereas Rent-Addiction Theory does.

5.5.2.2 *Military Modernization and the Northern Fleet*

Relatedly, one might be concerned that Russia's investment in the Arctic is driven by its efforts to modernize its military, given that a substantial proportion of its naval forces are stationed in the Arctic with the Northern Fleet. I deal with this issue in two ways. First, Russia's military modernization plan was not announced until 2008, and it was not funded with a substantial increase in absolute military spending until 2012.[148] Second, I focused only on assessing Russia's investment in

---

[148] For more on this modernization plan and its funding, see Susanne Oxenstierna, "Russian Military Expenditure," in *Russian Military Capability in a Ten-Year Perspective—2016* (Stockholm: Swedish Defence Research Agency, 2016), 133–50; Johan Norberg et al., "Russia's Armed Forces in 2016," in *Russian Military Capability in a Ten-Year Perspective—2016* (Stockholm: Swedish Defence Research Agency, 2016), 23–66.

Arctic-specific assets, such as icebreakers, Arctic bases, and specialized Arctic military units, and excluded dual-use assets, such as the ships, aircraft, and submarines of the Northern Fleet that could be used to project power to the Arctic but are also useful for projecting power elsewhere. Russia's substantial investments in upgrading the Northern Fleet are also not counted, removing this potential source of bias in the data on Russia's Arctic force structure.

It is important to note that I am not claiming that Russia's actions in the Arctic are unrelated to efforts to modernize its military or to its geopolitical concerns elsewhere. Russia's efforts to modernize its military and increase its geopolitical competition with NATO clearly influence its strategic calculus and actions in the Arctic. I am only claiming that these factors alone cannot explain Russia's renewed commitment to and investment in boosting its Arctic military presence. These investments are a continuation of well-documented plans and policies that began in the immediate aftermath of the shock, prior to Russia's major modernization efforts and more assertive foreign policy actions outside the Arctic. Additionally, the fact that Russia continued to prioritize the Arctic, even after its forces were more strained from frequent deployment to Crimea, Ukraine, and Syria, provides strong evidence of the Arctic's enduring importance to the Russian regime.

5.5.3 The Remaining Alternative Explanations

5.5.3.1 Responding to the Newly Exposed Northern Flank

Though the shock eliminates explanations based on constant or slow-moving factors, one might remain concerned about factors that covaried with the shock. Specifically, the melting ice exposed not only resources but also sea lanes, exposing Arctic countries' northern flanks. This is particularly important for Russia, given that the Northern Fleet, along with its submarine-based nuclear deterrent, is based in the Arctic. While these factors are no doubt important and likely explain at least some states' responses to the shock, there are several countervailing factors that suggest this was not the primary factor driving events. Even ten years after the shock, Arctic sea lanes are not viable; and they are unlikely to be for decades. Similarly, governments have realized that concerns over exposing a northern flank are overblown, given that any northern amphibious invasion would first have to navigate dangerous ice-choked waters. As Canada's chief of defense staff, General Natynczyk, quipped in 2009, "If someone were to invade the Canadian Arctic, my first task would be to rescue them." This explains why other Arctic nations are not racing to defend their coastlines.

5.5.3.2 Russia's Defense of Its Nuclear Deterrent

The desire to protect its undersea nuclear deterrent might explain why Moscow has invested so heavily in the Northern Fleet and in upgrading Arctic bases near its headquarters in Severomorsk, Murmansk. However, if protecting submarines is Russia's primary motivation, it is less clear why Russia has also invested in bases far from Murmansk along the Northern Sea Route. For a map of Russian bases, see Figure 5.3.

Moreover, it does not explain why Moscow projected power to claimed and disputed areas more frequently after the shock or why it has adopted a far more assertive force posture toward states with which it has maritime resource disputes, such as Norway. Nor does it explain why Russian officials have consistently made statements in both speeches and strategic documents linking the importance of securing Arctic resources with commitments to increase Russia's Arctic military presence. These outcomes would be puzzling if Russia only cared about protecting its nuclear deterrent. The answer to this puzzle, according to Russian Arctic experts Alexander Sergunin and Valery Konyshev, is that there was a major change in Russia's Arctic strategy:

> [In] contrast with the Cold War period, when Russian military strategies in the North were dictated by the logic of global political and military confrontation between two superpowers (USSR and USA) or two military blocs (Warsaw Pact and NATO), the current Moscow military policies in the region are driven by completely different

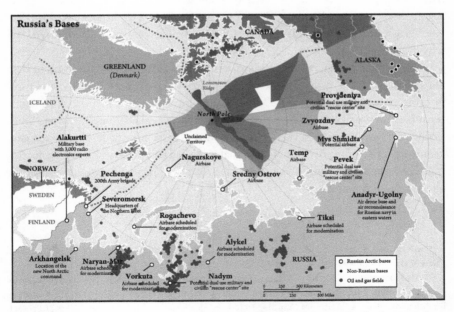

Figure 5.3 Map of Russia's Bases Source: I thank Jeremy Bender and Business Insider for permission to use this map. The original maps can be found at http://www.businessinsider.com/chart-of-russias-militarization-of-arctic-2015-8. Accessed on May 18, 2018.

motives. As the threat of a global nuclear war has disappeared, these strategies aim at three major goals: first, to demonstrate and ascertain Russia's sovereignty over the AZRF [Arctic Zone of the Russian Federation] (including the EEZ and continental shelf); second, to protect its economic interests in the North; and third, to demonstrate that Russia retains its great power status and has world-class military capabilities.[149]

The change in Russia's Arctic strategy can be explained by and is consistent with my theoretical predictions. The fact that Russian experts have also concluded that Russia's policy is driven primarily by defending its claims and economic interests rather than by safeguarding its nuclear deterrent lends strong support to my explanation.

5.5.3.3 International Legal Status Quo

Finally, it might be that those states with large shares of the resources within their EEZs, which stood to benefit under international law, were reluctant to respond to the shock by projecting power, whereas states that received fewer resources were more willing to pursue gunboat diplomacy as an extralegal option. However, a closer look reveals that, even if we only include hydrocarbons that were within Russia's EEZ and ECS and not claimed by another state, Russia received 53.3% of Arctic Ocean offshore hydrocarbons.[150] Given that Russia would benefit more than any other state from the status quo distribution of resources under international law, why did it back its claims by projecting force?

One might still argue that states' responses were driven by which stood to benefit the most. If this were the case, then Canada should have invested the most in projecting power, given that Ottawa would increase its relative stock of Arctic resources by nearly 19% if its potential claims were realized, while Russia's stock would increase by only 5.3%.[151] The fact that Russia has made more expansive claims than any other Arctic state and that it has backed these claims by projecting military force is especially strong evidence for my theory and casts doubt on the alternative explanations.

---

[149] Alexander Sergunin and Valery Konyshev, *Russia in the Arctic: Hard or Soft Power?* (New York: Columbia University Press, 2015), 147.

[150] Tina Praprotnik, "Arctic Offshore Energy Resources: Distribution Across International Boundaries and Climatic Impact" (master's thesis, Duke University, 2013), https://dukespace.lib.duke.edu/dspace/bitstream/handle/10161/6855/Praprotnik%20Master%27s%20Project.pdf?sequence=1.

[151] Praprotnik, "Arctic Offshore Energy Resources."

5.6 Conclusion

This chapter began with a puzzle: why did Russia invest so much more in projecting power to secure control over Arctic resources than any other state? This is especially puzzling given that Russia is less wealthy than Canada and far less economically and militarily powerful than the United States. The answer is that Russia's economy is highly land-oriented, making Russia far more financially dependent on resource rents than any other Arctic state. So, the Russian state has a far stronger preference to secure control over Arctic resources than production-oriented states that rely on income earned from producing goods and services. As Russian officials have stated clearly in public and private statements and government documents, they view the Arctic as a future source of resource rents and revenue that must be secured.

This case study began by assessing several observable implications of how the structure of Russia's economy influences the regime's preferences. First, as predicted by my theory, Russia's choice to proceed down the path of resource-driven development led to path-dependent effects that increased the switching costs associated with investing in production. More specifically, over time, Russia overinvested in natural resource extraction and underinvested in production-oriented inputs such as universities, intellectual property rights, basic research and development, and the health and human capital of its citizens. These *policies* drove up switching costs as Russia could not quickly generate income by substituting away from resource rents toward producing goods and services. This implies that Russia's leaders have a stronger preference to invest in securing control over resource rents than in transitioning to producing goods and services.

Second, I find that the structure of Russia's economy and the regime's dependence on resource rents gave the governing coalition a keen interest in pursuing policies that benefitted the land-oriented sectors of the economy. I found evidence for both causal pathways by which my theory predicts this should occur. First, money captured the state as oil oligarchs invested in securing influence over the ruler, namely Putin. Second, the state captured the money as Putin used the power of the state to regain control of the country's resource wealth and redistributed it to his cronies within his governing coalition. In both scenarios, I found that those who benefited from natural resources became entrenched interests by using the income generated by resource rents to buy the political support and influence needed to solidify their hold on power. They used this power to bend state policy to favor natural resource industries at the expense of industries that produced goods and services.

Third, I found evidence that the Russian leadership values the political benefits associated with land rents specifically because land rents can be appropriated by the state and their production is easier to monitor and control. This gives Russian leaders a stronger preference to secure income from resource rents as opposed to goods and services, whose production is harder to control and monitor. I also found that Russia's rulers use these rents to maintain political power by redistributing them to individuals within the governing coalition. Collectively, this evidence provides support for the causal pathways through which the economic structure of the state influences the preferences of the regime.

In the second part of this chapter, I demonstrated that Russia responded to the shock by making stronger commitments to defend its Arctic resource claims, boosting its Arctic military presence, and backing those commitments with a larger investment than any other Arctic state. Russian leaders explicitly identified the Arctic as a strategic resource base and linked the importance of enhancing Russia's Arctic military presence with securing control of these resources. Before the shock, Russia was much less active in the Arctic, but it already had the largest Arctic force structure and the highest level of Arctic military activity relative to the other Arctic states. Despite this higher baseline, I find that there was a more significant change in Russia's post-shock level of investment in its Arctic force structure, military activity, and willingness to deploy force to disputed areas, compared to the other Arctic states.

Russia's massive Arctic military investments were the more costly part of a two-track strategy that also included pursuing international legal claims via UNCLOS. Russia's military actions should be interpreted as an attempt to strengthen its bargaining position by demonstrating its ability to project power and increasing the risk that other Arctic states would have to take when pressing competing claims. Russia poured money into building nuclear-powered icebreakers, specialized Arctic military units and equipment, and a string of new and refurbished bases along the Northern Sea Route that provide a "coercive back-up or back drop to secure its interest to extend its continental shelf northward."[152]

In closing, Russia's behavior provides especially robust support for my theory and suggests that the change in Russia's level of investment was larger because Moscow had a much stronger preference to secure control over resources than wealthier and more powerful states, like Canada and the United States, that could better afford to make such investments.

Having found strong support for my theoretical predictions, I close with the implications of my findings for the future of Russian policy in the Arctic. First, Russia has continued to slide into autocracy, but no regime lasts forever. How would Russia's foreign policy preferences change if Putin was replaced by a different autocrat or if Russia were to democratize? Rent-Addiction Theory suggests that so long as Russia is economically dependent on resource rents, it will have a strong interest in securing control over additional sources of rent. This would be the case regardless

---

[152] Juha Käpylä and Harri Mikkola, *Continental Shelf Claims in the Arctic: Will Legal Procedure Survive the Growing Uncertainty?* (Helsinki: Finnish Institute of International Affairs, 2015), 7, http://www. fiia.fi/en/publication/516/continental_shelf_claims_in_the_arctic/.

of whether Russia is governed by Putin or some other despot, unless that leader had some alternative source of rents and revenue. Even if a democratically elected regime that was highly representative of societal interests was in power, it would still have a stronger interest in securing control over resources than a democratic state that was not economically dependent on land. That said, a shift to representative democracy should decrease the regime's preference for territory, by lowering its value for the political benefits associated with land rents.

Finally, the last several years have seen a major decrease in the price of energy, making offshore Arctic oil generally unprofitable. Could this cause Russia to withdraw from the Arctic again and instead invest in transitioning away from resource rents? My theory suggests that this is unlikely because Russia is still heavily dependent on resource rents and lacks the ability to generate income by substituting investment in other sectors of the economy. Instead, Russian leaders are hoping that energy prices recover or technology improves in ways that make development profitable. Russia's recent investments in its Arctic military presence, despite falling energy prices, suggest that Moscow recognizes it has little choice but to double down on the Arctic and pray that energy prices recover. As Arctic expert Marlene Laruelle writes, "A widespread impression among ruling elites is that there is 'no other choice' for Russia's future but to pursue such an Arctic policy. The country hopes nonetheless that new technologies, such as oil fracking, can save the day."[153] This does not suggest that conflict is likely, only that Russia is unlikely to withdraw militarily from the Arctic any time soon.

---

[153] Laruelle, "Resource, State Reassertion and International Recognition," 258.

The United States' Arctic Foreign Policy

The Big Dog That Does Not Bark

6.1 Introduction: Why Doesn't the Unipole Care More about the North Pole?

The United States' share of global power is so high that the United States is sometimes referred to as the "unipole."[1] It is the most powerful Arctic state in terms of both military potential, as measured by GDP, and actual military capabilities, as measured by the size and quality of its forces. It has the world's most impressive power projection capabilities and has chosen to project more military power than any other state in history.[2] Washington currently maintains hundreds of bases internationally and, for over seventy years, has deployed hundreds of thousands of troops overseas.[3] The United States has been so militarily active overseas that critics have suggested that Washington's grand strategy is driven too often by capabilities rather than a rational calculation of its interests.[4] If capabilities are, in fact, the principal driver of grand strategy, the United States should be the state most likely to project power into the Arctic. However, this is precisely the opposite of what we observe.

---

[1] Stephen G. Brooks and William C. Wohlforth, "The Rise and Fall of the Great Powers in the Twenty-First Century: China's Rise and the Fate of America's Global Position," *International Security* 40, no. 3 (2016): 7–53.

[2] For an assessment of current US military potential and capabilities, see Michael Beckley, "China's Century? Why America's Edge Will Endure," *International Security* 36, no. 3 (2012): 41–78; Barry R. Posen, "Command of the Commons: The Military Foundation of U.S. Hegemony," *International Security* 28, no. 1 (2003): 5–46; William C. Wohlforth, "The Stability of a Unipolar World," *International Security* 24, no. 1 (1999): 5–41.

[3] Stephen G. Brooks and William C. Wohlforth, "Assessing America's Global Position," in *America Abroad: The United States' Global Role in the 21st Century* (New York: Oxford University Press, 2016), 14–47.

[4] Eugene Gholz, Daryl G. Press, and Harvey M. Sapolsky, "Come Home, America: The Strategy of Restraint in the Face of Temptation," *International Security* 21, no. 4 (1997): 5–48.

Perils of Plenty. Jonathan N. Markowitz, Oxford University Press (2020). © Oxford University Press.
DOI: 10.1093/oso/9780190078249.001.0001

The Arctic is one of the few regions of the world where the United States has adopted a grand strategy of restraint.[5] Washington has demonstrated little interest in securing Arctic resources outside of its exclusive economic zone (EEZ) and has not prioritized the Arctic as a region of geopolitical concern. It has declined to invest in increasing its Arctic military presence or in building the capabilities to project power into the Arctic in the future. Because of its lack of interest in the Arctic, the United States has been branded the "reluctant Arctic power."[6]

This lack of interest in the Arctic is especially informative. Given that Washington maintains forces in virtually every other region of the world, America's behavior is puzzling. The United States' actions cannot be explained by theories that focus on relative power or by theories of the rent-seeking state, which suggest that all governments should seek rents.[7] Also, many leftist critiques of United States' grand strategy suggest that it is driven by a desire to control resources, pointing to American interventions in Latin America throughout the twentieth century and the presence of US forces in the Middle East since the Carter Doctrine.[8] However, if the United States is driven by a desire to control resources, why has it not acted to appropriate Arctic seabed resources?

Rent-Addiction Theory suggests that, as a democratic, production-oriented state, the United States' principal interest is in securing goods for its citizens by maintaining open access to markets globally, and it should have little interest in directly appropriating resources as a source of rents and revenue. Thus, the United States' desire to remain deeply engaged in virtually every region except the Arctic is not puzzling but stems from its ex ante preferences. These preferences are molded by the characteristics of the coalition of individuals who govern the United States, who generate income not by extracting wealth from territory but by producing goods and services for export.

While the United States is a major energy producer in absolute terms, natural resources account for only a tiny fraction of the American economy.[9] Rather than relying primarily on profits from resource rents, the United States ensures its citizens are prosperous and secure through a business model that depends on

[5] Barry Posen, *Restraint: A New Foundation for U.S. Grand Strategy* (Ithaca, NY: Cornell University Press, 2014).

[6] Huebert, *United States Arctic Policy*.

[7] Lane, *Profits from Power*.

[8] Klare, *Rising Powers, Shrinking Planet*, 182–208.

[9] Recall that resource rents are less than 1% of US GDP according to the World Bank. See World Bank, "Total Natural Resources Rents (% of GDP)," World Development Indicators, June 20, 2019, https://data.worldbank.org/indicator/NY.GDP.TOTL.RT.ZS?locations=US&view=chart.
Additionally, according to the US government's Bureau of Economic Analysis, mining accounted for just 1.6% of US GDP in 2018, the latest year for which data are available. See
Bureau of Economic Analysis, "BEA Industry Facts," US Department of Commerce, Bureau of Economic Analysis, June 20, 2019, https://apps.bea.gov/industry/factsheet/factsheet.cfm?IndustryId=21.

investments in human capital, secure property rights, and access to large, stable overseas markets. Since at least the end of World War II, US foreign policy has prioritized regions with the largest concentrations of wealth and purchasing power. For example, Kennan's strategy of containment was explicitly based on ensuring access to markets in Japan and Europe and preventing potential aggressors, such as Russia, from capturing those markets by force.[10] Later, the Carter Doctrine extended this strategy, explicitly threatening to use force to prevent any state from denying the United States access to markets in the Middle East. Washington did not make these costly investments because it wanted to directly control the wealth of these regions; it did so because its citizens had a strong interest in trading with them, and it wanted to ensure American access.

Washington chooses this strategy not out of benevolence but because its leaders believe it is the best strategy for ensuring security and prosperity for American citizens. This policy explains why the United States recently opted to pivot to Asia, rather than to the Arctic. The United States is far more interested in ensuring access to the world's largest and wealthiest markets in Asia than in appropriating natural resources in the Arctic. Previous work has suggested that American lack of interest in the Arctic is due to its other global interests and has taken those interests as given, rather than as a choice. In contrast, my theory explains why the United States has chosen to prioritize other regions over the Arctic and predicts the conditions that might change America's Arctic strategy. I discuss these conditions and their implications for future US foreign policy in the conclusion of this chapter.

6.1.1 Overview of Argument and Evidence

Rent-Addiction Theory suggests that all states should have some preference to seek control over resources; thus, even the production-oriented United States should have become more interested in the Arctic after the shock. The question is whether some states have a stronger preference than others to seek control over resources and whether this explains the strength of their response, as measured by changes in their level of investment in projecting power to the region. Given that the United States is highly production-oriented, my theory predicts that it should be among the least willing to invest in securing control over Arctic resources, unlike more land-oriented states. If this theory is correct, the overall change in American investment should be small.

More specifically, I code the change in the overall level of investment by assessing the change in foreign policy behavior in the Arctic across three categories of indicators: (1) *Arctic commitments*, claims expressed in government documents,

---

[10] Harry S. Truman, "Telegram, George Kennan to George Marshall [Long Telegram]" (Administration File, Elsey Papers, February 22, 1946).

statements by officials, and the Arctic's priority, relative to other regions, within the US foreign policy bureaucracy; (2) *Arctic force posture*, the level of US military activity in the Arctic and how much the United States has invested in deploying forces to areas that it has claimed and/or that are disputed; and (3) *Arctic force structure*, the level of US investment in Arctic-specific assets such as icebreakers, ice-hardened warships, and bases. Collectively, these indicators are used to code the overall level of investment in pursuing an exclusionary foreign policy (defined as the projection of power to seek control over rents).

A summary of the predicted and observed values of these indicators is given in Table 6.1. The first column shows my predicted change in the level of investment. The second column contains the observed level of investment in the pre-shock period. This allows me to establish a baseline for pre-shock investment. The third column displays the observed level of investment in the post-shock period. Comparing the pre-shock and post-shock levels of investment allows me to code the observed changes in the level of investment. By comparing my predictions to the observed changes, we can test my predictions.

Table 6.1 **Predicted and Observed Changes in the Level of American Investment**

	Predicted Change in Investment	*Observed Pre-shock Investment (Scale 1–5)*	*Observed Post-shock Investment (Scale 1–5)*	*Observed Change in Investment (Scale 0–4)*
Arctic commitments	Small	Very low (1)	Low (2)	Small (1)
Arctic military activity	Small	Very low (1)	Low (2)	Small (1)
Deploying force to claimed or disputed areas	Small	Very low (1)	Low (2)	Small (1)
Icebreakers and ice-hardened warships	Small	Very low (1)	Very low (1)	Almost none (0)
Arctic bases	Small	Very low (1)	Very low (1)	Almost none (0)
Overall investment in exclusionary foreign policy	Small	Very low (1)	Low (2)	Small (1)

As detailed in the following sections, the observed change is generally consistent with my predictions. After the shock, there was a small increase in US commitments as the Arctic was mentioned more frequently in strategic documents and statements by public officials. However, the commitments outlined in those documents are vague and not backed by a substantial increase in funding needed to enhance US Arctic presence. There was also a slight increase in US military activity, exercises, and the number of incidents in which the United States deployed force to areas under dispute; however, most of the events involve research missions and efforts to map the ocean floor. Finally, there was almost no change in Washington's investment in its Arctic force structure, even less than my theory expects. Collectively, these indicators provide strong evidence that the overall change in US willingness to invest in seeking control over Arctic resources after the shock was small.

In addition to predicting a general American reluctance to invest in projecting military power to the Arctic, Rent-Addiction Theory generates several more specific predictions that can be evaluated qualitatively with process evidence. First, the production-oriented sector should leverage its superior financial resources to obtain and keep a dominant share of political influence within the state's governing coalition. Second, this investment in influence should translate into more favorable policies, so we should observe the state pursuing policies that benefit the production-oriented sector. Third, because this sector's share of the nation's economic output is so dominant, production-oriented interests should be well represented and influential within the governing coalition regardless of changes in administration. As a result, we should see little evidence of land-oriented interest groups lobbying for policies likely to be opposed by the production-oriented sector, such as spending to secure control over resources by military means, because they know they would lose.

Thus, I would expect little change in the United States' willingness to invest in securing control over Arctic resources, regardless of the administration that is in power. This should be the case even if the administration includes people who have an economic or ideological interest in supporting land-oriented industries, such as oil and gas. This suggests not that leaders do not matter but only that the more a state's economy is dominated by the production-oriented sector, the more constrained leaders will be in their ability to pursue policies that this sector strongly opposes. Since the shock, there has been a shift in administrations from the relatively pro-oil and gas Republican Bush administration to the more environmentally friendly Democratic Obama administration and back to the more pro-oil and gas Trump administration. If there was little change in American willingness to invest in securing control over Arctic resources across these three administrations, this would be strong evidence for my theoretical predictions.

6.2   Coding the Characteristics of the United States' Governing Coalition

The United States is one of the world's oldest democracies and, by most measures, has highly representative and democratic political institutions.[11] Despite constitutional amendments and expansions in voting rights, these measures have been relatively constant over US history. However, American foreign policy interests have shifted dramatically over the past 250 years. Given that democratic political institutions have remained relatively constant, they alone cannot explain shifts in foreign policy preferences. What has changed is the structure of the US economy and, therefore, the economic interests of the governing coalition. Specifically, the United States has shifted away from land as the principal source of wealth and income and now depends on producing goods and services. Understanding the impact of these changes allows me to explain an outcome that remains puzzling for theories that focus solely on regime type: why the United States used to be so interested in projecting power to take territory, despite being democratic, and why it no longer is. My theory suggests that if the United States had remained economically dependent on land rents to generate income, rather than producing goods and accessing markets, it would have invested in pursuing an exclusionary foreign policy in the Arctic. I next illustrate how the shifts in the source of US income condition its preferences.

6.2.1   How the United States' Economic Structure Influences Its Governing Coalition

Like other states at the time, the United States in its first century was relatively dependent on income derived from land. The link between land and income was so tight that the Founding Fathers made the right to vote contingent upon owning property to prevent those without land from demanding redistribution. In 1850, sixty years after the founding of the republic, agriculture still accounted for 50% of US GDP and employed 70% of the workforce.[12] In 1869, farming's value added as a percentage of GDP was still 37.5%, but by 1900 it had dropped to 20% and, by 1929, below 10%.[13] After World War II, agriculture's share of the economy continued to

---

[11]   Monty G. Marshall, Ted R. Gurr, and Keith Jaggers, *Polity IV Project. Political Regime Characteristics and Transitions, 1800–2015, Dataset Users' Manual* (Vienna, VA: Center for Systemic Peace, 2016); Cheibub, Gandhi, and Vreeland, "Democracy and Dictatorship Revisited."

[12]   Robert Gallman and Thomas Weiss, "The Service Industries in the Nineteenth Century," in *Production and Productivity in the Service Industries*, ed. Victor R. Fuchs (New York: Columbia University Press, 1969), 287–352.

[13]   J. Alston et al., *Persistence Pays: U.S. Agricultural Productivity Growth and the Benefits from Public R&D Spending* (New York: Springer, 2010).

plunge, and today it constitutes less than 1.5% of US GDP and employs just 1% of the population. This is not because farming became less productive. In 2006, US farms produced six times as much value as in 1929. However, over the same time, measured in constant dollars, the US economy has grown thirteen times larger.[14] The takeaway is that land has become dramatically less important to the income of those who govern the United States.

Those skeptical of my contention that the United States is no longer economically dependent on land might point out that the fracking and tight oil boom has made the United States one of the biggest, if not the biggest, producers of oil and gas in the world.[15] They would be right. In terms of absolute production, the United States is a global titan in energy. However, although the US land-oriented sector is a global giant, it is domestically a pygmy, with a tiny relative share of GDP. Even with revolutionary advances in fracking that have resulted in a dramatic increase in absolute production, resource rents have remained a relatively small part of the economy, averaging less than 1% of GDP over the last decade.[16] According to Bureau of Economic Analysis (BEA) data, which include not just resource rents but the total value added of the oil, gas, and coal industries, these industries' value added went from 2.7% of GDP in 2008 to just 1.7% of GDP in 2015.[17] To provide some perspective, according to the BEA, from 2008 to 2015, the finance sector's value added as a percentage of GDP increased from a little over 6% to just over 7%, educational services and healthcare increased from 7.8% to 8.3%, and professional business services rose from 11.2% to 12.2%. These sectors are all part of the production-oriented sector of the economy and collectively dwarf the land-oriented sector. The overwhelming dominance of the production-oriented sector becomes apparent when we note that services are responsible for nearly 80% of US GDP.

The production-oriented sector of the economy also employs the vast majority of Americans. By comparison, data from the World Bank suggest that since the year 2000, agriculture has employed between 1% and 2% of the US working population.[18] The mining sector, which the Bureau of Labor Statistics defines as including all extractive industries such as oil, gas, and coal, employs just 0.06% of the working population.[19] In contrast, the service sector employs 81% of American workers.

[14] Alston et al., *Persistence Pays*.

[15] US Energy Information Administration, "Today in Energy: U.S. Remained World's Largest Producer of Petroleum and Natural Gas Hydrocarbons in 2014," April 7, 2015, https://www.eia.gov/todayinenergy/detail.php?id=20692.

[16] World Bank, "Total Natural Resources Rents (% of GDP)," June 25, 2018.

[17] Bureau of Economic Analysis, "Industry Data: GDP-by-Industry," n.d., https://www.bea.gov/iTable/iTable.cfm?ReqID=51&step=1#reqid=51&step=2&isuri=1.

[18] World Bank, "Employment in Agriculture (% of Total Employment)," http://data.worldbank.org/indicator/SL.AGR.EMPL.ZS?page=2.

[19] Bureau of Labor Statistics, "Industries at a Glance: Mining, Quarrying, and Oil and Gas Extraction: NAICS 21," accessed July 17, 2017, https://www.bls.gov/iag/tgs/iag21.htm:

In sum, the United States no longer relies on land to generate the vast majority of its income and instead relies on its citizens to produce innovative goods and services. This is not because land has become less productive over time. As discussed, due to technological innovation, American energy firms and farms have both dramatically increased their production. Despite the productivity of these land-oriented industries, their contribution to the US economy is dwarfed by production-oriented sectors. It is not the absolute value of a sector's productivity but its relative contribution to the state's economy that determines its domestic political representation and influence within the state's governing coalition.

6.2.2 How the Governing Coalition's Source of Income Influences Policy

Recall that if my causal mechanisms are present, we should expect to observe two outcomes: first, production-oriented sectors of the economy should invest in acquiring and retaining a dominant share of political influence within the governing coalition and, second, the state should pursue polices benefiting those sectors. As evidence that the first mechanism is present, consider the relationship between lobbying by sector and the corporate tax code in the United States. In 2014, of the ten firms that spent the most on lobbying, only one (ExxonMobil) was an energy company.[20] While oil and gas firms invest heavily in lobbying, they are outgunned by firms in production sectors such as healthcare, insurance, tech, and telecommunications.[21]

The US tax code reflects this balance of economic interests and influence, being skewed to benefit goods and services and disadvantage land-oriented interests. This provides evidence of my second mechanism: the dominant sector should use its political influence to obtain more favorable policies from the state. US energy companies paid the second highest corporate taxes of any industry (an average of 37%) and, in absolute terms, Exxon, Chevron, and ConocoPhillips each paid higher tax rates than similar-sized firms, such as General Electric, Verizon, and Boeing,[22]

"establishments that extract naturally occurring mineral solids, such as coal and ores; liquid minerals, such as crude petroleum; and gases, such as natural gas. The term mining is used in the broad sense to include quarrying, well operations, beneficiating (e.g., crushing, screening, washing, and flotation), and other preparation customarily performed at the mine site, or as a part of mining activity."

[20] Jesse Solomon, "Top 10 Companies Lobbying Washington," CNN Money, October 1, 2014, http://money.cnn.com/2014/10/01/investing/companies-lobbying-10-biggest-spenders/.

[21] For an analysis of lobbying by sector, see Rani Molla, "Tracking Lobbyist Spending in 2014," *Wall Street Journal* (blog), July 30, 2014, http://blogs.wsj.com/numbers/tracking-lobbyist-spending-so-far-in-2014-1625/.

[22] Mike Bostock et al., "Across US Companies, Tax Rates Vary Greatly," *New York Times*, May 25, 2013, http://www.nytimes.com/interactive/2013/05/25/sunday-review/corporate-taxes.html.

each of which spends more on lobbying than any energy company, including ExxonMobil.[23]

Although there are American energy companies whose economic interests depend on the control of territory, research suggests that American officials have been unwilling to intervene militarily on their behalf.[24] A telling example occurred when ExxonMobil appealed to the US military to help it secure its facilities against rebels in Nigeria. The American military's response was, "You need to work out the arrangement with that sovereign nation to your satisfaction. And if you can't, you might want to reconsider your investment. We are not the guarantor of your security."[25] This example illustrates how the interests of companies like ExxonMobil, which would benefit from military intervention to protect their foreign investments, are generally outweighed by other groups whose economic interests would be harmed if the United States projected military power on behalf of American oil companies. American elected officials are well aware that all Americans and production-oriented firms would have to foot the bill for any military intervention but would not necessarily reap the economic rewards, knowledge that adds further political disincentives to intervene. This example of an energy firm lobbying and losing also illustrates why we rarely observe energy firms lobbying for US military intervention today. Rather than wasting their political capital on lobbying for policies they expect not to get, energy firms focus on lobbying for policies that are less likely to be opposed by the powerful production-oriented sector, such as loosening environmental regulations. As we shall see in Section 6.4, this is exactly what energy firms chose to focus on while lobbying the US government about the Arctic.

Rather than pursuing policies that benefit land-oriented industries like oil and gas, my theory predicts that a state like the United States, whose economy is dominated by industries such as tech, healthcare, and finance, should favor the production-oriented sector. Consistent with my theoretical expectations, Washington has chosen policies that privilege the production-oriented sector over the land-oriented sector. For example, from 1975 until December of 2015, the United States banned the export of oil.[26] This policy explicitly benefited production-oriented industries by providing them with cheaper energy at the expense of US oil firms that were prohibited from selling oil overseas to the highest bidder. The government only lifted the ban after energy prices crashed to record lows.

[23] Daily Beast, "Top 20 Companies That Lobby the Most," March 24, 2011, http://www.thedailybeast.com/articles/2011/03/25/top-20-companies-that-lobby-the-most.

[24] See Stephen D. Krasner, Defending the National Interest: Raw Materials Investments and US Foreign Policy (Princeton, NJ: Princeton University Press, 1978).

[25] Coll, Private Empire, 475.

[26] Economist, "America Lifts Its Ban on Oil Exports," December 18, 2015a, https://www.economist.com/news/finance-economics/21684531-light-sweet-compromise-puts-end-crude-market-distortions-america-lifts.

Washington also invested in policies that benefited the production-oriented sectors of the economy. For example, the United States spends between 2.5% and 3% of its GDP on research and development, making it among the top ten states in terms of the share of its income that goes to research and development.[27] The United States also invests heavily in subsidizing its citizens' human capital, a critical input for the production-oriented sector of the economy. US government expenditures on education are between 5% and 5.5% of GDP. The federal government also subsidizes and guarantees student loans, makes donations to schools and universities tax-deductible, and allows private universities to maintain nonprofit status. This greatly benefits the production-oriented sector of the economy. It is also one reason why human capital–intensive industries, such as information technology, biotech, and pharmaceutical firms, tend to cluster around top American universities. In comparison, as stated in the previous chapter, autocratic land-oriented states like Russia tend to spend far less on education and research and far more on developing and maintaining the institutions and infrastructure to extract oil and gas.[28]

As predicted by Rent-Addiction Theory, the production-oriented sector outspends the land-oriented sector on lobbying and receives more favorable policies. The evidence presented here demonstrates the plausibility of my casual mechanisms but does not constitute proof of the causal link between the state's economic structure and the composition of its governing coalition. Having probed the plausibility of my causal mechanisms and defended my coding of the economic structure and interests of the United States, I will now assess how the United States responded to the exogenous shock of Arctic climate change. Doing so requires establishing the baseline level of US interest and investment in maintaining a regional military presence before the shock. As I will demonstrate, the United States maintained minimal commitments and invested little in projecting power to the Arctic for more than a decade before the shock.

6.3   Establishing a Baseline: US Arctic Foreign Policy Prior to the Shock

For much of the twentieth century, the Arctic was an important theater of military activity for the United States. In 1942, Japanese forces invaded and occupied two of the Aleutian Islands, Attu and Kiska. After the war, the Arctic became geopolitically important. During the Cold War, the United States maintained a high level of

---

[27] World Bank, "Research and Development Expenditure (% of GDP)," n.d., http://data.worldbank.org/indicator/GB.XPD.RSDV.GD.ZS.

[28] This specific example is in line with a larger trend that suggests that, on average, resource-dependent states spend less on education. For more on this trend, see Lara Cockx and Nathalie Francken, "Natural Resources: A Curse on Education Spending?," *Energy Policy* 92 (2016): 394–408.

military activity and presence in the Arctic. B-52 bombers armed with thermonu-
clear weapons circled the Arctic, ready to hit targets deep in the Soviet Union. US
ballistic missile submarines patrolled silently, lurking beneath the Arctic ice sheets;
and American nuclear-powered attack subs hunted their Soviet counterparts in a
seemingly never-ending game of cat and mouse.

However, as the Cold War drew to a close, the region faded in importance. The
United States pulled out of the Arctic, dramatically decreasing its Arctic submarine patrols and decommissioning much of its Arctic military force structure.[29] For
nearly two decades after the Cold War and before the shock, the United States occasionally sent icebreakers on mapping expeditions and held submarine military
exercises in the Arctic, but the overall level of US military activity was very low compared to other regions.

6.3.1 US Arctic Force Structure and Force Posture
before the Shock

On the eve of the shock, the United States maintained some residual military presence in the Arctic, mostly tied to ballistic missile defenses. The US Coast Guard,
the only arm of the US government with an Arctic surface capability, had no bases
above the Arctic Circle.[30] At the time of the shock, the Coast Guard owned just three
icebreakers, only two of which were active since the *Polar Star* was near-mothballed
and placed in caretaker status in 2006. The two operational icebreakers were responsible for covering both the Arctic and the Antarctic. Two years before the
shock, the icebreaker budget was transferred from the Coast Guard to the National
Science Foundation, emphasizing the ships' increasing role as a science platform,
rather than a power projection asset.[31]

The US military has only one base above the Arctic Circle, located in Thule,
Greenland. Thule, which was built during the Cold War, is a substantial base with a
deep-water port, a 10,000-foot runway, and a 20 million–gallon fuel farm. However,
in 2006 that base had no aircraft and was only used to house intercontinental ballistic missile warning radar.[32] Thule is primarily maintained as part of the US Ballistic
Missile Early Warning System; its main purpose is not to project conventional military force into the Arctic but to defend against ballistic missile attacks.[33] Prior to the

[29] *Newsday*, "U.S. Is Phasing out Attack Sub Patrols."

[30] Heather A. Conley, "The Colder War: U.S., Russia and Others Are Vying for Control of Santa's
Back Yard," *Washington Post*, December 25, 2011.

[31] Committee on the Assessment of U.S. Coast Guard Polar Icebreaker Roles and Future Needs,
Polar Icebreaker Roles and U.S. Future Needs: A Preliminary Assessment (Washington DC: National
Academies Press, 2005), 20–21, https://www.nap.edu/read/11525/chapter/1.

[32] Wezeman, "Military Capabilities in the Arctic."

[33] Michael Byers, *International Law and the Arctic*, Cambridge Studies in International and
Comparative Law (Cambridge: Cambridge University Press, 2013).

shock, in 2002, the United States chose to place its ground-based interceptors (i.e., ground-based antiballistic missiles) in Ft. Greely, Alaska.[34] The base is located well below the Arctic Circle, and the interceptors are there not to project power into the Arctic but rather to defend against missiles from North Korea, China, or Russia. The United States also maintained a few Coast Guard HC-130s on Kodiak Island that patrolled the Bering Sea.[35] However, this base is south of mainland Alaska and nearly 1,000 miles from the northern tip of the state.

The Pentagon maintains a force structure with many dual-use assets capable of operating in the Arctic environment, such as its fleet of nuclear-powered submarines, which can operate under Arctic ice, and the HC-130 Hercules, a military cargo plane outfitted with skis in place of landing gear. Some other assets, such as the P-3 Maritime Patrol Aircraft, F-22 Raptor, and Stryker vehicle, can reportedly operate in a variety of environments, including the Arctic.[36] The F-22s, currently the most capable US military asset near the Arctic, are stationed at Elmendorf Air Force Base in Alaska.[37] However, this base is in southern Alaska, 719 miles south of the Arctic Ocean. The United States also maintains Eielson Air Force Base, outside Fairbanks, where the F-16 aggressor training squadron is based; but this base is also well below the Arctic Circle (roughly 500 miles from Barrow [Utqiagvik], the northern tip of Alaska, and 1,745 miles from the North Pole). Thus, US fighter aircraft cannot patrol much of the Arctic without air-to-air refueling; and, even with refueling, their loiter time is significantly limited. This complicates using the aircraft to support maritime operations in the Arctic.[38]

6.3.2 Pre-shock Arctic Claims and Disputes

In 1990, the United States negotiated the Bering Sea Treaty with what was then a rapidly disintegrating Soviet Union. The treaty settled a 1,600–nautical mile maritime boundary between the two, delimiting each state's EEZ.[39] The United States' only remaining EEZ claim involves a disagreement with Canada, dating back to 1976, about their overlapping claims in the Beaufort Sea, which lies off the coast of Alaska and Canada's Yukon Territory.[40] The dispute remains unsettled to this day,

---

[34] Missile Defense Agency, "Ground-Based Miscourse Defense (GMD) Expanded Capability, Fort Greely Alaska: Proposed Final Environmental Assessment," Department of Defense, February 2018, https://mda.mil/global/documents/pdf/GMD_ECFinalEA13Feb18.pdf.

[35] Wezeman, "Military Capabilities in the Arctic."

[36] Wezeman, "Military Capabilities in the Arctic."

[37] James Kraska, "The New Arctic Geography and U.S. Strategy," in *Arctic Security in an Age of Climate Change*, ed. James Kraska (New York: Cambridge University Press, 2011), 256.

[38] Christopher Gray, Leif Bergey, and Walter A. Berbrick, "Fleet Arctic Operations Game: Game Report," Defense Technical Information Center, 2011, 33.

[39] Byers, *International Law and the Arctic*, 36.

[40] For an excellent discussion of this dispute, see Byers, *International Law and the Arctic*, 56–92.

but it is not contentious. The United States cannot legally make extended continental shelf (ECS) claims because it has not ratified the United Nations Convention on the Law of the Sea (UNCLOS). However, the United States has gathered data to support an Arctic ECS claim for if and when it ratifies UNCLOS. Overlap between potential ECS claims by the United States and Canada will have to be resolved via bilateral negotiations.[41]

With regard to the use of Arctic sea lanes, the United States has two ongoing disputes. The first is with Moscow over a portion of the Northern Sea Route, which runs over the northern coast of Russia. Moscow claims it as internal waters, whereas Washington claims it is an international strait. The second, similar dispute concerns the Northwest Passage and freedom of navigation.[42] The Canadian government claims the Northwest Passage as part of Canadian internal waters, where Canadian law applies, while Washington asserts that the area is an international strait, which would allow American ships to enter without permission. This issue was never a priority, given that, before 2007, the Northwest Passage had generally been clogged year-round with ice.[43] In sum, American interest and investment in projecting power to the Arctic were very low in the period before the shock. Having established this baseline, we can now compare how the United States responded to the shock.

6.4 The US Response to the Shock

In the summer of 2007, as the amount of Arctic ice fell to a historic low, international headlines reported that states like Russia and Canada were scrambling for Arctic resources. The following year, the US Geological Survey released a report suggesting that the Arctic contained 30% of the world's undiscovered natural gas and 13% of the undiscovered oil.[44] In contrast to other countries that responded to the shock by declaring the Arctic to be among their top foreign policy priorities and backed their claims by investing in their Arctic force structure and military activity, the United States was slow to respond and vague in its commitments. Also, unlike other states, the United States did not make expansive claims to Arctic resources beyond its EEZ, nor did it back its claims by projecting military force.

The lack of US interest is illustrated by statements made by Robert J. Papp, commander of the US Coast Guard, who, even when advocating for planning and investing in future Arctic capabilities, admitted that US "strategic interests in the

---

[41] Steven Groves, "US Accession to U.N. Convention on the Law of the Sea Unnecessary to Develop Oil and Gas Resources," The Heritage Foundation, May 14, 2012, 10–12, http://www.heritage.org/report/us-accession-un-convention-the-law-the-sea-unnecessary-develop-oil-and-gas-resources.

[42] Groves, "U.S. Accession to U.N. Convention"; Byers, International Law and the Arctic, 143–53.

[43] Byers, International Law and the Arctic, 142–43.

[44] US Geological Survey, "90 Billion Barrels of Oil."

region are not yet prominent enough to support anything but outreach, planning, and small-scale summer deployments."[45] As this chapter will show, a decade after the shock, the United States still has no new Arctic bases, ice-hardened warships, or icebreakers, nor has it made substantial investments in its Arctic military presence or activity.

The Bush administration was widely considered friendly toward the oil and gas industries, even lifting the ban on offshore Arctic drilling.[46] However, after the shock, they waited nearly two years before releasing a strategy document entitled "Arctic Region Policy (NSPD-66)." It was vague in outlining American commitments in the Arctic and made no commitments to allocate resources.[47] The document calls security America's number one Arctic priority, outlining interests in "missile defense and early warning; deployment of sea- and air-systems for strategic airlift, strategic deterrence, maritime presence, and maritime security operation; and ensuring operation of navigation and overflight."[48] These issues primarily concern general US security interests rather than control of maritime resources.

The Obama administration focused more on protecting the Arctic environment and cooperating with allies through multilateral institutions like the Arctic Council. However, there was relatively little change in the government's willingness to invest in maintaining a regional military presence in order to secure resources. The Arctic has played a relatively minor role in other US strategic planning documents. It is barely mentioned in the US National Security Strategy of 2010 and the US National Military Strategy of 2011.[49] It is not mentioned at all in 2012's *Sustaining US Global Leadership: Priorities for 21st Century Defense*.[50] The Obama administration issued an updated Arctic strategy, entitled "National Strategy for the Arctic Region" in 2013.[51] That document essentially reaffirms the priorities outlined in the Bush administration's NSPD-66 and remains vague on priorities or prospects for additional spending on Arctic capabilities. The document was widely criticized, considered by many to be a step backward in terms of providing guidance for funding

[45] Robert J. Papp Jr., "Charting the Coast Guard's Course," *Proceedings* 137, no. 3 (March 2011): 21. Cited in Wezeman, "Military Capabilities in the Arctic," 11.

[46] Sheryl Gay Stolberg, "Bush Calls for End to Ban on Offshore Oil Drilling," *New York Times*, June 19, 2008, https://www.nytimes.com/2008/06/19/washington/19drill.html.

[47] George W. Bush, "National Security Presidential Directive/NSPD 66—Homeland Security Presidential Directive/HSPD 25—Subject: Arctic Region Policy," January 9, 2009, http://media.adn.com/smedia/2009/01/12/15/2008arctic.dir.rel.source.prod_affiliate.7.pd.

[48] Bush, "National Security Presidential Directive," 3.

[49] M. G. Mullen, *The National Military Strategy of the United States of America, 2011: Redefining America's Military Leadership* (Washington, DC: Joint Chiefs of Staff, 2011).

[50] Barack Obama and Leon E. Panetta, *Sustaining US Global Leadership: Priorities for 21st Century Defense*, vol. 1 (Washington DC: Department of Defense, 2012).

[51] Barack Obama, "National Strategy for the Arctic Region," Washington, DC: Office of the President, May 2013.

decisions, and did not lead to any congressional appropriations.[52] Comparing the US response to that of Russia, Zysk and Titley write, "One striking example exists between US and Russian policies. While the United States has produced much documentation, policy activity has not been followed up with any real budgetary action."[53]

In addition to protecting the Arctic environment, the US has articulated an interest in securing open access to sea lanes and ensuring that maritime boundary disputes are handled peacefully.[54] The central issues are the previously mentioned ongoing disputes with Canada over the Northwest Passage and with Russia about the status of the Northern Sea Route. The United States considers both waterways to be international straits and thus not under the sovereign control of any state. Given that the United States is a highly production-oriented state, my theory suggests that it should have a keen interest in securing sea lanes to access markets.

The United States has had a relatively muted reaction to the exposure of Arctic resources and, thus far, has not made exclusionary claims to Arctic seabed resources or sought to exclude other actors from the region. Instead, Washington has insisted that regional forums like the Arctic Council be open to nonmember states seeking observer status.[55] The United States has not made formal claims to seabed resources beyond its EEZ, nor can it because it has not ratified UNCLOS. One might argue that the United States refuses to ratify UNCLOS because it can obtain more favorable terms by pursuing Arctic resources outside of international law. However, the United States has not made claims beyond international law or what it would be allowed to claim under UNCLOS.

Like all other Arctic states, the United States has conducted research on the seabed to determine the extent of its continental shelf, information that could be used to bolster future formal claims.[56] This would allow the United States to submit a claim to extend its EEZ, *if it ratifies UNCLOS*. However, the United States has not tried to appropriate, claim, or control Arctic resources outside of its EEZ, nor has it projected military force to back its informal claims or its position in disputes. Thus, American restraint is informative insofar as it demonstrates a lack of desire to compete militarily over Arctic resources.

---

[52] Mihaela David, "U.S. National Strategy for the Arctic Region: Strong Foothold or on Thin Ice?" Arctic Institute, May 13, 2013, http://www.thearcticinstitute.org/us-national-strategy-for-arctic-region/.

[53] Katarzyna Zysk and David Titley, "Signals, Noise, and Swans in Today's Arctic," *SAIS Review of International Affairs* 35, no. 1 (2015): 173.

[54] Kraska, "New Arctic Geography and U.S. Strategy," 260.

[55] Canadian Press, "Icy Clinton Leaves Arctic Summit," *The Telegram*, March 30, 2010, http://www.thetelegram.com/World/2010-03-30/article-1440150/Births-1847.

[56] Randy Boswell, "Arctic Sea Floor to Be Contested; Canada, U.S. to Spar over Rich Resources," *National Post*, February 13, 2008.

The key issue over which competing interest groups have lobbied the US government is not whether the United States should be scrambling to appropriate Arctic resources but rather the degree to which the United States should restrict Arctic drilling and environmental damage. The disputes focus mainly on areas within US territory and in uncontested offshore waters.[57] For instance, when Rex Tillerson was chief executive officer (CEO) of Exxon, he was also chair of the National Petroleum Council (NPC), an industry group that represents the views of the oil and gas industry and advises the Department of Energy. During his time as chair, the NPC commissioned a report stating "To remain globally competitive and to be positioned to provide global leadership and influence in the Arctic, the United States should facilitate exploration in the offshore Alaskan Arctic now."[58] Also, Shell spent millions on lobbyists who worked tirelessly to successfully convince the Obama administration to reverse its position and open the Arctic to drilling in 2011.[59] In short, energy firms have been primarily interested in opening up these uncontested Arctic waters to drilling and limiting environmental regulation, but as predicted by my theory, there is no evidence that they have lobbied for the United States to adopt a more assertive policy in its disputes. Even if US-based energy firms preferred an aggressive Arctic policy, they would understand that they have no hope of achieving it.

Despite opening the Arctic to limited drilling, the Obama administration made efforts to protect the Arctic environment, including placing a moratorium on fishing in certain areas until the effects of climate change on fish stocks could be better assessed.[60] Also, in 2011, Hillary Clinton became the first secretary of state to visit the Arctic Council.[61] The primary focus of her visit was on climate change and protecting the Arctic environment. When the United States held the chair of the Arctic Council, Secretary of State Kerry focused on protecting the Arctic Ocean and on global climate change, an agenda that was somewhat at odds with states, including Norway, that sought to develop offshore oil.[62] Finally, just before leaving

---

[57] For more on the battle between environmentalists and the oil lobby, see Bob Reiss, "Bolstered by Trump, Big Oil Resumes Its 40-Year Quest to Drill in an Arctic Wildlife Refuge," *Fortune*, September 15, 2017, http://fortune.com/2017/09/15/donald-trump-big-oil-alaska-arctic-wildlife-refuge/.

[58] Mia M. Bennett, "Discursive, Material, Vertical, and Extensive Dimensions of Post-Cold War Arctic Resource Extraction," *Polar Geography* 39, no. 4 (2016): 266.

[59] John M. Broder and Clifford Krauss, "New and Frozen Frontier Awaits Offshore Oil Drilling," *New York Times*, May 23, 2012, https://www.nytimes.com/2012/05/24/science/earth/shell-arctic-ocean-drilling-stands-to-open-new-oil-frontier.html?mtrref=undefined&gwh=75374EB1D55F1BC178BA3A0FBD55F79E&gwt=pay.

[60] Juliet Eilperin, "Commercial Fishing Is Barred in Parts of Arctic," *Washington Post*, February 6, 2009.

[61] Steven Lee Myers, "Hillary Clinton Takes Seat at Arctic Council," *New York Times*, Green (blog), May 12, 2011, https://green.blogs.nytimes.com/2011/05/12/hillary-clinton-takes-seat-at-arctic-council/.

[62] "Northern Exposure," *Arctic Journal*, accessed June 14, 2016, http://arcticjournal.com/politics/2386/northern-exposure.

office, Obama banned all offshore Arctic drilling. In general, the prioritization of the Arctic environment over the desire of US energy firms to open the Arctic up for drilling reflects the limited influence of these firms.

6.4.1 US Arctic Military Activity after the Shock

Even after the shock, the United States has been reluctant to boost its Arctic military presence or invest in the force structure needed to do so in the future. America's lack of interest in the Arctic becomes clearer when we consider how the United States has behaved in virtually every other region of the world. The United States has adopted a forward-deployed force posture for over seventy years, maintaining more forces overseas than any other state. Deep in the bowels of the Pentagon, these forces are tracked and assigned to regional combatant commands. Each region falls under the "area of responsibility" of one of these combatant commands, but some regions are so important that they receive their own commands.

Post-shock, the United States could have given the Arctic its own combatant command or set up a special military command center, as other Arctic states did. However, the United States declined to do so, signaling its general lack of interest in the region. Instead, in 2011, the United States decided to consolidate responsibility for the region by reducing the number of combatant commands in charge of the Arctic from three to two, taking responsibility away from the Pacific Command.[63] Responsibility for the Arctic is now shared between the European Command and the Northern Command, which has historically been charged with controlling US military activity in North America and protecting US borders.[64] Despite the fact that the Arctic encompasses one-sixth of the globe, it still has no dedicated combatant command.

Despite some recorded instances of US submarines transiting the Northwest Passage or surfacing near the North Pole, unlike Russia, the US Navy's surface ships did not start regularly patrolling the Arctic after the shock, nor did US bombers regularly patrol Arctic airspace. That said, the United States did engage in military exercises in the region with its NATO allies. The United States has participated in Operation NANOOK, an annual Arctic naval exercise hosted by the Canadian Maritime Command and Canadian Coast Guard.[65] The US Marine Corps also participated in military exercises with the Norwegian military in Operation Cold

---

[63] Heather A. Conley, *The New Foreign Policy Frontier: U.S. Interests and Actors in the Arctic* (Washington, DC: Center for Strategic and International Studies, 2013), 68, https://www.csis.org/analysis/new-foreign-policy-frontier.

[64] Ronald O'Rourke, *Coast Guard Polar Icebreaker Modernization: Background and Issues for Congress* (Washington, DC: Congressional Research Service, 2012).

[65] Department of Defense, *Report to Congress on Arctic Operations and the Northwest Passage* (Washington, DC: Department of Defense, 2011).

Response.[66] These operations show the importance the United States has placed on protecting its NATO allies. Every two years, the US Navy's Arctic Submarine Laboratory holds Ice Exercise (ICEX), in which it deploys submarines to the Arctic Ocean to conduct research and hardware tests.[67] However, in 2011, the Navy announced that it would reduce the frequency of ICEX to once every three years because of budgetary pressures.[68] Although they are only training missions, ICEX serves a second purpose of establishing a US presence in the Arctic. A former Coast Guard captain, Lawson Bingham, suggests that the US Navy ensures that when its submarines surface at the North Pole, the event is well documented by the news media as a signal to both American allies and potential aggressors that the US military still has a presence in the Arctic.[69]

The US military also carries out ARCTIC CARE, an annual military operation involving the Air National Guard and Army Reserve that is designed, in part, to provide services to remote areas in Alaska where communities receive little other outside assistance.[70] These operations allow the military to maintain some ability to operate in cold-weather environments, but they occur within the borders of the United States and are more about training and medical service provision than about power projection.

Since the end of the Cold War, the US military has prioritized projecting force into the deserts of the Middle East and the tropical waters of the South China Sea, rather than training to operate in the Arctic. Although the US Army sent 800 soldiers a year through the Cold Weather Training Center, as of 2011, the US Navy and Marine Corps remained curiously disengaged from the Arctic, considering that it is principally a maritime environment.[71] By 2011, US capabilities had degraded so significantly that a report by the National Research Council (NRC) concluded that the United States had lost its ability to conduct High Arctic warfare.[72]

The event that, arguably, most influenced American willingness to project power to the Arctic was not the sudden exposure of resources in 2007 but the Russian invasion of Crimea in 2014. After Russia invaded Crimea in late February and March of 2014, the United States made efforts to appear to be increasing its Arctic military activity in order to reassure its allies and deter further Russian aggression. For

[66] Department of Defense, *Report to Congress on Arctic Operations*.

[67] Geoff S. Fein, "ICEX 2011 Demonstrates Naval Research Projects," April 7, 2011, http://www.thenorthwestnavigator.com/news/2011/apr/07/icex-2011-demonstrates-naval-research-projects/.

[68] Perry and Andersen, *New Strategic Dynamics in the Arctic Region*, 126.

[69] Lawson Brigham, author interview, May 15, 2013.

[70] Guy Hayes, "Service Members Support Arctic Care in Rural Alaska," April 27, 2011, http://www.af.mil/news/story.asp?id=123253450.

[71] Kraska, "New Arctic Geography and U.S. Strategy," 265.

[72] National Research Council, *National Security Implications of Climate Change*, 5–7.

example, in late March of 2014, the United States held its first ICEX operation since 2011, deploying nuclear-powered attack subs 150 miles north of Alaska to test their ability to punch through Arctic ice. At the same time, 440 US marines took part in military exercises hosted by Norway. However, while these exercises were aimed at reassuring American allies, they were planned long before Russia's intervention in Crimea.[73] As relations with Russia soured, the United States canceled Operation Vigilant Eagle, a joint Arctic counterterrorism exercise with Russia and Canada that had been held every year since 2010.[74]

More recently, the United States has made greater efforts to reassure its NATO allies by increasing its military presence in both eastern Europe and the Arctic. For example, the United States deployed strategic bombers to the Arctic as part of Operations Polar Roar and Polar Growl in 2015 and again in 2016 and 2018.[75] The United States has also participated in joint Arctic military exercises such as Arctic Challenge, Cold Response, Trident Juncture, Arctic Edge, and Bold Quest.[76] Many of these exercises are hosted by allied nations and help both to reassure allies and to improve joint operability. In January 2017, the United States sent 300 marines on a six-month deployment in Norway.[77] However, it is important to note that these deployments have been largely symbolic. As we shall see in the next section, even after Crimea, the United States has not been willing to invest substantially in building the capabilities that would facilitate a more permanent Arctic military presence, such as new bases, icebreakers, or ice-hardened warships.

[73] Julian E. Barnes, "Cold War Echoes under the Arctic Ice," *Wall Street Journal*, March 25, 2014, https://www.wsj.com/articles/cold-war-echoes-under-the-arctic-ice-1395788949.

[74] For more on this, see CBS News, "Russian, NORAD Forces Unite for 'Hijack' Exercise," August 30, 2013, https://www.cbsnews.com/news/russian-norad-forces-unite-for-hijack-exercise/.

[75] For more on Polar Roar see US Strategic Command, "Strategic Bombers Participate in POLAR ROAR," August 1, 2016, http://www.usafe.af.mil/News/Article-Display/Article/881697/strategic-bombers-participate-in-polar-roar/; US Strategic Command Public Affairs, "Strategic Bomber Force Showcases Allied Interoperability During POLAR," August 3, 2016, http://www.stratcom.mil/Media/News/News-Article-View/Article/983671/strategic-bomber-force-showcases-allied-interoperability-during-polar-roar/. For more on Polar Growl, see Joseph Trevithick, "Russia Watched as American Bombers Showed Off over the Arctic," *Medium* (blog), April 3, 2015, https://medium.com/war-is-boring/russia-watched-as-american-bombers-showed-off-over-the-arctic-8302cebcc8ba. For more September 2018 deployments, see Thomas Nilsen, "U.S. and Russian Bombers Test Airspace over European Arctic," Eye on the Arctic, February 27, 2019, http://www.rcinet.ca/eye-on-the-arctic/2018/09/24/russia-usa-bombers-barents-norway-sea-airspace-military-mission/.

[76] Office of the Under Secretary of Defense for Policy, *Report to Congress: Department of Defense Arctic Strategy* (Washington, DC: Department of Defense, June 2019), 10, https://media.defense.gov/2019/Jun/06/2002141657/-1/-1/1/2019-DOD-ARCTIC-STRATEGY.PDF.

[77] Oriana Pawlyk, "No Additional Marines Bound for Norway as Cold-Weather Training Advances," Military.Com, May 14, 2019, https://www.military.com/daily-news/2019/05/14/no-additional-marines-bound-norway-cold-weather-training-advances.html.

6.4.2   US Post-shock Arctic Force Structure and Force Posture

In terms of force structure, the Arctic has remained a relatively low priority for the United States, even after the shock. The United States is the only Arctic nation that did not invest in a more capable Arctic force structure.[78] A decade after the shock, the United States has yet to appropriate any funding for this purpose. It is telling that Washington has done relatively little to alter or upgrade its Arctic force structure. In addition to refusing to invest in building ice-hardened warships, Washington has failed to even maintain its relatively small fleet of three icebreakers (one medium, two heavy), all of which were commissioned in the 1970s and have exceeded their intended life spans. Despite a 2006 NRC report warning that US icebreaking capacity was at risk due to deferred maintenance on existing icebreakers, little was done to implement service life extensions or replacement programs.[79] In May of 2010, one of the three American icebreakers, the *Polar Sea*, suffered catastrophic engine failure and was removed from service.[80] This left the United States with only one operational icebreaker, the USCG *Healy*, as the *Polar Star* was going through a retrofit from 2010 to 2012 and would not come back into service until 2013. The result is that for three years the US Coast Guard had no operational heavy icebreakers, and its medium icebreaker was used primarily for scientific research.[81]

Even after this decrease in US icebreaking capacity, the Defense Department (DoD) was reluctant to prioritize spending in this area. In May of 2010, Secretary of Defense Gates embodied American reluctance to invest in Arctic capabilities when he remarked, "we haven't done too much advanced planning in terms of additional icebreaker capability."[82] The planning and building of ships take years, if not decades. The secretary of defense openly admitted that the DoD had not even begun planning for additional icebreaker capability. This speaks volumes about the United States' lack of interest and investment in an Arctic force structure.

In 2010, the Coast Guard released a report suggesting it would need Congress to invest in three medium and three heavy icebreakers to meet minimum mission

---

[78] Linda Jakobson and Neil Melvin, *The New Arctic Governance*, SIPRI Research Report 25 (New York: Oxford University Press, 2016a), 17.

[79] Rebecca Pincus, "'The US Is an Arctic Nation': Policy, Implementation and US Icebreaking Capabilities in a Changing Arctic," *Polar Journal* 3, no. 1 (2013): 153.

[80] Heather A. Conley, *A New Security Architecture for the Arctic* (Washington, DC: Center for Strategic and International Studies, 2012), 31.

[81] Ronald O'Rourke, *Coast Guard Polar Icebreaker Modernization: Background, Issues, and Options* (Washington, DC: Congressional Research Service, September 29, 2010).

[82] Mia Bennett, "U.S. Defense Secretary Gates Talks Icebreakers, Cooperation with Canada," Foreign Policy Association (blog), May 4, 2010, https://foreignpolicyblogs.com/2010/05/04/us-defense-secretary-gates-interested-in-icebreakers/. See US Department of Defense, "Secretary of Defense Speech," May 3, 2010, http://archive.defense.gov/Speeches/Speech.aspx?SpeechID=1460.

requirements for operating in the Arctic.[83] During congressional testimony, Admiral Papp, commandant of the Coast Guard, clarified that in order to maintain a permanent Arctic presence, the United States would need six heavy icebreakers and four medium icebreakers.[84] Reports from self-interested bureaucracies should obviously be viewed with skepticism; however, an independent report from the Department of Homeland Security's Office of the Inspector General supports this assessment:

> Should the Coast Guard not obtain funding for new icebreakers or major service life extensions for its existing icebreakers with sufficient lead-time, the United States will have no heavy icebreaking capability beyond 2020 and no polar icebreaking capability of any kind by 2029. Without the continued use of icebreakers, the United States will lose its ability to maintain a presence in the Polar Regions, the Coast Guard's expertise to perform ice operations will continue to diminish, and missions will continue to go unmet.[85]

The report stated that among the missions that would go unmet was "assured access to ice-impacted waters through a persistent icebreaker presence in the Arctic and Antarctic."[86] Nearly a decade after the shock, in 2015, President Obama called for the United States to invest in new icebreakers to replace some of its aging fleet.[87] However, in the US fiscal year 2016 federal budget, only $4 million was requested for continued "pre-acquisition activities" for the next class of polar icebreaker, which are widely believed to cost $1 billion.[88] Thus, even if the United States invested in building icebreakers and ice-hardened warships today, it would be many years, if not decades, until they became operational.

To put the meager US fleet in perspective, recall that a decade after the shock, Canada had fifteen icebreakers, four ice-hardened patrol ships under construction, and two more on order. Russia had sixty-one ice-capable ships (icebreakers and

---

[83] ABS Consulting, *United States Coast Guard: High Latitude Region: Mission Analysis: Capstone Summary* (Arlington, VA: ABS Consulting, 2010).

[84] July 27, 2011, hearing on US economic interests in the Arctic before the Oceans, Atmosphere, Fisheries, and Coast Guard subcommittee of the Senate Commerce, Science, and Transportation Committee, as reported in Ronald O'Rourke, *Coast Guard Polar Icebreaker Program: Background and Issues for Congress* (Washington, DC: Congressional Research Service, 2018).

[85] US Department of Homeland Security, *The Coast Guard's Polar Icebreaker Maintenance, Upgrade, and Acquisition Program* (Washington, DC: US Department of Homeland Security, 2011), 10.

[86] US Department of Homeland Security, *Coast Guard's Polar Icebreaker Maintenance*, 9.

[87] Julie Hirschfeld Davis, "Obama to Call for More Icebreakers in Arctic as U.S. Seeks Foothold," *New York Times*, September 1, 2015, http://www.nytimes.com/2015/09/02/us/politics/obama-to-call-for-more-icebreakers-in-arctic-as-us-seeks-foothold.html?smprod=nytcore-iphone&smid=nytcore-iphone-share.

[88] Zysk and Titley, "Signals, Noise, and Swans," 173.

ice-hardened patrol ships), with ten under construction.[89] Even the raw numbers do not capture the true state of affairs as icebreakers, like any other asset, depreciate over time. Without new investments, the US icebreaker fleet has become even less capable than a decade ago. Not only does the United States have fewer, smaller, and less capable icebreaking ships than Russia, it has been unwilling to commit to even maintaining its capabilities.

Moreover, if the United States is to have any substantial Arctic presence, it will need more than just icebreakers. As James Kraska writes, "The American Arctic lacks deep water port facilities, air fields, aids to navigation and maritime domain awareness systems and associated infrastructure, all of which would have to be created to accommodate a greater US military and law enforcement presence in the region."[90] Currently, there is little support for funding any Arctic infrastructure. Four years after the shock, American Arctic naval surface capabilities were so weak that an independent report from the NRC stated the following:

> In the post–Cold War era, the US Navy has had a very limited surface ship presence in true northern latitude, cold-weather conditions. According to information presented to the committee, the US military as a whole has lost most of its competence in cold-weather operations for high-Arctic warfare.[91]

Later that year, the US Navy asked the War Gaming Department at the Naval War College to host the 2011 Fleet Arctic Operations Game. After running several scenarios, the participants concluded that the Navy lacked the capabilities needed to sustain military operations in the Arctic.[92] The report concluded that "the Navy has extremely limited capability to project power in a surface maritime environment, on behalf of the US in the Arctic, including our own US waters, regardless of the geopolitical or emergency situation."[93] In January of 2012, the Government Accountability Office released a report suggesting that DoD efforts in the Arctic were hampered by a lack of planning:

> Without taking steps to meet near- and long-term Arctic capability needs, DOD risks making premature Arctic investments, being late in obtaining

---

[89] Refer to the Icebreaker and Ice-Hardened Warships Data Set.

[90] Kraska, "New Arctic Geography and U.S. Strategy," 257.

[91] National Research Council, *National Security Implications*, 5–7.

[92] Nicole Klauss, "US Navy Lacks Ability to Operate in Arctic, Games Reveal," *Alaska Dispatch News*, September 29, 2016, https://www.adn.com/alaska-news/article/us-navy-lacks-ability-operate-arctic-games-reveal/2012/04/29/. See also Gray, Bergey, and Berbrick, "Fleet Arctic Operations Game," 32.

[93] Gray, Bergey, and Berbrick, "Fleet Arctic Operations Game," 17.

needed capabilities, or missing opportunities to minimize costs by collaborating on investments with the Coast Guard.[94]

The loss of US capabilities and competence is the result of Washington choosing not to prioritize investments in training and force structure in the Arctic relative to other regions. Virtually all of the former and current US officials and Navy and Coast Guard officers that I interviewed lamented the United States' utter lack of investment in Arctic infrastructure and capabilities. Although these individuals may have had bureaucratic or professional incentives for their opinions, it is worth noting that many of the academic researchers I spoke with agreed.

Just as the United States has been unwilling to invest in icebreakers or ice-hardened warships, it has declined to invest in building new Arctic bases or refurbishing existing ones. A decade after the shock, the US military maintained only one base above the Arctic Circle, at Thule, Greenland. Thule has a deep-water port, but the US Navy has no ice-hardened surface ships to operate there. This limits the United States' ability to project power above the Arctic Circle as ships must spend less time on station in the Arctic and more time traveling from home bases hundreds of miles away. Despite these limitations, the US government still has no plans to invest in new Arctic bases. The United States has made minor upgrades to bases located well below the Arctic Circle. For example, it added more antiballistic missiles to the base at Ft. Greely.[95] However, these assets are clearly aimed at defending the homeland, not projecting power to back American maritime resource claims.

6.4.3 The Trump Administration

The election of Donald Trump ushered into power an administration that was much less interested in environmental protection and much friendlier to the oil and gas industry. Trump even selected Rex Tillerson, former CEO of ExxonMobil, as secretary of state; note that Exxon invested heavily in developing Arctic offshore resources while Tillerson was CEO. This shift in power from an environmentally friendly Democratic administration to an oil and gas–friendly Republican administration provides me with an opportunity to address potential counterarguments by assessing how sensitive US Arctic policy was to a change in administration and leadership. One might be concerned that American restraint in the Arctic was

---

[94] US Government Accountability Office, "Arctic Capabilities: DOD Addressed Many Specified Reporting Elements in Its 2011 Arctic Report but Should Take Steps to Meet Near- and Long-Term Needs," GAO-12-180 (Washington, DC: US Government Accountability Office, 2012): 1, http://www.gao.gov/products/GAO-12-180.

[95] Associated Press, "Fort Greely to Get $50 Million toward Missile Defense System," *Army Times*, December 16, 2014, https://www.armytimes.com/news/pentagon-congress/2014/12/16/fort-greely-to-get-50-million-toward-missile-defense-system/.

leader- or administration-specific. Under this interpretation, had the United States been governed not by the environmentally friendly Democratic Obama administration but instead by a pro–oil and gas Republican one, it would have invested in projecting power to secure control over Arctic resources. If this is the case, then we should observe the Trump administration investing in projecting power to secure control over Arctic resources. However, if we see Trump continue the restrained Arctic foreign policies of the previous administration, that would cast doubt on this alternative explanation.

More than a year after Trump came to power, there was relatively little change in Washington's interest in securing control over Arctic resources or its willingness to invest in enhancing its Arctic military presence or capabilities. Rather than prioritize the Arctic, the Trump administration chose to invest less in diplomatic staff for the region. For example, in August of 2017 Secretary Tillerson eliminated the position of US special representative to the Arctic. This was not just part of the overall effort to shrink the State Department staff but rather a shift in personnel to other areas as Tillerson also created special representatives for other regions such as Ukraine and the Great Lakes region of Africa.[96] When I visited the State Department in May of 2017, I was informed by my hosts that the number of staffers covering the Arctic had been reduced to just six. Trump has sought to reverse the ban on drilling for offshore gas development within undisputed US waters that Obama put in place just before leaving office.[97] However, his administration has not tried to secure control over Arctic resources beyond those undisputed waters by escalating existing disputes, making new claims, or significantly enhancing US Arctic military presence or capabilities. Nor is there any evidence that energy firms have lobbied the Trump administration do so.

As with many issues, President Trump made bold claims, saying that "we will be building the first new heavy icebreakers the United States has seen in over 40 years. We're going to build many of them. . . . We're going to build six, but we're on the fast track to build just one."[98] However, in reality no funding has been provided to build six icebreakers, and the administration has generally continued the Obama administration's previous procurement process of providing modest incremental funding to eventually replace the existing, aging icebreaker fleet.[99] Moreover, the

---

[96] Joël Plouffe, *U.S. Arctic Foreign Policy in the Era of President Trump: A Preliminary Assessment* (Calgary: Canadian Global Affairs Institute, 2017), 19.

[97] Nick Allen, "Donald Trump Overturns Obama Bans on Drilling as He Moves to Vastly Expand US Offshore Oil," *The Telegraph*, January 4, 2018, https://www.telegraph.co.uk/news/2018/01/04/donald-trump-overturns-obama-bans-drilling-moves-vastly-expand/.

[98] Dan Lamothe, "Trump Pledges to Build Coast Guard Icebreakers, but It's Unclear How Different This Plan Is from Obama's," *Washington Post*, May 17, 2017, https://www.washingtonpost.com/news/checkpoint/wp/2017/05/17/trump-pledges-to-build-coast-guard-icebreakers-but-its-unclear-how-different-his-plan-is-than-obamas/?utm_term=.e6da0d6771ce.

[99] Plouffe, *U.S. Arctic Foreign Policy*, 14.

Trump administration has not proposed any major changes to Arctic policy with regard to military presence, bases, or other Arctic-specific assets. Despite noting the importance of many other regions, the Trump administration's 2018 National Defense Strategy did not even mention the Arctic.[100]

In sum, the United States has been remarkably consistent in its Arctic foreign policy and its reluctance to invest in projecting military force. That there has been no major change in US Arctic military policy under Trump lends strong support to my theory and casts doubt on competing theories. While I am not suggesting that individual leaders and administrations don't matter, my theory does suggest that they will be constrained by the economic interests of their governing coalitions, which, in turn, will be a function of the economic structure of the state. While oil and gas companies clearly had more influence in the Bush and Trump administrations, especially with regard to environmental regulation, there is no evidence that they lobbied the government to use the military to seek control over additional Arctic resources. Had they tried, they would undoubtedly have been counterbalanced by much more economically powerful production-oriented interests, which do not want to pay the costs of securing resources for oil and gas companies.

6.4.4 Summary of Findings

The US reaction to the rapid exposure of Arctic resources is consistent with my ex ante theoretical predictions. I expect production-oriented states to be more restrained in their pursuit of resources and territory than their land-oriented counterparts. My theory predicts that the United States, as a production-oriented state, should be less interested in capturing Arctic resources. As this case demonstrated, while US interest and military activity in the Arctic have increased slightly in the post-shock period, the overall level of US interest and investment has been low. Thus, insofar as the United States has exhibited more restraint than other Arctic powers, its behavior is consistent with the predictions of my theory.

6.5 Addressing Counterarguments

Having laid out the case for Rent-Addiction Theory, I will briefly cover the prominent counterarguments to the analysis presented here. First, critics may reasonably assert that in 2007 the United States was preoccupied with Iraq and otherwise would have projected power into the Arctic. However, as the United States withdrew from Iraq, it chose to rebalance to Asia, not the Arctic. Had the United States pivoted to the Arctic and boosted its military presence more than any other state, few from the

---

[100] James Mattis, *Summary of the 2018 National Defense Strategy* (Washington, DC: Department of Defense, 2018).

power preponderance school would have been surprised. The fact that the United States has still not invested in icebreakers and ice-hardened ships suggests that it currently has little interest in increasing its military presence in order to compete for Arctic resources. Moreover, even if the United States were to invest in these capabilities today, it would be many years until it could maintain a substantial military presence in the High North.

Second, one might argue that the United States would have projected power to compete over Arctic resources, but the discovery of fracking and tight oil and America's already abundant reserves of such resources made the Arctic less important. However, in the summer of 2007, few people understood the revolutionary impact that fracking would have on the American oil and gas industry. According to Daniel Yergin, in 2007—the year in which the Arctic shock occurred—the dominant outlook suggested that the United States would face a sharp decline in domestic energy production, and few people understood how much fracking would change energy production.[101] Moreover, the possession of massive reserves of resources did not stop Canada, Russia, and Norway from prioritizing the Arctic more than the United States did. These states were motivated to secure Arctic resources not because they lacked their own reserves but because they sought greater wealth.

Third, one might ask why, if my theory is correct, the United States did not become more interested in competing over additional resources, given that fracking should have made the US economy more dependent on resource rents. My response here is that fracking remains a relatively small part of the US economy compared to the production of goods and services. Recall that, even after the fracking revolution, resource rents made up less than 1% of US GDP. In short, the United States is still not very economically dependent on resource rents.

Fourth, one might suggest that the United States did not build or project power into the Arctic because it already had the military capabilities necessary to act in the Arctic if it so chose. While the United States, like Russia, certainly had aircraft, submarines, and missiles that could deploy to the Arctic, it did not deploy them there, nor did it invest in the capabilities, such as icebreakers and bases, required to do so in response to the 2007 shock. This stands in stark contrast to how the United States behaves in other regions. Historically, when the United States has chosen to prioritize projecting power to a region, such as Southeast Asia or the Middle East, it has increased its regional military presence and invested in region-specific bases and training operations. The United States has done none of these things in the Arctic. In fact, as the aforementioned NRC reports concluded, by 2012 the United States had invested so little in Arctic training that it had lost its ability to operate militarily in the Arctic. Additionally, a review of American Arctic capabilities and another NRC report concluded that existing US assets were insufficient, noting,

[101] Yergin, *The Quest*, 331.

"It is the judgment of this committee that this need is only partially fulfilled by airborne, spaceborne, and submarine assets and that a physical surface presence is necessitated by geopolitics."[102] However, despite these warnings, a decade after the shock the United States still lacks the assets needed to maintain a continuous presence. This state of affairs is captured by a statement made by Admiral Zukunft of the US Coast Guard in May of 2017 when he testified to Congress: "we need national assets, icebreakers, to exert sovereignty there. And right now, we're trying to do it with a ship that's 40 years old, is literally on life support."[103] The fact that the United States has not made greater investments in training, regional bases, and maintaining presence in the Arctic is revealing about its true preferences.

6.6 Conclusion

This chapter started with a puzzle: Why didn't the world's most powerful state project power to the Arctic after the shock? Other states declared the Arctic to be the strategic resource base of the future and backed their commitments to the region by significantly increasing their Arctic military presence. So why didn't the United States follow them north?

The United States' behavior is puzzling until we consider how the composition of a state's governing coalition influences its foreign policy preferences and behavior. The United States is a production-oriented state and is governed by a coalition that seeks to generate income by exporting goods and services, rather than extracting land rents. Simply put, there are no major groups within the US governing coalition that would benefit from shifting to a strategy of pursuing resource rents by expanding US claims to maritime territory in the Arctic. As a result, while the exposure of Arctic resources enticed other states to increase their Arctic military presence, the United States remained fundamentally uninterested in competing for control of those resources.

Although the United States has been reluctant to prioritize the Arctic, my theory provides guidance about conditions under which it would take a more active role. Washington is likely to invest in projecting power to the Arctic if one of two things occurs: first, if Russia further militarizes its maritime resource claims and threatens America's NATO allies or, second, if the Arctic becomes consistently ice-free in the summer over the next few decades, as most climate models predict. If either of

---

[102] Transportation Research Board and National Research Council, *Polar Icebreakers in a Changing World: An Assessment of U.S. Needs* (Washington, DC: National Academies Press, 2006), 98, https://doi.org/10.17226/11753.

[103] Megan Eckstein, "Zukunft: Changing Arctic Could Lead to Armed U.S. Icebreakers in Future Fleet," *USNI News*, May 18, 2017, https://news.usni.org/2017/05/18/zukunft-changing-arctic-environment-could-lead-to-more-armed-icebreakers-in-future-fleet.

these conditions is met, the United States, as well as many other states, will have a much stronger interest in projecting power in the Arctic to protect both its allies and global sea lanes.

There are some recent indications that the United States is starting to take a greater interest in projecting power to the Arctic in order to protect its NATO allies. For example, in mid-October of 2018, I was in Reykjavik, Iceland, and noticed that the bars were overrun with American and Canadian sailors and that the harbor was filled with warships. These sailors and ships were on their way to join the largest NATO operation since 2002, Operation Trident Juncture, which included more than 50,000 troops and seventy ships from thirty-one nations. The United States contributed over 14,000 troops and deployed an aircraft carrier strike group above the Arctic Circle for the first time since 1991.[104] The exercises involved a simulated Russian attack on Norway and were designed to give NATO forces experience operating in the Arctic's extreme environmental conditions. While such exercises are designed to reassure allies and deter Russia, it remains to be seen whether they represent a true shift in Washington's willingness to make major Arctic-specific investments. Thus far, the United States has remained unwilling to develop the regionally specific forces or organizations that would signal that it is prioritizing substantially increasing its Arctic military presence over the long term.

In addition to protecting its allies, my theory suggests that the biggest prize in the Arctic for the United States is not the resources but the shipping lanes. If much of the world's shipping were to shift north, my theory predicts that the US military would follow. So long as the United States depends upon sea lanes to access world markets, it will have a strong interest in protecting access to those sea lanes. Indeed, both the DoD and the Coast Guard recently released updates to their Arctic strategy documents, in which they directly identify Russia and, to a lesser extent, China as potential threats to America's ability to access Arctic sea lanes.[105]

One might ask, given that this outcome is likely and that it takes decades to build icebreakers and ice-hardened warships, why isn't the United States investing more heavily in its Arctic capabilities now? The principal issue is that there is great uncertainty about several things that will condition the specific capabilities the United States needs to secure Arctic sea lanes. First, while most climate models predict that the Arctic won't be entirely ice-free for decades, those estimates are highly uncertain, with some models suggesting a time much sooner and others much later.[106]

---

[104] Gina Harkins, "50,000 Troops Prep for NATO's Biggest Show of Force since the Cold War," Military.Com, October 22, 2018, https://www.military.com/daily-news/2018/10/22/50000-troops-prep-natos-biggest-show-force-cold-war.html.

[105] Office of the Under Secretary of Defense for Policy, "Report to Congress," 2, 4, 7; US Coast Guard, *Arctic Strategic Outlook* (Washington, DC: US Coast Guard, April 2019), 10, https://www.uscg.mil/Portals/0/Images/arctic/Arctic_Strategic_Outlook_APR_2019.pdf.

[106] James E. Overland and Muyin Wang, "When Will the Summer Arctic Be Nearly Sea Ice Free?" *Geophysical Research Letters* 40, no. 10 (2013): 2097–2101, https://doi.org/10.1002/grl.50316. For a

Second, the Arctic currently lacks the infrastructure to handle a large number of ships. It is unclear whether governments will be willing to make the enormously costly investments in deep-water ports and search-and-rescue capabilities necessary to make Arctic shipping lanes viable. The cost of building this infrastructure is far higher than in other regions around the world due to the Arctic's hostile environmental conditions, and returns on that investment might be decades away. Third, the Arctic's inhospitable environment and lack of infrastructure have deterred companies from offering shipping insurance at low enough rates to make voyages profitable. Unless this infrastructure is built and firms offer shipping insurance at lower rates, few ships will be willing to traverse the Arctic.

Given this uncertainty, the United States faces major risks if it invests heavily in (the wrong type of) Arctic force structure. One possibility is that the Arctic will melt much faster, and there will be little need for expensive heavy icebreakers for much of the year once the Arctic is largely ice-free. Another possibility is that the Arctic will not be ice-free during the summer until the second half of this century, and there will be little shipping for the US to protect.

In sum, if and when US policymakers expect the Arctic to become a vital artery for global commerce, they will have a stronger interest in increasing American Arctic military presence. So long as Arctic ice continues to decrease, my theory suggests that the region will increase in geopolitical importance, something that US policymakers should consider when investing in force structure over the long term.

helpful summary of this finding from this paper, see National Oceanic and Atmospheric Administration, "Arctic Nearly Free of Summer Sea Ice during First Half of 21st Century," *NOAA Research News*, April 12, 2013.

Canada

The Dog That Barks but Does Not Bite

7.1 Introduction

During the summer of 2007, the unexpected drop in the amount of Arctic ice resulted in the Northwest Passage being ice-free for the first time in recorded history. On July 9, 2007, Canadian prime minister Stephen Harper traveled to Esquimalt, a Canadian military base near Victoria, British Columbia. Flanked by lines of naval officers, Harper sounded the alarm, asserting that, "Canada has a choice when it comes to defending our sovereignty over the Arctic. Either use it or lose it. And make no mistake, this government intends to use it." Harper then announced plans to invest in Canada's ability to project power into the Arctic, promising billions to build ice-hardened patrol ships, new bases, and Arctic training facilities in order to "assert our sovereignty and protect our territorial integrity in the north."[1] This statement fueled media speculation about conflict in the Arctic as it appeared that states were scrambling to compete over Arctic resources.

Ottawa responded to the Arctic shock with the most assertive foreign policy of any of the production-oriented Arctic states.[2] Of all the Arctic states, Canada was perceived as taking one of the most aggressive stances about its sovereignty disputes.[3] Prime Minister Harper made a number of promises to upgrade Canada's Arctic force structure and increase its Arctic military presence. Canada's domestic debate over Arctic foreign policy featured much more prominently in political discourse than in Denmark or the United States. As Kristofer Bergh wrote, "The

---

[1] Perry and Andersen, *New Strategic Dynamics in the Arctic Region*, 86.

[2] Linda Jakobson and Neil Melvin, "Understanding National Approaches by Bergh and Kilemenko," in *The New Arctic Governance*, ed. Linda Jakobson and Neil Melvin (Oxford University Press, 2016b), 43.

[3] Frederic Lasserre, Jerome Le Roy, and Richard Garon, "Is There an Arms Race in the Arctic?" *Journal of Military and Strategic Studies* 14, no. 3–4 (2012): 11, http://jmss.org/jmss/index.php/jmss/article/view/496/492.

Perils of Plenty. Jonathan N. Markowitz, Oxford University Press (2020). © Oxford University Press.
DOI: 10.1093/oso/9780190078249.001.0001

top levels of US leadership may pay attention to the region, but the Arctic is not in the minds of the US public and is thus not a politicized issue. Canada, in contrast, has made the Arctic a top national priority, closely linked to Canadian identity and sovereignty."[4] Harper made it a point to visit the Canadian Arctic in every year of his tenure, during Canada's annual Arctic military exercises. During those visits, he announced new investments in Arctic military capabilities and made commitments to increase Canada's military presence in the Arctic. A recent statistical analysis finds a strong correlation between those visits and public support for Harper's Conservative government.[5] Moreover, numerous polls demonstrated that the Canadian public supported spending more money and sending more troops to increase Canada's Arctic military presence.[6]

However, despite the Arctic's prominent role in speeches by Canadian leaders, Ottawa has been reluctant to follow through on promises to upgrade its Arctic force structure and military presence. A decade later, the Canadian government has no ice-hardened warships, no major Arctic bases, and a very limited capacity to operate in the Arctic. Comparing Canada with Russia, the two countries are similar in a number of ways. Both control more Arctic territory than the other Arctic states, including vast swaths of tundra and long Arctic coastlines. Officials from both governments have made nationalistic claims that the Arctic represents part of their identity.[7] These claims have tended to include rhetoric about using military power to defend their state's Arctic sovereignty. However, whereas Russia has backed its rhetoric and commitments by investing in its Arctic force structure and military capabilities, Canada has not. Talk is cheap, but ships and bases are expensive; and, as this case will show, Canada was unwilling to back its commitments with costly investments. If the United States is the dog that does not bark, then Canada is the dog that barks but does not bite.

Why didn't Canada, like Russia, follow through on its commitments to build a more powerful Arctic force structure? Was it because Canada simply did not have the money? Hardly. Canada was better able than Russia to follow through on those commitments given that, at the time of the shock, it had a larger GDP ($1.5 trillion vs. $1.3 trillion in constant US dollars) and was much wealthier, as measured by per capita GDP ($44,544 vs. $9,101).[8] Was it because Russia has a larger Arctic

[4] Kristofer Bergh, *The Arctic Policies of Canada and the United States: Domestic Motives and International Context*, SIPRI Insights on Peach and Security 2012/1 (Stockholm: Stockholm International Peace Research Institute, 2012).

[5] Mathieu Landriault and Paul Minard, "Does Standing up for Sovereignty Pay off Politically? Arctic Military Announcements and Governing Party Support in Canada from 2006 to 2014," *International Journal* 71, no. 1 (2016): 41–61.

[6] Landriault and Minard, "Does Standing up for Sovereignty Pay off Politically?" 49.

[7] Todd L. Sharp, "The Implications of Ice Melt on Arctic Security," *Defence Studies* 11, no. 2 (2011): 305.

[8] World Bank, "GDP at Market Prices (Constant 2010 US$)," accessed January 11, 2017, http://data.worldbank.org/indicator/NY.GDP.MKTP.KD; The World Bank, "GDP per Capita (Constant

exclusive economic zone (EEZ) than Canada? No. Canada and Russia have nearly identically sized Arctic EEZs, and both states have Arctic sea routes—Canada's Northwest Passage and Russia's Northern Sea Route—that are becoming navigable due to climate change.[9] Neither of these explanations can account for why Russia chose to follow through on its commitments, while Canada did not.

However, it is important not to understate Canada's Arctic commitments by comparing it only to Russia. If we compare Canada to the United States, we see that Canada has made far greater commitments and a larger investment in boosting its Arctic military presence, despite being much less powerful. Even a decade after the shock, the United States had not built any new icebreakers or bases. In contrast, although funding was repeatedly delayed, Canada eventually invested several billion dollars in building new ice-hardened Arctic and offshore patrol vessels (AOPs). Why did Canada choose to invest far less in projecting power into the Arctic than Russia but more than the United States? The answer is that while Canada is much more dependent on resource rents for national income and government revenue than the United States, it is much less dependent than Russia.

7.1.1 Overview of Argument and Evidence

Rent-Addiction Theory predicts that Canada should be more interested in pursuing an exclusionary foreign policy (i.e., projecting military power to seek control over rents) than the United States but less so than Russia. If my theoretical predictions are correct, we should see Canada making stronger military and structural commitments to the Arctic than the United States but weaker commitments than Russia. Thus, I expect that in response to the 2007 shock we should see only a small increase in Ottawa's overall willingness to invest in projecting power to secure control over Arctic resources.

As in the previous chapter on the United States, Table 7.1 lays out my theoretical predictions and findings. The table compares the observed pre- and post-shock levels of investment in order to assess the change in Canada's overall commitment and investment. By comparing the expected and observed changes, we can test my predictions. As I demonstrate in this case, before the shock, Canada's commitment and investment were low in terms of both Arctic military activity and willingness to deploy forces to claimed or disputed areas. Moreover, during this period, Ottawa's

---

2010 US$)," accessed January 11, 2017, http://data.worldbank.org/indicator/NY.GDP.PCAP.KD?locations=RU.

[9] Note that neither sea route is likely to be an economically viable alternative in the near future. See Arctic Council, *Arctic Marine Shipping Assessment 2009* (Tromsø, Norway: Arctic Council, 2009). See also Pruyn, "Will the Northern Sea Route Ever Be a Viable Alternative?"

Table 7.1 **Predicted and Observed Changes in the Level of Canadian Investment[a]**

	Predicted Change in Investment	Observed Pre-shock Investment (Scale 1–5)	Observed Post-shock Investment (Scale 1–5)	Observed Change in Investment (Scale 0–4)
Commitments to the Arctic	Small	Low (2)	High (4)	Moderate (2)
Arctic military activity	Small	Low (2)	Medium (3)	Small (1)
Deploying force to claimed or disputed areas	Small	Low (2)	Low (2)	Almost none (0)
Icebreakers and ice-hardened warships	Small	Very low (1)	Low (2)	Small (1)
Arctic bases	Small	Very low (1)	Low (2)	Small (1)
Overall investment in exclusionary foreign policy	Small	Low (2)	Medium (3)	Small (1)

[a]For more on the how the change in the level of investment operationalized, see Appendix sections B and C.

willingness to invest in its Arctic force structure was very low, shown by its reluctance to invest in replacing its aging icebreaker fleet.

Right after the shock, Canada dramatically increased its commitments by promising to build new bases, training centers, and ice-hardened patrol ships. However, there was only a small change in its overall level of investment as the government was reluctant to pursue those commitments. Moreover, there was almost no change in Canada's willingness to deploy forces to areas under dispute.[10] In sum, the observed change in Canada's willingness to invest in an exclusionary foreign policy in the Arctic matched my prediction. Having laid out my theoretical predictions, the next section focuses on defending my coding of the structure of Canada's economy.

---

[10] As Chapter 4 reveals, there was actually a slight decrease in the number of events in which Canada deployed its forces to disputed areas.

7.2 Coding the Characteristics of Canada's Governing Coalition

Canada has a long history of maintaining stable democratic institutions and is coded as such using virtually all available indicators.[11] Canada is governed by a broad coalition that is generally representative of its citizens' interests. These institutions give the government an incentive to maintain the socioeconomic welfare of its citizens. Canadian leaders consider these interests carefully when making domestic and foreign policy. Given that my coding of Canada's domestic political institutions as representative is uncontroversial, I focus on illustrating how the structure of its economy influences the economic interests of its governing coalition. Specifically, I identify the primary sources of income for Canada's governing coalition and illustrate how they influence its foreign policy preferences.

7.2.1 How Canada's Economic Structure Influences Its Governing Coalition

Canada, like the United States, benefits from extensive natural resources, including lumber, minerals, and, most importantly, vast oil and gas reserves. Resources are an important part of Canada's economy: oil, gas, and refined petroleum products have constituted between 12% and 24% of Canada's exports since at least 2002.[12]. However, Canada is not a petro-state and is far less resource-dependent than Norway or Russia.[13] For comparison, since 2002 oil and gas have typically represented between 40% and 53% of Norway's exports and between 50% and 60% of Russia's.[14] Also, Norway and Russia derive two and three times as much of their GDP from resource rents, respectively, as Canada does (see Table 7.2). Thus, unlike Norway and Russia, I code Canada as a production-oriented state. However, Canada is the most resource-dependent of the production-oriented states. As Figure 7.1 and Table 7.2 demonstrate, Canada derives over three times as much of its income from

---

[11] Systemic Peace, *Polity IV Country Report 2010: Canada* (Vienna, VA: Systemic Peace), accessed September 30, 2016, http://www.systemicpeace.org/polity/Canada2010.pdf.

[12] Government of Canada, "Trade Data Online by Industry," August 27, 2019, https://www.ic.gc.ca/app/scr/tdst/tdo/crtr.html?&productType=NAICS&lang=eng

[13] According to *The Economist*, in 2015 Canada derived just 3% of its GDP from oil. See *Economist*, "Beyond Petroleum," January 29, 2015b, https://www.economist.com/news/americas/21641288-growth-shifting-oil-producing-west-back-traditional-economic-heartland.

[14] For more on Russian energy exports, see World Bank Group, *Russia Economic Report: The Long Journey to Recovery* (Washington, DC: World Bank, 2016). For data on Norway oil and exports, see Norwegian Ministry of Petroleum and Energy, "The Government's Revenues," May 16, 2018, http://www.norskpetroleum.no/en/economy/governments-revenues/.

Table 7.2 **Operationalizing Land-Oriented Economic Structure**

Country	Oil Exports % of GDP*[a]	Fuel Exports % of GDP**[b]	Resource Rents % of GDP**[c]
United States	0.325	0.171	1.01
Canada	1.04	4.88	3.75
Denmark	0.766	2.04	1.15
Norway	9.72	19.1	8.38
Russia	9.44	16.5	15.5

*Data only available through 2001 (average 1991–2001).

** Average 1997–2007.

[a]Ashford, "Oil and Violence"; Graham and Tucker, "International Political Economy Data."

[b]Calculated based on World Bank data on fuel exports as a percentage of merchandise exports. World Bank, "Fuel Exports."

[c]Estimates based on sources and methods described in World Bank, "The Changing Wealth of Nations."

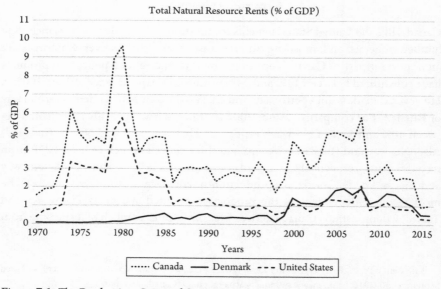

Figure 7.1 The Production-Oriented States: Economic Development on Resource Rents
Source: The World Bank, "Total Natural Resources Rents (% of GDP)," World Development Indicators, June 20, 2019, https://data.worldbank.org/indicator/NY.GDP.TOTL.RT.ZS?locations=US&view=chart.

resource rents as the United States and Denmark. Additionally, in terms of exports, the importance of the natural resource sector has grown since 1994, as oil and gas have surpassed automobile parts to become Canada's largest export every year since 2004, with the exception of 2016 (see Figure 7.2).

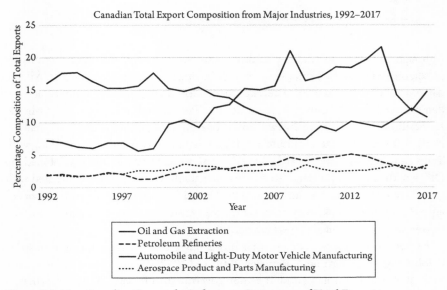

Canadian Total Export Composition from Major Industries, 1992–2017

——Oil and Gas Extraction
-- - Petroleum Refineries
——Automobile and Light-Duty Motor Vehicle Manufacturing
····· Aerospace Product and Parts Manufacturing

Figure 7.2 Top Canadian Exports by Industry as Percentage of Total Exports
Source: Government of Canada, "Trade Data Online by Industry," August 27, 2019, https://www.ic.gc.
ca/app/scr/tdst/tdo/crtr.html?&productType=NAICS&lang=eng.

Moreover, due to technological innovations and the discovery of oil tar sands in Alberta, Canada has the world's third-largest oil reserves. The Canadian government estimates that C$570 billion will be invested in the Canadian energy sector between 2014 and 2024.[15] Thus, resources are projected to remain a significant sector of Canada's economy, albeit never approaching the levels of resource dependence observed in Norway or Russia.

Given that Canada is more economically dependent on land than the United States, if my theory is correct, we should see several differences between the two states. First, Canada's land-oriented sector should have more money to capture the state by investing in lobbying and maintaining a greater share of political influence within the governing coalition. Second, the state should develop a greater interest in the productivity of the land-oriented sector, either because money has captured the state or because the state captured the money by coming to rely on that sector for revenue and the prosperity of its citizens. Third, this influence should result in land-oriented interests having greater representation in the governing coalition, allowing them to obtain more favorable policies.

---

[15] Natural Resources Canada, "10 Key Facts on Canada's Natural Resources," October 2016, https://www.nrcan.gc.ca/sites/www.nrcan.gc.ca/files/files/pdf/10_key_facts_nrcan_2016-access_ e.pdf.

7.2.2 Money from the Natural Resource Sector Seeks to Capture the State

Although there are no readily available public data on campaign contributions by sector, the Office of the Commissioner of Lobbying of Canada maintains a searchable database of lobbying activity. A recent independent analysis of this lobbying activity demonstrates that the Canadian Association of Petroleum Producers and the Mining Association of Canada were the two most active lobbying groups.[16] Additional analysis by the left-leaning Polaris Institute also found that these two associations, along with TransCanada Corporation, were among the top ten most active groups that lobbied the Office of the Prime Minister.[17] To the degree that lobbying efforts are associated with financial contributions, we can compare the United States and Canada and see that energy and mining groups occupy three of the top ten slots in Canada but only one of the top ten slots in the United States (ExxonMobil).

Moreover, the oil industry was far more active than manufacturing industries in lobbying the government. Between 2008 and 2012, the petroleum industry met with members of Parliament and senior government officials 734 times, whereas the next most active group, the motor vehicle industry, met with them only 157 times.[18] This is consistent with my theoretical expectation that because Canada's land-oriented industries own a larger share of the economy than their American counterparts, they should have a greater capacity to invest in lobbying and should have more political influence.

7.2.3 The State Captures the Money from the Natural Resource Sector

Just as a larger natural resource sector gives the land-oriented sector as a whole more money with which to capture the state, it generates more money for the state to capture. Natural resources generated an average of C$26 billion per year in tax revenues from 2010 to 2014, or approximately 10% of the federal government's revenue. The Canadian government's statistics suggest that, in 2015, natural resources were directly responsible for 12% of Canada's GDP and generated an additional 5% of GDP indirectly.[19] These statistics suggest that oil, gas, and mining are directly responsible for creating 654,000 jobs, or approximately 4% of all the jobs in Canada. Natural

---

[16] Daniel Cayley-Daoust and Richard Girard, "Big Oil's Oily Grasp: The Making of Canada as a Petro-State and How Oil Money Is Corrupting Canadian Politics," Polaris Institute, December 2012, https://www.polarisinstitute.org/big_oil_s_oily_grasp.

[17] Cayley-Daoust and Girard, "Big Oil's Oily Grasp."

[18] Cayley-Daoust and Girard, "Big Oil's Oily Grasp," 4.

[19] Natural Resources Canada, "10 Key Facts on Canada's Natural Resources." Note that these figures differ from those from World Bank data, which only measure the "revenues above the cost of extracting the resources" or the rents derived from fossil fuels and mining without measuring this

resources are also credited with indirectly generating an additional 900,000 jobs. This gives the government a vested interest in the economic productivity of the natural resource sector. This interest was succinctly expressed by Canada's minister of natural resources, John Oliver, in a 2012 speech when he remarked, "it is no exaggeration to say the resource sector is the cornerstone of our economy, our long-term prosperity and our quality of life."[20]

7.2.4 Land-Oriented Interests Exercise Influence within Canada's Governing Coalition

Rent-Addiction Theory suggests that greater investment in maintaining political influence should be associated with land-oriented interests being represented within the governing coalition and with the ruler pursuing policies that are more favorable to them. Perhaps no Canadian politician better represents those interests than Stephen Harper, prime minster from 2006 to 2015. Harper had long been regarded as an ally and champion of Canada's extractive industries. Prior to his political career, Harper worked in the oil industry for several years. He hails from and represented Alberta, a province highly reliant on oil, gas, and mining; oil and gas alone account for one-fifth of the province's GDP.[21] Royalties from oil and gas provide 18% of the provincial government's revenue.[22] Harper sought to pursue policies that generally favored the oil and gas industry and, by extension, his home province of Alberta. For illustration, in 2008 Alberta received C$2.1 billion in petroleum subsidies, or 73% of the total federal and provincial subsidies to the petroleum industry.[23]

In 2006, then-new prime minister Harper declared his plans to make Canada an energy superpower. In multiple speeches to both foreign and domestic audiences, Harper defended his vision of natural resource development as the key to Canadian economic development and prosperity.[24] Consistent with my expectations, at the same time that lobbying efforts by the oil and gas industries increased, Harper's Conservative government began rewriting and repealing environmental protection

---

sector's share of GDP. For more on this definition, see World Bank, "Total Natural Resources Rents," June 25, 2018.

[20] Joe Oliver, *Natural Resources: Canada's Advantage, Canada's Opportunity* (Vancouver, Canada: Canaccord Genuity Corporation, 2012).

[21] *Economist*, "Beyond Petroleum."

[22] Canada's Oil Sands, "Economic Contribution," accessed February 8, 2017, http://www.canadasoilsands.ca/en/explore-topics/economic-contribution.

[23] Bruce Campbell and Canadian Centre for Policy Alternatives, *The Petro-Path Not Taken: Comparing Norway with Canada and Alberta's Management of Petroleum Wealth* (Ottawa: Canadian Centre for Policy Alternatives, 2013), 44.

[24] P. Whitney Lackenbauer and Ryan Dean, *Canada's Northern Strategy under Prime Minister Stephen Harper: Key Speeches and Documents, 2005–15* (Calgary, Canada: Arctic Institute of North America, 2016).

laws that it claimed impeded the development of natural resources. Harper's government canceled 678 environmental reviews involving fossil fuels and another twenty-four related to pipelines.[25] During his tenure, Canada not only withdrew from the Kyoto Protocol, which would have impeded the development of Canadian oil sands, but also announced an end to fifteen climate change–related programs previously supported by the government. Many of those changes to environmental regulations were suggested by energy industry lobbyists. The Harper government also made major investments in Canada's energy infrastructure and advocated for the development of the Keystone XL pipeline.

It is important to note that Harper's successor and ideological opponent, Liberal Justin Trudeau, also supports the Keystone XL pipeline.[26] The fact that Trudeau, a liberal with a reputation for prioritizing environmental protection, still backs the pipeline is evidence of the enduring influence of the Canadian energy industry. This is not to argue that Trudeau has pursued the same policies as Harper but only to suggest that the Canadian energy industry is too economically and politically powerful for even a liberal, environmentally minded government to ignore. Note that in 2015 the oil and gas sectors received C$36 billion in capital investments, more than any other part of the Canadian private sector.[27]

The evidence examined thus far illustrates the causal pathways through which my theory suggests the state's economic structure and its dependence on resources shape the interests of those who govern the state. Canada is no petro-state, but it is far more resource-dependent than the United States. Therefore, land-oriented interests were more able to capture the state by seeking and securing influence within the governing coalition in order to bend policy in their favor. Alternatively, the more the state captures the money by coming to rely on a given sector to provide revenue and prosperity for its citizens, the more a government will have a vested interest in adopting policies to enhance that sector's productivity. Recall that according to Canadian government statistics, natural resources account directly for 12% of GDP and 10% of federal government revenue.

Canada's government is far more economically dependent on resources than the United States but far less than Russia or Norway. Thus, I expect Canadian leaders to have a stronger interest in investing in projecting power to secure Arctic resources than the United States but not as strong as Russia or Norway. In the following section, I evaluate how Canada responded to the shock. To do this, I must first establish

---

[25] Campbell and Canadian Centre for Policy Alternatives, *Petro-Path Not Taken*, 44.

[26] Ed Struzik, "Canada's Trudeau Is under Fire for His Record on Green Issues," *Yale Environment 360*, January 19, 2017, accessed June 20, 2018, https://e360.yale.edu/features/canada_justin_trudeau_environmental_policy_pipelines?utm_source=folwd.com.

[27] Natural Resources Canada, "Additional Statistics on Energy," August 18, 2011, http://www.nrcan.gc.ca/publications/statistics-facts/1239.

a baseline of Canada's pre-shock interest in the Arctic and the degree to which Canada chose to project power there.

7.3 Establishing a Baseline: Canada's Arctic Foreign Policy Prior to the Shock

During the Cold War, Canada maintained a strong interest in the Arctic as a potential theater of conflict. Canada's Arctic waters and airspace were the front lines as Russian submarines patrolled the coast just outside Canadian waters, and the threat of Soviet intercontinental ballistic missile attacks over the North Pole loomed in the background. To defend against such an attack, Canada worked with the United States to install the Distant Early Warning Line, a set of radar stations that allowed both countries to track incoming Russian aircraft and missiles. However, as the Cold War drew to a close, Canada's interest in the Arctic declined, as did its willingness to invest in its Arctic military capabilities.

While Canada was less interested in the Arctic after the end of the Cold War, it retained some Arctic interests and capabilities during the pre-shock period. Canada has long been concerned with maintaining its Arctic sovereignty, providing services to its citizens who live in remote Arctic areas, and utilizing and protecting the Arctic's natural resources and environment. The acceptance of Canada's Arctic sovereignty by other actors has even been made a precondition for cooperation on Arctic issues.[28] Protecting Canadian sovereignty involves defending its northern territories, internal waters, and maritime claims. Before the shock, Canada had four Arctic disputes with other states. As of today, none of them has been resolved.

First, Canada has a long-running dispute with the United States over the status of the Northwest Passage. The United States insists that the Northwest Passage is in international waters and is therefore subject to free navigation, but Canada considers it an internal waterway subject to Canadian jurisdiction and regulations.[29] The issue came to a head in 1969, when the SS *Manhattan*, a massive oil tanker converted into a giant icebreaker, attempted to sail the Northwest Passage. The Canadian government protested the move as a violation of its sovereignty and deployed icebreakers to escort the *Manhattan*. Canada also responded by initiating sovereignty patrols, sending aircraft and naval vessels to show the flag and monitor the Northwest Passage.[30] The issue was raised again in 1985, when a US Coast Guard icebreaker,

---

[28] Sebastian Knecht and Kathrin Keil, "Arctic Geopolitics Revisited: Spatialising Governance in the Circumpolar North," *Polar Journal* 3, no. 1 (2013): 178–203.

[29] For more on this dispute, see Michael Byers and Suzanne Lalonde, "Who Controls the Northwest Passage," *Vanderbilt Journal Transnational Law* 42 (2009): 192.

[30] Rob Huebert, "Canadian Arctic Security Issues: Transformation in the Post–Cold War Era," *International Journal* 54, no. 2 (1999): 219.

the *Polar Star*, passed through the Northwest Passage on its way to Alaska from Greenland without seeking permission from the Canadian government. Two years after the *Polar Star* incident, in 1987, Canada's Progressive Conservative government released a white paper in which it announced its plan to invest in ten to twelve nuclear-powered attack submarines with which to patrol Arctic waters.[31] The following year, the government also announced that it would build a base at Nanisivik, on Baffin Island. However, the plans to build submarines were scrapped, and the planned base at Nanisivik was downgraded and delayed. In 1988, the United States and Canada agreed to disagree over the status of the Northwest Passage, a novel arrangement in which the United States refused to change its position but agreed always to seek consent before entering, so long as the Canadians always granted it.

Second, Canada and the United States have overlapping EEZ claims in the Beaufort Sea. This dispute has been peaceful but remains unresolved. Both states have sought control over energy reserves and have sought to maintain their rights to fish in the area.[32] The Beaufort Sea is believed to be rich in natural resources, with some in the petroleum industry referring to it as the "next Gulf of Mexico."[33] In 2006, Devon Energy Canada discovered a major find of as much as 250 million barrels of oil in the area just east of the disputed zone. Following this find, BP paid $595 million and ExxonMobil paid $1.2 billion for exploration rights,[34] though rights have not been granted in the disputed areas.

Third, Canada has a dispute with Denmark over Hans Island and an overlapping EEZ claim in the Lincoln Sea. In 1973, Canada and Denmark delimited what was then the world's largest maritime boundary, between Greenland and Ellesmere Island, but failed to settle these two issues. Starting in the 1980s, Hans Island was the site of the "Battle of the Bottles," in which both the Danish and the Canadian military visited the island periodically to raise their flags and leave a bottle of the country's liquor—Canadian whiskey or Danish schnapps. In the summer of 2005, the Canadian military engaged in Exercise Frozen Beaver, in which Arctic Rangers landed on Hans Island, taking down the Danish flag and raising the Canadian flag. They then installed a plaque indicating that Hans Island belonged to Canada.[35] However, the two states subsequently agreed not to deploy their forces to Hans

---

[31] Lasserre, Le Roy, and Garon, "Is There an Arms Race in the Arctic?" 47.

[32] Ian G. Brosnan, Thomas M. Leschine, and Edward L. Miles, "Cooperation or Conflict in a Changing Arctic?" *Ocean Development & International Law* 42, no. 1–2 (2011): 196, https://doi.org/10.1080/00908320.2011.543032.

[33] Ebinger and Zambetakis, "Geopolitics of Arctic Melt," 1229.

[34] Michael Byers, "Cold Peace: Arctic Cooperation and Canadian Foreign Policy," *International Journal* 65, no. 4 (2010): 907.

[35] Jon D. Carlson et al., "Scramble for the Arctic: Layered Sovereignty, UNCLOS, and Competing Maritime Territorial Claims," *SAIS Review of International Affairs* 33, no. 2 (2013): 32, https://doi.org/10.1353/sais.2013.0033.

Island, and neither has visited since 2005.[36] The status of Hans Island and the EEZ dispute involving the Lincoln Sea remain unresolved, but neither has been a contentious issue since the shock.

The key feature of the Hans Island case is that the island is economically useless— it contains no natural resources, so owning it would not enable either state to make additional claims to resource-rich territory. It is clear that, for these production-oriented states, resources were not the key driver of the dispute. One might be concerned that while Hans Island contains no natural resources, states might instead be interested in the island as a jumping-off point to project power to other Arctic locations where they could claim resources. However, as we shall see in this chapter and in Chapter 8, since the 2007 shock neither state has projected military force to Hans Island. Moreover, as predicted by my theory, both Canada and Denmark have been relatively reluctant to project military force to claimed and disputed areas in which there are resources at stake.

Fourth, before the shock, Canada made informal claims (which have not yet been submitted to the Commission on the Limits of the Continental Shelf) to extend its continental shelf to include the Lomonosov Ridge and began the process of collecting geological data to support a formal claim to this area.[37] The government estimates that Canada would gain 650,000 square miles if it extended its continental shelf claims.[38] As previously discussed, the ridge is also claimed by Denmark and Russia and might be claimed by the United States if it ratifies the United Nations Convention on the Law of the Sea.

Having discussed Canada's pre-shock Arctic interests and disputes, I will now assess Canada's pre-shock investment in force structure and its level of military activity. At the beginning of 2007, the Canadian military had not a single ship designed to operate in Arctic waters. The only ships capable of operating in the Arctic were two ships built in the 1960s: a Protecteur-class auxiliary oiler replenishment ship and a Kingston-class maritime coastal defense vessel.[39] The Canadian government did have fifteen icebreakers; but sources have reported that only seven could be deployed to the Arctic, and most of these were approaching the end of their service

---

[36] Additionally, in May of 2010, the military chiefs of staff of both states signed a memorandum of understanding on Arctic defense, security, and operational cooperation, which committed both parties to enhancing cooperation on Arctic exercises and information exchange. In short, relations between Denmark and Canada have generally been cooperative since the shock. For more on this, see Ronald O'Rourke, *Changes in the Arctic: Background and Issues for Congress* (Washington, DC: Congressional Research Service, 2013), 18.

[37] Nikolaj Peterson, "The Arctic as a New Arena for Danish Foreign Policy: The Ilulissat Initiative and Its Implication," in *Danish Foreign Policy Yearbook 2009* (Copenhagen: Danish Institute for International Studies, 2009), 35–78.

[38] Kathryn Isted, "Sovereignty in the Arctic: An Analysis of the Territorial Disputes and Environmental Policy Considerations," *Transnational Journal of Law and Policy* 18, no. 2 (2009): 357.

[39] Lasserre, Le Roy, and Garon, "Is There an Arms Race in the Arctic?"

lives, given that they were first commissioned in the 1960s, 1970s, and 1980s.[40] In addition, the Canadian Navy had four submarines and fifteen surface warships with the range to operate in the Arctic, but none of those ships was ice-hardened.[41]

In the post–Cold War period, the Canadian political elite lost interest in projecting military power to the Arctic. Through the mid-1990s, the Canadian Army continued to conduct several Arctic exercises annually, but those stopped in 1999.[42] In 2002, the Canadian Navy returned to the Arctic for the first time since 1989, but its capabilities were insufficient: it was unable to even reach Hans Island.[43] Perhaps in response to this embarrassing incident, Canadian forces began holding Arctic exercises more frequently in the mid 2000s. In August of 2004, Canada sent 500 troops and two ships to complete a military exercise on Baffin Island. This was the largest military exercise in years and reversed a trend of a declining military presence in the Canadian Arctic. This was followed in 2006 by Operation Lancaster, a military exercise in Canada's eastern Arctic.[44]

Generally, Canada's level of interest, force structure, and military activity in the Arctic were relatively low prior to 2007. Canada had several minor disputes in the Arctic during the pre-shock period, some of which involved military force. However, all of these incidents were low-intensity and did not escalate. Canada's investment in its Arctic force structure and force posture was also relatively low. That said, Canada did begin to increase the frequency and intensity of Arctic military exercises in the middle of the first decade of the 2000s, although these exercises generally occurred on Canadian soil. Canada made relatively meager investments in its Arctic force structure until 2006, when Stephen Harper was elected on a platform that included promises to boost Canada's Arctic military presence.[45] He said, "you don't defend national sovereignty with flags, cheap election rhetoric, and advertising campaigns. You need forces on the ground, ships in the sea, and proper surveillance."[46] If Harper had maintained his commitment, especially after the shock, this would have been

[40] Pierre Leblanc, "Canada Needs More Coast Guard Icebreakers," *Arctic Deeply*, February 17, 2017, https://www.newsdeeply.com/arctic/community/2017/02/17/canada-needs-more-coast-guard-icebreakers.

[41] Barbora Padrtová, "Russian Military Build Up in the Arctic: Strategic Shift in the Balance of Power or Bellicose Rhetoric Only," *Arctic Yearbook* (2014): 1–19.

[42] David Pugliese, "Arctic Sovereignty at Risk: Military Warns North's Riches Open to Plunder by Foreign Lands; Threat Rises as Forces' Power Slips," *Ottawa Citizen*, December 7, 2000.

[43] Robert Huebert, "The Return of the Vikings," in *Breaking Ice: Renewable Resource and Ocean Management in the Canadian North*, ed. F. Berkes et al. (Calgary, Canada: University of Calgary Press, 2005), 329.

[44] Government of Canada, National Defence, "Joint and Integrated CF Operation in Canada's Eastern Arctic," August 11, 2006, http://www.forces.gc.ca/en/news/article.page?doc=joint-and-integrated-cf-operation-in-canada-s-eastern-arctic/hnocfocm.

[45] Knecht and Keil, "Arctic Geopolitics Revisited," 193.

[46] Quoted in Knecht and Keil, "Arctic Geopolitics Revisited."

crucially informative about the strength of Canada's interest in projecting military force to the Arctic after the shock. As we will see, Harper's words turned out to be hollow.

7.4 Canada's Response to the Shock

In the summer of 2007, after the drop in Arctic sea ice, the Canadian government made bold promises to boost its Arctic military presence and challenged the validity of other states' Arctic claims. Foreign Minister McKay forcefully asserted Canada's Arctic sovereignty: "There is no question over Canadian sovereignty in the Arctic. We've made that very clear. We established a long time ago that these are Canadian waters and this is Canadian property."[47] Following the infamous incident in which a member of Putin's United Russia Party planted a Russian flag on the bottom of the Arctic Ocean, McKay was quick to quip to the BBC, "This isn't the 15th Century. . . . You can't go around the world and just plant flags and say 'We're claiming this territory.' "[48]

The Canadian government followed these statements with a set of policy documents outlining Canada's Arctic interests and strategy. First, the governments of Canada's three Arctic territories released a document titled *A Northern Vision: A Stronger North and a Better Canada*.[49] Ottawa followed this in 2008 with the release of the "Canada First Defense Strategy," in which the Arctic played a vital role. Canada then released national-level Arctic strategy documents in 2009—*Canada's Northern Strategy*[50]—and 2010—"Statement of Canada Arctic Foreign Policy."[51] Sovereignty is listed as the country's first priority and is the primary focus of both documents. The Arctic and its potential resources were explicitly mentioned in the "Canada First Defense Strategy," which notes, "the military will play an increasingly vital role in demonstrating a visible Canadian presence in this potentially resource-rich

---

[47] CBC News, "Russia Plants Flag Staking Claim to Arctic Region," August 2, 2007, http://www.cbc.ca/news/world/russia-plants-flag-staking-claim-to-arctic-region-1.679445.

[48] BBC News, "Russia Plants Flag under N Pole," August 2, 2007, http://news.bbc.co.uk/1/hi/world/europe/6927395.stm.

[49] Polar Connection, *A Northern Vision: A Stronger North and a Better Canada* (London: Polar Research & Policy Initiative, 2007), http://polarconnection.org/northern-vision-stronger-north-better-canada-2007/.

[50] Canadian Government, Indian and Northern Affairs, and Federal Interlocutor for Métis and Non-Status Indians, *Canada's Northern Strategy: Our North, Our Heritage, Our Future* (Ottawa: Government of Canada, 2009).

[51] Government of Canada, "Achievements under Canada's Northern Strategy, 2007–2011," n.d.a, http://www.northernstrategy.gc.ca/cns/au-eng.pdf.

region, and in helping other government agencies such as the Coast Guard respond to any threats that may arise."[52]

These documents stress the importance of protecting the Arctic environment, Canada's sovereignty over its current territory, and the provision of basic government services to Canadians living in the Arctic. *Canada's Northern Strategy* lays out four principal Arctic foreign policy interests or "pillars" on which its foreign policy rests: (1) asserting Canada's sovereignty over its Arctic claims, (2) facilitating economic development and the provision of services to Canadian citizens living in remote areas, (3) protecting the Arctic environment, and (4) improving northern governance and facilitating greater political autonomy for people living in the North.[53]

Regarding sovereignty, Canada has been primarily concerned with maintaining control over its existing territory, rather than using force to expand its maritime borders. As other Arctic scholars have noted, "in terms of focus or emphasis, the importance of strengthening and protecting Canadian northern sovereignty seems to trump international oriented policy."[54] This domestic focus explains why Canada has mainly deployed its military forces to patrol Canadian territory, rather than projecting power beyond Canadian borders into the Arctic Ocean, as other states have done. Canada's focus on international issues has been on efforts to address Arctic climate change and strengthen Arctic science.[55]

However, following the shock, Canada, like many of the other Arctic states, increased its efforts to conduct underwater surveys to gather evidence supporting its continental shelf extension claims. In 2008 Canada budgeted an additional C\$40 million (approximately US\$30.5 million) to fund data collection and analysis. This increase was on top of the C\$69 million that had already been budgeted in 2004 for the following ten years.[56] This additional funding helped Canada deploy icebreakers to gather evidence to support its extended continental shelf (ECS) claims. Canadian scientists and government officials planned to submit this evidence as part of Canada's full and comprehensive ECS claim in early December of 2013. The claim was expected to include the Lomonosov Ridge but not the North Pole since Denmark and Canada had previously come to an informal agreement about what each state would claim.[57] Nonetheless, just days before the planned

---

[52] Government of Canada, "Canada First Defence Strategy," n.d.b, accessed June 21, 2016, https://www.canada.ca/en/department-national-defence/corporate/policies-standards/canada-first-defence-strategy-summary.html.

[53] Government of Canada, Foreign Affairs Trade and Development Canada, "Canada's Arctic Foreign Policy," accessed July 20, 2017, http://www.international.gc.ca/arctic-arctique/arctic_policy-canada-politique_arctique.aspx?lang=eng; Knecht and Keil, "Arctic Geopolitics Revisited."

[54] Knecht and Keil, "Arctic Geopolitics Revisited," 195.

[55] Knecht and Keil, "Arctic Geopolitics Revisited," 195.

[56] Elizabeth Riddell-Dixon, *Breaking the Ice: Canada, Sovereignty, and the Arctic Extended Continental Shelf* (Toronto: Dundurn, 2017), 154–55.

[57] Riddell-Dixon, *Breaking the Ice*, 222.

submission, Prime Minister Harper "ordered government bureaucrats back to the drawing board to craft a more expansive international claim for seabed riches in the Arctic after the proposed submission they showed him failed to include the geographic North Pole."[58]

Harper's move was controversial, given the lack of scientific evidence found for Canada's expanded claims and the prior agreement with Denmark. Canadian minister of foreign affairs John Baird admitted, "The reality is the Lomonosov Ridge wasn't fully mapped in the submissions that my department did."[59] Canada declared that its submission was a partial claim and that it reserved the right to submit additional data. Baird went on to claim that Canada would continue to gather data in order to obtain international recognition, which would be "vital to the future development of Canada's offshore resources."[60] However, in describing the incident, Canadian Arctic expert Michael Byers said, "The whole thing just reeks of amateurism."[61]

The last-minute nature of Canada's North Pole claim and its failure to collect adequate data in advance highlight the Harper administration's half-hearted commitment to pursuing Arctic resources. The next section further elaborates on Canada's reluctance, compared to Russia, to project military force to back its Arctic claims since the 2007 shock.

7.4.1 Canada's Post-shock Military Activity

Since 2007, Canadian forces have been more active in the Arctic, but Ottawa has rarely projected force beyond its own borders. The vast majority of its military activity has involved exercises and sovereignty operations on Canadian soil. Shortly after the Russians planted a flag on the Arctic seabed, the Canadian military hosted Operation NANOOK, a joint military exercise involving the navy, army, air force, Royal Canadian Mounted Police, and coast guard. Canada has held Operation NANOOK regularly since then and has increased the number of personnel and weapons systems involved.[62] These operations have also included allied forces, such

---

[58] Steven Chase, "Harper Orders New Draft of Arctic Seabed Claim to Include North Pole," *Globe and Mail*, December 4, 2013, https://www.theglobeandmail.com/news/politics/harper-orders-new-draft-of-arctic-seabed-claim-to-include-north-pole/article15756108/.

[59] Canadian Press, "Canada Makes Territorial Claim for North Pole," *The Star*, December 9, 2013, https://www.thestar.com/news/queenspark/2013/12/09/canada_makes_territorial_claim_for_north_pole.html.

[60] Canadian Press, "Canada Makes Territorial Claim."

[61] Bob Weber, "Stephen Harper's North Pole Bid Caught Bureaucrats by Surprise," CBC/Radio-Canada, November 9, 2014, https://www.cbc.ca/news/politics/stephen-harper-s-north-pole-bid-caught-bureaucrats-by-surprise-1.2829243.

[62] Munk School of Global Affairs, "Operation NANOOK," n.d., http://gordonfoundation.ca/sites/default/files/images/Operation%20NANOOK.pdf.

as the United States' Second Fleet. Operation NANOOK has expanded to include Operation NUNAKPUT, which is designed to enhance surveillance missions in the western Arctic, and Operation NUNALIVUT, which involves Ranger sovereignty patrols in the Canadian High Arctic.[63] Also, in 2009, Canadian Arctic training exercises expanded to include special antisubmarine warfare operations and other drills in response to Russian bomber and submarine patrols.

Canada has also regularly held Operation RAM, in which ground forces practice maneuvering in Arctic conditions. As part of Operation RAM 2010, Canadian armored forces were deployed to the Arctic for the first time since the end of the Cold War.[64] This operation was significant because it represented a shift of attention away from Afghanistan and toward the Arctic. Between 100 and 150 soldiers had participated in previous exercises; Operation RAM 2010 involved 1,500 soldiers. However, insufficient funding and inadequate cold-weather equipment have plagued even these modest exercises. Internal documents show that the Canadian government has failed to provide its troops with adequate warm clothing and cold-weather gear, limiting their ability to maintain even summer operations or conduct long-range patrols.[65]

A closer look at Canadian military activity reveals that, despite the increase in exercises and sovereignty patrols, Canada has rarely projected power beyond its borders to areas under dispute. Unlike Russia, Canada did not project power to the borders of states that it has disputes with, nor did it take assertive actions, such as mock bombing runs and live fire drills, in disputed areas. Moreover, the vast majority of incidents in which Canada deployed force beyond its borders involved scrambling Canadian jets to monitor Russian bombers that were approaching Canadian airspace. Canada's central interest seems to be protecting its existing Arctic territory and the sovereignty of its internal waters, rather than acquiring additional territory and resources in the Arctic.[66] When Canada did project power beyond its borders, it was often because it was invited to take part in NATO exercises. For example, Canada sent troops to participate in Operation Cold Response, a NATO exercise held in Norway. However, internal government documents reveal that, as of 2011, a number of officials in Harper's government were reluctant to engage in even this minimal level of power projection because they were concerned

---

[63] Perry and Andersen, "New Strategic Dynamics in the Arctic Region," 89.

[64] Perry and Andersen, "New Strategic Dynamics in the Arctic Region," 89.

[65] Murray Brewster, "'Critical Equipment Shortfalls' Plague Canadian Forces in Arctic," *Globe and Mail*, May 10, 2012, http://www.theglobeandmail.com/news/politics/critical-equipment-shortfalls-plague-canadian-forces-in-arctic/article4107383/.

[66] P. Whitney Lackenbauer, "Polar Race or Polar Saga? Canada and the Circumpolar World," in *Arctic Security in an Age of Climate Change*, ed. James Kraska (New York: Cambridge University Press, 2011).

that it might be "misconstrued to contradict (Government of Canada) policy for the Arctic."[67]

7.4.2   Canada's Post-shock Investment in Its Arctic Force Structure and Force Posture

After the shock, Harper announced that Canada would make a major investment in increasing its Arctic forces and presence. Specifically, he reiterated the government's commitment to invest in six to eight ice-hardened armed patrol ships and to build new icebreakers and several new Arctic bases. Canadian plans also called for investing in dual-use platforms that would enhance Canada's power projection capabilities, which were intended specifically for use in the Arctic. These plans included replacing Canada's older C-130s with seventeen new search-and-rescue aircraft and enhancing Arctic domain awareness by investing in unmanned drones and enhanced surveillance satellite capabilities.[68]

Although there was a small increase in the number of Canadian Arctic military exercises, Ottawa has not followed through on its commitments to invest in its Arctic military capabilities and presence. Despite promises to invest in Arctic capabilities, a decade later Canada had no ice-hardened patrol ships and no bases above the Arctic Circle from which its navy could operate. Out of the six to eight ice-hardened patrol ships that Harper committed to building in 2007, only five were ordered and none had been built, let alone commissioned, by the end of 2017. Construction on the first ice-hardened patrol ship, the HMCS *Harry DeWolf*, did not begin until December 2015. At the end of 2017, a full decade after the shock, Canada still had no ice-hardened patrol ships and only limited ability to sustain an Arctic military presence beyond its borders. Defense officials have highlighted this shortcoming, but funding for ships capable of operating in the Arctic has been repeatedly delayed.

In August of 2008, Harper announced that Canada would invest in building a Polar-class icebreaker capable of operating in ice as thick as 2.5 meters (8 feet).[69] The Coast Guard expected to build the *John G. Diefenbaker*, a $720 million icebreaker, in 2017.[70] However, this program has been repeatedly delayed, and the ship is not

---

[67] Canadian Press, "Canada Uncertain about Joining NATO's Arctic War Games," CBC, August 24, 2012, https://www.cbc.ca/news/politics/canada-uncertain-about-joining-nato-s-arctic-war-games-1.1166218.

[68] Perry and Andersen, "New Strategic Dynamics in the Arctic Region," 90.

[69] Rob Huebert, "Canada and the Newly Emerging International Arctic Security Regime," in *Arctic Security in an Age of Climate Change*, ed. James Kraska (New York: Cambridge University Press, 2011).

[70] Huebert, "Canada and the Newly Emerging International Arctic Security Regime."

expected to be operational until the mid-2020s at the earliest.[71] One new icebreaker will not be enough to maintain the status quo, given that Canada's aging icebreakers are between thirty and fifty years old and will need to be refurbished or replaced in the coming years.[72] Moreover, most of Canada's icebreakers are too small to deploy year-round and reportedly can only operate in the Arctic during the summer.[73]

In 2007, Harper also committed to increasing Canada's Arctic military presence by building bases and increasing the size of the Canadian Rangers, an Arctic reserve force made up primarily of Inuit who live in the Arctic. These units exist to provide basic surveillance, carry out search-and-rescue missions, and occasionally engage in sovereignty patrols. They also train regular Canadian troops to move and survive in the Arctic. Despite promises from Harper to upgrade the Rangers' World War II–era Lee Enfield bolt-action rifles by the fall of 2013, Canadian Army internal documents suggest that the efforts are at least three years behind schedule and that the new weapons will not arrive until sometime between 2017 and 2021.[74] The lack of funding is so acute that many of the Rangers must provide their own snowmobiles because the government has refused to purchase any replacement vehicles until 2021.[75] This is yet another example of Harper's unwillingness to follow through on his Arctic promises.

In efforts to increase Canada's cold-weather combat capabilities, in August of 2007, Harper announced that the base at Resolute Bay would be upgraded in order to build a Canadian Armed Forces Arctic training center.[76] After repeated delays, this center was finally opened in 2013 and is capable of housing up to 120 troops.[77] Harper also committed to building an Arctic base at Nanisivik on Baffin Island. The plan was to upgrade what had been mining facilities so that Canadian Navy and Coast Guard vessels could refuel there. Nanisivik is strategically located

[71] Canadian Press, "Feds Close to Deal with Quebec Shipyard Davie for Coast Guard Icebreakers," *Vancouver Courier*, June 5, 2018, http://www.vancourier.com/feds-close-to-deal-with-quebec-shipyard-davie-for-coast-guard-icebreakers-1.23325548.

[72] Jonathan Hayward, "Canadian Coast Guard May Be Forced to Lease Icebreakers as Aging Fleet Increasingly at Risk of Breakdowns," *National Post* (blog), November 18, 2016, http://nationalpost.com/news/canada/canadian-coast-guard-may-be-forced-to-lease-icebreakers-as-aging-fleet-increasingly-at-risk-of-breakdowns/wcm/4d424729-80b0-4d5f-8de0-7076650571ba.

[73] Padrtová, "Russian Military Build Up in the Arctic."

[74] David Pugliese, "No Money for New Guns for Arctic Rangers," Who Owns the Arctic?, September 27, 2013, http://byers.typepad.com/arctic/2013/09/no-money-for-new-guns-for-arctic-rangers.html.

[75] Pugliese, "No Money for New Guns."

[76] Government of Canada, National Defence, "Canadian Rangers," March 8, 2013, http://www.army-armee.forces.gc.ca/en/canadian-rangers/index.page.

[77] David Pugliese, "Canadian Forces to Expand Nunavut Training Centre as Russia Plans More Bases in the Arctic," *National Post* (blog), February 23, 2016, http://nationalpost.com/news/canada/canadian-forces-to-expand-nunavut-training-centre-as-russias-plans-more-bases-in-the-arctic/wcm/bfaf4835-78c9-4927-aec5-f9c97048d2cf.

at the eastern opening of the Northwest Passage, increasing Canada's ability to monitor and control the passage. The plans for refurbishing the base, which were running years behind schedule, have been scaled back to making some modest improvements to a few 1970s-era trailers that can house six people. The base will no longer be equipped with a runway and will only be staffed for part of the year.[78] While the base was supposed to open in 2015, construction did not even begin until July of that year.[79]

7.4.3 The Trudeau Administration

In October 2015, the Liberal Party and its leader Justin Trudeau swept into power, winning a staggering 148 additional seats, giving them a majority of the seats in Parliament. Although the change in government occurred more than eight years after the shock, and near the end of my period of analysis, it is important to briefly evaluate whether there was a major change in Canada's Arctic foreign policy after Trudeau came to power. Existing analyses suggest there was not.[80] The Trudeau government has neither made more expansive claims nor projected military power to disputed areas. If anything, Trudeau appears even less interested in developing Arctic resources. For example, in 2016, the Trudeau government joined the Obama administration in placing a temporary ban on offshore Arctic drilling, to be reviewed every five years.[81]

That said, the government has made some minor changes in policy. For instance, Trudeau reversed Harper's policy that sought to keep NATO out of the Arctic and now supports closer cooperation with Canada's NATO allies regarding Arctic exercises.[82] This change is likely driven by Russia's continued military buildup and more assertive posture, especially after the invasion of Crimea. Canada's 2017 defense policy explicitly mentions Russia's actions in Crimea and the need to deter increased Russian

---

[78] It should be noted that one potential reason that the runway was scrapped is that there was a neighboring civilian airfield at Arctic Bay approximately sixteen miles away.

[79] CBC News, "Nanisivik, Nunavut, Naval Facility Breaks Ground," July 18, 2015, http://www.cbc.ca/news/canada/north/nanisivik-nunavut-naval-facility-breaks-ground-1.3158798.

[80] Greg Sharp, "Trudeau and Canada's Arctic Priorities: More of the Same," Arctic Institute, December 6, 2016, https://www.thearcticinstitute.org/trudeau-canadas-arctic-priorities/.

[81] Levon Sevunts, "Ottawa Commits to Complete Fleet Renewal for Canada's Coast Guard," Radio Canada International, May 22, 2019, https://www.rcinet.ca/en/2019/05/22/canadian-coast-guard-fleet-renewal-justin-trudeau/.

[82] Rob Huebert, "The Arctic and the Strategic Defence of North America: Resumption of the 'Long Polar Watch,'" in *North American Strategic Defense in the 21st Century: Security and Sovereignty in an Uncertain World*, ed. Christian Leuprecht, Joel J. Sokolsky, and Thomas Hughes, Advanced Sciences and Technologies for Security Applications (Cham, Switzerland: Springer International Publishing, 2018), 183–84, https://doi.org/10.1007/978-3-319-90978-3_14.

aggression.[83] Also, in 2018, the government committed to purchasing three used icebreakers to replace Canada's rapidly aging fleet, as well as a sixth AOP ice-hardened patrol ship.[84] Canada has one of the oldest ice-breaking fleets in the world, and its aged ships badly need replacement. More recently, in May of 2019 the government made a commitment to a complete fleet renewal for Canada's coast guard ships.[85]

However, it remains to be seen whether the government will follow through on these commitments. As these chapters have demonstrated, the Canadian government has a long history of making big commitments and then failing to follow through, leaving Canadian forces ill-equipped and underprepared. Recall that Canadian forces were so ill-prepared during exercises in 2010 that they lacked basic cold-weather clothing, limiting soldiers' ability to carry out patrols. Embarrassingly, Canadian soldiers were forced to buy their own cold-weather clothing. As of April 2019, the government has still failed to solve this problem; and as a result, at least eighty soldiers developed frostbite during a recent Arctic military exercise.[86] The person in charge of examining the soldiers, Wendy Sullivan-Kawntes, remarked, "Many people are spending their own money to get better mitts." Again, Canadian soldiers were forced to spend their own money to buy the gear their government was unwilling to invest in.

7.5 Summary of Findings

Canada has a long history of jealously guarding its Arctic sovereignty. However, it has generally been less willing to project military force to disputed areas. Despite rhetoric to the contrary, in the post-shock period Canada has been unwilling to invest in the force structure necessary to project power into the Arctic. Canada's relatively modest investment in its Arctic force structure appears to be designed to allow it to continue sovereignty operations on its own territory but not far beyond.

---

[83] Canadian Armed Forces and Ministère de la défense nationale, *Strong, Secure, Engaged—Canada's Defence Policy* (Ottawa: Ministère de la défense nationale, 2017), 51, http://dgpaapp.forces.gc.ca/en/canada-defence-policy/docs/canada-defence-policy-report.pdf.

[84] Murray Brewster, "Ottawa Makes Deal to Buy Three Icebreakers for Canadian Coast Guard—Eye on the Arctic," CBC News, June 22, 2018, https://www.rcinet.ca/eye-on-the-arctic/2018/06/22/ottawa-makes-deal-to-buy-three-icebreakers-for-coast-guard/; Andrea Gunn, "Sixth Arctic and Offshore Patrol Ship about Readiness, Not Fairness, Experts Say," *Chronicle Herald*, November 6, 2018, https://www.thechronicleherald.ca/news/local/sixth-arctic-and-offshore-patrol-ship-about-readiness-not-fairness-experts-say-256850/.

[85] Sevunts, "Ottawa Commits to Complete Fleet Renewal."

[86] Helene Cooper, "Military Drills in Arctic Aim to Counter Russia, but the First Mission Is to Battle the Cold," *New York Times*, April 12, 2019, https://www.nytimes.com/2019/04/12/world/europe/global-warming-russia-arctic-usa.html.

Despite some basic upgrades to the Canadian military, most of its force structure is dedicated to protecting Canadian sovereignty and providing basic surveillance and search-and-rescue operations. Ottawa has made a few upgrades to its Arctic force structure, but it has not built a force that would allow it to project substantial amounts of military power. Its main investments have been for the purposes of ensuring that it can operate within its own territory and maintaining the ability to monitor the actions of others in the Arctic, particularly in the Northwest Passage. These limited developments led officials from other nations to privately suggest that Harper was all talk and no action and that the Arctic was not in fact a high priority for the Canadian government.[87]

7.6 Addressing Counterarguments

Before closing, I will address some of the most prominent potential counterarguments to my analysis. First, one might reasonably argue that Canada chose to hold more military exercises in the Arctic and respond with bombastic rhetoric not because it is more economically dependent on resource rents than the United States but because the Arctic plays a much larger role in Canada's identity and domestic politics. While it is almost certainly true that Canadian citizens care more about the Arctic than Americans, this is not necessarily at odds with my explanation. I would argue that one of the reasons Canadians care more about the Arctic than Americans is that many of them derive income from the development of Arctic natural resources. A larger percentage of Canadians than Americans are employed in mining, oil and gas extraction, and forestry; and much of this activity occurs in Canada's Arctic and sub-Arctic regions. Prime Minister Harper was keenly aware of this and routinely connected defending Arctic sovereignty with developing Canada's natural resources as a means to generate jobs and economic growth. The Canadian government specifically highlighted oil and gas exploration, mining, and diamonds as the three priority economic sectors for northern Canada.[88]

Second, one might wonder whether Russia chose to project more power than Canada because of geographic factors. However, Canada and Russia have virtually identically sized Arctic EEZs, so this factor cannot explain why Russia has invested so much more than Canada. One might argue that confounding geographic factors, such as the amount of resources at stake, were driving behavior. A closer look at the evidence reveals that Canada actually had the most to gain

[87] Wikileaks, "Canada's Conservative Government and Its Arctic Focus," January 21, 2010, https://wikileaks.org/plusd/cables/10OTTAWA29_a.html.

[88] Geneviève King Ruel, "The (Arctic) Show Must Go on: Natural Resource Craze and National Identity in Arctic Politics," *International Journal* 66, no. 4 (2011): 827.

by filing an ECS claim. If Canada realized its potential ECS claims, it would increase the total amount of Arctic resources under its control by 19%, more than any other state.[89]

Third, one might argue that Canada does not project power to the Arctic because it doesn't need to, because of its membership in NATO. Canada might be choosing to free-ride off NATO and the United States. However, as discussed in Chapter 6, the United States has not substantially increased its Arctic military activity either, making it difficult to argue that Canada is free-riding off its allies. Moreover, following the shock, the Harper government did not encourage NATO to take a more active role in the Arctic, as Norway has, and instead actively sought to prevent NATO and European Union involvement in Arctic security issues. In fact, after the shock, but before Russia's invasion of Crimea, the Canadian government adopted a hard-line policy that NATO had no security contribution to make in the region, a view that was not supported by other NATO states.[90] It was only after Russia's invasion of Crimea and Trudeau's election that the government backed a more active role for NATO in the Arctic.[91]

7.7 Conclusion

As predicted by Rent-Addiction Theory, Canada invests more in its Arctic military presence than its production-oriented counterparts, as shown by its larger, more intense military exercises. However, also in line with the theory, Canada is less willing to invest in an exclusionary Arctic foreign policy than Norway or Russia. Canada has talked a big game and has made some minor upgrades to its capabilities, allowing it to patrol its own territory; but unlike Norway and Russia, it has failed to follow through on building a military capable of projecting power to contest control over Arctic resources.

With regard to the future, my theory suggests that Canada will continue to be more interested in maintaining an Arctic military presence than the United States or Denmark but is unlikely to deploy force to coercively compete over territory. Canada's principal interests will be in managing tensions between NATO and Russia, maintaining sovereignty over its existing Arctic territory, and overseeing maritime traffic and drilling activity. Another issue that will continue to be important to Canada is the future of the Northwest Passage. The control of this sea lane is at the center of an ongoing, but peaceful, dispute between the United States and Canada. In closing, as climate change continues to rapidly alter the Arctic environment, Canada will continue to take a greater interest in the region than the United States but will be unlikely to pursue its claims to Arctic resources through gunboat diplomacy.

---

[89] Praprotnik, "Arctic Offshore Energy Resources," 61.

[90] Valur Ingimundarson, "Managing a Contested Region: The Arctic Council and the Politics of Arctic Governance," *Polar Journal* 4, no. 1 (2014): 188, https://doi.org/10.1080/2154896X.2014.913918.

[91] Huebert, "Arctic and the Strategic Defence of North America," 183–84.

A Tale of Two Nordic Powers

8.1 Introduction

On August 13, 2007, a Danish team embarked for the North Pole to gather evidence to support Denmark's claim to the extended continental shelf protruding from Greenland along the Lomonosov Ridge.[1] This mission, paid for by Denmark's Ministry for Science, Technology and Innovation, launched the Danish Continental Shelf Project, which invested $42 million to map Denmark's continental shelf. Seven years later, in December 2014, Denmark submitted this evidence to the UN Commission on the Limits of the Continental Shelf (CLCS) in support of its claim to the Lomonosov Ridge, an area that includes the North Pole, which has also been claimed by Russia and is likely to be claimed by Canada.[2] In this submission, Denmark also claimed an area in the Norwegian Sea that Norway had claimed in 2006.[3] The total area claimed by Denmark is approximately 455,000 square miles, or roughly the size of Germany and France combined.[4]

Denmark had seven years between the 2007 shock and the submission of its formal claims to the CLCS to invest in boosting its Arctic military presence to back those claims. However, despite the massive areas that Denmark claimed, Copenhagen has not backed these claims by substantially increasing its Arctic military presence or investing in its Arctic force structure to do so in the future. Instead, Copenhagen has responded to the exposure of Arctic resources in a relatively measured and cooperative manner. Denmark has not used the belligerent rhetoric of states like Canada nor dramatically increased its Arctic military activity, like Russia and Norway. To illustrate the general lack of assertive military behavior, Denmark's

---

[1] Isted, "Sovereignty in the Arctic," 362.
[2] Jakobson and Melvin, "Understanding National Approaches," 61.
[3] Andrei Zagoriski, "Russia Arctic Governance Policies," in *The New Arctic Governance*, ed. Linda Jakobson and Neil Melvin (Oxford University Press, 2016), 83.
[4] Rahbek-Clemmensen, "Carving up the Arctic," 1.

Perils of Plenty. Jonathan N. Markowitz, Oxford University Press (2020). © Oxford University Press.
DOI: 10.1093/oso/9780190078249.001.0001

Sirius dogsled patrols remain one of its principal military activities in the Arctic.[5] If Canada was the dog that barks but doesn't bite, then Denmark is the state that doesn't bark but deploys dogsled teams.

At first glance, it might appear that Denmark's reaction can be entirely explained by its small size and inability to afford to project power into the Arctic. However, Norway—a country similar in size and wealth—reacted to the shock by increasing its Arctic military presence and training activity and moving its military headquarters above the Arctic Circle. Norway's increased Arctic military presence suggests that Denmark could have done the same. Although Norway has publicly adopted a cooperative and diplomatic tone, it has also made expansive claims to Arctic seabed resources that are dubious under international law. Norway is also the only democratic state to back its Arctic claims by regularly projecting military force to patrol disputed areas. In sum, Oslo responded to the shock with the resoluteness of its Viking ancestors, choosing to stand its ground regarding its more expansive claims, despite having these claims challenged by much more powerful states, such as Russia.

The divergence between Norway and Denmark poses two questions: Why did a tiny liberal democratic state like Norway invest so heavily in enhancing its Arctic military presence? And, given that Norway boosted its Arctic military presence, why didn't Denmark do the same? Rent-Addiction Theory suggests that the answer to the puzzle is that Oslo is highly economically dependent on resource rents, while Copenhagen is not. Denmark, unlike Norway, does not rely on oil and gas revenues to provide basic public services for its citizens. This suggests not that Denmark was uninterested in Arctic resources but that Norway had a stronger preference to secure those resources, so it was more willing to invest in boosting its Arctic military presence.

In answering this puzzle, I illustrate how my theory can explain an outcome that prior theories of the democratic and capitalist peace cannot. In doing so, I highlight the limitations of those theories and where my theory has additional explanatory power. Not only are Denmark and Norway both democratic but both have economies that are highly advanced, capital- and contract-intensive, trade-dependent, and fully integrated into the global economy. Given this, virtually all prior theories predict that *both* states should have a weak preference to secure control over territory.[6]

---

[5] Michael Finkel, "The Cold Patrol," *National Geographic*, January 2012, https://www.nationalgeographic.com/magazine/2012/01/cold-patrol/.

[6] Theories of the democratic peace suggest that both states should have a weaker preference to control additional territory given their highly democratic political institutions. Moreover, virtually every theory that uses economic structure and trade to explain states' foreign policy preferences would expect the Nordics to have a weak interest in seeking territory. Those, such as Rosecrance (1986) and Brooks (2005), who suggest that economically advanced trading states should not be interested in territory cannot explain this divergence. Most variants of the capitalist peace cannot explain this away, given that both states are contract-intensive, wealthy, and financially integrated into the global economy. See Rosecrance, *Rise of the*

Table 8.1 **Denmark versus Norway: Predicted and Observed Change in the Level of Investment[a]**

	Predicted Change in Investment	Observed Pre-shock Investment (Scale 1–5)	Observed Post-shock Investment (Scale 1–5)	Observed Change in Investment (Scale 0–4)
Denmark	Small	Very low (1)	Low (2)	Small (1)
Norway	Moderate	Low (2)	High (4)	Moderate (2)

[a]For more on how the change in the level of investment operationalized, see Appendix sections B and C.

In contrast, my theory instead predicts that only Denmark should have this weak preference, while Norway should have a stronger preference to secure control over Arctic resources. Comparing cases illustrates why it is important to examine not just whether states develop economically but how. My theory suggests that states following a path of resource-driven development will have a stronger preference for territory than if they developed primarily by producing goods and services. This is because states that develop primarily by extracting resources remain or become more dependent on territory, whereas states that develop by producing goods and services become less dependent.

8.1.1   Overview of Argument and Evidence

If my theory is correct, we should observe a greater change in Norway's post-shock willingness to project power to secure control over Arctic resources than in Denmark's. A summary of my theoretical predictions can be found in Table 8.1.

Trading State; Brooks, *Producing Security*. For more on contract intensity, see Mousseau, "Comparing New Theory with Prior Beliefs." For more on the effect of wealth and financial integration, see Erik Gartzke, "The Capitalist Peace," *American Journal of Political Science* 51, no. 1 (2007): 166–91; Erik Gartzke and Dominic Rohner, "The Political Economy of Imperialism, Decolonization and Development," *British Journal of Political Science* 41, no. 3 (2011b): 1–32. The only strain of the theory of the capitalist peace that explains some of Norway's behavior is McDonald (2009), who suggests that states with large amounts of public property should be more willing to pursue assertive foreign policies because the public goods provide them with a source of revenue to fund military investments and buy off the domestic political opposition. However, although McDonald can explain why Norway's large stock of public goods might allow it to pursue a more assertive foreign policy, he cannot explain why Norway chose to be assertive with regard to one foreign policy objective rather than another. More specifically, the question I am interested in is not why Norway became more assertive but rather why Oslo chose to become more assertive with regard to securing control over Arctic resources. See McDonald, *Invisible Hand of Peace*.

Before the shock, Denmark's commitment to and investment in projecting power to the Arctic were very low. Denmark maintained a few small outposts in Greenland, with patrol ships capable of managing fisheries along Greenland's coast; and its principal Arctic military activity involved deploying dogsled teams to patrol Greenland. After the shock, Copenhagen slightly increased its commitment and investment in the Arctic, promising to build a small Arctic command center and continue to build previously ordered ice-hardened patrol ships. However, Denmark was reluctant to project power to claimed or disputed areas except through research missions that gathered data for its extended continental shelf claims. Thus, as predicted by my theory, there was only a small change in Copenhagen's willingness to invest in projecting power to the Arctic after the shock.

Although Norway's pre-shock commitment and investment were low, they were higher than Denmark's. Norway began to take a more active interest in the Arctic as early as 2005 and in 2006 released a High North Arctic strategy. In terms of Arctic-specific force structure, Norway maintained a number of Cold War–era bases and a small fleet of ice-hardened patrol ships that were used to manage fisheries in Norway's large exclusive economic zone (EEZ). After the shock, Norway made a large investment in enhancing its Arctic-specific force structure and military activity. Oslo backed its commitment to making the Arctic its number one foreign policy priority by moving its military and Coast Guard headquarters north of the Arctic Circle, refurbishing its Arctic bases, building additional icebreakers, and creating specialized Arctic military units. The Norwegian military also began to hold larger and more frequent Arctic military exercises. The navy and coast guard deployed more frequently to claimed and disputed areas, such as the Barents Sea and the waters around Svalbard. In sum, although Norway had a higher level of investment prior to the shock than Denmark, we observe a greater difference following the shock as Oslo invested much more in projecting power to the Arctic than Copenhagen.

The remainder of this chapter proceeds as follows. I begin by describing the characteristics of Denmark's and Norway's governing coalitions and illustrate the causal pathways by which the economic structure of each state influences its foreign policy preferences. I then evaluate each country's pre-shock Arctic foreign policy to establish a baseline for its level of interest and investment in projecting power to the Arctic. I use this baseline to compare the two states' responses to the shock by assessing the changes in their levels of Arctic commitment, force structure, and military activity. Finally, I briefly address potential counterarguments before closing with the implications of my findings for theory and policy.

8.2 Comparing the Characteristics of Norway and Denmark

As discussed in Chapter 3, comparing the economic structures of Norway and Denmark offers an ideal opportunity for causal inference for two reasons. First, in the late 1960s Norway struck it rich with the discovery of oil in the North Sea, while Denmark's share of North Sea resources was much smaller. As a result, Norway became highly economically dependent on oil, while Denmark did not. This exogenous shock is a natural experiment that randomly assigns Norway to the treatment (by altering its economic structure to make it more land-oriented) while assigning Denmark as the control.[7] No state could have anticipated the discovery of North Sea oil, nor did either realize at the time how large the reserves were. Because neither state could predict or select into the treatment, this design allows me to rule out the possibility that differences between them are driven by some unobservable confounding factors that caused them to select in or out of the treatment.

Second, comparing Denmark and Norway allows me to match many potential covariates. The two states share a common Nordic history, heritage, and cultural norms because Norway used to be part of Denmark. Additionally, the two states are extraordinarily similar in their economic and demographic characteristics and domestic political institutions. Both have small, ethnically homogeneous, highly educated populations as well as strongly democratic, representative, and transparent political institutions with low levels of corruption. Both states are highly economically developed, with low levels of income inequality, a large public sector, and a strong social safety net.[8] Moreover, these factors remained constant or changed in tandem for each state, both before and after the discovery of North Sea oil. In short, the two states' similarity enhances our confidence that differences between them are driven by the treatment, not by other observable differences between them.

8.2.1 The Structure of Norway's Economy

Before the discovery of North Sea oil, both Denmark and Norway were trading states that relied on exporting agrarian and manufactured goods to generate revenue. The oil extracted from the bottom of the North Sea transformed Norway's economic structure and sources of income. This newfound wealth allowed Norway to grow faster than Denmark.[9] Norway changed rapidly. According to Norwegian

---

[7] For another paper that uses this as a natural experiment to examine the effect of oil on the Norwegian economy relative to other Nordic states, see Larsen, "Escaping the Resource Curse and the Dutch Disease?"

[8] Prior to the discovery of North Sea oil, Norway lagged slightly behind Denmark. Today, both states are highly economically developed, but because of its oil, Norway is wealthier than Denmark.

[9] Larsen, "Escaping the Resource Curse and the Dutch Disease?"

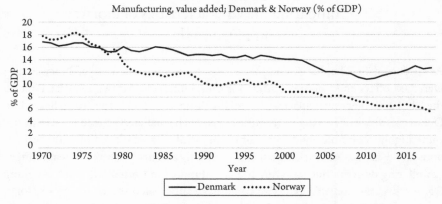

Figure 8.1 Manufacturing's Value Added as a Percentage of GDP
Source: The World Bank, "Manufacturing, Value Added (% of GDP) | Data," The World Bank, 2018,
https://data.worldbank.org/indicator/NV.IND.MANF.ZS?locations=DK-NO.

government data, in 1974 income from petroleum represented approximately 0% of GDP, but by 1980 it had jumped to 13% of GDP (see Figure 8.1). Oil made up an increasing share of the country's exports, and Norway became more dependent on resource rents. In 1974 the petroleum sector accounted for just 2% of Norway's exports, but by 1983 this share had exploded to 37%.[10]

This is not a story of how Norway became cursed by oil. To the contrary, Norway is considered an exemplar for successfully managing resource wealth.[11] Instead, this is a story about how even a state that mostly escaped the resource curse came to rely on income from oil extraction to pay its bills. This gave Norway a much stronger preference to secure control over resources than its production-oriented cousin, Denmark. Norway may have escaped the resource curse, but it did not escape becoming more dependent on resource rents.

Having established that Norway is following a path of resource-driven economic development, we can assess the evidence for two causal pathways through which my theory suggests a state's economic structure influences its preference for territory. First, a resource-driven development path should be associated with path-dependent effects that generate positive feedback loops, increasing the switching costs associated with shifting to a production-oriented economy. Specifically, if my theory is correct, the further Norway proceeds down a path of resource-driven development, the more it should invest in assets to bring its resources to market, such as oil wells, refineries, and infrastructure. These investments should increase the productivity of the land-oriented sector. As the resource sector becomes more

[10] Norwegian Ministry of Petroleum and Energy, "The Government's Revenues."
[11] Andrzej Polus and Wojciech J. Tycholiz, "The Norwegian Model of Oil Extraction and Revenues Management in Uganda," *African Studies Review* 60, no. 3 (2017): 181–201.

productive, costs rise in other sectors that use the same inputs (i.e., capital and skilled labor). This is known as the *Baumol effect*, and it makes it more difficult for the non-resource sectors in Norway to remain globally competitive.[12] The Dutch disease compounds the problem. The inflow of oil revenue boosts the value of the Norwegian currency, further increasing the costs of domestic production and further undermining the competitiveness of Norway's non-oil exports.

The funds invested in developing the technology, expertise, and infrastructure to extract deep-sea oil are sunk costs that, of course, cannot be unsunk. Each dollar invested in extracting resources is a dollar that is not spent on the infrastructure and training necessary to produce other goods and services. This increases the switching costs associated with reorienting the economy toward production. The higher the switching costs, the lower the expected return from investing in production relative to continuing to invest in resource extraction. In sum, if the path dependency mechanism is present, we should see income from natural resources continuing to make up a large share of Norway's exports and GDP, while production-oriented sectors, such as manufacturing, stagnate or fall as a share of national income and exports.

Second, because so much of Norway's income is derived from land and the state captures the money directly because it owns the natural resources, the members of the Norwegian governing coalition should have a vested interest in developing and securing natural resources. This is because the income from these resources is critical for providing prosperity, security, and other public goods that Norwegian citizens rely upon. Therefore, despite Norway's best efforts to diversify away from oil and gas, we should see the government continuing to prioritize investing in resource extraction.

I begin by assessing the evidence for the path-dependent effects associated with resource-driven development. Norwegian leaders were highly aware of the risks of proceeding down this path and adopted a number of strategies to manage them. However, despite managing its oil wealth better than virtually any other state, Norway's economy still became highly dependent on resource rents. The petroleum sector's share of national investment increased markedly over time, as did its share of exports, GDP, and government revenue.[13]

At the same time, rising wages made production-oriented sectors of the Norwegian economy less competitive as oil flowed into the economy in the 1970s. Resource-driven development made producing goods and services more costly and harmed the manufacturing sector.[14] Wages rose 25% between 1974 and 1977.[15]

---

[12] William J. Baumol and William G. Bowen, *Performing Arts, the Economic Dilemma: A Study of Problems Common to Theater, Opera, Music, and Dance* (Cambridge, MA: MIT Press, 1966).

[13] Norwegian Ministry of Petroleum and Energy, "The Government's Revenues."

[14] Rolf Jens Brunstad and Jan Morten Dyrstad, "Booming Sector and Wage Effects: An Empirical Analysis on Norwegian Data," *Oxford Economic Papers* 49, no. 1 (1997): 89–103. See also, Michael M. Hutchison, "Manufacturing Sector Resiliency to Energy Booms: Empirical Evidence from Norway, the Netherlands, and the United Kingdom," *Oxford Economic Papers* 46, no. 2 (1994): 311–29.

[15] Karl, *Paradox of Plenty*, 214.

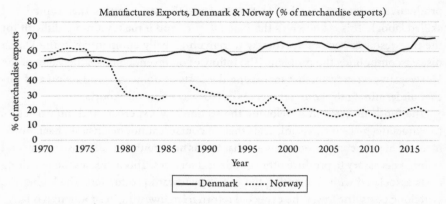

Figure 8.2 Manufacturing Exports as a Percentage of Merchandise Exports
Source: The World Bank, "Manufactures Exports (% of Merchandise Exports) | Data," The World Bank, 2018, https://data.worldbank.org/indicator/TX.VAL.MANF.ZS.UN?locations=NO-DK.

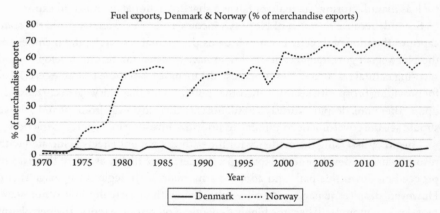

Figure 8.3 Fuel Exports as a Percentage of Merchandise Exports
Source: The World Bank, "Fuel Exports (% of Merchandise Exports) | Data," The World Bank, 2018, https://data.worldbank.org/indicator/TX.VAL.FUEL.ZS.UN?locations=DK-NO&view=chart.

Higher wages meant higher costs, making Norwegian manufacturing less competitive. As a result, the production-oriented sector's share of exports and output began to fall. In just nine years, from 1974 to 1983, oil's share of GDP and exports overtook manufacturing's. In 1974 manufacturing represented 18.3% of Norwegian GDP, but by 1983 it had fallen to 11.6% (see Figure 8.1). Over the same period, manufacturing's share of merchandise exports fell from 61.5% to 29% (see Figure 8.2). In comparison, fuel exports shot up from 5.5% to 52.8% of merchandise exports (see Figure 8.3). The Norwegian government's own data show a similar spike, in which oil's share of GDP shot up from 2.1% to 15% and its share of all exports went from 2% to 37% (see Figure 8.4).

Comparing the Danish and Norwegian economies before and after oil began flowing into the Norwegian economy in the mid-1970s provides a useful

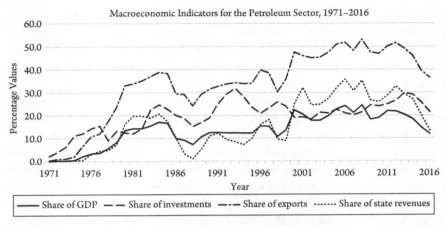

Figure 8.4 Macroeconomic Indicators for the Norwegian Petroleum Sector, 1971–2016
Source: Norwegian Ministry of Petroleum and Energy, "The Government's Revenues."

counterfactual. Specifically, because Denmark did not discover and exploit vast amounts of North Sea oil, we can infer what would have happened to Norway's manufacturing sector had Norway not discovered and exploited those reserves. Figures 8.1 and 8.2 reveal that, in 1970, manufacturing's value added as a share of GDP and its share of merchandise exports were similar for both countries. However, after Norwegian oil production took off in the mid-1970s, manufacturing's share of Norway's GDP and exports fell dramatically, while there was little change in its share of the Danish economy. In contrast, fuel exports as a share of merchandise exports shot up in Norway but remained low in Denmark (see Figure 8.3).

The decline in manufacturing's share of national income and exports and the increasing importance of oil are indicative of the broader shift in Norway's economy from production to resource extraction. However, unlike other states, Norway avoided the worst effects of the resource curse and the Dutch disease by limiting the amount of oil revenue the government could use and reinvesting most of the profits in finding and extracting more oil.[16] This policy, combined with low energy-processing costs in the mid-1980s, caused oil's percentage of government revenue to plunge (see Figure 8.4). However, because of Norway's policy of reinvesting the profits from oil into additional extraction and exploration, it soon developed world-class infrastructure and expertise, allowing Norway to find and extract more oil and gas. For example, by 2014 Norway was estimated to have built approximately seventy offshore oil platforms.[17] As Minister of Petroleum and Energy Tord Lien remarked in 2015, "We obviously have the resources and a fantastic infrastructure

---

[16] Larsen, "Escaping the Resource Curse and the Dutch Disease?"

[17] Charles Recknagel, "What Can Norway Teach Other Oil-Rich Countries?" RadioFreeEurope/RadioLiberty, November 27, 2014, accessed July 30, 2017, https://www.rferl.org/a/what-can-norway-teach-other-oil-rich-countries/26713453.html.

built up over several decades. This delivers high regularity, we have the expertise, and are a trusted exporter both as a nation and an industry. Everything's in place."[18] This policy of reinvesting the oil income delayed the flow of that money into the economy, but it enhanced Oslo's ability to extract oil in the future, which eventually generated a tidal wave of revenue.

Norway's efforts to slow the flow of income into the economy were somewhat successful in holding back the tide of resource revenues. As a result, Norway was relatively successful in avoiding the most severe symptoms of resource dependence, especially its effects on economic growth.[19] However, these policies could only hold back the tide for so long. By the late 1990s, petroleum prices had begun to rise and the symptoms associated with the Dutch disease and the Baumol effect became more pronounced.[20] The 50,000 engineers employed in Norway's offshore oil sectors are not available to work in the country's tech sector, which must compete with the highly productive resource sector for talent and capital.[21] According to the Norwegian government, in 2012 the petroleum sector was approximately twice the size of the manufacturing sector.[22] Thus, although Norway has worked hard to diversify its economy and invest in the human capital of its citizens, oil and gas remain the dominant sources of income for the state and its governing coalition.

In short, in spite of Norway's judicious attempts to avoid becoming economically dependent on income from natural resources, that income eventually began to dominate the Norwegian economy as energy prices rose through the early 2000s. Since 2000, the petroleum industry has made up a much greater share of Norway's economy and government revenue. This matches my predictions that income from natural resources would come to make up a greater share of Norway's exports, GDP, and government revenue.

Despite largely escaping the worst effects of the resource curse, Norway's choice to pursue resource-driven development has resulted in path-dependent effects that increased the switching costs associated with shifting to a production-oriented economy. Income from natural resources has inflated the cost of the labor needed to produce goods and services. Just as every dollar invested in the oil and gas industry is a dollar not invested in the tech sector, every citizen trained to become a petroleum engineer is a citizen not trained to become a software engineer.

---

[18] Norwegian Petroleum Directorate, "Norwegian Continental Shelf," 12, no. 2 (2015), 7, https://www.npd.no/globalassets/1-npd/publikasjoner/norsk-sokkel-en/arcive/norwegian-continental-shelf-no-2-2015.pdf.

[19] Larsen, "Escaping the Resource Curse and the Dutch Disease?"

[20] Larsen, "Escaping the Resource Curse and the Dutch Disease?," 637.

[21] Economist, "The Rich Cousin: Oil Makes Norway Different from the Rest of the Region, but Only up to a Point," February 2, 2013.

[22] Government of Norway, "Norway's Oil History in 5 Minutes," Redaksjonellartikkel, October 9, 2013, https://www.regjeringen.no/en/topics/energy/oil-and-gas/norways-oil-history-in-5-minutes/id440538/.

The implication of these path-dependent effects is that Norwegian leaders cannot just turn a key and quickly generate an alternative source of income by moving investment away from natural resources and into production. If Norway is to develop an alternative source of revenue, it will first need to pay the switching costs. However, each dollar invested in paying these costs is a dollar not invested in securing and developing the natural resources that generate the income that Norwegian citizens depend on and have grown accustomed to.

Norway has made impressive efforts to make its economy less dependent on oil income. For example, in the mid-1990s Norway was generating so much resource revenue that it chose to create a sovereign wealth fund where it could invest its income.[23] The government has made a rule that it will spend no more than 4% of the fund's annualized return. This is one of the largest sovereign wealth funds in the world, and Norway hopes to one day use income from the fund to replace its oil revenues. However, this will take many decades as the fund has grown slowly. From 1998 to 2017 it returned an average of only 3.9%.[24] Thus, for many years to come, Norway will remain economically dependent on resource rents for both income and government revenue.

Once a state and its citizens become addicted to the income and revenue from natural resources, it becomes difficult to quickly substitute away. As anyone who has been to Norway can tell you, Norwegians are acutely aware that their high standard of living depends on oil and gas. Norway's resource rents allow the enjoyment of first-rate healthcare, public transport, infrastructure and a generous social safety net.[25] This fact was not lost on Terje Søviknes, Norway's minister of petroleum, when he defended the importance of continued oil and gas development, admitting that "We have better welfare than we could ever have imagined before.... For the government, it's important to offer new acreage to oil and gas companies."[26] Søviknes also pointed out that "Oil revenues finance the welfare state."[27]

"We still need oil."[28] Tord Lien was minister of petroleum and energy from 2013 to 2017, and his succinct statement makes clear that Norwegian officials are well aware of their long-term dependence on natural resources. Despite their efforts to diversify away from oil and gas, it will take decades before Norway is able to develop alternative sources of income and government revenue to replace natural resources.

---

[23] Recknagel, "What Can Norway Teach Other Oil-Rich Countries?"

[24] Norges Bank, "Returns," accessed July 31, 2017, https://www.nbim.no/en/the-fund/return-on-the-fund/.

[25] Economist, "Rich Cousin."

[26] Richard Milne, "Oil and the Battle for Norway's Soul," Financial Times, July 26, 2017, https://www.ft.com/content/c2dad93c-7192-11e7-aca6-c6bd07df1a3c.

[27] Bente Bergøy, "Out of the Echo Chamber," Norwegian Petroleum Directorate, June 28, 2017, http://www.npd.no/en/Publications/Norwegian-Continental-Shelf/No-1-2017/The-interview/.

[28] Norwegian Petroleum Directorate, "Norwegian Continental Shelf," 9.

For example, Ola Borten Moe, minister of petroleum and energy from 2011 to 2013, suggested that oil and gas would "still be dominant and crucial in Norwegian society thirty years from now."[29] A decade after the shock, Norwegian leaders have continued to defend their investment in developing offshore Arctic resources. For example, Prime Minster Erna Solberg defended her support of controversial Arctic offshore drilling by claiming that the energy industry would be Norway's largest economic sector for the next "ten, twenty, thirty years."[30]

Some environmental groups and political parties, such as the Green Party and more recently the Liberal Party, have pushed to rapidly end Norway's economic dependence on oil and gas because of their environmental impact. These efforts have been opposed by larger, more powerful mainstream political parties such as the Conservative, Labor, and Progress Parties, which have significantly more seats in the Norwegian Parliament. For seventy-one of the past seventy-five years, the Conservative and Labor Parties have been included in the coalition of political parties that make up the government.[31] Members of the Progress Party have long backed the natural resource sector, which is valuable not only as a source of government revenue but as a source of employment. Speaking in opposition to a proposal to limit oil and gas development on environmental grounds, Tord Lien, a leading member of the Progress Party, caustically asked "whether we should shut down the country's biggest oil value creation by far, which employs people all along the coast, to save the world from one per cent of its oil."[32] As head of energy issues for the Conservative Party, Tina Bru remarked, "We can't dismantle the most lucrative industry in Norway by replacing it with pipe dreams and wishful thinking."[33] Thus, although the government has paid lip service to environmental protection by banning drilling in the Lofoten Islands, it has opened up areas of the Barents Sea with much larger reserves.[34]

In sum, I find evidence for both of the causal pathways through which I expect the state's economic structure to influence leaders' preferences for investing in securing territory and resources. First, Norway's resource-driven development

---

[29] Bjørn Rasen, "A Rich Inheritance," Norwegian Petroleum Directorate, November 16, 2011a, http://www.npd.no/en/Publications/Norwegian-Continental-Shelf/NO2-2011/The-interview/.

[30] Milne, "Oil and the Battle for Norway's Soul."

[31] Ministry of Security and Service Organization, "Norway's Governments since 1945," Regjeringen.no, accessed July 2, 2018, https://www.regjeringen.no/en/the-government/previous-governments/regjeringer-siden-1814/historiske-regjeringer/governments-since-1945/id438715/.

[32] Bjørn Rasen, "The Oil Industry Must Also Have Two Ideas in Its Head at Once," Norwegian Petroleum Directorate, November 16, 2011b, http://www.npd.no/en/Publications/Norwegian-Continental-Shelf/No2-2015/The-interview/.

[33] AFP News, "Oil-Rich Norway Struggles to Beat Its 'Petroholism,'" The Local.no, September 8, 2017, https://www.thelocal.no/20170908/oil-rich-norway-struggles-to-beat-its-petroholism.

[34] Richard Milne, "Norway Opens up Record 93 Blocks for Arctic Oil Exploration," *Financial Times*, June 21, 2017, https://www.ft.com/content/a120d578-567e-11e7-9fed-c19e2700005f.

Table 8.2 **Resource Orientation: Norway versus Denmark**

	Oil Exports % of GDP*ᵃ	Fuel Exports % of GDP**ᵇ	Resource Rents % of GDP**
Norway	9.72	19.1	8.38
Denmark	0.766	2.04	1.15

*Data only available through 2001, average 1991–2001.

**Average 1997–2007.

ᵃAshford, "Oil and Violence," 21–23. Data calculated using BP and EIA. Graham and Tucker, "International Political Economy."

ᵇCalculated based on fuel exports as a percentage of merchandise exports from World Bank, "Fuel Exports."

led to path-dependent effects that restructured the Norwegian economy and increased the switching costs associated with shifting to a production economy. Second, just as the Norwegian economy became more dependent on income from energy resources, its citizens, and subsequently their elected representatives in the government, developed a vested interest in the natural resource sector. As a result, Norwegian leaders have continued to prioritize investing in natural resource development. Unless Norwegians are willing to suffer a massive loss of income and government services, they will be forced to continue investing in developing and securing the natural resources on which their prosperity depends until they can generate a substitute source of income. Thus, as we shall see in the section on Norway's response to the shock, this gives Norwegian citizens—and their government—a stake in securing control over the source of these rents.

8.2.2 The Structure of Denmark's Economy

If Norway is a story of how a state escaped the resource curse and became wealthy from resource rents, then Denmark is a story of a state that became wealthy without those North Sea oil reserves. Denmark is arguably the most production-oriented and least land-oriented state in the Arctic. Because Denmark produces only a small amount of natural resources, it is almost entirely economically dependent on income from producing goods and services. In the decade before the shock, fuel exports accounted for approximately 2% of GDP, oil exports accounted for less than 1%, and resource rents accounted for just over 1%.[35] As Table 8.2 shows, this stands

---

[35] On agriculture as a percentage of GDP, see World Bank, "Agriculture, Value Added (% of GDP)," accessed September 16, 2016, http://data.worldbank.org/indicator/NV.AGR.TOTL.ZS. On services as a percentage of GDP, see World Bank, "Exports of Goods and Services (% of GDP)," accessed September 16, 2016, http://data.worldbank.org/indicator/NE.EXP.GNFS.ZS.

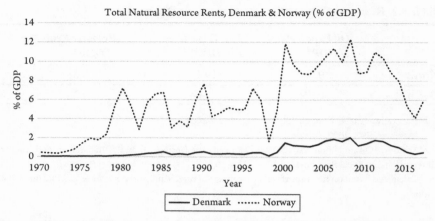

Figure 8.5 Resource Rents as a Percentage of GDP, Norway versus Denmark
Source: The World Bank, "Total Natural Resources Rents (% of GDP)," June 25, 2018.

in stark contrast to Norway. Moreover, as Figure 8.5 shows, Denmark has never derived a large share of its income from resource rents.

Instead of oil, Denmark has relied on the human capital and productivity of its citizens. Anyone who has visited Copenhagen and Oslo, including most Norwegians,
will tell you that they would much prefer to dine in Copenhagen. However, this
has not always been the case. Before 2000, Nordic cuisine would not have been
at the top of any foodie's list. New Nordic cuisine has taken off since the turn of
the new century. Copenhagen's flagship establishment in this category, Noma, has
won what is arguably the most prestigious title in the culinary world—"World's Best
Restaurant," awarded by the World's 50 Best Restaurant Academy—more times
than any other restaurant since 2010.[36] Copenhagen has become one of the most
innovative culinary cities in the world as aspiring cooks flock from all over the world
to learn their craft. Local bar and restaurant owners will tell you it is much easier to
do business in Denmark than Norway. This is no accident. Not having oil to rely
on, Denmark has generated income by producing services rather than extracting
wealth. Rather than a curse, this may have been a blessing. Because the Danish state
and its citizens rely on income from goods and services, the Danish government
has adopted policies that enhance the productivity of that sector. For example,
Denmark has implemented policies that have consistently made it ranked as one of
the best places in the world to do business. Eliminating much of the red tape and
regulation associated with doing business enhances the incentive for Danes to produce wealth in this way.

---

[36] For more on this academy, see World's 50 Best Restaurants Academy, "About the Academy,"
accessed August 1, 2019, https://www.theworlds50best.com/the-academy/about-us.

Table 8.3 **World Bank Ease of Doing Business Rank[a] (1 is the highest rank out of 190 economies)**

	2016	*2017*
Norway	8	6
Denmark	2	3

[a]See World Bank, "Doing Business: Measuring Business Regulations. Historical Data Sets and Trends Data," n.d.," accessed July 26, 2017, http://www.doingbusiness.org/Custom-Query.

Table 8.4 *US News and World Report* **Open for Business 2017 (1 is the highest rank out of 80 countries surveyed)**

	Rank
Norway	9
Denmark	4

Nordic states, including Norway, have typically ranked near the top on business-friendliness indicators. However, the relevant comparison group is not the rest of the world but rather those states that are most similar to Norway. Comparing only Nordic countries reveals that Norway consistently lags behind its Nordic cousins that cannot rely on oil and must produce rather than extract their wealth.[37] Focusing directly on the comparison between Denmark and Norway, we can see that Denmark consistently outpaces Norway across a broad set of these measures (see Tables 8.3–8.5). Table 8.3 shows that Denmark ranks higher on the World Bank's Ease of Doing Business measure. Table 8.4 shows that Denmark also outranks Norway on the *US News and World Report* Open for Business measure. These are both measures of the degree to which regulation hinders or helps business. Table 8.5 shows the Heritage Foundation's Economic Freedom Indicators. While Denmark and Norway's overall economic freedom scores (column 1, Table 8.5) are similar, a closer look at the indicators used to code business shows a sharper divergence. Denmark's lead is particularly pronounced with regard to labor freedom (Table 8.5, column 3). Copenhagen has combined a policy of allowing businesses to more easily hire and fire employees with a generous social safety net.[38] This allows companies to lay off workers

---

[37] For a comparison of all the Nordic states on these indicators, see Appendix section D.

[38] Paul N. Gooderham et al., "The Labor Market Regimes of Denmark and Norway—One Nordic Model?" *Journal of Industrial Relations* 57, no. 2 (April 1, 2015): 166–86, https://doi.org/10.1177/0022185614534103.

Table 8.5 **Heritage Index of Economic Freedom Indicators Averaged 1997–2007[a]**
(100 Is the Best Score)

	Mean Economic Freedom Score	Mean Business Freedom Score	Mean Labor Freedom Score*	Mean Monetary Freedom Score	Mean Trade Freedom Score	Mean Investment Freedom Score	Mean Financial Freedom Score
Norway	67.3	73.9	49.6	82.7	81.9	57.3	50.0
Denmark	71.3	90.9	99.9	88.9	79.9	70.9	80.9

*Data only available 2005–2007 (average is taken from 2005–2007).

[a]Heritage Foundation, "Index of Economic Freedom," n.d., accessed August 2, 2017, http://www.heritage.org/index/visualize.

Table 8.6 **Norway versus Denmark: Production-Oriented Indicators, Pre-shock (1997–2007 Average)[a]**

	Education Spending (% of GDP)*	R&D Spending (% of GDP)**	Healthcare Spending (% of GDP)
Norway	6.99	1.57	8.93
Denmark	8.02	2.30	9.21

*Denmark data missing: 1997.
**Denmark data missing: 2000.
[a]World Bank "Government Expenditure on education, total (% of GDP).
World Bank "Research and Development expenditure(% of GDP)
World Bank "Current health expenditure (% of GDP)

when they are no longer needed and enables workers to shift to sectors with the highest demand for labor.

8.2.3 Denmark vs. Norway: Indicators of Ease of Doing Business and Economic Freedom

While Norway, like most Nordic states, has made substantial investments in its citizens' health and human capital, Denmark outpaced Norway in the share of its GDP dedicated to education and healthcare. Denmark has not only invested a larger share of its GDP in developing the human capital on which a production-oriented economy runs; it has invested more in research and development (R&D). In the ten years before the shock, Norway, on average, spent 1.6% of its GDP on R&D, whereas Denmark spent 2.3%. Norway would have needed to increase its spending by approximately 46% to reach Denmark's spending level during this period (see Table 8.6). Moreover, this gap has only widened in recent years as

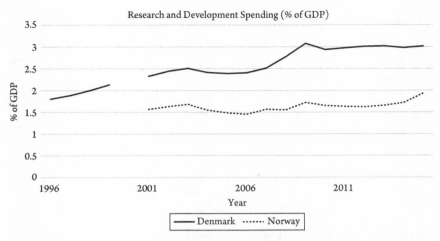

Figure 8.6 Research and Development Spending as a Percentage of GDP, Norway versus Denmark

Source: The World Bank, "Research and Development Expenditure (% of GDP)."

Denmark has increased spending during its transition to a knowledge economy, while Norway's spending has remained flat (see Figure 8.6). As of 2014 (the last year for which data are available), Denmark spent 3.1% of its GDP on R&D, nearly double Norway's 1.7%.

Denmark's income relies almost entirely on the skill and drive of its citizens to produce goods and services, while a large share of Norway's income derives from extracting land rents. This is a direct result of Norway's discovery of North Sea oil, which allowed it to enrich itself to an unprecedented degree but also made it economically dependent on resource rents. To exemplify how dependent Norway is on oil, consider this: when global commodity prices collapsed during the Great Recession, Norway's per capita GDP fell from $61,676 in 2008 to $55,459 in 2009, a drop of over 10%, whereas Denmark's fell from $41,278 in 2008 to $40,380 in 2009, only slightly more than 2%.[39] As Figure 8.7 reveals, when global energy prices slumped again in 2014, Norway's per capita GDP plummeted, while Denmark's continued to grow. Oslo is still searching for ways to transition away from oil, but until it does, it will have a stronger interest in securing control over the resources that underwrite its prosperous standard of living. As we shall see in the following section, this gave Norway a stronger incentive to secure control over Arctic resources, leading to a greater change in Oslo's willingness to project power relative to Copenhagen's.

---

[39] Per capita GDP is represented as purchasing power parity using current international dollars. See World Bank, "GDP per Capita, PPP (Current International $)," 2018, https://data.worldbank.org/indicator/NY.GDP.PCAP.PP.CD?locations=DK-NO.

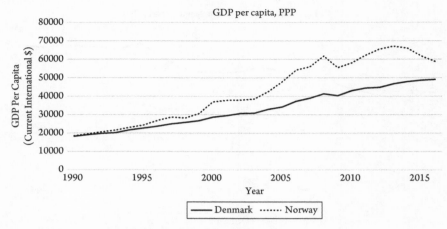

Figure 8.7 Per capita GDP, Norway versus Denmark
PPP, purchasing power parity
Source: The World Bank, "GDP per Capita, PPP (Current International $)," The World Bank, 2018,
https://data.worldbank.org/indicator/NY.GDP.PCAP.PP.CD?locations=DK-NO.

8.3   Establishing a Baseline: Norway and Denmark's Arctic Foreign Policy Prior to the Shock

During the Cold War, Norway's and Denmark's interest in the Arctic stemmed from their participation in NATO and their control of strategically valuable Arctic territory that was of great interest to both the United States and the Soviet Union. Norway's Arctic territory directly borders Russia, which put Oslo on the front lines. As a result, Norway maintained a network of Arctic bases near its border with Russia. Norway's northern coast borders the Barents Sea, which, as anyone who has watched the first scene of the film *Red October* knows, makes it an ideal location for NATO to monitor Russian nuclear submarines coming in and out of Russia's naval base at Murmansk.

Denmark's role stemmed from its control over Greenland, with its proximity to the North Pole. In the new nuclear world, the ability to detect bombers and missiles flying over the North Pole might make the difference between survival and obliteration, so Greenland's unique position in the north represented the commanding heights. Therefore, Greenland has served as a valuable bargaining chip for Denmark in its relationship with the United States. As a small nation, Denmark sought US protection; and its relationship with Greenland allowed it bring something to the table that the United States valued.[40] In fact, even before

---

[40] Anders Henriksen and Jon Rahbek-Clemmensen, "The Greenland Card: Prospects for and Barriers to Danish Arctic Diplomacy in Washington," in *Danish Foreign Policy Yearbook 2017* (Copenhagen: Danish Institute for International Studies, 2017), 75–98.

the Cold War began, strategic thinkers were aware of Greenland's strategic importance. In 1946, the United States offered to buy Greenland from Denmark, an offer Denmark declined.[41]

In 1951, Denmark and the United States signed the Defense of Greenland Agreement. The United States opened three air bases in Greenland that year, one of which, at Thule, is still in operation. Thule is particularly valuable for tracking ballistic missiles. Another of those bases, Camp Century, was considered as a potential site to host US ballistic missiles underneath the Arctic ice sheet as part of a feasibility study called Project Iceworm.[42] These missiles would have been buried deep under the ice field to protect them from attack. Although it may seem like an evil plan from a Bond movie, Project Iceworm envisioned a subsurface railway that would support 600 ballistic missiles underneath the Arctic ice sheet.[43] Shockingly, this plan was deemed infeasible. However, Greenland did host nuclear-armed American bombers and controversial stockpiles of American nuclear weapons.

After the Cold War, geopolitical tensions and Arctic military activity decreased. During the 1990s and early 2000s, the Cold War rivalry was replaced by cooperative relations between the Arctic nations.[44] In 1996 the Arctic Council was formed, providing a forum for Arctic nations to discuss and coordinate on issues such as environmental protection. However, despite the region's decreased geopolitical importance, both Denmark and Norway still had Arctic interests prior to the shock.

8.3.1 Denmark Pre-shock Interests

Denmark has long had three principal interests in the Arctic. First and foremost is its relationship with Greenland. Though Greenland is now politically autonomous, it has been part of Denmark for hundreds of years, first as a colony and then formally as part of the Kingdom of Denmark after 1953.[45] To this day, Denmark remains in charge of Greenland's defense and foreign policy. Defending Greenland and ensuring that the Danish military can maintain a presence in the waters around Greenland is the main reason Copenhagen has historically invested in the capability to project power to the Arctic. For example, in the early 1990s, Denmark acquired

---

[41] Hans W. Weigert, "Iceland, Greenland and the United States," *Foreign Affairs* (October 1944).

[42] William Colgan et al., "The Abandoned Ice Sheet Base at Camp Century, Greenland, in a Warming Climate," *Geophysical Research Letters* 43, no. 15 (2016): 8091–96, https://doi.org/10.1002/2016GL069688.

[43] Weigert, "Iceland, Greenland and the United States."

[44] Teemu Palosaari and Frank Möller, "Security and Marginality: Arctic Europe and the Double Engagement," *Journal of the Nordic International Studies* 39, no. 9 (2004): 255–81.

[45] Kathrin Keil, "The Arctic: A New Region of Conflict? The Case of Oil and Gas," *Cooperation and Conflict* 49, no. 2 (June 6, 2013): 177, https://doi.org/10.1177/0010836713482555.

four Thetis-class ice-hardened frigates that allowed it to patrol the ice-choked waters around Greenland.[46]

Without Greenland, Denmark would have no Arctic territory. Therefore, Copenhagen has an interest in ensuring that Greenland remains a part of Denmark and does not pursue total independence, which would result in Denmark losing its Arctic territory, Arctic EEZ claims, and claims to the extended continental shelf (ECS) in the Arctic.[47] Greenland has fewer than 60,000 residents, but if it were an independent country, it would be the twelfth largest geographically in the world. The landmass of Greenland has approximately fifty times the area of Denmark. In terms of population and landmass, Greenland and Denmark are each other's opposites: Denmark is tiny geographically and has more than 5 million people, while Greenland is enormous geographically but has the population of a middle-sized town.

Second, and relatedly, Denmark has a long-term interest in maintaining close ties with the United States, its key NATO ally, without provoking Russia.[48] Copenhagen viewed the Arctic as an area where it had something to offer the United States, principally the right to station forces at Thule Air Base. To this day, Denmark maintains influence with the United States because Washington seeks Danish cooperation regarding security and economic issues both in and outside the Arctic. Copenhagen has sought to walk a fine line by pleasing the United States, to ensure cooperation on economic and security issues, without antagonizing Russia through actions that it finds threatening, such as the upgrades to US missile defense radars in Greenland that occurred in 2004.[49]

Third, Copenhagen has an interest in defending its Arctic claims and in protecting the Arctic environment. Denmark had a number of disputes with Canada, Iceland, and Norway that were settled peacefully via bilateral agreements prior to 2007. However, Denmark also had a number of disputed claims and potential claims it could make by submitting a continental shelf extension claim. Because I am interested in whether Denmark chose to escalate these disputes after the shock, I focus on disputes that existed when the shock occurred. The first is a disagreement over Hans Island. Although Canada and Denmark settled the continental shelf boundary between Canada and Greenland in the 1973 Delimitation Treaty, they did not settle the issue of who owned Hans Island. Hans Island is a small, uninhabited rock that lies between Canada's Ellesmere Island and Greenland.[50] It contains no resources and would not change the boundary.

[46] S. Torp Petersen, THETIS Class Patrol Frigate (Copenhagen: Royal Danish Navy), accessed July 5, 2019, http://www.marinehist.dk/orlogsbib/THETIS-class.pdf.

[47] Rahbek-Clemmensen, "Carving up the Arctic."

[48] Rahbek-Clemmensen, "Carving up the Arctic."
Jakobson and Melvin, "Understanding National Approaches," 61.

[49] Sharp, "Implications of Ice Melt on Arctic Security," 309–10.

[50] Carlson et al., "Scramble for the Arctic," 33.

The second issue concerns potential continental shelf extensions that might overlap other states' claims. In November 2004, Denmark ratified the United Nations Convention on the Law of the Sea (UNCLOS), giving it ten years to submit ECS claims to the CLCS. Although there were some areas where Denmark could claim continental shelf extensions off the coast of Greenland and the Faroe Islands, there is only one area north of Greenland that could overlap with claims made by other states. This area contains the Lomonosov Ridge, which extends from the northern tip of Greenland to the North Pole. These continental shelf extensions have the potential to give Denmark control over hundreds of thousands of square miles of seabed.

8.3.2 Norway's Pre-shock Interests

Before the shock, Norway had three core interests in the Arctic. First, Norway has a larger portion of its population (approximately 10%) living above the Arctic Circle than any other state. Thus, Oslo has a long-term interest in providing the infrastructure and logistical capabilities necessary to sustain economic activity and provide basic services for its citizens living in the High North. Second, Norway has sought to ensure peaceful and stable relations with its Arctic neighbors. Like Denmark, Norway faces the tricky balance of maintaining ties with the United States and NATO, which provide for its security, without antagonizing Russia.

Third, and most important for this analysis, consider Norway's offshore Arctic interests. Oslo, like Copenhagen, confronts the challenge of patrolling a large Arctic EEZ and managing its claims and disputes. At the time of the shock, Norway had two unresolved offshore disputes with Russia. The first concerned an overlapping EEZ claim in the Barents Sea, and the second was a dispute over the right to exploit resources in the Fishery Protection Zone around Svalbard. Under the Spitsbergen Treaty of 1920, Norway administers Svalbard, but any nation that signed the treaty can develop the area's land resources. However, Norway has also claimed a fishery protection zone in the 200 nautical miles around Svalbard and claims the exclusive right to develop Svalbard's offshore resources, a claim that Russia and many other nations dispute. Also, in 1996, Norway ratified UNCLOS, giving it ten years to submit ECS claims.[51] On November 27, 2006, Norway submitted a claim to extend its continental shelf in the Barents Sea and Arctic Ocean to include another 91,000 square miles of undersea territory. In 2009, the CLCS determined that Norway's claim was supported by the evidence that had been submitted.

In short, both Norway and Denmark had Arctic interests, but since the Cold War, neither had invested heavily in projecting military force there. Denmark maintained its dogsled patrols of Greenland and a few ice-hardened patrol ships that it used to

---

[51] Perry and Andersen, "New Strategic Dynamics in the Arctic Region," 45.

patrol the ice-choked waters around Greenland. However, overall, Denmark's investment in projecting force in the Arctic was very low before the shock. Norway
had a slightly greater investment because of its shared border with Russia and
sought to patrol the waters around Svalbard to prevent illegal fishing from Russia.
Norway began to take a greater interest in the Arctic starting in 2005, and in 2006 it
released a new High North strategy that prioritized developing the Arctic and providing additional support for Norwegians living above the Arctic Circle. However,
despite Norway's increasing interest in the Arctic, before the shock, Oslo's level of
investment in boosting its Arctic military activity and force structure was relatively
low.[52] In sum, although Norway had a slightly higher level of commitment and investment than Denmark, both states maintained relatively low levels of investment
in projecting military force to the region before the shock. However, as we shall see
in the next two sections, the two states responded very differently to the shock.

8.4   Denmark's Response to the Shock

In the summer of 2007, the reality that the ice-choked waters around Greenland
might soon be ice-free for much of the summer confronted Danish officials.
Following the shock, in May of 2008 the Danish Ministry of Foreign Affairs and
Greenlandic Home Rule published an initial draft of its Arctic strategy called *The
Arctic at a Time of Transition: Draft Strategy for Activities in the Arctic Region*. This was
followed by a number of defense documents that named the Arctic as a priority.[53] In
2011, a more comprehensive policy document designed to guide Denmark's Arctic
strategy through 2020 was released.[54] These documents stressed peaceful cooperation between states, particularly on issues such as resolving maritime boundaries
and search and rescue. They also highlighted opportunities for economic development in the realms of shipping, minerals, oil and gas extraction, and fisheries, while
still managing climate change and protecting the Arctic environment.

8.4.1   Denmark's Post-shock Arctic Force Structure

These Arctic strategy documents discuss protecting Danish sovereignty through a
visible military presence. After the shock, Denmark's intelligence services warned
that armed conflict in the Arctic was a significant possibility in the next twenty

[52] *Economist*, "Norway's Election: Rich but Worried," September 17, 2009.
[53] GeoPolitics in the High North, "Danish Arctic Strategy," accessed July 20, 2016,
http://www.geopoliticsnorth.org/index.php?option=com_content&view=article&id=15
7:danish-preliminary-arctic-strategy&catid=40&Itemid=108.
[54] GeoPolitics in the High North, "Danish Arctic Strategy."

years.[55] However, Denmark has not made major investments in boosting its Arctic military presence, force posture, or force structure.[56] Despite claiming to value demonstrating sovereignty through presence, Denmark has been reluctant to invest in building more ice-capable warships and icebreakers. Since 2007, Denmark has received two Knud Rasmussen–class ice-strengthened offshore patrol vessels (OPVs), commissioned in February of 2008 and January of 2009. However, these ships were ordered before the shock and designed to replace existing obsolete ships. In 2010, Denmark was considering refurbishing three icebreakers and deploying them to Greenland but instead decided to retire them.[57] Since the shock, the only new ship that has been announced is a third Knud Rasmussen ice-hardened OPV.[58] The Danish parliament did not announce that it would purchase this ship until 2013, half a decade after the shock.[59] Although ships of the Knud Rasmussen class are more capable than the ships they replaced, the total number of ice-hardened ships Denmark can deploy to the Arctic has actually decreased.

Since 2007, the Danish government has made some modest investments in reorganizing its Arctic force structure and force posture.[60] In 2009, Denmark announced that it would create an Arctic military headquarters. However, it is unclear whether this represented a major shift in Denmark's total Arctic presence as the 2010–2014 National Defense Agreement that established the Arctic headquarters simultaneously closed the Greenland Command and Faroe Command. The Joint Arctic Command launched in October 2012 maintains personnel at Nuuk, Greenland, and in the Faroe Islands. The command is relatively small, hosting a few dozen soldiers and civilians. In 2009, the Danish government decided to create the Arctic Task Force to augment this command. However, rather than creating a new military unit, which the name implied, this only meant training existing units for emergency search-and-rescue operations.[61]

[55] Andreas Lindqvist, *Danish Defence Intelligence Service: Danger of Military Clashes in the Arctic*, BBC Monitoring International Reports (London: BBC, 2011).

[56] Nikolai Petersen, "The Arctic Challenge to Danish Foreign and Security Policy," in *Arctic Security in an Age of Climate Change* (New York: Cambridge University Press, 2011).

[57] Lasserre, Le Roy, and Garon, "Is There an Arms Race in the Arctic?," 44.

[58] Jon Rahbek-Clemmensen, "'Arctic-Vism' in Practice: The Challenges Facing Denmark's Political–Military Strategy in the High North," *Arctic Yearbook* 2014 (2014): 9.

[59] Siemon T. Wezeman, "Military Capabilities in the Arctic: A New Cold War in the High North?" SIPRI Background Paper (Stockholm: Stockholm International Peace Research Institute, 2016), http://www.css.ethz.ch/content/dam/ethz/special-interest/gess/cis/center-for-securities-studies/resources/docs/SIPRI%20Military-capabilities-in-the-Arctic.pdf.

[60] W. Rodgers, "War over the Arctic? Global Warming Skeptics Distract Us from Security Risks," *Christian Science Monitor*, March 2, 2010. See also Atland, "Interstate Relations in the Arctic," 156.

[61] Jon Rahbek-Clemmensen, "The Arctic Turn—How Did the High North Become a Foreign and Security Policy Priority for Denmark?" in *Greenland and the International Politics of a Changing Arctic: Postcolonial Paradiplomacy between High and Low Politics* (Abingdon: Routledge, 2017), 64.

Other than this relatively minor reorganization of its forces, Denmark has not built any new Arctic bases or made any major upgrades or refurbishments to existing bases since 2007. As of December 2016, according to the Danish government, only eighty Danish military personnel are stationed on the entire island of Greenland.[62] Moreover, there are reasons to doubt that these developments represent a substantial shift in the resources being dedicated to the Arctic. In September of 2013, the Danish state auditors issued a report criticizing the government for not providing adequate funding to enable the Danish Defense Forces to carry out fundamental defense and surveillance missions in the Arctic.[63]

However, it is important to note that after Russia's invasion of Crimea in 2014, Denmark began to make modest investments in upgrading its military capabilities. For example, in 2016 Denmark opted for the more expensive F-35 over a cheaper but less capable Swedish aircraft.[64] Denmark has also made minor investments in increasing its Arctic military presence. In 2016, Denmark's Arctic Defense Commission recommended an increase in spending for Arctic operations from 50 million Danish kroner (approximately US$7.8 million) a year to 120 million kroner a year (about US$18.5 million), which was later confirmed in the 2018–2023 defense agreement.[65] This increase in funding did not occur until nearly a decade after the shock and was a relatively small increase in the capabilities that Denmark will be able to project to the Arctic. Thirty-eight million kroner, or over one-third of this budget, will be used to deploy a single frigate to the Arctic during the summer.[66] Moreover, even after the increase, Arctic spending still represents less than 1% of Denmark's defense budget, which was approximately 22 billion kroner in 2018.[67] The 2018–2023 defense agreement reveals that Copenhagen has no plans to substantially upgrade its Arctic bases or other Arctic military capabilities in the next five years.[68]

---

[62] Danish Ministry of Defence, "Tasks in the Arctic and the North Atlantic," accessed August 6, 2017, http://www.fmn.dk/eng/allabout/Pages/TasksintheArcticandtheNorthernAtlantic.aspx.

[63] Gerard O'Dwyer, "Denmark Boosts Resources for Arctic Security," *Defense News*, October 8, 2013, http://archive.defensenews.com/article/20131008/DEFREG01/310080012/Denmark-Boosts-Resources-Arctic-Security.

[64] Danish Ministry of Defence, "Type Selection of Denmark's New Fighter Aircraft," n.d., accessed July 5, 2019, https://www.fmn.dk/temaer/kampfly/Documents/type-selection-denmarks-new-fighter-aircrafts-english-summary5.pdf.

[65] See Danish Ministry of Defence, *Forsvarsministeriets fremtidige opgaveløsning I Arktis* (The Ministry of Defence's future assignments in the Arctic), June 2016, pp. 19, http://www.fmn.dk/nyheder/Documents/arktis-analyse/forsvarsministeriets-fremtidige-opgaveloesning-i-arktis.pdf. See also Danish Ministry of Defence, Agreement for Danish Defence 2018–2023, accessed on June 12, 2018, https://www.fmn.dk/eng/allabout/Pages/danish-defence-agreement.aspx.

[66] See Danish Ministry of Defence. (MoD) in the Arctic, 19.

[67] Danish Ministry of Finance, Danish Finance Act of 2018, accessed June 26, 2018, pp. 7, https://www.fm.dk/publikationer/2018/finanslov-for-2018.

[68] Danish Ministry of Defence, Agreement for Danish Defence 2018–2023.

8.4.2 Denmark's Post-shock Arctic Military Activity

Denmark's Arctic military activity has not increased substantially since the shock. Just like before the shock, the Danes have used their navy to perform constabulary duties within their EEZ. Denmark does not maintain a separate coast guard; therefore, the Danish armed forces are in charge of duties normally reserved for the coast guard, such as inspecting commercial vessels.[69] For example, in 2010 Denmark deployed a warship to defend a drilling rig that had been boarded by Greenpeace protesters.[70] In general, Denmark's military activity in the region has been to protect its territorial sovereignty. It has not deployed forces in a provocative manner to back resource claims outside its EEZ.

Instead of using gunboat diplomacy, Denmark has led the way in seeking a cooperative and legalistic approach to disputes. In 2008, the Danish foreign minister initiated and held an Arctic Ocean Conference for the five Arctic littoral states. This conference resulted in the Ilulissat Declaration, in which each state pledged to uphold the use of international law enshrined in UNCLOS to settle their disputes.[71] Not all of these states have kept their pledges, as Denmark has. While they have all used UNCLOS to make claims to Arctic resources, some have also backed their claims with gunboat diplomacy by increasing their Arctic military presence and projecting power to disputed areas. Recall that my theory suggests that states will use both cooperative tools, such as claims through UNCLOS, and more coercive tools, such as projecting power to back their claims. However, the weaker a state's preference to secure control over resources, the less willing it should be to employ coercive tools, such as projecting power, because they are far costlier. As predicted by Rent-Addiction Theory, after the shock, Denmark has pursued its claims purely within the confines of international law. It has generally chosen not to deploy military forces to the areas that are or might be disputed. Denmark's claim to Hans Island remains unresolved, but neither Canada nor Denmark has projected power there since both agreed to stop deploying forces to the island in 2005.

Since the 2007 shock, rather than escalating the dispute over Hans Island, Denmark's focus has been on gathering data to submit a claim for a continental shelf extension. Since 2007, these claims have been complicated as climate change rapidly altered the Arctic environment. For example, in October of 2007, Arctic explorer Dennis Schmitt made a remarkable discovery when shifting ice packs revealed a small landmass off the northern coast of Greenland now named Stray Dog. If the CLCS rules that Stray Dog is an island, Denmark might be able to claim additional seabed and fishing rights north of Greenland.[72] Denmark has

---

[69] Rahbek-Clemmensen, "'Arctic-Vism' in Practice," 7.

[70] Uchenna Izundu, "The Race Is on for Greenland's Arctic Oilfields," *Sunday Telegraph*, September 26, 2010, http://search.proquest.com.libproxy1.usc.edu/docview/754922030?pq-origsite=summon&.

[71] Peterson, "Arctic as a New Arena."

[72] Ebinger and Zambetakis, "Geopolitics of Arctic Melt," 1230.

spent most of the decade after the shock carefully mapping the five areas off the coast of Greenland and several areas around the Faroe Islands, for which it could submit ECS claims. A map of Denmark's claims vis-à-vis other states' can be seen in Figure 8.8.

Denmark made partial submissions to the CLCS in June 2012 to extend its continental shelf by approximately 44,000 square miles in the area south of Greenland. Part of this claim overlaps with Iceland's submission from 2009 and Canada's partial submission from 2013.[73] In November 2013, Denmark submitted another ECS claim for an area northwest of Greenland, of approximately 24,000 square miles. This claim partially overlaps with Norway's submission from 2006. Finally, as mentioned in the introduction, in 2014 Denmark submitted an ECS claim to approximately 455,000 square miles north of Greenland. This claim includes the North Pole, overlaps with Russia's submission from 2015, and is expected to overlap with Canada's claim once it is submitted. Denmark's claims thus have the potential to increase tensions with both Russia and Canada.[74] However, as predicted by my theory, Denmark has not backed its claims by projecting power to these areas or substantially increasing its Arctic military presence

In sum, since the shock, Denmark has chosen to pursue its claims cooperatively within the confines of international law, without projecting force to support its position. As predicted by my theory, there was only a small increase in Copenhagen's willingness to invest in projecting power to the Arctic. Its Arctic foreign policy behavior is generally consistent with my theoretical predictions across a range of indicators that capture its behavior. Denmark has approached its Arctic interests in a cooperative manner and has handled its disputes through formal international legal challenges, without projecting force. Also, Denmark has not significantly boosted its Arctic military presence or force structure. Denmark has made relatively modest investments in maintaining and modernizing its existing forces, but it has not made a major investment in increasing its Arctic military capabilities. As Danish Arctic expert John Rahbek-Clemmensen has concluded, "Most of Denmark's defence investment in the Arctic has been directed towards boosting its military's ability to conduct coast guard activities—search and rescue, surveillance, environmental protection—rather than actual warfighting capabilities."[75]

[73] Ministry of Foreign Affairs of Denmark, "Greenland and Denmark Present Claims Relating to the Continental Shelf to the United Nations in New York," n.d., accessed July 5, 2019, http://um.dk/en/news/newsdisplaypage/?newsid=3a2bd941-d477-4df9-8ad7-ef6f15ae9ec8.

[74] Rahbek-Clemmensen, "Carving up the Arctic," 327.

[75] Levon Sevunts, "Denmark's New Defence Agreement Renews Focus on Protecting the Baltic," Eye on the Arctic, October 16, 2017, https://www.rcinet.ca/eye-on-the-arctic/2017/10/16/denmarks-new-defence-agreement-renews-focus-on-protecting-the-baltic/.

Maritime jurisdiction and boundaries in the Arctic region

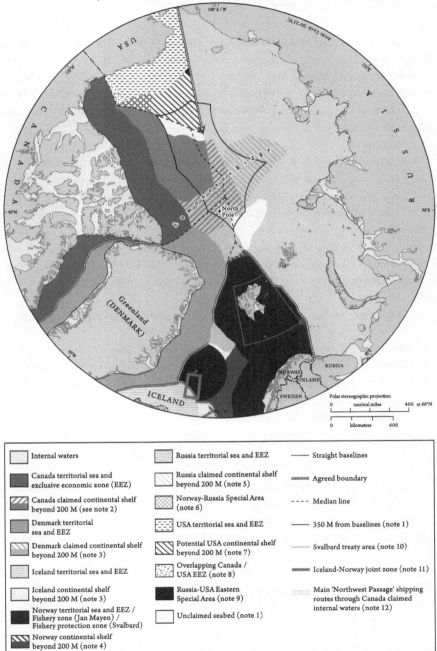

Figure 8.8 Map of Arctic Claims

Source: Special thanks to IBRU, Durham University for allowing use of this map. Note that the full color version on the website, see https://www.dur.ac.uk/resources/ibru/resources/Arcticmap2019/IBRUArcticmapJune2019.pdf.

8.5 Norway's Response to the Shock

If my theory is correct, we should see several things. First, Norway's leaders and officials should express a strong interest in developing Arctic resources. Second, Norwegian leaders should make strong commitments to defending their claims to Arctic resources. Third, they should back those commitments by making larger investments in increasing their Arctic military presence than production-oriented states with a similar economic capacity, like Denmark. As we shall see, this is exactly what we observe.

At the time of the shock, Norway was governed by a Labor Party–led coalition with Jens Stoltenberg as prime minister (from 2005 to 2013). Formerly minister of the oil and gas industry, Stoltenberg viewed resources as a "blessing," not a curse,[76] and emphasized the importance of developing natural resources, especially in the Arctic.[77] Norway has a major economic interest in protecting its offshore Arctic EEZ due to its reliance on offshore energy resources and fisheries. The Norwegian Petroleum Directorate estimates that nearly 30% of the Arctic's undiscovered resources lie in the Barents Sea, where Russia and Norway have ongoing disputes.[78]

In 2008, Oslo released the Norwegian Defence and Security Policy, asserting

> The northern regions are Norway's prime area for strategic investment. Norway's position as a significant energy exporter and as a country responsible for the administration of important natural resources extending over large sea areas, has an important bearing on security policy. We must be able to uphold our sovereignty and our sovereign rights, and to exercise authority in a proper way in areas under Norwegian jurisdiction.[79]

Although Norway always had interests in the Arctic, the region has become a much greater strategic priority since the shock. Norway responded to the shock by making a much larger investment in projecting power to the Arctic than Denmark, Canada, or the United States. Oslo increased its Arctic military presence in disputed areas and shifted the entire focus of its military to prioritize the Arctic. In 2009, the

[76] Phillip Inman, "Norway's Sovereign Wealth Fund 'Is Example for Oil-Rich Nations,'" *The Guardian*, September 30, 2013, https://www.theguardian.com/business/2013/sep/30/norway-oil-sovereign-wealth-fund.

[77] Konstantin Rozhnov, "Norway and Russia 'Open up for Business' in the Barents Sea," BBC News, September 15, 2010, http://www.bbc.co.uk/news/business-11299024.

[78] Norwegian Petroleum Directorate, *Undiscovered Resources*, n.d., http://www.npd.no/en/Publications/Resource-Reports/2011/Chapter-2/.

[79] Norwegian Ministry of Defence, *Norwegian Defence 2008* (Oslo: Norwegian Ministry of Defence, 2008), https://www.regjeringen.no/globalassets/upload/fd/dokumenter/fakta2008_eng.pdf.

Norwegian government released an update to its 2006 High North strategy, entitled *New Building Blocks in the North* and, in 2011, unveiled an Arctic white paper called *The High North: Visions and Strategies*.[80] Both of these documents note the importance of Norway maintaining a military presence in its High Northern territory and EEZ. Additionally, in September 2009, the new strategic concept for the Norwegian Armed Forces was published under the title *Capable Force*. It strongly prioritized the Arctic and explicitly mentioned securing maritime resource areas and offshore oil and gas installations.[81] Norwegian defense officials have stressed that these documents guide the development of their Arctic capabilities. Grete Faremo, Norwegian defense minister from 2009 to 2011, remarked, "We are developing a series of new military capabilities and upgrading others, not least those which are of particular importance in safeguarding our interests in the northern areas. There is thus a close linkage between the Government's Northern Area strategy and the development of the Armed Forces."[82]

These developments have coincided with increased interest and investments in developing Arctic offshore resources. The Norwegian government granted exploration licenses for forty-three blocks of seabed territory in Norwegian territory and fifty-one blocks in the Barents Sea in 2011.[83] In October 2013, Foreign Minister Børge Brendes gave a speech at the University of Tromsø, proudly asserting that, "The petroleum industry has made major discoveries in the north in recent years, and there is more drilling activity in the Barents Sea than ever before." He also noted that "Norway has valuable mineral resources that are estimated to be worth around 1400 billion kroner, and most of these are in the north."[84]

According to interviews I conducted with Norwegian academics and government officials, the Arctic will be Norway's primary security and foreign policy concern for years to come. My interviews with officials suggest that the government's primary objective in the Arctic is maintaining peace and stability, especially in

---

[80] Norweigan Ministry of Foreign Affairs. *New Building Blocks in the North*. 2006. https://www.regjeringen.no/globalassets/upload/ud/vedlegg/nordomradene/new_building_blocks_in_the_north.pdf.

Norweigan Ministry of Foreign Affairs. *The High North: Visions and Strategies*. 2011. https://www.regjeringen.no/globalassets/upload/ud/vedlegg/nordomradene/ud_nordomrodene_en_web.pdf. Huebert et al., *Climate Change and International Security*, 7.

[81] Norwegian Ministry of Defence, *Capable Force: Strategic Concept for the Norwegian Armed Forces* (Oslo: Norwegian Ministry of Defence, 2009), 49–50, accessed August 6, 2017, https://www.regjeringen.no/globalassets/upload/FD/Dokumenter/Capable-force_strategic-concept.pdf.

[82] Quoted in Andreas Osthagen, "Coastguards in Peril: A Study of Arctic Defense Collaboration," *Defense Studies* 15, no. 2 (2015): 5–6, http://dx.doi.org/10.1080/14702436.2015.1035949.

[83] Keil, "The Arctic," 175.

[84] Børge Brendes, "An Active High North Policy – Growth and Innovation in the North," University of Tromsø, October 28, 2013.

relation to issues of jurisdiction and maritime boundaries.[85] Although the government publicly sought to project a cooperative disposition about the region and its claims, officials have also expressed concerns about threats to Norway's offshore resource claims.

As a small state that has disputes with a much more powerful neighbor, Norway faced a strategic trade-off of whether to accommodate Russia by acceding to its demands or to invest in the capabilities to deter Russia at the risk of antagonizing it. Not wanting to give up its resource claims, Oslo has generally opted for the latter strategy. Thus, on the one hand, Norway has pursued a cordial and cooperative relationship with Russia, offering to partner with Russia in the development of offshore energy reserves and holding joint military exercises. On the other hand, Norway has also assertively maintained its claims and refused to accommodate Russian demands to develop resources in the Svalbard Fishery Protection Zone or to back down with regard to overlapping EEZ claims in the Barents Sea.

Oslo has opted to increase its coercive leverage in the Arctic by pursuing a two-pronged strategy. First, it has invested in the capability to maintain a presence in the disputed areas that it considers under its jurisdiction. Second, it has sought to boost its cooperation with NATO and increase NATO member states' Arctic presence, while improving its own ability to operate in the Arctic. Norway has pursued this objective by hosting a set of large-scale Arctic war games and exercises called Operation Cold Response, eliciting the participation of NATO states.[86] These operations involve tens of thousands of troops, aircraft, and ships from over a dozen states. They improve the ability of NATO states to operate together in the Arctic, while also sending a message to Russia.

8.5.1 Norway's Post-shock Arctic Force Structure

As part of the first prong of this strategy, Norway has made significant investments in its Arctic force structure. Whereas Denmark took years to build a small Arctic command center below the Arctic Circle, Norway announced in 2008 that it would move its Joint Military Headquarters for its entire armed forces north, above the Arctic Circle. Norway is the only state to have moved its headquarters to the Arctic, signaling its prioritization of the region.[87] Oslo made a substantial investment in these new headquarters by upgrading a Cold War–era base located inside

[85] Rolf Einar Fife, interview by author, June 28, 2013; Levi Lunde, interview by author, June 28, 2013.

[86] Huebert et al., *Climate Change and International Security*, 31.

[87] Tammes, "Arctic Security and Norway," 59.

a mountain and designed to withstand a nuclear attack. Deep inside the base, past the blastproof doors and long underground tunnels, the Norwegian military has installed state-of-the-art equipment that allows it to monitor foreign military activity in the Arctic and coordinate and command Norwegian forces.[88] In August of 2009, the minister of defense, Anne-Grete Strøm-Erichsen, officially opened the base with a speech that explicitly mentioned the role of climate change in the competition for Arctic resources: "It is in the High North that we can see increased competition for strategic resources . . . [and] we have unsettled boundary issues. . . . Global climate change will make the extraction and transport of energy in the Arctic an even more central issue in the future."[89]

In 2010, the Norwegian Coast Guard also moved its headquarters, to Sortland, far above the Arctic Circle. This move entailed relocating the entire coast guard staff, command, and logistical support system. The Norwegian Coast Guard is in charge of patrolling Norway's massive EEZ, including its disputed zone; and shifting the headquarters north is consistent with Norway's enhanced interest in patrolling its Arctic waters. Moving the base to the Arctic allowed ships to spend more time patrolling the Arctic and less time transitioning to and from their home base.

In addition to upgrading these two bases so that they could serve as the headquarters for the Norwegian military and coast guard, Oslo invested in upgrading four other bases. Table 8.7 describes the six bases that received upgrades or substantial investments. In 2010, Oslo invested approximately US$7.8 million in building a new kitchen, mess hall, and barracks at the Sør-Varanger garrison.[90] An additional US$28 million was invested in consolidating six border stations into two much larger facilities.[91] In 2012, Norway spent approximately $116 million on a major renovation to the base facilities at Setermoen Garrison, Norway's largest garrison, housing approximately 1,500 soldiers.[92] In addition, in 2016 a new 200-person Ranger company was added to the garrison at Sør-Varanger.[93]

---

[88] BBC News, "Inside Norway's Underground Military HQ," September 22, 2010, http://www.bbc.com/news/av/world-europe-11386699/inside-norway-s-underground-military-hq.

[89] Quoted in Colonel Jon M. Mangersnes, *The Role of the National Joint Headquarters of Norway* (Carlisle, PA: US Army War College, 2012), 1.

[90] Trude Pettersen, "New Garrison for the Norwegian Border Guards," *Barents Observer*, October 19, 2009, https://barentsobserver.com/en/topics/new-garrison-norwegian-border-guards.

[91] Pettersen, "New Garrison for the Norwegian Border Guards."

[92] Memim Encyclopedia, s.v. "setermoen," accessed June 2, 2018, https://memim.com/setermoen.html.

[93] Thomas Nilsen, "Norway Creates New Army Unit on Border to Russia," *Independent Barents Observer*, June 17, 2016, https://thebarentsobserver.com/en/security/2016/06/norway-creates-new-army-unit-border-russia.

Table 8.7 **Norwegian Arctic Base Upgrades and Investments[a]**

Base Name	Base Upgrade/Investment Details
Norwegian Joint Headquarters	Upgraded to host Joint Headquarters for Norwegian Military
Sortland Naval Base/ Kystvaktskvadron Nord	Upgrade to host Headquarters for Coast Guard
Garrison of Sør-Varanger	Upgraded base infrastructure (barracks, kitchen, and mess hall)
Setermoen Garrison	Major infrastructure upgrades for base that hosts 1,500 troops
Evenes	Upgraded facilities to host F-35 joint strike fighter and P-8 maritime patrol aircraft NASAM II medium and long-range air defense system
Bardufoss Air Station	Upgraded facilities to house 250 full-time employees and operate fourteen NH90 helicopters.

[a]Note sources on base upgrades can be found in Arctic Bases Data Set and in the Arctic Base Details Document located in the online supplementary materials.

Norway has also invested in increasing its ability to project air power into the Arctic. In 2012 major renovations were approved to upgrade the facilities at Evenes airbase.[94] In 2014 Norway approved $30 million to upgrade the facilities at Bardufoss Air Station to house 250 full-time staff and operate fourteen NH-90 helicopters. This was part of Oslo's plan to move its air power closer to the Arctic. Norway closed Bodø, its main Arctic air base, and instead stationed some of its F-35s at Evenes airbase, which is even farther north, close to Harstad.[95] Toward this end, Norway invested in substantial upgrades to the facilities at Evenes to allow it to support up to fifteen aircraft simultaneously.[96] Oslo also announced plans in 2016 to upgrade the facilities at Evenes to accommodate NASAMS II

[94] Anders Horne, "Skal rustes for 15 fly," Fremover, June 28, 2012, https://www.fremover.no/lokale_nyheter/article6127882.ece?ns_campaign=article&ns_mchannel=recommend_button&ns_source=facebook&ns_linkname=facebook&ns_fee=0.

[95] News in English, "Fighter Jet Base Landed at Ørland," March 2, 2012, http://www.newsinenglish.no/2012/03/02/fighter-jet-base-landed-at-orland/.

[96] Horne, "Skal rustes for 15 fly."

medium- and long-range air defense missile systems as well as the P-8 maritime patrol aircraft.[97] These P-8s will replace the older P-3s that are currently being used to patrol Norway's Arctic EEZ. Evenes is much closer to Svalbard and the Barents Sea, where Norway has a major stake in maintaining a military presence to protect its offshore resources.

Norway also invested heavily in its Arctic-specific and dual-use capabilities that enhance its capacity to project power to the Arctic. In 2008, the government ordered the F-35 Joint Strike Fighter, which, at US$133.6 million each, is a major investment in cutting-edge, high-intensity warfare capabilities.[98] Wikileaks cables reveal that Oslo chose the F-35 over the less expensive Swedish Gripin because of its ability to operate in the Arctic.[99] In 2009 Norway restructured its land forces to increase the number of soldiers in the winter-trained Brigade Nord, making it by far the largest unit in the Norwegian Army. This Arctic battalion is stationed in the Arctic and equipped with snowmobiles and other specialized equipment which allow it to patrol Norway's vast Arctic wilderness.[100]

The Norwegian government made these investments while continuing to fund the construction and commissioning of five Fridtjof Nansen–class frigates armed with state-of-the-art Aegis weapons systems, which at the time was the most expensive defense program in Norwegian history. These larger ships, commissioned between 2006 and 2011, can project power at great distances, allowing Oslo to maintain a surface presence in the Arctic. Although the ships were ordered before the shock, the government chose not only to continue funding these programs but to invest further in upgrading Norway's Arctic capabilities. Recall from Chapter 4 that Norway's willingness to follow through on such commitments stands in stark contrast to other Arctic nations, such as Canada. Ottawa announced plans to build six to eight icebreakers before the shock but did not follow through on this commitment, repeatedly delaying funding and the start of construction.

Norway's Aegis frigates are substantially more capable than the ships they are replacing. Concurrently, in the summer of 2007 Norway ordered the RV *Kronprins Haakon*, a 9,000-ton icebreaker capable of breaking 1-meter-thick ice. This ship was

---

[97] Norwegian Ministry of Defence, *Capable and Sustainable: Long Term Defence Plan* (Oslo: Norwegian Ministry of Defence, 2016), https://www.regjeringen.no/globalassets/departementene/fd/dokumenter/rapporter-og-regelverk/capable-and-sustainable-ltp-english-brochure.pdf.

[98] Andrew Chuter, "Norway F-35 Deliveries to Begin in 2017," *Defense News*, April 23, 2013, http://www.defensenews.com/article/20130426/DEFREG01/304260023/Norway-F-35-Deliveries-Begin-2017; Bob Cox, "Defense Department Says F-35 Fighter Program's Costs to Signficantly Rise," Fort Worth Star-Telegram, April 7, 2010.

[99] Wikileaks, "U.S. Force Reductions in Europe: View from Norway," September 15, 2009, https://search.wikileaks.org/plusd/cables/09OSLO564_a.html.

[100] Trude Pettersen, "Norway Establishes 'Arctic Battalion,'" *Barents Observer*, March 29, 2012, http://barentsobserver.com/en/topics/norway-establishes-arctic-battalion.

commissioned in February 2017, adding a second icebreaker to Norway's fleet, which already included the *Svalbard*, an armed icebreaker that is the largest ship in the Norwegian fleet, specially designed to patrol the waters around its namesake islands. In sum, in comparison to Denmark—which now has fewer ice-capable ships than at the time of the shock and no dedicated icebreakers capable of operating in the Arctic—Norway now has nine ice-hardened patrol ships and two icebreakers, for a total of eleven ice-capable ships, more than double the number it had at the time of the shock.

Moreover, following Russia's recent more assertive behavior in both Crimea and the Arctic, Norway has invested more in dual-use capabilities that will enhance its ability to defend its Arctic claims. As Bård Vegard Solhjell, a member of Parliament who sits on the Standing Committee on Foreign Affairs and Defense, remarked in August of 2017, "given all that is happening in the region, Norway needs to have the strongest defense that it can afford."[101] As part of this effort, Norway has invested in new, more capable submarines to replace the aging Ula class. In the words of then–minister of defense Eriksen Søreide, "Submarines are amongst the Norwegian Armed Forces' most important capabilities and [are]of great significance for our ability to protect Norway's maritime interests."[102] Chief among these maritime interests are Norway's offshore resource claims, which have been increasingly challenged by Russia since the shock. As we shall see in the following section, Norway has stood its ground about these claims and has projected power to the areas under dispute.

8.5.2 Norway's Post-shock Arctic Military Activity

Before the shock, Norway's level of Arctic military activity was relatively low. The Norwegian Coast Guard regularly patrolled Norway's EEZ in the Barents Sea and the Fishery Protection Zone. Norway's claim to the exclusive right to develop resources around Svalbard has long been contested by Russia. Although there have been a number of incidents both before and after the shock involving Norwegian efforts to prevent Russian fishing in the waters around Svalbard, it seems likely that these disputes over the Fishery Protection Zone are driven by conflicting claims to the rights to develop seabed resources. Some senior Russian officials have admitted as much, saying, "The real reason for

---

[101] *Defense News*, "Eying Russia, Norway Pumps Prior Savings into Its Defense Budget," August 8, 2017, https://www.defensenews.com/global/2017/02/03/eying-russia-norway-pumps-prior-savings-into-its-defense-budget/.

[102] Thomas Nilsen, "Norway Teams up with Germany for New Submarines," *Independent Barents Observer*, February 3, 2017, https://thebarentsobserver.com/en/security/2017/02/norway-teams-germany-new-submarines.

the arguments is the oil rather than fish."[103] Russia strongly contests Norway's claim, which would limit Russia's ability to develop the area's resources and allow Oslo to extract most of the income. As Russian legal expert Alexander Oreshenkov has written,

> If a deposit beginning within the limits of the archipelago's territory extends beyond its territorial waters, the Russian companies working on Svalbard will be expected (in violation of the Svalbard Treaty) to observe the norms of Norway's continental mainland petroleum legislation in the sea areas adjacent to the archipelago. This means that 78% of their earnings from the hydrocarbons produced outside Norway's territorial waters will go away in tax payments to the Norwegian treasury.[104]

Russia has gone so far as to deploy ships to explore for oil and gas in the waters around Svalbard.[105]

Norway has been careful not to provoke Russia, by only leniently enforcing its ban on energy exploration in the Fishery Protection Zone; but it has refused to relinquish these claims despite their dubious international legal standing and increasing pressure from Russia. Instead, Norway has sought to secure control over these seabed resources and deter Russia by projecting power to the waters around Svalbard.

Since the shock, Norway has increased its patrols around Svalbard and its military presence in the Barents Sea. My interviews with Norwegian journalists revealed that, since the shock, Norway has begun to deploy not just lightly armed coast guard vessels but also heavily armed Aegis frigates to the waters around Svalbard.[106] According to the same reporters, Norway has been careful not to broadcast these deployments in order to avoid antagonizing Russia, but they are occasionally captured by local media, such as when Norway deployed KNM *Thor Heyerdahl*—Norway's newest warship—in the waters around Svalbard.[107]

---

[103] Lennart Simonsson and Nick Allen, "Russia and Norway Wrestle over Barents Sea," June 14, 2006, http://www.lngplants.com/TurkistanGasNewsletterJune152006.html. Also cited in Perry and Andersen, *New Strategic Dynamics in the Arctic Region*, 44.

[104] Alexander Oreshenkov, "Arctic Square of Opportunities," *Russia in Global Affairs* (December 25, 2010), http://eng.globalaffairs.ru/number/Arctic-Square-of-Opportunities-15085.

[105] Perry and Andersen, *New Strategic Dynamics in the Arctic Region*.

[106] Thomas Nilsen, personal interview, October 7, 2016.

[107] Trude Pettersen, "Norway Sends Warship to Svalbard," *Barents Observer*, November 15, 2012b, accessed August 14, 2013, http://barentsobserver.com/en/security/norway-sends-warship-svalbard-15-11

Svalbard is located nearly 1,200 miles from Norway's main naval base. To over-
come the tyranny of distance and enhance its situational awareness, Oslo has
invested in the logistical and intelligence capabilities needed to project power to
the disputed waters around Svalbard. For example, in 2010, Norway ordered a
highly advanced spy ship for the explicit purpose of monitoring developments in
the Barents Sea. This ship cost approximately US$188 million, making it one of the
most expensive military purchases in Norwegian history, and more than doubled
Norway's capabilities.[108] In 2013, Norway ordered its first ever combat support
ship, which significantly improved the range of its newly acquired Aegis frigates by
increasing the time they can spend on patrol.[109] This was followed in 2014 by a decision to acquire three or four A330 tanker aircraft, which will allow Norway's F-16s
and F-35s to patrol farther from its shores.[110]

The Spitsbergen Treaty prohibits any state from maintaining military forces on
the island. However, Norway has focused on increasing its presence in Svalbard
with dual-use assets that are ostensibly for search-and-rescue operations and fishery
patrols but could also have military applications. For example, Norway's decision to
base Super Puma helicopters on Svalbard both boosts its ability to maintain maritime domain awareness in the region and helps establish presence there.[111] A map
of the Svalbard Fishery Protection Zone and Norway's other claims can be seen in
Figure 8.9.

The evidence suggests that Norway's choice to increase its Arctic military presence in disputed areas is calculated and driven by its concern over potential Russian
incursions. Norwegian Coast Guard commodore Geir Osen, who was charged with
patrolling Svalbard's waters, warned that competition over Svalbard's resources is
"a potential source of conflict."[112] Olsen further stressed that "the situation can become particularly difficult" from the Norwegian standpoint if it were to involve "a
Russian company enjoying passive support from the Russian government. How
should Norwegian authorities deal with such a situation? Should one only protest
or use military force?"[113]

Norwegian officials were not alone in their assessment of the potential for conflict in the region. In 2008, the European Union's top two foreign policy officials,
Javier Solana and Benita Ferrero-Waldner, issued a special report to the European

---

[108] Pettersen, "Norway Sends Warship to Svalbard."

[109] Wezeman, "Military Capabilities in the Arctic."

[110] Wezeman, "Military Capabilities in the Arctic," 11.

[111] Trude Pettersen, "New Helicopters Give Better Preparedness in the Arctic," *Barents Observer*,
December 11, 2012, http://barentsobserver.com/en/arctic/2012/12/new-helicopters-give-better-
preparedness-arctic-11-12.

[112] Torbjørn Pedersen, "The Constrained Politics of the Svalbard Offshore Area," *Marine Policy* 32,
no. 6 (2008): 916, https://doi.org/10.1016/j.marpol.2008.01.006.

[113] Pedersen, "Constrained Politics of the Svalbard Offshore Area."

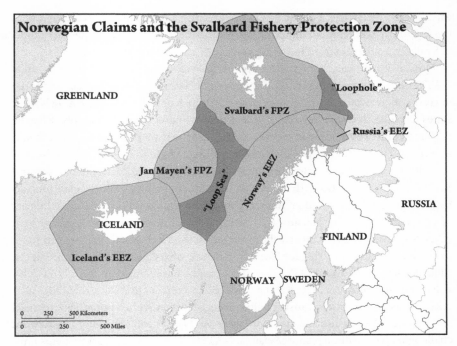

Figure 8.9 Maps of Norwegian Claims and the Svalbard Fishery Protection Zone
Source: Special thanks to Áslaug Ásgeirsdóttir and Mathieu Duval for permission to use this map which was originally published in Aslaug Asgeirsdottir, "Who Gets What?: Domestic Influences on International Negotiations Allocating Shared Resources" (SUNY Press, 2009).

Union on climate change and international security in which they warned that "a serious conflict could emerge between Russia and Norway" over the "large deposits of gas and oil that are currently locked under a frozen continental shelf around the islands of Svalbard."[114] Additionally, a WikiLeaks cable written by a US diplomat stationed at the embassy in Oslo mentions that their Norwegian counterparts were "increasingly aware that Russia is willing to at least consider force as a legitimate tool of international politics. A few recognize that Russia could take a step short of force (e.g. sending an oil rig to Svalbard) to provoke."[115] The cable goes on to say that Norwegian foreign minister Jonas Gahr Støre had publicly claimed that Svalbard

---

[114] Quoted in Perry and Andersen, *New Strategic Dynamics in the Arctic Region*, 45. For more on the report, see Ian Traynor, "Climate Change May Spark Conflict with Russia, EU Told," *The Guardian*, March 10, 2008, http://www.theguardian.com/world/2008/mar/10/eu.climatechange.

[115] Wikileaks, "Norway, Russia and Georgia; Opportunity to Strengthen Ties to Norway," Public Library of US Diplomacy, September 16, 2008, https://search.wikileaks.org/plusd/cables/08OSLO513_a.html.

was covered by Article 5 of the NATO treaty. The US diplomat specifically noted the risk of Russia's gunboat diplomacy in Svalbard, writing, "The unique legal status of Svalbard could provide a tempting place for Russia to flex its muscles."[116]

Norway's assertion that Article 5 applies to Svalbard is part of its effort to enlist NATO's help in protecting its offshore resource claims. While a Russian territorial invasion of Norway would certainly trigger Article 5 of the treaty, obligating NATO states to come to Oslo's defense, it is less clear whether this would apply if Russia declared control over some of Norway's EEZ and the resources that lie beneath it. It is even less clear whether NATO would be willing to fight to defend Norway's claim to exclusive rights to develop resources in the Fishery Protection Zone around Svalbard. My interviews with American officials suggest that Norwegian officials have sought to clarify whether Norway's maritime claims are considered to be part of its territory.[117] In an allusion to Norway's Arctic maritime claims, Norwegian officials have expressed concern about threats in the High North that are too small to involve NATO but too big for Norway to handle on its own.[118] While some states, such as Russia and even NATO member Canada, have sought to limit NATO involvement in the Arctic, Norway has worked to enhance NATO's role. NATO is critical to Norway both because it helps protect Norway from a potential territorial invasion from Russia and because Norway hopes NATO will help deter Russia from challenging its maritime resource claims. NATO's protection of Norway helps limit how much Russia can coerce Norway in any negotiation.

Norway's efforts to increase NATO's engagement in the Arctic represent the second prong of its strategy to secure its offshore resource claims. While Norway has long focused on training its forces to operate in the Arctic and encouraging NATO involvement in its Arctic exercises, these exercises have become larger and more frequent since the shock. For example, in the decade prior to the shock, Norway hosted Operation Cold Response only once, in 2006. However, since the shock, it has hosted Operation Cold Response five times, in 2007, 2010, 2012, 2014, and 2016.[119] These operations have also grown larger, going from 8,500 troops to 16,000 troops from over a dozen NATO-allied nations.[120] Since 2013 Norway has also joined Sweden and Finland in cohosting a number of NATO

---

[116] Wikileaks, "Norway, Russia and Georgia."

[117] Interview on background with senior American official, January 2015.

[118] See Justyna Gotkowska, *Norway and the Bear: Norwegian Defence Policy—Lessons for the Baltic Sea Region* (Warsaw, Poland: Center for Eastern Studies), 20.

[119] Terry Macalister, "US and Russia Stir up Political Tensions over Arctic," *The Guardian*, July 6, 2011.

[120] For information on these operations, see Norwegian Armed Forces, "Exercise Cold Response 2016," updated March 4th, 2016, https://forsvaret.no/en/ForsvaretDocuments/Information%20 Folder.pdf; The Royal House of Norway, "Cold response 2007," https://www.royalcourt.no/nyhet. html?tid=31115&sek=27262;

countries for Arctic Challenge, a set of Arctic military exercises designed to improve interoperability.[121]

By hosting joint military exercises, Norway ensures that Russia sees the forces of NATO member states preparing to fight in the Arctic on Norwegian territory and in Norwegian waters. Norway has signaled both its own willingness and that of its allies to fight to protect its offshore maritime resource claims by engaging in joint exercises designed to deal with such scenarios. For example, in 2009, as part of Operation Cold Response, Norway engaged in war-gaming exercises in which "the large non-democratic state 'Nordland' has declared its rights to an oil deposit located in the territorial waters of the small democratic state 'Midland.' However, the entry of Midland's allies into the war leads to victory."[122] The authors of the war game, who were from the Norwegian Defense Ministry, revealed that the war games were practice for possible conflict in the area around Svalbard as well as other areas where conflict might arise.[123]

Norway's efforts to boost its Arctic power projection ability are tightly connected to its efforts to engage NATO. Conversation with Norwegian defense experts at the Peace Research Institute at Oslo revealed that part of Oslo's motivation for acquiring capabilities is not to defeat Russian forces at sea but rather to project enough power to assert its interests and deny Russia the ability to create a fait accompli without engaging Norwegian forces. Any threatening action by Russia toward Norway would put Moscow in the position of engaging Norwegian forces, which would risk making the dispute large enough to involve NATO. Thus, Norway's ability to project power to back its Arctic claims may deter Russia even if Moscow knows it could quickly send Norway's frigates and patrol ships to the bottom of the Barents Sea.

In sum, Norway has maintained expansive claims over Arctic resources and, since the shock, has made major investments in projecting power to uphold them. Norway's expansive claims are dubious under international law and have been challenged by some NATO member states, such as Britain.[124] Its Fishery Protection

Trude Pettersen, "Cold 'Cold Response'," *Barents Observer*, February 24th, 2010, http://barentsobserver. com/en/sections/topics/cold-cold-response?qt-popular_content=0; NATOSource, "Sixteen Nations Participating in Norway's Cold Response Military Exercise This Week," *Atlantic Council*, March 10th, 2014, http://www.atlanticcouncil.org/blogs/natosource/sixteen-nations-participating-in-norway-s-cold-response-military-exercise-this-week. All accessed June 13, 2018.

[121] Abby L. Finkel, "Arctic Challenge Exercise Aims to Increase Interoperability," US Department of Defense, May 24, 2017.

[122] Sergunin and Konyshev, *Russia in the Arctic*, 111.

[123] Sergunin and Konyshev, *Russia in the Arctic*, 111.

[124] Ole Andreas Lindemann, "Norwegian Foreign Policy in the High North. International Cooperation and the Relations to Russia," *Forsvaret*, 2009, https://brage.bibsys.no/xmlui/handle/11250/99637.

Zone around Svalbard is well beyond 200 nautical miles from Norway's shores and thus beyond any EEZ that it could claim from its territory. Svalbard is technically administrated by Norway, but Norway does not have exclusive rights to develop its resources but must share them with more than forty other countries that signed the Spitsbergen Treaty of 1920.[125] It is thus far from clear whether Norway has the exclusive right to develop seabed resources in the 200 nautical miles surrounding Svalbard.[126] Yet Norway has maintained its claims even though it may be damaging its reputation as a state that upholds and adheres to international law.

Perhaps more informative is that Norway has been willing to endure increasing pressure from Russia and accept a greater risk of conflict rather than relinquish its resource claims. As we saw in Chapter 5, Norway was unwilling to back down in its EEZ disputes with Russia over the Barents Sea, even as Moscow increased its efforts to intimidate Norway via gunboat diplomacy. The dispute was finally settled in 2010, but Russia was unable to get Norway to back down from its long-standing demand that the two countries split the difference between their claims.[127] Rather than backing down, Norway invested in projecting power capabilities to defend its resource claims. These capabilities have allowed the military to engage in what Norwegian defense planners call "threshold defense." This refers to Norway's ability to independently defend its interests over issues that are below the threshold that would trigger NATO's Article 5, such as its offshore resource claims and in partic-ular its legally dubious claims around Svalbard.[128] These actions are evidence of the strength of Norway's preference to secure its resource claims and provide strong support for my theoretical predictions.

8.6 Addressing Counterarguments

Before concluding, I will briefly deal with the most prominent counterarguments to my analysis. A critic might argue that Norway invests more in projecting power to the Arctic than Denmark not because it has a stronger preference to secure resources but because it has a larger percentage of its population living above the Arctic Circle.

---

[125] Lindemann, "Norwegian Foreign Policy in the High North." See also Robin Churchill and Geir Ulfstein, "The Disputed Maritime Zones around Svalbard," in *Changes in the Arctic Environment and the Law of the Sea*, ed. Myron Nordquist, John Norton Moore, and Tomas H. Heider (Leiden, The Netherlands: Brill, 2010), 551–93.

[126] For an in-depth discussion of this issue of Svalbard's legality, see Lindemann, "Norwegian Foreign Policy in the High North." See also Churchill and Ulfstein, "Disputed Maritime Zones around Svalbard."

[127] James Kraska, ed., *Arctic Security in an Age of Climate Change* (New York: Cambridge University Press, 2011), 61.

[128] Jokela, *Arctic Security Matters*, 62. See also Pezard et al., *Maintaining Arctic Cooperation with Russia*, 55–57.

This might explain why Norway was more interested in and committed to the Arctic than Denmark before the shock, but it cannot explain the change in Norway's investment in the region after the shock. This is because the number of Norwegians living above the Arctic Circle did not change much, but Norway's investment increased substantially.

Perhaps Norway invests more in projecting power to the Arctic because it shares a border with Russia, while Denmark does not. Once again, the shared border is a constant and explains why Oslo had a higher baseline investment than Denmark. But it cannot explain the differences between the two states' levels of investment after the shock (i.e., why Norway's investment increased so much more than Denmark's). However, as Chapters 4 and 5 demonstrated, Russia invested much more in projecting power to the Arctic after the shock. Thus, a critic might suggest that the shared border, combined with Russia's newly assertive Arctic foreign policy, drove Norway to enhance its Arctic military presence to defend against an overland territorial invasion rather than to deter threats to its maritime resources. There are two reasons to doubt this alternative explanation.

First, if a more assertive Russian Arctic foreign policy is threatening to Arctic states that have a border with Russia, we should also observe other small Nordic states that share a border with Russia increasing their Arctic military presence right after the shock. Here, comparing Norway to Sweden and Finland is particularly informative. Sweden and Finland are both Nordic Arctic states that share maritime and land borders, respectively, with Russia. However, although Sweden and Finland have territory above the Arctic Circle, they do not border the Arctic Ocean, so they cannot claim Arctic seabed resources. Thus, if these states had increased their Arctic military activity after the shock, this would be strong evidence that fears of a potential Russian invasion, rather than securing resources, were driving their behavior. However, unlike Norway, these states did not increase their Arctic military activity immediately after the shock. In fact, Finland and Sweden both have more people living above the Arctic Circle than Norway but maintain a smaller Arctic military presence.[129] Only seven years after the shock, in 2014, the year that Russia invaded Crimea, did Sweden and Finland begin to increase their investments in defending themselves against an invasion from Russia. In fact, Finland was forced to rearm, given that in 2012, before Crimea, it drastically reduced the size of its army, from 350,000 to 230,000.[130] Figure 8.10 demonstrates that Norway increased its military spending much more post-shock than Sweden, Denmark, and Finland, although they are all small Nordic states geographically close to Russia.

---

[129] "Chapter 5: Geopolitical Impacts of the Changing Arctic," *Adelphi Series* 53, no. 440 (2013): 119–40, https://doi.org/10.1080/13569783.2013.872863.

[130] Jokela, *Arctic Security Matters*, 62.

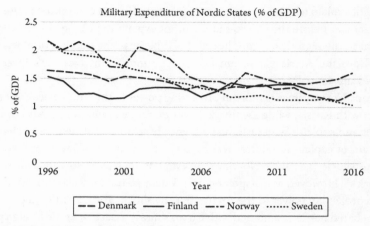

Figure 8.10 Nordic State Military Expenditures (1996–2016)
Source: The World Bank, "Military Expenditure (% of GDP)," n.d., http://data.worldbank.org/
indicator/MS.MIL.XPND.GD.ZS?order=wbapi_data_value_2012+wbapi_data_value+wbapi_data_
value-last&sort=desc.

Second, if Norway was only concerned about its territorial borders, why did it allocate scarce funds to investing in the capability to project power to secure its offshore resource claims? Moreover, why did it focus its war game exercises on defending these claims instead of focusing exclusively or even primarily on a possible territorial invasion? If Norway was principally concerned about territorial invasion, we should observe greater investment in land forces rather than maritime military assets. This is the opposite of what we observe because, after the shock, Norwegian defense officials were much more worried about a potential conflict over resources than about territorial invasion. For example, in 2008 Sverre Diesen, Norwegian chief of defense, asserted that competition over maritime resources, rather than Russian territorial invasion, was the most likely cause of conflict in the region.[131] Thus, it appears Norway's concerns over its resource disputes with Russia, and not the land border, were the principal factors driving its Arctic foreign policy.

Finally, one might wonder if the difference between the quantity of potential resources at stake and the degree to which they have been contested by other states explain the difference between Norway and Denmark. Several pieces of evidence help to eliminate this possibility. First, Norway and Denmark have similar-sized Arctic EEZs, which have similar estimated reserves of oil and gas (see Table 8.8). Also, a larger percentage of Denmark's total Arctic EEZ claims are disputed, 16.1%

---

[131] Håkon Lunde Saxi, *Norwegian and Danish Defence Policy* (Oslo: Norwegian Institute for Defence Studies, 2010).

Table 8.8 **Norway and Denmark's EEZ Areas and Resources**

	Total Potential EEZ Area[a]	% of EEZ Area That Is Disputed, Potentially Claimable Area, or Treaty Area[b]	Distribution of Estimated Oil and Natural Gas Resources (Total Estimated Resources in Oil Equivalent [billion barrels])[c]	Percentage of Total Arctic Gas and Oil[d]
Denmark	1,695,011	16.1%	44.49	11%
Norway	1,920,762	10.9%	47.46	12%

[a]Tina Praprotnik, "Boundaries and Climatic Impact" (master's thesis, Duke University, 2013), 43–44, https://dukespace.lib.duke.edu/dspace/bitstream/handle/10161/6855/Praprotnik%20 Master%27s%20Project.pdf?sequence=1.

[b]Praprotnik, "Boundaries and Climatic Impact," 43–44.

[c]Keil, "The Arctic."

[d]Keil, "The Arctic."

compared to only 10.1% for Norway.[132] Second, both countries have overlapping claims with Russia. Recall that Denmark and Russia both claim the North Pole, and Norway and Russia have ongoing disputes over the Fishery Protection Zone around Svalbard. Moreover, Russia has increased the frequency with which it projects power to the disputed areas with both Norway and Denmark.[133]

Thus, both states face challenges to their territorial claims from a state that is willing to back its claims by projecting military force. The very fact that Russia still has disputes with Norway is because Oslo chose to maintain claims over Svalbard's EEZ that exclude Russia. Recall that Norway not only claimed an EEZ and an ECS but went beyond what it would receive under international law by making an exclusive claim to the right to develop the resources in the Fishery Protection Zone around Svalbard. In contrast, Denmark has not made any claims beyond its unambiguous claims under international law. Thus, Denmark and Norway have similar-sized EEZs, with similar amounts of resources at stake, but have approached their claims differently, in terms of both what they have claimed and the degree to which they have backed those claims by projecting force.

8.7 Conclusion

The Nordic states have a long history of territorial conquest in the North. For centuries Viking ships sailed through ice-covered waters to raid and conquer distant

---

[132] Praprotnik, "Arctic Offshore Energy Resources," 43–44.

[133] Sergunin and Konyshev, "Russia in Search of Its Arctic Strategy."

lands. By 1800 tiny Denmark ruled all of Norway, Greenland, and Iceland as well as a number of smaller colonial outposts scattered across the Caribbean, India, and the East Indies. For most of its history leading up to that time, Denmark, like most states, was ruled by a narrow governing coalition composed of a king and his followers, who could control the rents extracted by the state. The primary source of these rents was territory and exclusive access to trade routes, giving the king substantial incentives for an expansionist foreign policy.

However, like most of Europe, Denmark's economic engine no longer relies on controlling territory or on rents gleaned from monopolizing lucrative trade routes. Instead, Denmark is one of the wealthiest countries in the world because its highly educated and technically capable citizens produce high-end goods and services. This does not mean Denmark is no longer interested in territory and resources; recall that Rent-Addiction Theory assumes that all states seek rents. However, land rents have become dramatically less important to the individuals in the Danish governing coalition and the citizens whose support they need, reducing Denmark's preference to secure territory. Today, no Danish politician could win office by promising to increase economic growth by investing in the military capabilities to conquer Arctic resources: there is no constituency in favor of doing so and no public debate over the desirability of such a strategy. In short, the structure of the Danish economy has altered the preferences of those who rule Denmark so much that what once seemed like an obvious way to generate wealth, territorial conquest or the acquisition of exclusive trade routes, seems absurd today.

Norway, once part of Denmark, shares its culture, norms, heritage, history, and demographics and has followed a similar path in many respects, becoming one of the most democratic, wealthy, and well-educated countries in the world. However, there is one key difference: Norway is highly dependent on resource rents, while Denmark is not. The fact that these two states are so similar, except for the source of their income, provided a rare opportunity to conduct a comparative case study to assess the impact of a state's economic structure on its foreign policy preferences and behavior. Two exogenous shocks made this causal inference possible. First, over half a century ago, in the late 1960s, Norway discovered vast stocks of petroleum in the North Sea, while Denmark did not. The fact that Norway received these resources was determined millions of years ago by geological factors and hence assigned as if randomly. This caused Norway to become economically dependent on resource rents.

Over forty years later. in the summer of 2007, a second exogenous shock occurred in the form of a rapid drop in the amount of Arctic ice, which exposed vast energy reserves. As this chapter has demonstrated, Denmark and Norway have similar-sized Arctic EEZs, with comparable amounts of resources at stake, and each claimed some of the same areas as a much more powerful competitor, Russia. Additionally, both countries were members of NATO and had similar military capabilities that could be used to project power to the Arctic right after the shock and similar levels of income that could be invested in enhancing their future ability to do so. The similarity of these two states in all of these dimensions provided a remarkable opportunity to assess whether the structure of each state's economy influenced how it responded to the shock, while effectively holding these other factors constant.

Confirming my theoretical predictions, the findings clearly show a much greater change in Norway's willingness to invest in projecting power to the Arctic than in Denmark's. This strongly supports my argument that what states make influences what they take or, more precisely, the source of states' income influences their preferences about what goods to secure. My theory suggested that because Norway was more economically dependent on resource rents, it should have a stronger preference for pursuing an exclusionary foreign policy to secure control of the source of such rents, in this case, Arctic maritime resource reserves. All else being equal, this preference should give Norway a stronger incentive to invest in projecting power to secure control over these resources. I found that Norway was more willing than Denmark to boost its Arctic military presence and project power to areas under dispute. Norway also made greater investments in its Arctic force structure by moving the headquarters for its military and coast guard to the Arctic; upgrading its bases, ice-hardened patrol ships, and icebreakers; and more frequently hosting Arctic military exercises.

Norway is perhaps the last country in the world to have grown wealthy from a combination of luck and territorial expansion. Five hundred years ago Columbus "discovered" the New World, allowing Spain to extract land rents from its colonies. Half a millennium later, Norway discovered North Sea oil. Instead of heading across the oceans to extract wealth from distant colonies, Norway was able to use international law to declare an EEZ out to 200 nautical miles from its shores, giving it the exclusive right to extract wealth from its newly acquired territory. Today, Norway controls an EEZ (and, more importantly, the resources that lie under the seafloor) that is seven times the size of its territory on land. However, just as Spain sought new sources of booty after it had depleted the gold and silver reserves of the Americas, Norway is looking to the Arctic to replace the rapidly depleting North Sea oil and gas reserves which generate the income on which it depends.

In contrast, Denmark, which ceased being economically dependent on income derived from the control of territory long ago, faces no such dilemma. Denmark offers another case of a highly production-oriented, democratic state being presented with an exogenous shock that dramatically increased the incentives to secure control over Arctic resources and then declining to make a substantial investment in projecting force to do so. The fact that all three of the Arctic's production-oriented states—Denmark, Canada, and the United States— declined to employ gunboat diplomacy to back their resource claims strongly supports my conjecture that a state's economic structure conditions its foreign policy preferences and behavior.

These findings support my theoretical predictions and have important implications for the future of Arctic geopolitics and international security policy. My findings demonstrate that Norway has a strong preference to secure control over Arctic resources and has backed its claims by investing in power projection capabilities. Also, Norwegian defense officials suggest that Norway is likely to continue investing in an enhanced Arctic military presence. In April of 2018, Chief of Defense Bruun-Hanssen asserted that a "higher level of military presence in the High North is now a new normality. The navy carried out 48% of its activity in the High North in 2017 and with a continuous presence of at least one submarine."[134] Russia's renewed Arctic presence is a key reason why Norway has pushed for a stronger NATO presence in the Arctic. For example, as discussed in Chapter 5, in October of 2018 Norway hosted Operation Trident Juncture, the largest NATO-led exercise held on Norwegian territory since the end of the Cold War. A stronger NATO presence bolsters Oslo's ability to defend its territory on land as well as its offshore Arctic claims.

Thus, just because Norway is smaller and weaker militarily than Russia does not mean it will back down if Russia attempts to seize control of the waters around Svalbard.[135] This is something that NATO member states, especially the United States, should be aware of when considering whether it is in their interest to protect Norway's offshore resource claims. If the United States and its NATO allies believe that this is in their interest, they should make it clear to Russia, just as the United States has made it clear to China that the disputed Senkaku Islands fall under the American alliance commitment to Japan.

Leaving unclear whether a violation of Norway's claims would activate Article 5 invites Norway to pursue a more assertive policy than it might be willing to adopt if it would have to defend those claims on its own. This ambiguity also encourages Russia to test the waters, presenting the potential for conflict between the two states that might drag the United States and NATO into a preventable conflict over issues that may not be in their interest to fight over. As Chapter 5 demonstrated, not only does Russia have a stronger preference to secure control over Arctic resources than any other state, but its leaders have signaled that they are willing to use gunboat diplomacy; they explicitly reference Russia's expansion in Crimea when discussing Svalbard. US policymakers would be wise to consider the strength of both states' preferences to secure Arctic resources when managing American security commitments in the region.

---

[134] Solrun F. Faull, "The Armed Forces Strengthened in the High North," *Norway Today*, April 3, 2018, http://norwaytoday.info/news/armed-forces-strengthened-high-north/.

[135] For more on a possible fait accompli, see Altman, "By Fait Accompli, Not Coercion."

Conclusion

9.1 Introduction

We began with a puzzle: why are some states more willing than others to project power to compete over the control of resources and territory? The answer is that what countries make influences what they want to take. More precisely, a state's economic structure determines the source of income for its governing coalition, which in turn conditions the set of goods rulers will project power to secure. States seek profit because it is necessary both to ensure the government's political survival and to fund its other objectives. History and security studies tell us that income is the crucial input for maintaining the military power needed to guard against threats to the state and its interests.[1] Generating income allows rulers to buy the loyalty of their governing coalition and maintain the military power necessary to protect themselves and their interests.

Walt argued that states balance (i.e., arm and ally) against threats, not power.[2]

If power projection is a form of arming, then, following Walt's logic, states should invest in projecting power against threats to their interests. However, Walt had no theory of foreign policy interests. This left him unable to explain what states sought to secure themselves against, beyond immediate threats to their territorial integrity and survival. This book argues that, because income is the basis of the security of those who govern the state, states will balance against threats to their sources of income. This insight allows us to explain why states arm and project power to

---

[1] For work on the relationship between wealth and military power, see Richard Bean, "War and the Birth of the Nation State," *Journal of Economic History* 33, no. 1 (1973): 203–21; Paul Kennedy, *The Rise and Fall of the Great Powers: Economic Change and Military Power from 1500 to 2000* (New York: Random House, 1987); Michael C. Horowitz, *The Diffusion of Military Power: Causes and Consequences for International Politics* (Princeton, NJ: Princeton University Press, 2010); Michael Beckley, "Economic Development and Military Effectiveness," *Journal of Strategic Studies* 33, no. 1 (2010): 43–79.

[2] Stephen M. Walt, *The Origins of Alliances* (Ithaca, NY: Cornell University Press, 1987).

Perils of Plenty. Jonathan N. Markowitz, Oxford University Press (2020). © Oxford University Press.
DOI: 10.1093/oso/9780190078249.001.0001

secure foreign policy goals beyond immediate threats to their territorial integrity and survival.

To understand the origins of states' foreign policy interests, we must understand the sources of their income, such as rents extracted from territory or profits from the production of goods and services.[3] The more a state depends on a given source of income, the stronger the state's incentive to keep it. The central claim of Rent-Addiction Theory is that the more a state depends on land rents for income, the stronger its preference for territory, and the more willing it is to invest in projecting power to secure its control of that territory.

I test this proposition by evaluating how states responded to an exogenous shock, namely climate change that resulted in a rapid decrease in Arctic sea ice, exposing seabed resources. Specifically, I assess whether states that were more economically dependent on land rents responded to the shock by investing more in projecting power to the Arctic than states that were less dependent on land rents. Contrary to conventional wisdom, which suggests that resource-scarce states should have a stronger preference to secure control over resources, I find that the most resource-rich states invested far more in projecting power to secure control over Arctic resources. This strongly supports my theory. I briefly summarize the findings from each of the empirical chapters. I then discuss how these findings are complemented by additional work that demonstrates how the theory generalizes beyond the Arctic.

9.2 Summary of Findings

Chapter 4 tests my theory via a systematic cross-national comparison of how each of the Arctic states reacted to the shock of Arctic climate change. I employ three original data sets that capture variation in how much countries responded by enhancing their Arctic-specific military capabilities and projecting power to back their maritime resource claims. I find that the states that were already most resource-dependent invested the most in boosting their Arctic military presence and projecting power to disputed areas. The findings strongly support my theoretical predictions and are bolstered by the more detailed qualitative evidence discussed in the case studies.

Chapter 5 explains how the political economy of Putin's predatory state led Moscow to invest more than any other Arctic state in pursuing an exclusionary foreign policy. Russia is the most economically dependent on resource rents, and the regime relies on these rents for survival. Russia spent decades underinvesting in its citizens' health and human capital, property rights, and the research and development needed to generate income by producing goods and services. As a result, the governing coalition cannot easily substitute away from natural resource rents and

---

[3] I have chosen to focus on material goods, but there is nothing in my theory that suggests that states will necessarily prefer material goods to nonmaterial goods.

desperately needs to find additional revenue. As detailed in strategic documents and in public and private statements, Russian leaders view the Arctic as a strategic resource base and consider it critical to secure. This is why Russia, the poorest of all the Arctic states,[4] responded to the shock by investing by far the most in projecting power to back its maritime resource claims.

Chapter 6 tells the story of the big dog that didn't bark. That is, it explains why the United States, the Arctic's most powerful but least land-oriented state, was so reluctant to invest in projecting power to secure control over the region's maritime resources. Despite the fracking boom, the United States derives less income from resource rents than any other Arctic state, except Denmark. Instead, the United States relies on income from producing and selling goods and is much more interested in securing access to markets than in control over resources. This is one of the reasons why the United States pivoted to Asia rather than the Arctic.

Chapter 7 tells the story of the dog that barked but didn't bite. Canada's leaders responded to the shock by making major commitments to enhance their investment in projecting power to the Arctic. But while talk is cheap, bases and ships are expensive; Ottawa repeatedly delayed, scaled back, and cut funding. Canada is more dependent on resource rents than the United States but still derives the vast majority of its income from producing goods rather than extracting resource rents. As a result, Canadian leaders were largely unwilling to actually invest in projecting power to secure control over resources. Chapters 6 and 7 demonstrate that the more production-oriented a state is, the less it will invest in an exclusionary foreign policy.

Chapter 8 tells the tale of two Nordic states. Norway, through essentially random chance, won the geological lottery and struck it rich with the discovery of North Sea oil, while Denmark received minimal oil reserves. But, surprisingly, losing the lottery may have been a stroke of luck for Denmark. Having little natural capital forced Copenhagen to generate wealth by tapping into its citizens' human capital. As a result, at the time of the shock in 2007, Norway was highly dependent on resource rents, while Denmark was not. Comparing these two states provides an especially strong test of the internal validity of my theory because they are extraordinarily similar except for the fact that geology led Norway to become economically dependent on resource rents. Subsequently, Oslo had a much stronger incentive to secure control over resources, and it responded to the shock by investing heavily in projecting power to the Arctic. In contrast, production-oriented Denmark had little interest in projecting force to seek control of the region's resources. The findings from this

---

[4] At about \$1.5 trillion in 2007, Russia did not have the smallest GDP of the Arctic states (Denmark and Norway were both below \$500 billion), but its per capita income (\$12,000) was less than one-fourth of the next poorest state's (Canada, at \$55,000). World Bank, "GDP per Capita (Constant 2010 US\$)," accessed January 11, 2017. http://data.worldbank.org/indicator/NY.GDP.PCAP.KD?locations=RU.

natural experiment are consistent with a causal relationship between the economic structure of a state and how willing it is to invest in an exclusionary foreign policy.

9.2.1   Implications for the Future of Arctic Geopolitics: Will We See a Return of the Great Game?

The subtitle of this book asks whether climate change will lead to a return to the Great Game in the Arctic. I have demonstrated that some states have a much stronger interest in projecting power to compete over Arctic resources than others. However, the Great Game was historically pivotal not just because it involved power projection. The Great Game also featured coercive bargaining over the control of valuable territory, with the possibility of a great-power war looming over negotiations. So, the question is, what is the likelihood of conflict for control over Arctic territory?

My view offers a corrective to both sensationalist news accounts predicting imminent resource wars among Arctic nations and assertions that there is little or no military resource competition and that conflict is unthinkable. My theory suggests that some, but not all, states will have a strong interest in projecting power to compete over Arctic resources. While I expect all states to seek resources non-coercively via international law, states with the strongest interests will also bargain coercively over these resources, with the shadow of military power in the background. My theory suggests that so long as Russia and Norway remain economically dependent on income derived from natural resources and view the Arctic as a future source of that income, they will have a strong interest in maintaining an Arctic military presence to secure their claims.

In contrast, the United States and its production-oriented NATO allies, Denmark and Canada, should be less interested in projecting power to secure control over Arctic resources. However, this does not mean that they will not become more interested in projecting power to the Arctic for other reasons.

Two issues could cause the United States, Denmark, and Canada to take a greater interest in projecting power to the region. First, if the Arctic Ocean becomes a major shipping route for global trade, then the United States, as well as other nations that are heavily dependent on maritime trade such as China, will have a stronger interest in ensuring its access to those sea lanes. Indeed, as I discuss in Section 9.6.2, China has already indicated an interest in Arctic shipping lanes.

There has been a great deal of hype about the opening of Arctic shipping lanes and an increase in Arctic ship traffic. The reality is that these increases are just a drop in the bucket compared to the shipping that passes through the Panama and Suez Canals, which in 2018 received 13,795 and 18,174 ships, respectively.[5] In contrast,

[5] Statistics and Models Administration Unit, "Panama Canal Traffic: Fiscal Years 2016 through 2018, Table No. 1" (Statistics and Models Administration Unit, 2018), http://pancanal.com/eng/op/transit-stats/2018/Table-01.pdf; Suez Canal Authority, "Suez Canal Authority Navigation

while estimates vary, the number of commercial voyages along the Northern Sea Route in 2018 was between 27 and 130.[6] While Arctic shipping is likely to increase, it has a long way to go before it can rival the volume of shipping on the current trade routes. Moreover, a survey of major Japanese shipping companies suggests that there is "very little interest in the trans-Arctic option" because of "higher construction and operational costs, unpredictable ice-situation for some of the year, and limitations on vessel size due to shallow straits, impeding economies of scale."[7] In short, existing analyses suggest that the Arctic is unlikely to become a major thoroughfare for global trade for decades.[8] However, if and when this does happen, production-oriented states like the United States and Denmark will have a strong interest in securing their access to those sea lanes.

Second, if Russia increases its Arctic military presence and further threatens Norway, the United States and its NATO allies will have a stronger interest in projecting power to the region. As discussed in the conclusion to Chapter 6, there is some indication that this has already begun to occur. After Russia's intervention in Crimea in 2014, the United States and NATO began taking a more active role in the Arctic. Recall that in 2018, the United States deployed an aircraft carrier battle group and 14,000 troops to the Arctic to participate in Operation Trident Juncture, a NATO war game hosted by Norway.

9.2.2   Where Is the Risk of Militarized Arctic Resource Conflict Greatest, and How Should Policymakers Manage This Risk?

Given that Russia and Norway are the two states with the most interest in securing control over Arctic resources, the risk of military resource conflict in the Arctic is greatest between them. Of particular concern is the ongoing dispute over the right to develop resources in the resource-rich seabed around Svalbard. As discussed in Chapters 5 and 8, Norway claims the sole right to develop the resources in the 200 nautical miles around Svalbard. Russia disputes this claim. Oslo is especially concerned about issues, such as its offshore resource claims, that might be too small to involve NATO but too big for Norway to defend on its own.[9]

Statistics: Yearly Statistics," 2019, https://www.suezcanal.gov.eg/English/Navigation/Pages/ NavigationStatistics.aspx.

[6] For the 27 ship figure, see Nord University CHNL Information Office, "27 Transit Voyages during the Year 2018," June 14, 2019, http://arctic-lio.com/27-transit-voyages-during-the-year-2018/ ; for the 130 ship figure, see *Wall Street Journal*, "The Future of Arctic Shipping," October 24, 2018, http://www.wsj.com/graphics/the-future-of-arctic-shipping/.

[7] Moe Arild and Olav Schram Stokke, "Asian Countries and Arctic Shipping: Policies, Interests and Footprints on Governance," *Arctic Review* 10 (2019): 33–34.

[8] Orts Hansen et al., *Arctic Shipping*.

[9] See Gotkowska, *Norway and the Bear*, 20.

My theory and findings suggest that Norway's fears are well founded. Russia is both autocratic and even more resource-dependent than Norway; thus, it should have an even stronger interest in securing control over additional resource-rich territory. Recall from Chapter 5 that Russia's public statements have become more assertive, and it has increased its military activity in the waters around Svalbard. Yet, despite facing greater pressure from a much more powerful Russia, Norway has been unwilling to back down.

In areas where it is clear that Russian expansion would provoke NATO intervention, such as Norway's mainland, Russia can likely be deterred. However, in gray zones, such as the ocean around Svalbard, it is less clear that Russian expansion would trigger NATO intervention. Norway is well aware of this and has pursued a tripwire strategy. It has invested in the capability to project enough power to those waters that if Russia were to attempt a fait accompli, it would be forced to engage Norwegian forces and risk triggering NATO action.

This gray zone dynamic has the potential to entrap the United States, by pulling it into a dispute between Norway and Russia over the rights to develop those maritime resources. Having briefed the air force, the State Department in 2017, and members of the intelligence community, I was shocked to learn just how little American policymakers had considered the risk of becoming entrapped in a crisis over offshore resource claims by NATO allies, such as Norway. My book suggests that, given Norway's strong interest in its offshore resource claims, US policymakers should not count on Norway backing down if it is challenged by Russia. If Washington's goal is to avoid being dragged into conflict with Russia, it should take steps to manage this risk. US officials should either clarify to Oslo that Norway is on its own if Russia challenges its claims around Svalbard or redouble their efforts to deter Russia by clarifying that such a challenge would trigger an Article 5 NATO intervention.

9.3 How Well Do the Findings Generalize beyond the Arctic?

The empirical tests in the book focus on testing my theoretical predictions in the Arctic; the scope of the theory, however, is global. The core argument of the theory is consistent not just with the cases presented here but also with related work that uses a much more representative sample of all states from 1816 to 2001.[10] This broader work shows that, as states grow less economically dependent on territory, they become much less likely to engage in militarized territorial disputes. A more recent paper provides additional quantitative tests demonstrating that the more

---

[10] Markowitz, Fariss, and McMahon, "Producing Goods and Projecting Power."

economically dependent states are on territory, the more likely they are to engage in militarized disputes over resource-based territorial claims and to engage in territorial rivalries.[11] This paper also develops a new measure of economic dependence on territory, taking into account income from agriculture as well as from natural resources.

Critically, this large-*n* work allows us to demonstrate that the theory developed in this book generalizes beyond petro-states or resource-dependent countries to states that are economically dependent on land rents derived from agriculture. The results demonstrate that such states, like those that depend on resource rents, are more likely to compete over territory. These broader statistical findings provide evidence for the external validity of the theory and demonstrate that it can be applied generally to explain why some states are more likely to compete militarily over territory and resources.

In the remainder of this chapter, I first discuss the book's core contribution. I then apply Rent-Addiction Theory to illuminate the past, present, and future of territorial and resource competition and conflict globally. In doing so, I am able to highlight the strengths and limitations of the theory. I then conclude with a discussion of avenues for future research.

9.4 The Core Contribution: A Theory of Foreign Policy Interests for Territory

Scholars and governments face a fundamental challenge, anticipating how countries will behave and what policies they will pursue. The problem is that it is nearly impossible to explain how states behaved in the past or predict what they will do in the future without knowing their goals. This book develops a theoretical foundation that allows us to think systematically about the origins of state interests and how those interests condition foreign policy goals. International relations cannot be explained through interests alone, but virtually nothing can be explained without talking about interests. My core contribution is to develop a theory of states' interests regarding two key issues that have historically been among the key drivers of international conflict: territory and resources.

Interests are not entirely absent from existing theories of international politics, but we lack a generally accepted theory of states' foreign policy interests. For example, scholarship suggests that states with revisionist preferences, especially with regard to territory, play a key role in driving states to arm and engage in international conflict.[12] Building on this work, Fearon finds that the stronger a state's preference

---

[11] Markowitz et al., "Productive Pacifists."

[12] For other work on this question, see Glaser, *Rational Theory of International Politics*; Schweller, "Bandwagoning for Profit."

for another's territory, the greater its incentive to arm and the higher the risk of war.[13] However, none of this prior work can explain why some states have a stronger preference for territory or more revisionist foreign policy goals than others. As Fearon writes, "There has been little analysis in [international relations] of the determinants of states' intrinsic value for controlling additional territory, whether by critics of realism or realist critics of Waltz's and offensive realists' skepticism."[14]

Interests alone cannot explain why coercive bargaining ends in war, but without interests, we cannot explain why states bargain coercively in the first place. Bargaining failure can be thought of as an end point of a causal process, and that process begins when two actors develop incompatible preferences over an issue, such as territory. The stronger a state's preference for another's territory, the more incompatible the two states' preferences and, thus, the greater the incentive they will have for coercive bargaining.[15] Also, the more incompatible states' preferences, the smaller the bargaining space (i.e., the set of outcomes that both actors would prefer to war).

To be clear, my theory is not designed to explain why coercive bargaining breaks down into conflict; rather, it informs our understanding of why some states have a stronger preference for coercive bargaining over territory in the first place. If countries do not bargain coercively, there can be no bargaining failure that ends in war. Thus, to explain why states engaged in resource competition and territorial conflict in the past and to anticipate whether they are likely to do so in the future, we must understand why states have a stronger or weaker preference for territory. The theoretical foundation developed in this book allows us to do precisely this.

9.5 Implications of the Theory: Explaining Trends in Resource-Driven Conquest over Time

The decline in territorial conflict and a related decrease in the frequency and severity of war are two of the most important trends in international politics. Understanding states' preferences for territory and how they have changed over time has implications for our ability to explain these trends and, perhaps more importantly, predict whether they are likely to continue. As Pinker and others have pointed out, the world today is dramatically more peaceful than it was in the past.[16]

---

[13] James D. Fearon, "Cooperation, Conflict, and the Costs of Anarchy," *International Organization* 72, no. 3 (2018): 537.

[14] Fearon, "Cooperation, Conflict, and the Costs of Anarchy," 538.

[15] For more on this point, see Andrew J. Coe, "The Modern Economic Peace" (Working paper, Stanford, CA: Stanford University, 2016).

[16] Steven Pinker, *The Better Angels of Our Nature: Why Violence Has Declined* (New York: Viking, 2011).

One of the principal reasons for this is that territorial conflict among the major powers, which used to be rampant, has declined dramatically.[17]

Historically, the world's most powerful states competed violently for territory and resources. During the 127 years between 1689 and 1815, France and Britain were at war for 64 years, fighting over territory from Europe to North America to the West Indies to India.[18] Although the severity of violent conflict among the major European powers declined from 1815 to 1913, those states engaged in regular territorial conquest in the rest of the world.[19] Europe represents only 8% of the world's land area, yet by 1800 the major powers of Europe controlled 37% of the world's territory. By 1878 this share had increased to 67%, and by 1914 it had reached 84%.[20] However, since World War II we have witnessed a remarkable decline in the prevalence of large-scale territorial conflict and conquest.[21] We have shifted from a world in which the goal of most major powers was to secure as much territory and resources as possible to a world in which the wealthiest and most powerful states rarely engage in imperialism or large-scale territorial aggrandizement.[22]

Yet, despite this decline, resource competition and territorial conflict have not disappeared. Much of the Middle East remains engulfed in a set of intertwined regional conflicts and proxy wars over the political control of the region and, with it, the enormous land rents that lie beneath the earth. Similarly, many conflicts in Africa are motivated by the desire to control land rents as a source of power, patronage, and profits. In Latin America, an ongoing dispute between Guyana and Venezuela over enormous natural gas fields threatens to escalate into violent conflict. Beijing's efforts to assert control over the South China Sea have pundits and policymakers concerned about whether China's rise will be peaceful. Recent clashes

---

[17] For more on the decline of territorial conflict and the decline in conflict more generally, see Gary Goertz, Paul F. Diehl, and Alexandru Balas, *The Puzzle of Peace: The Evolution of Peace in the International System* (New York: Oxford University Press, 2016). See also Andrew P. Owsiak, Paul F. Diehl, and Gary Goertz, "Border Settlement and the Movement toward and from Negative Peace," *Conflict Management and Peace Science* 34, no. 2 (2017): 176–93. See also Marie Henehan and John A. Vasquez, "The Changing Probability of Interstate War, 1816–1992: Identifying Peaceful Eras," in *The Waning of Major War: Theories and Debates*, ed. Raimo Väyrynen, Contemporary Security Studies Series (London and New York: Routledge, 2006), 280–99.

[18] Ronald Findlay and Kevin H. O'Rourke, *Power and Plenty: Trade, War, and the World Economy in the Second Millennium*, The Princeton Economic History of the Western World (Princeton, NJ: Princeton Univeersity Press, 2009), 247.

[19] Mark W. Zacher, "The Territorial Integrity Norm: International Boundaries and the Use of Force," *International Organization* 55, no. 2 (2001): 236.

[20] Daniel R. Headrick, *The Tools of Empire: Technology and European Imperialism in the Nineteenth Century* (Oxford: Oxford University Press, 1981).

[21] For an analysis that shows that while large-scale conquest has declined, small-scale conquest remains prevalent, see Altman, "Evolution of Territorial Conquest after 1945."

[22] Oona Anne Hathaway and Scott Shapiro, *The Internationalists: How a Radical Plan to Outlaw War Remade the World* (New York: Simon & Schuster, 2017).

arising from these disputes have thrust resource competition to the forefront of international politics.

These empirical patterns motivate three questions of significant interest to scholars and policymakers alike. First, why did most of the world's powerful states stop taking territory and resources? Second, why are some states still competing over territory and resources? Third, what are the prospects for resource competition in the future? I demonstrate that by illuminating why states have different interests with regard to territory and resources, Rent-Addiction Theory enhances our ability to answer all three questions. To be clear, I am arguing not that other factors do not matter but, rather, that variation in states' interests plays a vital role in explaining these trends. In this section, I cover the historical trends; in section 9.6, I consider the future.

9.5.1 Why Did Most of the World's Powerful States Stop Conquering Territory and Resources?

Rent-Addiction Theory suggests there has been a fundamental shift in the interests of most of the states that are rich enough to project significant power. From the fifteenth to the mid-twentieth centuries, the majority of the world's most powerful states were ruled by narrow coalitions whose primary source of wealth was rents extracted either from territory they controlled or by limiting market competition through exclusive access to trade routes and colonies.[23] Their income and therefore their political survival depended on building and projecting military power to compete over territories from which they could extract rents. Securing and controlling wealth represented states' raison d'être. As Edmund Burke wrote, "The revenue of the state is the state."[24] To paraphrase Tilly, the competition over these land rents made the state, and the state made war. But, over time, most states have followed a path of economic development that has made them much less dependent on territory, which has fundamentally altered their foreign policy interests. Industrialization and the declining importance of agriculture and commodities compared to services and technology have transformed one state after another from a land orientation to

---

[23] For more on the rent-seeking exclusionary policies of these states, see Leo J. Blanken, *Rational Empires: Institutional Incentives and Imperial Expansion* (Chicago: University of Chicago Press, 2012); Daron Acemoglu, Simon Johnson, and James Robinson, "The Colonial Origins of Comparative Development," *American Economic Review* 91, no. 5 (2001): 1369–1401; Charles Ralph Boxer, *The Dutch Seaborne Empire, 1600–1800* (London: Knopf, 1965); Kenneth R. Andrews, *Trade, Plunder and Settlement: Maritime Enterprise and the Genesis of the British Empire, 1480–1630* (Cambridge: Cambridge University Press, 1984); Charles Tilly, *Coercion, Capital, and European States, AD, 990–1992* (Malden, MA: Blackwell, 1990).

[24] Burke, *Reflections on the Revolution in France*, quoted in Karl, *Paradox of Plenty*, 222.

a production orientation. Not coincidentally, the incidence of territorial conflict has decreased dramatically.[25]

So long as rulers were addicted to land rents for the income needed to purchase the loyalty of their governing coalitions and to raise the armies necessary to defend themselves from foreign and domestic threats, they had strong incentives to secure territory. This was true even in democracies as Britain, France, and the United States adopted democratic institutions long before they stopped taking territory. Democratically elected governments still pursued expansionist foreign policies because their governing coalitions, which were highly dependent on income derived from the control of land, wanted them to do so.[26] This may explain why, before World War I, democracies were much more willing to engage in territorial aggrandizement and why prior work has found evidence that the democratic peace may not hold during this period.[27] It implies that there may be not just a democratic or capitalist peace but also a production-oriented peace. The decline of interstate warfare may not just be a result of states becoming more economically independent, financially integrated, or economically developed but also the result of their source of income shifting from land rents to the production of goods and services. As democracies became more production-oriented, they became less interested in territory and had fewer incentives to fight over it.

The Industrial Revolution, globalization, and the rise of the knowledge-based economy changed how states could acquire wealth.[28] States that mastered industrial technologies could produce goods much more efficiently. Rather than having to rely primarily on revenue from agrarian surplus, production provided a far larger, and therefore more attractive, source of income. This allowed industrializing states to break their addiction to land rents. So long as production-oriented states could access the markets necessary to export their products and import the inputs needed

[25] Paul K. Huth, "Territory: Why Are Territorial Disputes between States a Central Cause of International Conflict," in *What Do We Know about War*, ed. John A. Vasquez (New York: Rowman & Littlefield, 2000), 85–110.

[26] For illustration, recall from Chapter 6 that, in 1850, agriculture accounted for 50% of US GDP and 70% of the workforce. During the United States' first century as an independent country, its governing coalition had a strong interest in securing control over territory and invested in projecting power to coercively bargain over and conquer vast swaths of territory. The end of the nineteenth century witnessed a vigorous debate over whether the United States should continue its expansion abroad and add to the collection of colonies it had acquired as part of the spoils of war with Spain. By 1900, however, the structure of the US economy had already begun to shift in favor of producing goods as agriculture had dropped to 20% of GDP. With this shift in economic structure, the US governing coalition decided that what the United States needed was not colonies but access to markets.

[27] For a related review of the research on why the democratic peace does not hold before World War I, see Patrick J. McDonald, "Great Powers, Hierarchy, and Endogenous Regimes: Rethinking the Domestic Causes of Peace," *International Organization* 69, no. 3 (2015): 557–88.

[28] Rosecrance, *Rise of the Trading State*; Brooks, *Producing Security*; Gartzke and Rohner, "Political Economy of Imperialism, Decolonization and Development."

to produce goods and provide for their citizens, they no longer needed to conquer territory to prosper.

While the Industrial Revolution eventually freed states from their economic dependence on territory, nearly all the major powers remained economically dependent on territory until after World War II. In 1939, twenty of the world's twenty-five largest economies were still dependent on territory. This is according to a new measure of land orientation that takes into account both the share of national income that is derived from natural resources and the share from agriculture (which prior to the 1970s was the largest source of land rents).[29] By this measure, of the major power belligerents in World War II, only the United States and the United Kingdom had transitioned to a production-oriented economy before the war. Even major powers that were rapidly industrializing prior to World War II, such as Germany, remained dependent on income from agriculture. This measure matches the historical record. According to Adam Tooze, "Germany under Hitler was still only a partially modernized society in which upwards of 15 million people depended for their living either on traditional handcraft or on peasant agriculture."[30] In 1925, 25% of Germans were employed in agriculture.[31]

However, since at least World War II, the world's most powerful states have grown increasingly production-oriented, and open global markets have provided relatively secure access to resources. In 1940 only five of the world's twenty-five largest economies were production-oriented. By 1950 ten were, and by 1960 fifteen, including all the major powers except the Soviet Union and China.[32] Thus, the post–World War II norm against large-scale territorial aggrandizement, which scholars have argued began to be enforced after 1945 but did not reach full strength until after 1975,[33] became most effective just after a majority of the world's most powerful states became production-oriented. This is consistent with the view that their material economic interests played a role in states choosing to adopt and enforce this norm.[34]

As a result, the states with the greatest power to conquer territory have had less interest in doing so and a strong preference to deter other states from engaging in conquest. This helps explain why the world's most powerful states have not only adhered to the norm against territorial aggrandizement but have been willing to

[29] For more on this measure and how it was created, see Markowitz et al., "Productive Pacifists."

[30] Adam Tooze, *The Wages of Destruction: The Making and Breaking of the Nazi Economy* (New York: Viking, 2007), xxxiii, 29.

[31] Tooze, *Wages of Destruction*, xxxiii, 29.

[32] Note that this compares the twenty-five largest GDPs over the years 1950–2010, using data from the World Bank in 2010 constant dollars. For more on how this measure of land orientation was created, see Markowitz et al., "Productive Pacifists."

[33] For a review of the literature on the norm and an interesting argument regarding its limits, see Altman, "Evolution of Territorial Conquest after 1945," 1–19.

[34] Tanisha Fazal, *State Death: The Politics and Geography of Conquest, Occupation, and Annexation* (Princeton, NJ: Princeton University Press, 2007), 46–47.

invest in enforcing this norm.[35] These production-oriented states have a strong interest in preventing conquest because it could disrupt markets and the access to resources those markets provide.

In contrast, states that are still economically dependent on territory are the ones that have been willing to violate the norm. For example, in 1990, when one of the world's most resource-dependent states, Iraq, invaded the oil-rich country of Kuwait, a coalition of production-oriented nations, led by the United States, enforced the norm. By reversing the invasion and restoring the previous territorial status quo, the coalition sent a powerful signal that major violations of this norm would be punished. This coalition was made up of former colonial powers, such as the United Kingdom, France, Germany, and Japan, which less than half a century before had either acquired or sought to acquire vast empires through conquest. By 1990 Britain and France were decades removed from relying on income extracted from their colonial territories, and Germany and Japan no longer believed that they needed to secure access to vital natural resources through conquest, as they had before World War II.[36] Instead, these economically powerful production-oriented states were able to buy all the resources they needed on open markets and had grown wealthier from producing goods and services than they ever had from territory.[37]

In sum, the world's most powerful states stopped fighting over territory because they found a more attractive source of income and could buy all the resources they needed. This coalition of powerful production-oriented states has been investing in enforcing the norm against territorial aggrandizement, which has deterred conquest and suppressed resource competition among less powerful, land-oriented countries.

9.5.2 What about the United States in the Middle East?

If production-oriented states are uninterested in seeking resources via territorial conquest, why did the highly production-oriented United States expand its military presence in the Middle East, where most of the world's oil production is concentrated, after the First Gulf War? If the United States was not interested in profiting from direct control of the region's resource rents, why did it invade Iraq? One might conclude that the US presence in the Middle East and its invasion of Iraq are inconsistent with my theoretical prediction and represent a highly problematic and puzzling case for the theory. This would be wrong. The expanded American military

[35] For more on this point, see Coe and Markowitz, "Crude Calculations"

[36] For more on Germany's and Japan's need to secure resources prior to World War II, see Daniel Yergin, *The Prize: The Epic Quest for Oil, Money, and Power* (New York: Simon & Schuster, 1992), chapters 16–19.

[37] Piketty, *Capital in the Twenty-First Century*, 120–21.

presence in the Middle East after the First Gulf War and the invasion of Iraq in 2003 are entirely consistent with my theory.

First, recall from Chapter 2 that my theory is designed to explain why some states have a stronger preference for territory, assuming that they already have secure access to resources and other critical inputs via markets. Even production-oriented states will have a strong preference for securing control over resources if open markets do not give them that access.

Second, as I discussed in detail in the US case chapter, as a production-oriented state, the United States has a strong interest in maintaining secure and open access to resource markets for both itself and its allies. Thus, Washington expanded its position in the Middle East after the First Gulf War precisely because Iraq's interest in monopolizing control over Persian Gulf energy reserves threatened to disrupt the flow of oil onto global markets. Since the First Gulf War, the United States has maintained a strong military presence in the Middle East, not to directly control the resource rents there but rather to contain Saddam Hussein and deter other actors from attempting to monopolize those resources.

As Coe convincingly argues, the costs of containing Saddam eventually grew so large that the United States was forced to remove him from power by invading Iraq.[38] However, the US government did not seek to control or profit from Iraq's resource rents. Rather, the new Iraqi government was given control over those resource rents. One might wonder whether the Iraqi government, despite controlling the oil, was compelled to allow American companies preferential access to contracts to develop it. However, the evidence suggests that American energy firms did not benefit disproportionately and, in fact, largely lost out to French and Russian firms.[39] This is not to say that resources did not play a role in Washington's decision to remove Saddam from power. To the contrary, one of the rationales provided to the Bush administration by then-chair of the Federal Reserve Alan Greenspan for overthrowing Saddam was that he could threaten the free flow of oil, which is essential for maintaining low and stable energy prices, which were critical for the global and US economies.[40] This rationale is entirely consistent with my theory, which suggests that, as a production-oriented state, the United States will care deeply about maintaining open access to global markets.

---

[38] Andrew J. Coe, "Containing Rogues: A Theory of Asymmetric Arming," *Journal of Politics* 80, no. 4 (2018): 1197–1210.

[39] For more on this, see Eric Bonds, "Assessing the Oil Motive after the U.S. War in Iraq," *Peace Review* 25, no. 2 (2013), 291–98; Vivienne Walt, "U.S. Companies Shut Out as Iraq Auctions Its Oil Fields," *Time*, December 19, 2009, http://content.time.com/time/world/article/0,8599,1948787,00.html.

[40] Bob Woodward, "Greenspan: Ouster of Hussein Crucial for Oil Security," *Washington Post*, September 17, 2007, http://www.washingtonpost.com/wp-dyn/content/article/2007/09/16/AR2007091601287.html.

Third, as I argued in the previous section, it is precisely because the United States and its production-oriented allies have such a strong interest in maintaining open access to markets that they have been willing to invest heavily in deterring and punishing actors, like Saddam, who might disrupt that access. This has implications for understanding why some oil-rich states in the Middle East, such as Saudi Arabia, might at first glance look like a "dog that does not bark." My theory suggests that while many resource-dependent states in the Middle East do, in fact, have a strong interest in securing additional resources and territory, they are deterred from acting on these preferences by the United States and its allies. Someone who did not take this into account might incorrectly infer that the United States and its allies no longer needed to deter conquest in the region because Middle Eastern countries have little interest in each other's territory, given that there have been no attempts at large-scale conquest since 1991. This highlights the importance of having a theory of state interests that can identify their preferences ex ante—before they act on them, rather than after the fact.

9.5.3 Why Are Some States Still Competing over the Control of Territory and Resources?

If states can generate more wealth from production than conquest and can purchase the resources they need on open markets, then why are some still engaged in territorial and resource competition? The answer, as laid out in Chapter 2, is that the very forces of industrialization that weakened the link between territory and wealth for some states strengthened it for others. As production-oriented states shifted away from agriculture to producing goods and services, their demand for natural resources exploded. The surge in demand sent a flood of income into the economies of states that were blessed (or cursed) with large natural resource reserves.

Income from natural resources represented a new, highly addictive form of land rents called *resource rents*, which dwarfed the revenue that could be generated by agrarian land rents. For many states, this source of income was too strong to resist, and they became more addicted than ever to land rents. These states chose a path of resource-driven economic development, investing in the infrastructure needed to extract natural resources rather than the education and rule of law needed to produce goods and services. This enabled them to extract ever greater amounts of resources, which, in many cases, led to a tidal wave of resource rents so powerful that it swept away any emerging production-oriented sector.

Resource-driven development resulted in path-dependent effects that made these states even more dependent on resource rents and less able to transition to a production-oriented economy. Having spent years underinvesting in the capital stocks, institutions, and infrastructure needed to sustain a production-oriented economy, such as human capital, property rights, and manufacturing centers, these states could not just turn a key and immediately generate revenue by producing goods. They would first have to make those investments, delaying the returns on that investment for years or even decades. This is one reason that many resource-dependent states have had so much difficulty diversifying their economies and transitioning away from natural resources. Because these states cannot easily substitute by producing goods, they have stronger incentives to invest in generating income by securing control over territory.

The tidal wave of income from natural resources also shaped the domestic political institutions and economic interests of the political coalitions that governed these states. As demonstrated by research on the resource curse, as these states became more dependent on resource rents, their governments generally became more autocratic.[41] Following the logic laid out in Chapter 2, autocratic regimes tend to have a stronger preference for the political benefits of land rents because land rents are a source of revenue and patronage that is easier to control directly and to deny to the political opposition. However, even in states that managed to remain democratic, such as Norway, as long as the country and its citizens came to rely on resource rents, they developed a stronger interest in securing control over the source of these rents.

These factors collectively explain why, even in an era when states can purchase resources on open markets and generate wealth through production rather than conquest, some resource-dependent states still seek control over territory and the resources that lie beneath it. These land-oriented states are primarily motivated not by a desire for access to resources as a source of inputs but rather by a desire to control resources as a source of the rents on which they depend. To be clear, I am not claiming that this is the only factor that drives states to seek control over territory or that non-resource-dependent states do not value resource rents. My claim is only that states that are more dependent on resource rents tend to have a stronger interest in securing control over resources, which explains why they are more willing to compete for that control.

9.6   Implications of the Theory: The Future of Resource Competition and Conflict

I begin by discussing the potential for resource-driven territorial competition and conflict among the major powers in the future. I then take a regional perspective, identifying the areas where the risk of resource competition will be lowest and highest.

---

[41]   Michael L. Ross, "What Have We Learned about the Resource Curse?" *Annual Review of Political Science* 18, no. 1 (2015): 239–59.

9.6.1 Major Powers

Historically, the world's wealthiest and most powerful states competed against one another, each trying to gain control of the lion's share of the world's resources and wealth. If what states make does influence what they take, what does that tell us about the prospects for territorial and resource competition among major powers in the future? The good news is that most of the world's wealthiest and most powerful states are democratic and no longer generate wealth primarily from the control of territory and resources. Among the fifteen largest economies, thirteen are democracies and only one generates more than 10% of its GDP from resource rents. [42] Given this, as long as markets remain open and states can purchase the resources they need on those markets, my theory suggests that nearly all of the world's most powerful states should have a relatively weak preference to seek territory and resources as a source of rents and wealth. Only two of these states are not both democratic and production-oriented: Russia, which is both autocratic and land-oriented, and China, which is autocratic but production-oriented. I will next discuss my theory's implications for both states.

Until Russia is able to kick its addiction to resource rents, its rulers will have a strong preference to secure territory. This interest is likely to endure even if there are changes in Russia's leadership and domestic political institutions. Russia has experienced many changes to its domestic political institutions, from the October Revolution of 1917 to Yeltsin's democratization attempts to Putin's return to authoritarianism. Yet the Russian state has always been dependent on land rents, giving its various governing coalitions an enduring incentive to secure control over territory.[43] Thus, even if Putin resigned today and Russia democratized overnight, its citizens would still have a strong incentive to secure control of territory. Democratic political institutions might moderate the rent-seeking impulses of the state, or a different leader might be more or less restrained than Putin. But until Russia no longer depends on land rents, it will continue to have a strong interest in securing control over the source of those rents. As discussed in the conclusion to Chapter 5, this explains why Russia has invested so heavily in seeking to control Arctic resources and suggests that it is likely to continue to do so in the future.

Russia is the largest land-oriented economy in the world. Yet, at $1.6 trillion, Russia's GDP ranks eleventh in the world, behind that of Canada; and, in fact,

---

[42] Note that 10% is an arbitrary cutoff. I adopt it here because it is commonly used to identify rentier states. See Paul Collier and Anke Hoeffler, "Testing the Neocon Agenda: Democracy in Resource-Rich Societies," *European Economic Review* 53, no. 3 (2009): 293–308.

[43] For a more detailed discussion of the rent-seeking tendencies of the Russian state, see David A. Lake, "The Rise, Fall, and Future of the Russian Empire A Theoretical Interpretation," in *The End of Empire? The Transformation of the USSR in Comparative Perspective*, ed. Karen Dawisha and Bruce Parrott, The International Politics of Eurasia 9 (Armonk, NY: M. E. Sharpe, 1997), 30–62.

Russia's economy is little more than half the size of California's.[44] Thus, Russia's economic power and military potential are dwarfed by NATO's, with a combined GDP of over $36 trillion. Yet, as recent events in Syria, Crimea, and Ukraine have demonstrated, Russia is still powerful enough to take territory and generate instability. So long as NATO is willing to go to war with Russia, it should be able to deter Moscow from acting on its rent-seeking preferences, at least with regard to large-scale territorial aggrandizement. However, for countries outside NATO and countries that have offshore assets whose seizure might not trigger NATO intervention, the threat of Russian territorial expansion remains very real.

9.6.2 What about China?

Given China's rapid economic rise and growing power, a key question for the future of territorial conflict and resource competition is what China's interests will be. Of the world's ten largest economies, China is the only autocracy. My theory suggests that China's autocratic institutions should give it a stronger preference to seek rents than if it were democratic. However, unlike Russia, China no longer relies primarily on land rents for income. Instead, China makes its money by producing and exporting manufactured goods, technology, and services. This gives it a fundamentally different set of interests than Russia. Unlike Russia, China's business model does not rely primarily on the physical control of territory to generate wealth and power. Instead, China relies on the ability to generate globally competitive goods and maintain access to markets both to export those goods and to secure the inputs needed for their production.

To illustrate just how successful China's strategy has been in comparison to previous major powers that sought wealth from conquest, consider the following. At the turn of the twentieth century, when the sun never set on the British Empire, England controlled a massive stock of foreign assets in its colonies that were worth about double its national income. The income it earned from these assets made its annual national income approximately 10% higher than its domestic product. Put another way, England enjoyed an income stream that was 10% larger than it would have been if it had lost its colonies and their assets.[45] France, which then had the second largest empire, had accumulated foreign assets in its colonies that made its national income 5% to 6% higher than it would have been without those colonial assets.

---

[44] Associated Press, "California Is Now the World's Fifth-Largest Economy, Surpassing United Kingdom," *Los Angeles Times*, May 4, 2018, http://www.latimes.com/business/la-fi-california-economy-gdp-20180504-story.html.

[45] Piketty, *Capital in the Twenty-First Century*, 120–21. There were also some additional indirect economic gains, such as increased specialization, that trade with the colonies allowed.

Now imagine a colonizer so successful that it was able to increase its national income by 10% from the assets it conquered in a single year. Then suppose that this country was able to do this again the following year and the year after that and so on and that this pattern continued for thirty-five years. China is that country. Only China did not need to conquer a single colony to acquire this wealth. Instead, it adopted a production-oriented economy and exported goods to the world. The Chinese economy has grown by nearly 10% a year since 1982, a far greater economic expansion than Britain or France achieved by colonization: the French economy grew at around 1% to 1.5% a year during the nineteenth century, and Britain's grew 1.9% to 2.2% per year.[46]

As a more direct comparison of the two strategies for generating wealth, let us compare how much nineteenth-century Britain's economy grew over thirty-five years of a policy of conquest and colonialism with how much China's economy grew over thirty-five years of a policy of producing and exporting goods. To stack the deck in favor of finding that conquest pays more, we will make two assumptions: first, that Britain sustained its highest growth rate during the late nineteenth century, 2.2%, for all thirty-five years and, second, that all British growth was due to the colonies.[47] Making these two assumptions, we find that successfully pursuing a strategy of conquest would have increased British national income by 225% in thirty-five years.[48] In contrast, by producing and exporting goods, China's economy has grown by over 2,500% in the past thirty-five years.[49] In sum, in terms of generating income, Britain was arguably the most prosperous empire of all time, having conquered the world's most lucrative colonies, such as India. However, compared to Britain's triumph, China's strategy of production was more than ten times as successful at generating wealth.

That being said, China clearly lives in a different world from that of the British in the nineteenth century. Might China have grown even more wealthy by pursuing a strategy of conquest today? To illustrate just how much more profitable it has been for China to adopt a strategy of producing goods, rather than seeking to conquer

---

[46] On France's growth rates, see Piketty, *Capital in the Twenty-First Century*, 352. On the British growth rate, see N. R. S. Crafts, "British Economic Growth 1760–1913: A Challenge for New Growth Theory," Warwick Economic Research Papers 415 (University of Warwick, Department of Economics, 1993), 2.

[47] This assumption obviously overstates the benefits of the colonies as much of Britain's growth during the late nineteenth century was generated not by the colonies but by increasing domestic production. For more on this, see Findlay and O'Rourke, *Power and Plenty*, chapter 7.

[48] I arrive at this number by compounding 2.2% growth over 35 years. I then add 10% to that final figure to represent the additional income that the colonies added. See Piketty, *Capital in the Twenty-First Century*, 120–21.

[49] In 1982 the value of China's GDP was just $391 billion (using 2010 constant dollars to make the figures comparable over time while accounting for inflation). In 2017 it had grown to $10.1 trillion, over twenty-five times larger than it was in 1982.

and extract resource rents, consider another hypothetical example. The most valuable conquerable assets on earth are the energy reserves in the Persian Gulf. The combined reserves of Saudi Arabia, Iraq, Kuwait, Qatar, and the United Arab Emirates represent 635 billion barrels of oil and 1.5 trillion cubic feet of natural gas.[50] From 1981 to 2015 (the last year for which data are available), the combined annual profits from the oil and gas production of all these states ranged between $51 billion, when energy prices were at their lowest in 1998, and $676 billion, when they were at their highest in 2008.[51] Now imagine that China could magically conquer these countries and capture their profits at zero cost. Even during their most profitable year, at $676 billion, these resources would add less than 7% to China's GDP. At the low end, they would add less than half a percent.[52]

At the high end of this estimate, 7% would be larger than the increase in national income that France enjoyed from all its colonies. However, it would still be a far smaller increase in China's national income than it has enjoyed, on average, for the last third of a century by producing goods. The appeal of gaining profits from production rather than conquest becomes even clearer when we consider that, in reality, China would need to pay enormous costs to conquer Persian Gulf resources, which would significantly decrease and potentially wipe out any profits. In sum, because China's economy is structured to produce globally competitive goods, it has far more attractive opportunities for generating income, which decreases its preference for acquiring income by conquest.

China is a production-oriented state, but that does not necessarily mean that it has no interest in projecting power. Like other states that rely on trade, China has a fundamental interest in secure access to vital sea lanes and markets. In previous eras, the British and Dutch built large navies to ensure that they could secure sea lanes and maintain access to foreign markets. In the post–World War II era, states that rely on trade have largely been content to free-ride off the secure sea lanes provided by Washington, and no state has been powerful enough to challenge US naval dominance even if it wanted to. Assuming China continues to grow economically, it will eventually have the resources to, at the very least, contest US naval dominance. Given Beijing's concern that Washington might seek to limit its access to sea lanes in the event of a crisis over Taiwan or some other issue, China is unlikely to remain

[50] Coe and Markowitz, "Crude Calculations."

[51] Following standard practice, the profits are calculated by subtracting the cost of production from the sale prices. For details on the data and procedures used to calculate these figures, see Coe and Markowitz, "Crude Calculations." Note that these calculations come from a working paper that was presented at the Annual Meeting of the Midwest Political Science Association in 2018. This paper is available from the authors upon request. A more recent version of this paper is also available that estimates the cost of conquering Persian Gulf Energy Reserves using a slightly different set of states that would arguably be easier to conquer.

[52] Coe and Markowitz, "Crude Calculations."

content to allow America to dominate the sea lanes upon which its economic life-blood depends.

Given Beijing's interests, my theory suggests that its actions in the South China Sea are motivated less by the desire to extract resource rents from fisheries or undersea oil than by a desire to gain control over its littoral waters to prevent foreign powers from restricting China's access to vital sea lanes in the event of a crisis.[53] This does not suggest that China does not value these resources or that resources play no role in driving the behavior of China and other states in the region. To the contrary, my theory suggests that all states value resources and rents and that an autocracy like China should have a stronger preference to seek rents than if it were a democracy. Also, China should have an interest in securing access to resources as a source of inputs for its production-oriented economy.

However, estimates suggest that the reserves in the South China Sea are comparatively small.[54] They are not large enough to make China energy-independent, and their value as sources of rents is relatively small compared to the size of China's economy and its other economic opportunities.[55] Thus, China's interest in the resources under the South China Sea pales in comparison to its interest in the trade that flows on the surface. Given how much China's economy depends on trade, the gains from preventing a disruption in the flow of this trade likely far exceed any potential resource rents. All these factors suggest that resources are not the primary reason for China to seek control of these waters.[56]

---

[53] For an analysis that suggests that Chinese strategists view securing control over the South China Sea as critical for securing access to sea lanes, see Feng Zhang, "Chinese Thinking on the South China Sea and the Future of Regional Security," *Political Science Quarterly* 132, no. 3 (2017): 435–66, https://doi.org/10.1002/polq.12658. For several Chinese writings on these issues, see Chen Zhe (陈者) and Yang Chao Zhao (杨朝钊), 海洋是国家战略的坚实支点[The ocean is the crux of strong national strategy] (Beijing: Ministry of National Defense of the People's Republic of China [中华人民共和国国防部]), October 10, 2016), http://www.mod.gov.cn/jmsd/2016-10/10/content_4743783.htm; Foreign Ministry of the People's Republic of Chin,a中国坚持通过谈判解决中国与菲律宾在南海的有关争议 [China insists on resolving the South China Sea dispute with the Philippines through negotiations] (Beijing: Foreign Ministry of the People's Republic of China [中华人民共和国外交部]), accessed June 20, 2018, http://www.fmprc.gov.cn/web/ziliao_674904/tytj_674911/zcwj_674915/t1380600.shtml.

[54] For a comparison of the size of the South China Sea to other regions, see US Energy Information Administration, "South China Sea," February 7, 2013, https://www.eia.gov/beta/international/regions-topics.php?RegionTopicID=SCS., accessed June 20, 2018.

[55] For more on why South China Sea energy reserves would represent just a drop in the bucket in meeting China's energy demands, see Bonnie S. Glaser and Gregory Poling, "Vanishing Borders in the South China Sea," *Foreign Affairs*, June 5, 2018, 2–3, https://www.foreignaffairs.com/articles/china/2018-06-05/vanishing-borders-south-china-sea.

[56] Emily Meierding, "The Real Reason Tensions Are Rising in the South China Sea," Vox, May 24, 2015, https://www.vox.com/2015/5/24/8646571/the-real-reason-tensions-are-rising-in-the-south-china-sea.

If China's production-oriented economy makes it less interested in securing territory and resources as a source of rents, this should condition its future foreign policy goals in regions beyond the South China Sea. It suggests that China's actions in the South China Sea do not necessarily represent the beginning of a more territorially expansionist foreign policy. In short, China is not Germany in 1939, and the South China Sea is not Czechoslovakia.

Instead of territory, China should be more interested in securing access to markets and sea lanes. This has implications for understanding China's goals in resource-rich regions, such as Central Asia, the Middle East, and Africa. The theory suggests that China views these resource-rich regions not as sources of rents to conquer but as opportunities for investment and for securing access to raw material to power its production-oriented economy. China also views these regions, which are continuing to develop, as increasingly valuable markets for Chinese exports. China's Belt and Road initiative is aimed both at developing the infrastructure needed to export its goods to foreign markets and at importing vital natural resources. By developing several pipelines that allow China to import energy from Kazakhstan, Turkmenistan, and Russia, Beijing is diversifying its supply lines, making it less dependent on vulnerable sea lanes.[57]

China is also increasingly interested in the Arctic, as detailed in a recent Arctic white paper, which outlined its intention to build a "Polar Silk Road."[58] China has invested in building new icebreakers, conducting research missions in the Arctic, and seeking to partner with Arctic states to develop the region's resources.[59] China's interest in the region has prompted alarmist warnings that Beijing might try to appropriate those resources. For example, in his congressional testimony, Admiral Zukunft of the US Coast Guard stated the following:

We have seen China, for example, with their icebreakers [in the region]. . . . We have not ratified the Law of the Sea Convention so it is treated like it is a global commons. So, if at some point in the future we ratify the Law of the Sea, we stake our claim, I would be naïve to believe the claim would not be challenged by others who claim they have operated there repeatedly and this is now a global commons and next thing we know we see a Chinese mobile offshore drilling unit going into the extended continental shelf to extract what otherwise would be US oil.[60]

---

[57] For more see Jennifer Lind and Daryl G. Press, "Markets or Mercantilism? How China Secures Its Energy Supplies," *International Security* 42, no. 4 (2018): 191–94.

[58] State Council Information Office, *China's Arctic Policy* (Beijing: People's Republic of China, January 2018).

[59] Nong Hong, "Emerging Interests of Non-Arctic Countries in the Arctic: A Chinese Perspective," *Polar Journal* 4, no. 2 (2014): 271–86.

[60] Eckstein, "Zukunft."

These concerns are overblown. My theory suggests that while China will be interested in developing and purchasing Arctic resources, its goal will not be to appropriate them. In addition, China will have a long-term interest in developing and maintaining access to Arctic sea lanes if they become a viable global shipping route. However, as discussed in Chapter 5, it will likely be decades before these sea lanes are economically viable. China's recent investments in enhancing its Arctic presence and the white paper demonstrate that its interest in the region is increasing, but there is no evidence that China will seek to appropriate Arctic resources or that it would be willing to project military power to do so.

In sum, in contrast to previous rising powers such as pre–World War II Germany and Japan, for now, China lives in a world in which markets are relatively open, allowing it to export its goods and secure the resources it needs without conquering territory. Also, unlike previous empires, China does not rely primarily on the physical control of territory to extract income: it generates far higher profits from production rather than conquest. As long as these factors do not change, China should have a weak interest in securing control over territory and resources as a source of rents and wealth. Instead, China will be primarily interested in obtaining and maintaining access to the foreign markets and sea lanes upon which its economy depends.

9.6.3 Where Should We Be Least and Most Worried about the Future of Resource Competition?

The discussion in the previous section suggests that resource-driven territorial aggrandizement by the major powers is far less likely than in the past. Existing arguments suggest that there is a norm against large-scale territorial aggrandizement.[61] This norm is enforced by the most powerful production-oriented states. However, the empirical record suggests that there is a threshold below which this norm is not always enforced.[62] As a result, most incidences of territorial aggrandizement and militarized resource competition have occurred within states and between states over small pieces of territory or over gray zones, in which it is less clear which state exercises sovereign control (e.g., overlapping offshore resource claims).[63] So long as states expect norms to be enforced, they should be less likely to engage in large-scale territorial aggrandizement, even if they have a strong interest in doing so. However, we should still expect to observe intrastate conflict over resources, as well as interstate conflict over gray zones and smaller pieces of territory. This conflict will be most likely in regions where states are still land-oriented

---

[61] Fazal, *State Death*; Zacher, "The Territorial Integrity Norm."

[62] Altman, "Evolution of Territorial Conquest after 1945."

[63] See Altman, "By Fait Accompli, Not Coercion."

and resource-dependent and least likely where they have transitioned to producing goods and services.

9.6.4 Where Is the Risk of Resource-Driven Territorial Competition and Conflict Lowest?

The good news is that most of the world's states are far more production-oriented now than in the past. Some regions, such as Europe and North America, are almost exclusively populated by democratic production-oriented states, suggesting that the probability of territorial conflict and resource competition in these regions is extremely low. This should be the case even if technological advances in deep-sea drilling lead to discoveries of large deposits of natural resources in areas where countries have overlapping claims. So long as the states involved are democratic and production-oriented, militarized resource competition is unlikely. This does not suggest that these states will not compete to own these resources, but they should be less likely to engage in gunboat diplomacy and coercive bargaining.

It is helpful to compare the response to the sudden discovery of oil and gas reserves in the North Sea with the response to the exposure of resources in the Arctic. In June 1964 West Germany made the first offshore discovery of North Sea gas thirty-four miles north of the island of Juist.[64] In September 1965 the British made their first large offshore discovery of gas near the Humber estuary.[65] These discoveries were made possible by technological advances in offshore drilling and increased the expectation that the North Sea held commercially exploitable quantities of oil and gas.[66] Thus, undersea territory that had been of little economic or geopolitical interest suddenly became potentially valuable. Several states bordered the North Sea and could therefore make claims to those resources, including Britain, Norway, Denmark, the Netherlands, and West Germany.[67] This exposure of resources in an area that no one state owned, but to which many could lay claim, provides an additional opportunity to observe how states react to the exposure of contestable resources.

---

[64] Keith Chapman, *North Sea Oil and Gas: A Geographical Perspective*, Problems in Modern Geography (North Pomfret, VT: David and Charles, 1976), 48.

[65] Brent F. Nelsen, *The State Offshore: Petroleum, Politics, and State Intervention on the British and Norwegian Continental Shelves* (New York: Praeger, 1991), 26.

[66] Gerry Corti and Frank Frazer, *The Nation's Oil: A Story of Control* (London: Graham & Trotman, 1983), 29. In 1950 the effective limit was 20 feet; by 1973, drilling down to depths of 350 feet was routine, and some exploratory wells had gone below 1,000 feet. The impact of these new drilling technologies on the development of offshore resources was profound. In 1950 the amount of oil produced offshore was negligible, but two decades later submarine reservoirs made up 19% of global production. See Chapman, *North Sea Oil and Gas*, 33.

[67] Belgium and France technically border the North Sea, but since both had only marginal claims to North Sea oil, I do not include them in the analysis.

The principal difference between the Arctic and North Sea cases is the presence in the Arctic of land-oriented and autocratic states that had a stronger incentive to seek rents. In both the North Sea and the Arctic, states reacted to the exposure of resources by claiming resources within the framework prescribed by international law. The key difference is that, whereas in the North Sea the bargaining occurred solely within international institutions, in the Arctic some states employed a dual-track policy of making formal legal claims while also building and deploying military force to protect or further their resource claims.

What explains this difference? My theory suggests that in the Arctic, states with a strong preference for territory, such as land-oriented Norway and land-oriented, autocratic Russia, backed their claims by projecting military force. The very presence of these land-oriented states increased the incentives for even the production-oriented states to invest in increasing their Arctic military presence to defend their claims, albeit at a much lower level than the land-oriented states. In contrast, in the North Sea, all the states were democratic and highly production-oriented and, thus, while interested in the resources, all had a relatively weak preference to secure their control.[68] As a result, they were all willing to bargain over their interests without investing in or deploying power-projection capabilities. Rather than engaging in gunboat diplomacy, a group of production-oriented democratic states divided these resources peacefully.

The implication is clear. As states become less interested in securing territory and the resources that lie beneath, their willingness to invest in coercive bargaining over territory decreases. The weaker their preference for territorial control, the more likely they are to handle their disputes purely through international legal institutions, without the shadow of military power. This suggests that regions where states are less economically dependent on territory should have less territorial competition and conflict.

9.6.5 Where Is the Risk of Resource-Driven Territorial Competition and Conflict Greatest?

The largest concentrations of land-oriented states are in the Middle East and Africa, where states are, on average, much more economically dependent on resource rents than in the rest of the world (see Figure 9.1). Given this, my theory predicts that the risk of militarized resource competition and conflict is highest in these regions. I will give a number of examples of recent incidents of resource competition within and between highly resource-dependent states. It is important to note that these examples are meant to be illustrative and are not intended as empirical tests or

---

[68] Recall from Chapter 8 that when North Sea oil reserves were discovered, Norway was largely production-oriented and produced and exported virtually no oil or gas.

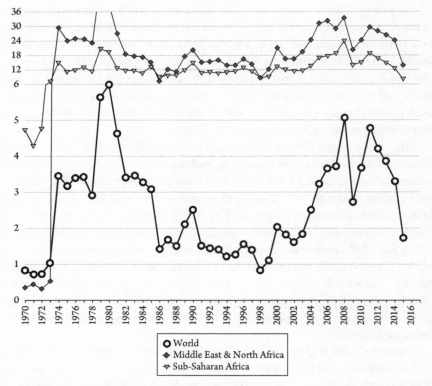

Figure 9.1 Resource Rents as a Percentage of GDP
Source: The World Bank, "Total Natural Resources Rents (% of GDP)," World Development Indicators,
June 25, 2018, https://data.worldbank.org/indicator/NY.GDP.TOTL.RT.ZS.

demonstrations that my theory alone can explain these cases. They merely show
that my theory can be applied to resource-dependent states beyond the Arctic and
foreshadows the potential for future resource conflict.

The Middle East contains the world's largest energy reserves and its most
resource-dependent states. It would be naive to suggest that competition over the
region's land rents is the only driver of conflict, but it would be equally absurd to
assert that land rents play no role in motivating and sustaining regional competition and conflict. Put simply, the Middle East contains a set of states that are economically dependent on land rents and, as a result, have a strong preference to
secure control over territory. As Fearon has recently argued, the stronger a state's
preferences to secure control over territory in a given region, the higher the levels of
arming and territorial rivalry are likely to be.[69] My theory provides an explanation
for why the states in the Middle East have a stronger preference for territory, which

---

[69] Fearon, "Cooperation, Conflict, and the Costs of Anarchy," 23.

makes them more likely to engage in territorial rivalries, arms races, and territorial conflict.

It is no coincidence that the region has a long history of violent territorial conflict both between and within highly resource-dependent states. In the 1980s, Iran and Iraq, two autocratic, resource-dependent states, fought a long, bloody eight-year war over resource-rich territory that largely ended in stalemate.[70] This was followed by Iraq's invasion of oil-rich Kuwait in 1990, which was reversed by a US-led coalition that had a strong interest in both enforcing the norm against territorial aggrandizement and ensuring that no one state could monopolize Middle Eastern energy reserves. Saddam Hussein's Iraq was a land-oriented state that depended on resource rents for the wealth needed to generate military power and maintain the support of the governing coalition. The Iran–Iraq War and Iraq's annexation of Kuwait are examples of a land-oriented state projecting power to seek control over additional resource rents.

After 1991, the United States clearly understood Iraq's expansionist interests and maintained a heavy military presence in the Middle East, containing and eventually invading Iraq.[71] The heavy US presence deterred the resource-dependent states in the region from pursuing or even openly making claims on one another's resource-rich territory but did not prevent proxy wars fought via civil conflicts within these states. Moreover, the rapid American exit from Iraq was associated with a renewed civil conflict that involved control over Iraq's resources.

The logic of Rent-Addiction Theory can also be applied to secessionist conflicts in highly resource-dependent states.[72] Perhaps nowhere is the link between resource dependence and resource competition clearer than in the secessionist conflicts between Kurdistan and Iraq. Iraqi Kurdistan has been politically autonomous since 2003 and is highly resource-dependent. In 2014, Kurdish Peshmerga forces seized oil fields near Kirkuk after Iraqi forces fled from advancing ISIS forces.[73] These oil

---

[70] For more on this conflict, see Kenneth M. Pollack, *Arabs at War: Military Effectiveness, 1948–1991*, Studies in War, Society, and the Military (Lincoln: University of Nebraska Press, 2002).

[71] As noted in Chapter 4, the United States has now projected military power into the Middle East for over forty years, but it has never sought to directly control the land rents, despite their enormous value. Even when the United States invaded Iraq, it did not keep the oil, despite suggestions by some that it would do so. Instead, the core US goal in the Middle East, as explicitly laid out by the Carter Doctrine, was to maintain the free flow of oil onto global markets. Because of his expansionist tendencies, Saddam Hussein represented a threat to this objective. For more on the need to contain Iraq, see Coe, "Containing Rogues."

[72] The link between resource dependence and civil conflict has already been well established as groups within the state face strong incentives to compete over control of the largest source of wealth and rents. For a review of the literature, see Michael L. Ross, "What Do We Know About Natural Resources and Civil War?" *Journal of Peace Research* 41, no. 3 (2004): 337–356.

[73] Diego Cupolo, "It's Never a Good Time for the Iraqi Kurds to Become Independent," *The Atlantic*, September 24, 2017, https://www.theatlantic.com/international/archive/2017/09/turkey-kurds-barzani-iraq-referendum/540909/.

fields reportedly contain nine billion barrels of oil, or 6% of the world's total reserves and 40% of Iraq's.[74] In October of 2017 the central government of Iraq, which is one of the most resource-dependent states in the world, deployed tanks not only to reconquer Kirkuk but to seize large tracts of disputed territory in northern and eastern Iraq, conquering far more area than Kurdish forces had taken in 2014.[75]

Even if Kurdistan became independent, it would still be resource-dependent and would share a border with Iraq, as well as with other rent-addicted states, such as Syria and Iran.

Thus, an intrastate competition over resources could morph into an interstate competition over those resources. This dynamic will be illustrated by the case of resource competition in the Sudan, an intrastate conflict that turned into an interstate conflict.

In 2005, after a brutal civil war that was motivated in part by control over natural resources, the warring parties made an agreement that gave South Sudan some degree of political autonomy from Sudan.[76] Natural resource rents were the economic lifeblood for both sides, giving them a strong preference to secure control over territory. The two sides continued to compete, sometimes violently, over the control of resource-rich territory, such as the oil fields near the town of Abyei, which reportedly contain 25% of the oil reserves of the formerly united Sudan.[77] In early 2011, just as South Sudan was preparing to declare formal independence, Sudan deployed militias to attack this oil-rich territory, and South Sudan responded in May of 2011 by invading the area.[78] Fighting erupted again in March of 2012, when South Sudan invaded the oil-rich area of Hejlij.[79] While United Nations intervention has temporarily reduced the level of conflict, the two states remain highly resource-dependent and continue to dispute the area near Abyei.[80]

---

[74] Michael Rubin, "An Independent Kurdistan Would Be a Failed State," *Newsweek*, July 4, 2017, https://www.newsweek.com/independent-kurdistan-would-be-failed-state-631778.

[75] Joost Hiltermann and Maria Fantappie, "Twilight of the Kurds," *Foreign Policy*, January 16, 2018, https://foreignpolicy.com/2018/01/16/twilight-of-the-kurds-iraq-syria-kurdistan/.

[76] Note that South Sudan was considered an autonomous region in 2005 and did not formally become an independent state until July of 2011. For more on Sudan's dependence on oil, see Samia Satti Osman Mohamed Nour, "Assessment of the Impacts of Oil: Opportunities and Challenges for Economic Development in Sudan," MERIT Working Paper (United Nations University—Maastricht Economic and Social Research Institute on Innovation and Technology, Maastricht, The Netherlands, 2011), https://econpapers.repec.org/paper/unmunumer/2011006.htm.

[77] On Abyei oil reserves, see Fred Oluoch, "South Sudan Risks Losing Oil-Rich Abyei," *The East African (Nairobi)*, February 21, 2017, https://allafrica.com/stories/201702210653.html.

[78] On the conflict over Abyei, see Joshua Craze, *Dividing Lines: Grazing and Conflict along the Sudan–South Sudan Border* (Geneva, Switzerland: Small Arms Survey, 2013), 79–80, 82.

[79] Luke Patey, *The New Kings of Crude: China, India, and the Global Struggle for Oil in Sudan and South Sudan* (London: Hurst, 2014), 235.

[80] Ted Dagne, "The Republic of South Sudan: Opportunities and Challenges for Africa's Newest Country," *Current Politics and Economics of Africa; Hauppauge* 5, no. 1 (2012): 64.

9.6.6 The Prospects of Resource Competition beyond Africa and the Middle East

Beyond the Middle East and Africa, there are many other resource-dependent states that I predict have a strong preference for territory. For example, central Asia contains a number of resource-dependent states that border the Caspian Sea, including Russia, Kazakhstan, Azerbaijan, Turkmenistan, and Iran. The Caspian Sea has major oil and gas reserves, and highly resource-dependent Iran has ongoing disputes over the division of resources in the region.[81] Also, two other resource-dependent states, Azerbaijan and Turkmenistan, have overlapping claims to resource-rich sections of the Caspian Sea.[82]

In Latin America, Guyana and Venezuela are resource-dependent states with an ongoing dispute over a large section of Guyana called Guayana Esequiba.[83] Venezuela also claims the waters off the coast of Guayana Esequiba, and in 2013 it evicted a ship that was surveying for oil in the disputed zone.[84] The dispute escalated in May of 2015, when the Guyanese government announced a massive oil discovery off the coast of Guayana Esequiba.[85] Venezuela reacted by making claims to the maritime resources and deploying troops to its border with Guyana, where they began conducting military exercises.[86] The dispute is ongoing, but for now the Venezuelan government is preoccupied with managing the domestic political turmoil associated with its recent economic collapse.

These cases provide illustrative evidence that the link between resource dependence and territorial competition is not just an Arctic phenomenon but generalizes to explain the potential for resource competition between land-oriented states in multiple regions of the world. The theory and evidence suggest that policymakers should be most concerned about the prospect for resource competition among

---

[81] Ziyad Ziyadzade, "Drilling for Black Gold: The Demarcation for Hydrocarbon Resources in the Caspian Sea," *Chicago Journal of International Law* 16, no. 1 (2015): 312–39.

[82] Douglas Green, "Caspian Sea Dispute: Where Solutions Jump ahead of Problems," *Times of Central Asia*, June 1, 2017, https://timesca.com/index.php/news/26-opinion-head/18120-caspian-sea-dispute-where-solutions-jump-ahead-of-problems.

[83] Venezuela has long been a petro-state. Guyana, on the other hand, is highly dependent on rents from timber and minerals. From 2008 to 2016, resource rents for both states averaged approximately 14.6% and 20.8% of GDP, respectively. See World Bank, "Total Natural Resources Rents (% of GDP)," June 25, 2018.

[84] Daniel Lansberg-Rodríguez, "An Oil Strike in No Man's Land," *Foreign Policy*, June 16, 2015, https://foreignpolicy.com/2015/06/16/an-oil-strike-in-no-mans-land/.

[85] William Neuman, "In Guyana, a Land Dispute with Venezuela Escalates Over Oil," *New York Times*, November 18, 2015, https://www.nytimes.com/2015/11/19/world/americas/in-guyana-a-land-dispute-with-venezuela-escalates-over-oil.html?ref=nyt-es&mcid=nyt-es&subid=article.

[86] Jose de Arimateia da Cruz, "Strategic Insights: Guyana-Venezuela: The Essequibo Region Dispute" (Strategic Studies Institute and US Army War College Press, December 14, 2015), http://publications.armywarcollege.edu/pubs/3338.pdf.

states that are highly economically dependent on resource rents. The bad news is that existing evidence suggests that once states become economically dependent on and addicted to resource rents, it is extremely difficult for them to transition to a production-oriented economy.[87] Unless these states can kick their addiction, the risk of resource competition will be high and the prospect for sustained peace limited, especially in regions such as the Middle East and Africa.

The good news is that, partially because of a shift in the interests of the world's most powerful states, a coalition of production-oriented and largely democratic states has supported an international order that facilitates open markets and largely upholds the norm against territorial conquest. This has significantly reduced the incentives for territorial conquest by allowing production-oriented states to buy the resources they need on open markets and generally deterring land-oriented states from attempting large-scale conquest. However, the cracks in the international order are starting to show, and it remains to be seen whether it will continue to hold. If states do not believe that markets will continue to provide them with vital natural resources, even production-oriented states will have a strong interest in gaining control over territory to ensure access to resources.

Also, if the coalition of powerful production-oriented states that has upheld the existing international order fractures and is no longer willing to enforce the norms against territorial aggrandizement, land-oriented states may no longer be deterred from acting on their preference to gain control over territory and resources. If this happens, territorial competition and conquest may no longer be confined to intrastate conflict, gray zones, and small pieces of territory. If land-oriented states do not believe they will be punished for large-scale violations of the norms against territorial aggrandizement, the frequency and scale of resource competition and territorial conquest may increase.

9.7 Future Research

Politics is ultimately about interests, and policy is simply a means to realize a given set of interests. Every day, world leaders wake up and make life-and-death decisions based on their interests and their beliefs about the interests of others. Without some basic understanding of an actor's interests, it is impossible to explain or anticipate that actor's behavior. Our ability to solve the world's most critical challenges

[87] Michael L. Ross, "What Do We Know about Economic Diversification in Oil-Producing Countries?" Energy and Economic Growth State-of-Knowledge Paper Series 5.2 (Berkeley: University of California Berkeley Center for Effective Global Action, 2017), 44. Diversification is difficult but not impossible. For some hopeful evidence, see Cullen S. Hendrix, "Kicking a Crude Habit: Diversifying away from Oil and Gas in the Twenty-First Century," *International Review of Applied Economics* 33, no. 2 (2019): 188–208.

related to war and peace, poverty and prosperity, environmental catastrophe and sustainability depends on our understanding of the actors involved, their interests, and how their incentives can be manipulated to realize the desired outcome. Given this, it is remarkable how little political science knows about where states' foreign policy interests come from, especially with regard to issues relating to international security.

Scholars of international political economy take for granted that states differ enormously in terms of trade and investment policy goals, based on the structure of their economies. Unfortunately, in the realm of international security, we know far less about how states' goals differ based on their domestic political economies. I have sought to remedy this by developing a theory of how states' economic structures and domestic political institutions influence their foreign policy preferences with regard to two key issues: territory and resources. The findings demonstrate that the strength of states' interests regarding these issues can be identified ex ante, that they vary in predictable ways, and that this variation can be used to explain changes in their behavior. These first steps represent the beginning rather than the end of what I hope will become a much wider area of research on the origins and impacts of foreign policy preferences. I close by offering three potential avenues for future research on the political economy of international security generally and the origins and impact of states' foreign policy goals more specifically.[88]

Research on the political economy of security is united by a core assumption: that actors' material interests shape their behavior with regard to policies and outcomes that involve the threat or use of violence.[89] While this book answers questions about the effects of economic structure on state preferences for territory, how does a state's source of income shape its foreign policy goals with regard to other issues? History shows that states can employ military force to seek wealth through means other than direct territorial control, such as securing preferential access to markets, exclusionary spheres of influence, or enforcing property rights for their citizens. Future research should explore the conditions under which a state's source of income influences its security policy goals and grand strategies and how those policies, in turn, create prosperity for those who govern the state.

Similarly, how do political and economic systems that reward elites for rent-seeking at home encourage them to pursue rent-seeking foreign polices?[90] This question is relevant not only for understanding the foreign policy objectives of increasingly powerful autocracies such as China but also for understanding

---

[88] For a review of this emerging subfield, see Paul Poast, "Beyond the 'Sinew of War': The Political Economy of Security as a Subfield," *Annual Review of Political Science* 22, no. 1 (2019): 223–39.

[89] I am indebted to Andrew Coe for this insight.

[90] For some promising pioneering work in this area, see Andrew J. Coe, "The Modern Economic Peace" (unpublished manuscript, University of Southern California, 2015).

consolidating democracies such as India, Indonesia, and Nigeria, whose domestic policies are rife with corruption and rent-seeking.

Thus, an expanded theory is needed to explain the conditions under which states prefer to generate income by producing value (making the world wealthier) rather than by taking goods from other states. At best, taking another state's goods simply redistributes wealth, but generally it results in at least some value being destroyed. Future research should explore the conditions under which states have an incentive to seek wealth via transfers from other states and, in particular, the conditions under which they have incentives to do so using military force.

Finally, the theory and empirical tests in this book are focused on the origins of states' foreign policy interests and how these interests condition behavior. States' domestic economic structure conditions their strategic interaction on a host of foreign policy issues. The next step is to incorporate my theory of foreign policy interests into a more fully developed theory of international relations. Doing so would allow us to examine the degree to which a given state's strategic environment is conditioned not just by the distribution of power but also by the distribution of interests.[91] This would make it easier to assess the degree to which states' foreign policy behavior is conditioned both by their own material interests and by the degree to which those interests are compatible with those of the other states in their strategic environments.

---

[91] For some initial work that examines how variation in a state's interests conditions its strategic environment, see Therese Anders, Christopher J. Fariss, and Jonathan N. Markowitz, "Bread before Guns or Butter: Introducing Surplus Domestic Product (SDP)," *International Studies Quarterly* (forthcoming).

APPENDIX

Table of Contents

Introduction to the Appendix

The key purpose of this appendix is to provide additional detail about how I operationalize my theoretical constructs, along with additional evidence supporting the core claims made in the book *Perils of Plenty: Arctic Resource Competition and the Return of the Great Game*.

The R code, data, and codebooks necessary to replicate the key figures and tables are available upon request.

A Measuring the Independent Variable: The Economic Structure of the State

As described in the main text, my measure of ruling coalition type assesses the *economic structure of the state*. I assess the degree to which a state's economy is organized to generate income from land, as opposed to from producing goods and services. States at either extreme of this dimension I call *land-oriented* and *production-oriented*.

My theory assumes a tight relationship between a given sector's share of the state's wealth and income and the degree to which the individuals in the governing coalition have an interest in that sector. This assumption is plausible because money generally finds its way into politics. This can happen through two pathways: either money captures the state or the state captures money.

Pathway 1: Money captures the state. Those who control the state's wealth generally invest in securing political influence to ensure that the government pursues policies favorable to their economic interests. The greater their share of the state's wealth, the greater their ability to outbid other sectors of the economy that are competing for this influence. Political economists refer to this as "capture" because a sector controls the entities that are intended to regulate it.

Pathway 2: The state captures the money. States often appropriate the commanding heights of the economy, especially in the case of resource wealth, thereby making state interests and industry interests one and the same. For my theory, whether these resources are owned by the state or privately makes little difference. The state will still act to protect the economic interests of those who control it.

Note that I am not arguing that there is a perfect correlation between the size of an economic sector and its political representation within the state's governing coalition. Rather, I only assert that states with more land-oriented economies will have governing coalitions in which the land-oriented sector has a greater influence on policy than in states with less land-oriented economies.

In order to measure the degree to which the economic interests of the governing coalition are reliant on land rents, I need a measure of the share of the state's economy or economic output that is derived from land. Historically, a useful measure was the value of the agrarian surplus, which was by far the largest source of land-based wealth. This is still the case for extremely poor states, which tend to have agrarian economies. However, in developed states today, such as those examined in this book, agriculture's value added as a percentage of GDP is extremely small, generally 5% for Russia and under 2% for the United States.[1] The largest source of land-based wealth today is not agriculture but rents from natural resources.[2] For this reason, I adopt indicators used by scholars of the resource curse, specifically resource rents as a percentage of GDP from the World Bank Development Indicators.[3] As a robustness check on this measure, I include data on several measures of the flow of income generated from land, including fuel and oil exports as a percentage of GDP.[4] All of these additional indicators tend to strongly covary, further increasing my confidence that the measure is capturing the degree to which a state is economically dependent on resource rents. As an additional robustness check on these quantitative indicators, I rely on area specialists' qualitative assessments of the economic interests of the individuals in the governing coalition. Given that income can only be generated from land or by producing goods and services, I deduce that any income not generated from land must be created by the production of goods and services. Therefore, the production-oriented sector's share of the economy is simply the amount remaining after subtracting income derived from land.

A.1 Why Not Only Use Government Revenue?

I choose to operationalize the economic interests of the governing coalition of a state as resource rents as a percentage of GDP. This indicator is better than government revenue or whether the state owns the energy sector because a highly influential sector of the economy might use its influence to privatize state resources and/ or lower the tax rate on its industry. For example, the US economy is dominated by production-oriented industries, which vastly outspend extractive industries in terms of political contributions. It is perhaps not a coincidence that gas companies, such as Exxon and Chevron, pay the second-highest tax rates of any industry, while information technology firms, such as Apple and Google, pay the second-lowest rate of any industry. If we only judged the influence of a sector by whether it was controlled by the state or the degree to which the government depended on it for

---

[1] World Bank, "Agriculture, Value Added (% of GDP)," accessed July 15, 2018, https://data.worldbank.org/indicator/NV.AGR.TOTL.ZS?end=2016&start=1988&view=chart.

[2] For more on this see, the World Bank's Inclusive Wealth Index.

[3] Collier and Hoeffler, "Testing the Neocon Agenda."

[4] For a review of the literature and various ways to measure the resource curse, see Ross, "What Have We Learned about the Resource Curse?"

revenue, we might incorrectly conclude that the information technology sector was not very influential, when in fact the opposite is true.

Russia also provides an excellent illustration of why ownership of a sector might not matter in terms of its influence on state policy. In the 1990s, Russia was run by a group of land-oriented oligarchs who used their influence to privatize the state's resources and bend policy to benefit their extractive industries at the expense of the production-oriented sector and the rest of society. Today, most of Russia's resource wealth is owned by the state and controlled by a small group of ex-KGB officials who manipulate state policy to benefit personally from extractive industries. In both cases, the extractive sector influenced state policy and rents flowed to individuals in the governing coalition. This relationship applies to autocratic as well as democratic states.

The key difference between autocracies and democracies is not whether the dominant sectors will receive preferential treatment but whether the profits will be enjoyed by a small, politically influential elite or distributed throughout society. For example, in both Russia and Norway, the state owns the resource wealth, giving those two states a stronger interest in policies that benefit the extractive sector of the economy. In contrast to Russia, Norwegian profits from extracting oil and gas are more broadly distributed throughout society in the form of public goods provision.

B Measuring the Dependent Variable: Investment in Exclusionary Foreign Policy

This section provides more detail about how I operationalize my dependent variable. Some of this detail is in the body of the main text, but I include and expand upon it here for the sake of clarification. As described in the main text, pursuing an exclusionary foreign policy is defined as investing in the projection of power to seek land rents.[5] I operationalize this variable as the relative investment that states make in pursuing an exclusionary foreign policy. Specifically, I compare states' foreign policy behavior using three categories of indicators:

1) *Arctic commitments*, expressed in strategic documents and statements made by officials, including claims to Arctic resources
2) *Arctic force posture*, or investment in deploying state forces to the Arctic

---

[5] Despite numerous attempts to measure the concept of power, there are relatively few studies that have sought to measure power projection in a systematic way. For previous attempts to systematically measure power projection, see Lemke, *Regions of War and Peace*; Fordham, "Who Wants to Be a Major Power?"

3) *Arctic force structure,* or investment in building military assets specifically designed for use in the Arctic

A state's investment across five ordinal indicators within these three categories is combined to measure its overall level of investment in an exclusionary foreign policy in the Arctic. Note that I take the average of the five indicators to represent the overall level of investment and round if the average is not a whole number. The advantage of using an ordinal measure for the dependent variable is that it is simple and easy to understand and allows me to draw on many different types of qualitative and quantitative evidence. However, the measure is less precise than an interval or ratio-level operationalization and requires a more detailed defense of my coding choices. But, given my theory, an ordinal level of operationalization is precise enough to evaluate my predictions about whether certain states will invest more than others in pursuing an exclusionary foreign policy in order to seek control over Arctic resources.

The first category is Arctic commitments. The second category, Arctic force posture, includes the indicators *Arctic military activity* and *deploying force to claimed or disputed areas.* The third category, Arctic force structure, contains the final two indicators: *icebreakers and ice-hardened warships* and *Arctic bases.* I provide a more detailed description and defense of my decision to include each of the indicators in section C.

Depending on its value, each indicator is assigned one of five ordinal values that reflect the relative interest or investment: (1) very low, (2) low, (3) medium, (4) high, and (5) very high. For illustration, if state A's investment prior to the shock was very low, its pre-shock level of investment would be coded as 1.

It is important to note that each state's investment is scored *relative to its own capacity to invest* because I use a state's level of investment as an observable implication of the strength of its preference for securing Arctic resources. This choice is analogous to measuring each state's Arctic military spending as a percentage of its GDP,[6] with higher percentages implying stronger preferences. Thus, the key comparison is each state's relative level of investment given its capacity, not its absolute level of investment.

C Measuring the Change in the Level of Investment

Comparing states' pre-shock levels of investment with their post-shock levels allows me to code the change in each state's level of investment. Based on the size

---

[6] Unfortunately, it is not possible to determine what each state spends on projecting power in the Arctic because it is not separated out in state budgets. Because of this, I look at changes in each state's Arctic military activity and force structure as proxies for the degree to which it is investing in projecting force to the region.

of the change, I assign each indicator one of five ordinal values: (0) almost none, (1) small, (2) moderate, (3) large, and (4) very large. It is helpful to use an example to illustrate how comparing a state's investment before and after the shock allows us to code the change. Suppose that prior to the shock state A made little mention of the Arctic in public statements or strategic planning documents; rarely deployed forces to the region; and invested little in maintaining and upgrading its Arctic-specific capabilities such as bases, icebreakers, and ice-hardened warships. Given this, I would code its pre-shock investment as very low, or 1. Now suppose that after the shock state A expressed a high level of interest in the Arctic, making bold commitments to enhancing its Arctic military presence in order to secure its claims in public statements and strategic documents; but there was only a small increase in its actual Arctic military activity, no increase in its willingness to deploy forces to areas under dispute, and only a small increase in its investment in enhancing its ice-capable fleet and Arctic bases. Given this, I would code state A's post-shock investment as low. However, this is still a change, given that state A's overall pre-shock investment was very low (coded as 1) and its post-shock level was low (coded as 2). Thus, the change in its level of investment would be coded as $2 - 1 = 1$ (small). This example is represented graphically in Table A.1.

Table A.1 summarizes the indicators used to code the level of, and change in, each state's investment in pursuing an exclusionary foreign policy. A version of this table appears in the introduction to each case study in Chapters 5–8 and previews the theoretical predictions and findings for each state.

C.1   Operationalizing a State's Level of Commitment to the Arctic

The first category of indicators used to assess states' investments in pursuing an exclusionary foreign policy considers Arctic commitments and resource claims. The nature and level of a state's commitment are assessed by observing the degree to which the Arctic, and Arctic resources specifically, are prioritized relative to other issues and commitments in strategic documents and statements by officials. I consider the nature of a state's resource claims by examining (1) what the state claimed and (2) the degree to which those claims were consistent with international legal norms. My theory suggests that production-oriented states should be most likely to make and pursue their claims purely within the confines of international law and should be reluctant to project power. I assess whether resource claims were pursued via international law or whether states chose extra-legal methods, such as building and projecting military power, to bargain coercively over claims.

To assess the degree to which states' claims adhere to international legal norms, I note whether claims to territory or sea lanes are formal (i.e., submitted to the

Table A.1 **State A's Overall Level of Investment**

	Predicted Change in Investment	Observed Pre-shock Investment (Scale 1–5)	Observed Post-shock Investment (Scale 1–5)	Observed Change in Investment (Scale 0–4)
Arctic commitments	Small	Very low (1)	High (4)	Large (3)
Arctic military activity	Small	Very low (1)	Low (2)	Small (1)
Deploying force to claimed or disputed areas	Small	Very low (1)	Low (2)	Small (1)
Icebreakers and ice-hardened warships	Small	Very low (1)	Very low (1)	Almost none (0)
Arctic bases	Small	Very low (1)	Low (2)	Small (1)
Overall investment in exclusionary foreign policy	Small	Very low (1)	Low (2)	Small (1)

International Seabed Authority [ISA] to extend the state's Exclusive Economic Zone [EEZ]) or informal (not submitted to the ISA).[7] I also assess whether states pursued their disputes using the principles of international law and prevailing legal norms or whether they made claims beyond what they would have received if they had relied on existing international legal norms; for instance, did they adopt the equidistance principle when delimiting overlapping EEZ claims? To capture state

[7] All states are accorded an EEZ under the United Nations Convention on the Law of the Sea and effectively own the seabed resources within their EEZ. States can make claims beyond their EEZs, but for these claims to be consistent with international law, states must submit evidence of an extended continental shelf (ECS) to the Commission on the Limits of the Continental Shelf. If a state's claimed EEZ or ECS overlaps with another state's, the two states must settle their boundary through bilateral negotiations; but the international legal norm is to delimit each side's boundaries using the equidistance principle.

claims, I rely on several indicators, including public statements from government officials, policy documents (including legislation), diplomatic communications, and formal legal claims.

C.2 Defining the Constructs of Interest

There are many conceptions and definitions of power projection. I am interested in power projection as an observable manifestation of a state's preference to seek some objective or good. I focus on states' choices to invest in power projection capabilities (Arctic force structure) and their decisions to deploy those capabilities (Arctic force posture).[8] It is critical to note that in this study I am less interested in whether a state's attempt to generate influence by projecting power is successful than in the relative level of investment in generating influence. For these reasons, I focus on indicators that capture changes in a state's relative level of investment in projecting power. This definition of power projection is useful because it allows me to operationalize power projection ex ante and to separate the act of projecting power from its intention or effect.

Projecting power requires two types of investments. First, states must adopt the appropriate force posture by deploying their (always limited) forces to a specific region (and paying the costs of deployment). Second, they must create and maintain the force structure and logistical infrastructure required to deploy force over distance, which I define as power projection capabilities. I am interested in how states responded to the shock in terms of their willingness to make both types of investments.

C.3 Operationalizing a State's Level of Investment in Its Arctic Force Posture

First, because I am interested in whether states chose to respond by increasing their Arctic military presence, I focus on changes in the frequency, intensity, and nature of each state's Arctic military deployments. In order to assess each state's Arctic military activity and changes in this activity over time, I created a new Military Activity Event Data Set. This data set includes all publicly reported events that involved state-owned or state-controlled forces being deployed to the Arctic from January 1, 2005, to December 31, 2009.[9] This is sufficient to cover the immediate post-shock period, and the cost of collecting data over a longer period is prohibitive.

---

[8] In other work, I focus on the effects of power projection; see Paul Avey, Robert Reardon, and Jonathan Markowitz, "Do US Troop Withdrawals Cause Instability? Evidence from Two Exogenous Shocks on the Korean Peninsula," *Journal of Global Security Studies* 3, no. 1 (2018): 72–92.

[9] I include all state forces, both military and nonmilitary, for two reasons. First, any state-owned unit deployed to the Arctic is a signal of the state's willingness to invest in maintaining a regional presence. Also, these forces can help the state project force by enhancing situational awareness or providing logistical support (such as icebreakers clearing sea lanes). Second, the distinction between military and

Collecting these data took the better part of a decade and required sifting through and hand-coding a sample of over 5,000 news articles collected from LexisNexis. These codes are robust under multiple intercoder reliability tests.[10]

In addition to recording the frequency of deployments, the Military Activity Event Data Set codes (a) where and (b) how each state deployed military force. The sum of these coded events gives a picture of the frequency and intensity of deployments. Regarding location, I coded the data using three criteria:

1) whether the state deployed forces beyond its borders or territorial waters
2) whether it deployed forces to areas under dispute
3) whether it deployed to the borders or airspace of other states with which it had disputes

If a state deployed forces to areas under dispute (criterion a2) or against states with which it had disputes over resources (criterion a3), this is informative about the strength of its preferences. The more a state invests in boosting its military presence and projecting power to disputed areas, the more evidence there is for the strength of the state's preferences to seek resource rents. These behaviors are costly signals of a state's interests and intentions.

The descriptive statistical analysis in Chapter 4 focuses on comparing the frequency and location of each of the states' deployments. The case study analyses in Chapters 5–8 then utilize and supplement these data by including additional qualitative evidence that illuminates how each state deployed its forces. In assessing how states deployed their forces, I record the date of deployment and the number of units that were deployed. I also code attributes of the deployment such as whether states engaged in confrontational behavior including live fire drills, violating another state's airspace or territorial borders, buzzing other states' ships, or conducting mock bombing runs on other states' territory. I also consider the attributes of the military units or forces that were deployed (e.g., heavily armed bombers versus unarmed reconnaissance aircraft). The type of units a state deploys can convey important information about its intentions, resolve, and willingness to escalate. For example, if a state deployed dogsled teams, we would infer that it was less resolved than if it deployed a nuclear-powered icebreaker. Both the frequency and the intensity with which states choose to deploy their forces are informative about the strength of their preferences. All else being equal, the more frequently a

---

nonmilitary is often blurred. For example, while some states have no coast guard, deferring the operation of their ships to a navy, others have what are effectively warships that are operated by the coast guard. To obtain the most accurate account of a state's efforts to project power into a region, I code all reported deployments of state forces to the Arctic and then code whether formal state military forces were involved.

[10] For more detail on the procedures used to identify this sample of articles and in the coding of the data, see the Arctic Military Activity Events Codebook which is available upon request.

state deploys forces and the more militarily capable and costly these forces are to deploy, the stronger its preference to project power into a given region.

C.4 Operationalizing a State's Level of Investment in Its Arctic Force Structure

Second, I must consider the degree to which states invested in Arctic-specific power projection capabilities. As described in the main text, I do this using two original data sets, the Arctic Bases Data Set and the Arctic Icebreakers and Ice-Hardened Warships Data Set. These data sets capture variation in how much states invested in their Arctic bases and ice-hardened warships.[11] The cases then build on these data by including additional qualitative detail on the purposes and capabilities of the ships and bases. The qualitative case analysis also allows me to consider a more complete set of evidence about each state's Arctic-specific investments. I consider shifts in training and operations, the establishment of Arctic commands, and special Arctic military units and dual-use capabilities that would enhance the state's ability to project power into the Arctic. These include naval, air, and land forces that are Arctic-capable as well as logistical capabilities, such as surveillance and communication technology, that could enhance a state's ability to project power into the Arctic.

Acquiring military hardware and training military units is a lengthy process—measured in years or decades. Governments often announce plans to acquire military units that never materialize due to a lack of funds; however, these announcements are informative about the strength of their preferences. The costliest behaviors are the most informative. Investments in site-specific force structure and force posture are the costliest behaviors and are therefore most informative about a state's willingness to invest in pursuing one type of foreign policy over another. Thus, the greater a state's investment in its geographically specific force structure and force posture, the stronger the signal that it has invested in projecting power to a specific geographic region. Conversely, the less a state invests in such capabilities, the less willing it is to invest in projecting power to a specific region. Many states have promised to invest in their Arctic force structures but have not followed through on those commitments. Therefore, the empirical section focuses on whether or not states actually invested in altering their Arctic military presence.

D   Robustness Checks and a More Nuanced Look at the Data

In this section, I demonstrate that my operationalization of the change in each state's investment in its Arctic military capabilities is robust to alternative measures and specifications.

---

[11] Additional detail on both data sets is available in the Arctic Bases and Ice-Capable Ships Codebook in the online supplementary materials.

D.1 Ship Tonnage versus Ship Count

In the main text, I measure investment in icebreakers and ice-hardened warships based on tonnage and show that, consistent with my theory, Norway and Russia made the largest increases in investment after the shock. Here, Figure A.1 shows the same comparisons but measures the number of ships, rather than the total tonnage. As we can see, Norway and Russia still show the largest increase, indicating that my results are robust to alternate measures of investment. The key difference when measuring the dependent variable using the number of ships rather than tonnage is that this measure tends to understate the size of Russia's post-shock investment because Russia built much larger, more expensive ships than did Norway.

D.2 New Ships versus Operational Ships

In the main text I argue that, because I am interested in measuring the change in investment, the most appropriate measure is the change in the number of new ships commissioned in the ten years before and after the shock, rather than the change in the total number of operational ships. However, one might wonder if my results would hold if instead I considered the change in count and tonnage of ships that were operational before and after the shock.

In this alternate specification, the pre-shock ship count includes all ships that were commissioned at any time before the shock and still operational as of June 1, 2007. There are two advantages to this specification. First, it allows us to see the total tonnage and number of ships that each state had at the time of the shock. This is important because it allows us to assess the possibility that some states might have been much further behind and therefore invested more, in order to try to

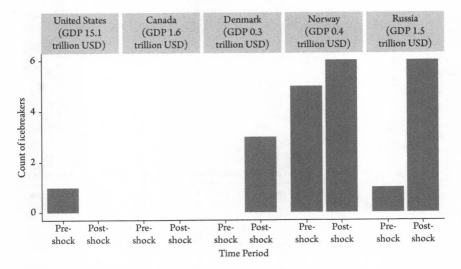

Figure A.1 Count of New Investments in Ice-Capable Ships

catch up. Second, it permits us to see if the amount of new investment after the shock was enough to offset ships that were taken out of commission in the ten years after the shock.

Figures A.2 and A.3 show that my results are robust to measuring the change using either the total number or the tonnage of operational ships. In fact, these results support my theoretical predictions more strongly as they show that Russia and Norway had a larger increase in both the number of operational ships and the operational tonnage. Moreover, as discussed in the main body of the text, these

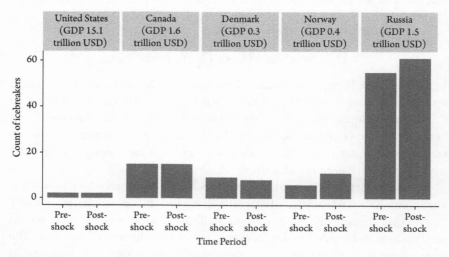

Figure A.2 Count of Operational Icebreakers

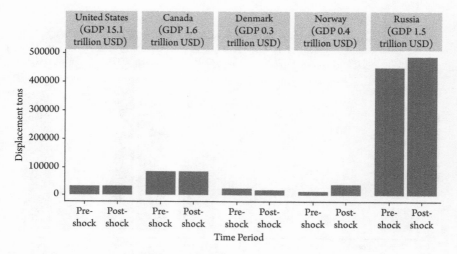

Figure A.3 Tonnage of Operational Icebreakers

figures illustrate that while Denmark commissioned new ships after the shock, those investments were not large enough to offset the decommissioning of several large icebreakers. As a result, both the number of Danish ships and the total tonnage of Denmark's ice-capable fleet actually decreased after the shock. This is shown below in Figure A.2 and Figure A.3.

D.3 New and Upgraded Bases versus Operational Bases

Similarly, one might wonder if my results hold if I measure states' level of investment in their Arctic bases using the change in the number of operational bases rather than just the number of new or upgraded bases. Here, as discussed in the main text, the results appear mixed as the number of operational Norwegian bases decreased after the shock. However, as discussed in both Chapter 4 and Chapter 8, this is not because Norway decreased its investment but rather because it closed two obsolete Cold War–era bases while simultaneously upgrading six bases and moving its military headquarters north of the Arctic Circle. Moreover, the results show that, despite the fact that Russia already had fourteen operational bases above the Arctic Circle at the time of the shock, Moscow still chose to increase its investment by building four new bases and reopening and/or upgrading another thirteen. As a result, a decade after the shock Russia has twenty-seven operational bases, more than any other state (Figure A.4).

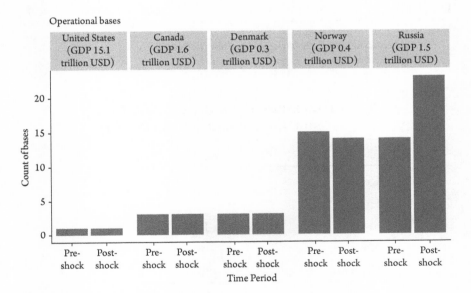

Figure A.4 Operational Bases

E Comparing Norway to the Other Nordic States

Chapter 8 claims that Norway consistently lags behind other Nordic states that do not have the luxury of relying on oil for their income. Tables A.2–A.4 provide evidence for this claim by showing that Norway scores below the average for the Nordic states on seven out of nine economic freedom indicators, while Denmark scores above average on all nine. Also, Denmark is the top performer among the Nordic states on six out of these nine indicators. In contrast, Norway is the top performer on only one indicator, trade freedom, and is the worst performer on six out of the nine indicators which can be seen in the following tables.

Table A.2 **Heritage Index of Economic Freedom Indicators Averaged 1997–2007 (Scale 0–100)** [a]

	Mean Economic Freedom Score	Mean Business Freedom Score	Mean Labor Freedom Score*	Mean Monetary Freedom Score	Mean Trade Freedom Score	Mean Investment Freedom Score	Mean Financial Freedom Score
Iceland	73.4	80.0	65.4	85.1	80.7	67.3	59.1
Finland	69.6	80.1	47.6	87.4	79.1	70.0	61.8
Sweden	67.6	74.6	65.1	88.9	80.1	80.0	77.3
Norway	67.3	73.9	49.6	82.7	81.9	57.3	50.0
Denmark	71.3	90.9	99.9	88.9	79.9	70.9	80.9

*Data only available 2005–2007 (average is taken from 2005–2007).
[a]Heritage Foundation, "Index of Economic Freedom."

Table A.3 **World Bank Ease of Doing Business Rank 2018 (1 is the highest rank, of 190 states)**

	Rank[a]
Iceland	23
Finland	13
Sweden	10
Norway	8
Denmark	3

[a]World Bank, "Ease of Doing Business Index (1=most Business-Friendly Regulations) | Data," accessed July 26, 2018, https://data.worldbank.org/indicator/IC.BUS.EASE.XQ.

Table A.4 **US News and World Report Open for Business 2018 (1 is the highest rank, of 80 countries surveyed)**

	Rank[a]
Iceland*	N/A
Finland	6
Sweden	5
Norway	8
Denmark	4

*Iceland was not among the countries surveyed.

[a]"The 80 Best Countries for Open for Business," U.S. News and World Report, accessed July 26, 2018, https://www.usnews.com/news/best-countries/open-for-business-full-list.

BIBLIOGRAPHY

ABS Consulting. *United States Coast Guard: High Latitude Region: Mission Analysis: Capstone Summary*. Arlington, VA: ABS Consulting, 2010.

Acemoglu, Daron, Simon Johnson, and James Robinson. "The Colonial Origins of Comparative Development." *American Economic Review* 91, no. 5 (2001): 1369–1401.

Advanced Resources International. *EIA/ARI World Shale Gas and Shale Oil Resource Assessment*. Arlington, VA: Advanced Resources International, 2013. http://www.adv-res.com/pdf/A_EIA_ARI_2013%20World%20Shale%20Gas%20and%20Shale%20Oil%20Resource%20Assessment.pdf.

AFP News. "Oil-Rich Norway Struggles to Beat Its 'Petroholism.'" The Local.no, September 8, 2017. https://www.thelocal.no/20170908/oil-rich-norway-struggles-to-beat-its-petroholism.

Air Force Technology. "Tu-160 Blackjack Strategic Bomber." n.d. http://www.airforce-technology.com/projects/tu160/.

Allen, Nick. "Donald Trump Overturns Obama Bans on Drilling as He Moves to Vastly Expand US Offshore Oil." *The Telegraph*, January 4, 2018. https://www.telegraph.co.uk/news/2018/01/04/donald-trump-overturns-obama-bans-drilling-moves-vastly-expand/.

Alston, J., M. A. Andersen, J. S. James, and P. G. Pardey. *Persistence Pays: U.S. Agricultural Productivity Growth and the Benefits from Public R&D Spending*. New York: Springer, 2010.

Altman, Dan. "By Fait Accompli, Not Coercion: How States Wrest Territory from Their Adversaries." *International Studies Quarterly* 61, no. 4 (2017): 881–91.

Altman, Dan. "The Evolution of Territorial Conquest after 1945 and the Limits of the Norm of Territorial Integrity," June 18, 2019. http://www.danielwaltman.com/uploads/3/2/3/1/32312379/evolution_of_territorial_conquest.pdf.

American Embassy Copenhagen. "Second Cable." August 27, 2009. http://news.bbc.co.uk/2/shared/bsp/hi/pdfs/12_05_11_wikicables_artic.pdf.

Anders, Therese, Christopher J. Fariss, and Jonathan N. Markowitz. "Bread before Guns or Butter: Introducing Surplus Domestic Product (SDP)." *International Studies Quarterly* (forthcoming).

Andrews, Kenneth R. *Trade, Plunder and Settlement: Maritime Enterprise and the Genesis of the British Empire, 1480–1630*. Cambridge: Cambridge University Press, 1984.

Antrim, Caitlyn L. "The Russian Arctic in the Twenty-First Century." In *Arctic Security in an Age of Climate Change*, edited by James C. Kraska, 107–28. New York: Cambridge University Press, 2011.

Arctic Council. *Arctic Marine Shipping Assessment 2009 Report*. Tromsø, Norway: Arctic Council, 2009.

Arild, Moe, and Olav Schram Stokke. "Asian Countries and Arctic Shipping: Policies, Interests and Footprints on Governance." *Arctic Review* 10 (2019). https://doi.org/10.23865/arctic. v10.1374.

Ashford, "Oil and Violence": The Foreign Policy of Resource Rich States" (ISA ISSS Conference, 2013).

Askin, Osman. "The High North: Challenges and Opportunities." NATO Parliamentary Assembly, n.d.https://www.nato-pa.int/sites/default/files/documents/2015%20-%20135%20 STC%2015%20E%20%20-%20Summary%20Budapest.doc.

Associated Press. "California Is Now the World's Fifth-Largest Economy, Surpassing United Kingdom." *Los Angeles Times*, May 4, 2018. http://www.latimes.com/business/la-fi-california-economy-gdp-20180504-story.html.

Associated Press. "Canada to Claim North Pole as Its Own." *The Guardian*, December 9, 2013, sec. World news. http://www.theguardian.com/world/2013/dec/10/canada-north-pole-claim.

Associated Press. "Fort Greely to Get $50 Million toward Missile Defense System." *Army Times*, December 16, 2014. https://www.armytimes.com/news/pentagon-congress/2014/12/16/ fort-greely-to-get-50-million-toward-missile-defense-system/.

Atland, Kristian. "Interstate Relations in the Arctic: An Emerging Security Dilemma?" *Comparative Strategy* 33, no. 2 (2014): 145–66. https://doi.org/10.1080/01495933.2014.897121.

Avey, Paul, Robert Reardon, and Jonathan Markowitz. "Do US Troop Withdrawals Cause Instability? Evidence from Two Exogenous Shocks on the Korean Peninsula." *Journal of Global Security Studies* 3, no. 1 (2018): 72–92.

Baev, Pavel K. *Russia's Arctic Policy*. Helsinki: Finnish Institute of International Affairs, December 17, 2010.

Baev, Pavel K. *Russia's Race for the Arctic and the New Geopolitics of the North Pole*. Washington, DC: Jamestown Foundation, 2007.

Bailes, Alyson J. K., and Lassi Heininen. *Strategy Papers on the Arctic or High North: A Comparative Study and Analysis*. Reykjavik: University of Iceland, Institute of International Affairs, Centre for Small State Studies, 2012.

Baker, Betsy. "Law, Science, and the Continental Shelf: The Russian Federation and the Promise of Arctic Cooperation." *American University International Law Review* 25, no. 2 (2010): 10–38.

Barents Observer. "Russian Aircraft Carrier Training Next to Norwegian Oil Platform." November 12, 2007.

Barnes, Julian E. "Cold War Echoes under the Arctic Ice." *Wall Street Journal*, March 25, 2014. https://www.wsj.com/articles/cold-war-echoes-under-the-arctic-ice-1395788949.

Batanov, Vasiliy. "Russia Increases Combat Capabilities in Arctic." Sputnik. February 10, 2010. http://en.rian.ru/russia/20101002/160804543.html.

Baumol, William J., and William G. Bowen, *Performing Arts, the Economic Dilemma: A Study of Problems Common to Theater, Opera, Music, and Dance*. Cambridge, MA: MIT Press, 1966.

BBC Monitoring. *Arctic Strategically Important for Russia*. September 17, 2008.

BBC News. "Inside Norway's Underground Military HQ." September 22, 2010. http://www.bbc. com/news/av/world-europe-11386699/inside-norway-s-underground-military-hq.

BBC News. "Putin Orders Russian Military to Boost Arctic Presence." December 11, 2013. http:// www.bbc.com/news/world-europe-25331156.

BBC News. "Russia Plants Flag under N Pole." August 2, 2007. http://news.bbc.co.uk/1/hi/world/ europe/6927395.stm.

BBC News. "Russia's New Arctic Trefoil Military Base Unveiled with Virtual Tour." April 18, 2017. http://www.bbc.com/news/world-europe-39629819.

Bean, Richard. "War and the Birth of the Nation State." *Journal of Economic History* 33, no. 1 (1973): 203–21.

Becker, Gary S., and Kevin M. Murphy. "A Theory of Rational Addiction." *Journal of Political Economy* 96, no. 4 (1988): 675–700.

Beckhusen, Robert. "Russia's New Arctic Ice Breaker Has One Very Special Feature: Anti-Ship Missiles and Naval Guns." *The National Interest*, May 14, 2017.

Beckley, Michael. "China's Century? Why America's Edge Will Endure." *International Security* 36, no. 3 (2012): 41–78.

Beckley, Michael. "Economic Development and Military Effectiveness." *Journal of Strategic Studies* 33, no. 1 (2010): 43–79.

Bennett, Mia. "Arctic Population Map from Russia." Foreign Policy Association, May 25, 2010. https://foreignpolicyblogs.com/2010/05/25/arctic-population-map-from-russia/.

Bennett, Mia M. "Discursive, Material, Vertical, and Extensive Dimensions of Post-Cold War Arctic Resource Extraction." *Polar Geography* 39, no. 4 (2016): 258–73.

Bennett, Mia. "U.S. Defense Secretary Gates Talks Icebreakers, Cooperation with Canada." Foreign Policy Association (blog), May 4, 2010. https://foreignpolicyblogs.com/2010/05/04/us-defense-secretary-gates-interested-in-icebreakers/.

Bergh, Kristofer. *The Arctic Policies of Canada and the United States: Domestic Motives and International Context*. SIPRI Insights on Peach and Security 2012/1. Stockholm: Stockholm International Peace Research Institute, 2012.

Bergøy, Bente. "Out of the Echo Chamber." Norwegian Petroleum Directorate, June 28, 2017.

Blanken, Leo J. *Rational Empires: Institutional Incentives and Imperial Expansion*. Chicago: University of Chicago Press, 2012.

Bonds, Eric. "Assessing the Oil Motive after the U.S. War in Iraq." *Peace Review* 25, no. 2 (2013): 291–98.

Bostock, Mike, Matthew Ericson, David Leonhardt, and Bill Marsh. "Across U.S. Companies, Tax Rates Vary Greatly." *New York Times*, May 25, 2013. http://www.nytimes.com/interactive/2013/05/25/sunday-review/corporate-taxes.html.

Boswell, Randy. "Arctic Sea Floor to Be Contested; Canada, U.S. to Spar over Rich Resources." *National Post*, February 13, 2008.

Bower, Tom. *The Squeeze: Oil, Money and Greed in the Twenty-First Century*. London: HarperCollins UK, 2009.

Boxer, Charles Ralph. *The Dutch Seaborne Empire, 1600–1800*. London: Knopf, 1965.

Brendes, Børge. "An Active High North Policy—Growth and Innovation in the North." University of Tromsø, October 28, 2013. https://www.regjeringen.no/en/aktuelt/growt-innovation-norsh/id744676/.

Brewster, Murray. "'Critical Equipment Shortfalls' Plague Canadian Forces in Arctic." *Globe and Mail*, May 10, 2012. http://www.theglobeandmail.com/news/politics/critical-equipment-shortfalls-plague-canadian-forces-in-arctic/article4107383/.

Brewster, Murray. "Ottawa Makes Deal to Buy Three Icebreakers for Canadian Coast Guard—Eye on the Arctic." CBC News, June 22, 2018. https://www.rcinet.ca/eye-on-the-arctic/2018/06/22/ottawa-makes-deal-to-buy-three-icebreakers-for-coast-guard/.

Broder, John M., and Clifford Krauss. "New and Frozen Frontier Awaits Offshore Oil Drilling." *New York Times*, May 23, 2012. https://www.nytimes.com/2012/05/24/science/earth/shell-arctic-ocean-drilling-stands-to-open-new-oil-frontier.html?mtrref=undefined&gwh=75374EB1D55F1BC178BA3A0FBD55F79E&gwt=pay.

Brooks, Stephen. *Producing Security: Multinational Corporations, Globalization, and the Changing Calculus of Conflict*. Princeton, NJ: Princeton University Press, 2005.

Brooks, Stephen. "The Globalization of Production and the Changing Benefits of Conquest." *Journal of Conflict Resolution* 43, no. 5 (1999): 646–70.

Brooks, Stephen G. "Economic Actors' Lobbying Influence on the Prospects for War and Peace." *International Organization* 67, no. 4 (2013): 863–88. https://doi.org/10.1017/S0020818313000283.

Brooks, Stephen G., and William C. Wohlforth. "Assessing America's Global Position." In *America Abroad: The United States' Global Role in the 21st Century*, 14–47. New York: Oxford University Press, 2016.

Brooks, Stephen G., and William C. Wohlforth. "The Rise and Fall of the Great Powers in the Twenty-First Century: China's Rise and the Fate of America's Global Position." *International Security* 40, no. 3 (2016): 7–53.

Brosnan, Ian G., Thomas M. Leschine, and Edward L. Miles. "Cooperation or Conflict in a Changing Arctic?" *Ocean Development & International Law* 42, no. 1–2 (2011): 173–210. https://doi. org/10.1080/00908320.2011.543032.

Brunstad, Rolf Jens, and Jan Morten Dyrstad. "Booming Sector and Wage Effects: An Empirical Analysis on Norwegian Data." *Oxford Economic Papers* 49, no. 1 (1997): 89–103.

Bueno de Mesquita, Bruce, Alastair Smith, Randolph M. Siverson, and James D. Morrow. *The Logic of Political Survival.* Cambridge, MA: MIT Press, 2003.

Bureau of Economic Analysis. "BEA Industry Facts." US Department of Commerce, Bureau of Economic Analysis, June 20, 2019. https://apps.bea.gov/industry/factsheet/factsheet. cfm?IndustryId=21.

Bureau of Economic Analysis, "Industry Data: GDP-by-Industry." n.d. https://www.bea.gov/ iTable/iTable.cfm?ReqID=51&step=1#reqid=51&step=2&isuri=1.

Bureau of Labor Statistics. "Industries at a Glance: Mining, Quarrying, and Oil and Gas Extraction: NAICS 21." Accessed July 17, 2017. https://www.bls.gov/iag/tgs/iag21.htm.

Burgess, Philip. "Foundations of the Russian Federation's State Policy in the Arctic until 2020 and Beyond." International Polar Year, December 1, 2010. http://icr.arcticportal. org/index.php?option=com_content&view=article&id=1791:foundations-of-the-russian-federations-state-policy-in-the-arctic-until-2020-and-beyond&catid=45:news-2007&Itemid=111&lang=sa.

Burke, Edmund. *Reflections on the Revolution in France.* 1790. Reprint, edited by Conor O'Brien. London: Penguin Classics, 1982.

Bush, George W. "National Security Presidential Directive/NSPD 66—Homeland Security Presidential Directive/HSPD 25—Subject: Arctic Region," January 9, 2009. https://fas.org/ irp/offdocs/nspd/nspd-66.htm

Byers, Michael. "Cold Peace: Arctic Cooperation and Canadian Foreign Policy." *International Journal* 65, no. 4 (2010): 899–912.

Byers, Michael. *International Law and the Arctic.* Cambridge Studies in International and Comparative Law. Cambridge: Cambridge University Press, 2013.

Byers, Michael, and Suzanne Lalonde. "Who Controls the Northwest Passage." *Vanderbilt Journal Transnational Law* 42 (2009): 1133.

Campbell, Bruce, and Canadian Centre for Policy Alternatives. *The Petro-Path Not Taken: Comparing Norway with Canada and Alberta's Management of Petroleum Wealth.* Ottawa: Canadian Centre for Policy Alternatives, 2013.

Campbell, Donald T., and H. Laurence Ross. "The Connecticut Crackdown on Speeding: Time-Series Data in Quasi-Experimental Analysis." *Law & Society Review* 3, no. 1 (1968): 33–54. https://doi.org/10.2307/3052794.

Canada's Oil Sands. "Economic Contribution." Accessed February 8, 2017. http://www. canadasoilsands.ca/en/explore-topics/economic-contribution.

Canadian Armed Forces and Ministère de la défense nationale. *Strong, Secure, Engaged—Canada's Defence Policy.* Ottawa: Ministère de la défense nationale, 2017. http://dgpaapp.forces.gc.ca/ en/canada-defence-policy/docs/canada-defence-policy-report.pdf.

Canadian Coast Guard. "Icebreaking Operations Services." Accessed June 5, 2018. http://www.ccg-gcc.gc.ca/icebreaking/home.

Canadian Government, Indian and Northern Affairs, and Federal Interlocutor for Métis and Non-Status Indians. *Canada's Northern Strategy: Our North, Our Heritage, Our Future.* Ottawa: Government of Canada, 2009.

Canadian Press. "Arctic Naval Base Plans Scaled Back after Costs Soared: Document." CBC News, September 8, 2014. http://www.cbc.ca/news/canada/north/arctic-naval-base-plans-scaled-back-after-costs-soared-document-1.2759743.

Canadian Press. "Canada Makes Territorial Claim for North Pole." *The Star*, December 9, 2013. https://www.thestar.com/news/queenspark/2013/12/09/canada_makes_territorial_claim_for_north_pole.html.

Canadian Press. "Canada Uncertain about Joining NATO's Arctic War Games." CBC, August 24, 2012. https://www.cbc.ca/news/politics/canada-uncertain-about-joining-nato-s-arctic-war-games-1.1166218.

Canadian Press. "Feds Close to Deal with Quebec Shipyard Davie for Coast Guard Icebreakers." *Financial Post*, June 5, 2018.https://business.financialpost.com/pmn/business-pmn/feds-close-to-deal-with-quebec-shipyard-davie-for-coast-guard-icebreakers.

Canadian Press. "Icy Clinton Leaves Arctic Summit." *Red Deer Advocate*, March 29, 2010. https://www.reddeeradvocate.com/national-news/icy-clinton-leaves-arctic-summit/.

Carlson, Jon D., Christopher Hubach, Joseph Long, Kellen Minteer, and Shane Young. "Scramble for the Arctic: Layered Sovereignty, UNCLOS, and Competing Maritime Territorial Claims." *SAIS Review of International Affairs* 33, no. 2 (2013): 21–43. https://doi.org/10.1353/sais.2013.0033.

Cayley-Daoust, Daniel, and Richard Girard. "Big Oil's Oily Grasp: The Making of Canada as a Petro-State and How Oil Money Is Corrupting Canadian Politics." Polaris Institute, December 2012. https://www.polarisinstitute.org/big_oil_s_oily_grasp.

CBC News. "Nanisivik, Nunavut, Naval Facility Breaks Ground." July 18, 2015. http://www.cbc.ca/news/canada/north/nanisivik-nunavut-naval-facility-breaks-ground-1.3158798.

CBC News. "Russia Plants Flag Staking Claim to Arctic Region." August 2, 2007. http://www.cbc.ca/news/world/russia-plants-flag-staking-claim-to-arctic-region-1.679445.

CBS News. "Russian, NORAD Forces Unite for 'Hijack' Exercise." August 30, 2013. https://www.cbsnews.com/news/russian-norad-forces-unite-for-hijack-exercise/.

Central Intelligence Agency. "Russia." In *World Factbook*, n.d. https://www.cia.gov/library/publications/the-world-factbook/geos/rs.html.

Chapman, Keith. *North Sea Oil and Gas: A Geographical Perspective*. Problems in Modern Geography. North Pomfret, VT: David and Charles, 1976.

"Chapter 5: Geopolitical Impacts of the Changing Arctic." *Adelphi Series* 53, no. 440 (2013): 119–40. https://doi.org/10.1080/13569783.2013.872863.

Chase, Steven. "Harper Orders New Draft of Arctic Seabed Claim to Include North Pole." *Globe and Mail*. December 4, 2013. https://www.theglobeandmail.com/news/politics/harper-orders-new-draft-of-arctic-seabed-claim-to-include-north-pole/article15756108/.

Cheibub, Antonio Jose, Jennifer Gandhi, and James Raymond Vreeland. "Democracy and Dictatorship Revisited." *Public Choice* 143, no. 2–1 (2010): 67–101.

Chen, Zhe (陈者), and Yang Chao Zhao (杨朝钊). 海洋是国家战略的坚实支点 [The ocean is the crux of strong national strategy]. Beijing: Ministry of National Defense of the People's Republic of China (中华人民共和国国防部), October 10, 2016. http://www.mod.gov.cn/jmsd/2016-10/10/content_4743783.htm.

CHNL Information Office. "Transit Statistics." Accessed July 9, 2017. http://www.arctic-lio.com/nsr_transits.

Churchill, Robin, and Geir Ulfstein. "The Disputed Maritime Zones around Svalbard." In *Changes in the Arctic Environment and the Law of the Sea*, edited by Myron Nordquist, John Norton Moore, and Tomas H. Heider, 551–93. Leiden, The Netherlands: Brill, 2010

Chuter, Andrew. "Norway F-35 Deliveries to Begin in 2017." *Defense News*, April 23, 2013.

Climate Change.ru. "Sovet Bezopasnoti RF Provel Zasedanie Po Problem Izmeneniia Klimata" [RF Security Council holds session on the problem of climate change]. March 17, 2010. http://www.climatechange.ru/node/423.

Cockx, Lara, and Nathalie Francken. "Natural Resources: A Curse on Education Spending?" *Energy Policy* 92 (2016): 394–408.

Coe, Andrew J. "Containing Rogues: A Theory of Asymmetric Arming." *Journal of Politics* 80, no. 4 (2018): 1197–1210.

Coe, Andrew J. "The Modern Economic Peace." Working Paper. Stanford, CA: Stanford University, 2016.

Coe, Andrew J., and Jonathan N. Markowitz. "Crude Calculations: When Does Conquest Pay?" Paper presented at the 76th Annual MPSA Conference, Chicago, April 5–8, 2018.

Cohen, Ariel. "Russia in the Arctic: Challenges to U.S. Energy and Geopolitics in the High North." In *Russia in the Arctic*, edited by Stephen J. Blank, 1–42. Carlisle, PA: Strategic Studies Institute, 2011.

Colgan, Jeff. "Fueling the Fire: Pathways from Oil to War." *International Security*, 38, no. 2 (2013a): 147–80.

Colgan, Jeff. "Modern Energy and the Political Economy of Peace." *Notre Dame*, October 7th, 2015.

Colgan, Jeff. "Oil and Revolutionary Governments: Fuel for International Conflict." *International Organization* 64, no. 4 (2010): 661–94. https://doi.org/10.1017/S002081831000024X.

Colgan, Jeff. *Petro-Aggression: When Oil Causes War*. Cambridge: Cambridge University Press, 2013b.

Colgan, William, Horst Machguth, Mike MacFerrin, Jeff Colgan, Dirk van As, and Joseph A. MacGregor. "The Abandoned Ice Sheet Base at Camp Century, Greenland, in a Warming Climate." *Geophysical Research Letters* 43, no. 15 (2016): 8091–96. https://doi.org/10.1002/2016GL069688.

Coll, Steve. *Private Empire: ExxonMobil and American Power*. New York: Penguin Press, 2012.

Collier, Paul, and Anke Hoeffler. "Testing the Neocon Agenda: Democracy in Resource-Rich Societies." *European Economic Review* 53, no. 3 (2009): 293–308.

Committee on the Assessment of U.S. Coast Guard Polar Icebreaker Roles and Future Needs. *Polar Icebreaker Roles and U.S. Future Needs: A Preliminary Assessment*. Washington, DC: National Academies Press, 2005. https://www.nap.edu/read/11525/chapter/1.

Conant, Eve. "Breaking the Ice: Russian Nuclear-Powered Ice-Breakers." *Scientific American* (guest blog), September 8, 2012. https://blogs.scientificamerican.com/guest-blog/breaking-the-ice/.

Congleton, Roger D., Arye L. Hillman, and Kai A. Konrad. "Forty Years of Research on Rent Seeking: An Overview," June 16, 2008. http://www.tax.mpg.de/fileadmin/TAX/pdf1/2008-introduction_rent_seeking_june_16_2008.pdf.

Conley, Heather A. *A New Security Architecture for the Arctic*. Washington, DC: Center for Strategic and International Studies, 2012.

Conley, Heather A. "The Colder War: U.S., Russia and Others Are Vying for Control of Santa's Back Yard." *Washington Post*, December 25, 2011.

Conley, Heather A. *The New Foreign Policy Frontier: U.S. Interests and Actors in the Arctic*. Washington, DC: Center for Strategic and International Studies, 2013. https://www.csis.org/analysis/new-foreign-policy-frontier.

Conley, Heather A. *The New Ice Curtain: Russia's Strategic Reach to the Arctic*. Washington, DC: Center for Strategic and International Studies, 2015.

Cooper, Helene. "Military Drills in Arctic Aim to Counter Russia, but the First Mission Is to Battle the Cold." *New York Times*, April 12, 2019. https://www.nytimes.com/2019/04/12/world/europe/global-warming-russia-arctic-usa.html.

Corden, Warner Max. "Booming Sector and Dutch Disease Economics: Survey and Consolidation." *Oxford Economic Papers* 36, no. 3 (1984): 359–80.

Corti, Gerry, and Frank Frazer. *The Nation's Oil: A Story of Control*. London: Graham & Trotman, 1983.

Cox, Bob. "Defense Department Says F-35 Fighter Program's Costs to Significantly Rise." *Fort Worth Star-Telegram*, April 7, 2010.

Cox, Gary W., and Mathew D. McCubbins. "Electoral Politics as a Redistributive Game." *Journal of Politics* 48, no. 2 (1986): 370–89.

Crafts, N. R. S. "British Economic Growth 1760–1913: A Challenge for New Growth Theory." Warwick Economic Research Papers 415. University of Warwick, Department of Economics, 1993.

Craze, Joshua. *Dividing Lines: Grazing and Conflict along the Sudan–South Sudan Border*. Geneva, Switzerland: Small Arms Survey, 2013.

Crisher, Brian Benjamin, and Mark Souva. "Power at Sea: A Naval Power Dataset, 1865–2011." *International Interactions* 40, no. 4 (2014): 602–29. https://doi.org/10.1080/03050629.2014.918039.

Cupolo, Diego. "It's Never a Good Time for the Iraqi Kurds to Become Independent." *The Atlantic*, September 24, 2017. https://www.theatlantic.com/international/archive/2017/09/turkey-kurds-barzani-iraq-referendum/540909/.

Dagne, Ted. "The Republic of South Sudan: Opportunities and Challenges for Africa's Newest Country." *Current Politics and Economics of Africa; Hauppauge* 5, no. 1 (2012): 53–85.

Daily Beast. "Top 20 Companies That Lobby the Most." March 24, 2011. http://www.thedailybeast.com/articles/2011/03/25/top-20-companies-that-lobby-the-most.

Danish Ministry of Defence. Agreement for Danish Defence 2018 – 2023. Last updated February 1st, 2019. https://www.fmn.dk/eng/allabout/Pages/danish-defence-agreement.aspx.

Danish Ministry of Defence. *Forsvarsministeriets fremtidige opgaveløsning I Arktis*. June 2016. https://www.fmn.dk/nyheder/Documents/arktis-analyse/forsvarsministeriets-fremtidige-opgaveloesning-i-arktis.pdf

Danish Ministry of Defence. "Tasks in the Arctic and the North Atlantic." Accessed August 6, 2017. http://www.fmn.dk/eng/allabout/Pages/TasksintheArcticandtheNorthernAtlantic.aspx.

Danish Ministry of Defence. *Type Selection of Denmark's New Fighter Aircraft*. n.d. Accessed July 5, 2019. https://www.fmn.dk/temaer/kampfly/Documents/type-selection-denmarks-new-fighter-aircrafts-english-summary5.pdf.

Danish Ministry of Finance. *Finanslov for 2018*. December 22nd, 2017. https://www.fm.dk/publikationer/2018/finanslov-for-2018.

David, Mihaela. "U.S. National Strategy for the Arctic Region: Strong Foothold or on Thin Ice?" Arctic Institute, May 13, 2013. http://www.thearcticinstitute.org/us-national-strategy-for-arctic-region/.

Dawisha, Karen. *Putin's Kleptocracy: Who Owns Russia?* New York: Simon & Schuster, 2015.

de Arimateia da Cruz, Jose. "Strategic Insights: Guyana–Venezuela: The Essequibo Region Dispute." Strategic Studies Institute and US Army War College Press, December 14, 2015. http://publications.armywarcollege.edu/pubs/3338.pdf.

Deboer, Sally. "Yours, Mine, and Moscow's: Breaking Down Russia's Latest Arctic Claims." Center for International Maritime Security, November 27, 2015. http://cimsec.org/mine-moscows-breaking-russias-latest-arctic-claims/18252.

Debs, Alexander, and Hein Goemans. "Regime Type, the Fate of Leaders, and War." *American Political Science Review* 104, no. 3 (2010): 430–45.

Defense News. "Eying Russia, Norway Pumps Prior Savings into Its Defense Budget." August 8, 2017. https://www.defensenews.com/global/2017/02/03/eying-russia-norway-pumps-prior-savings-into-its-defense-budget/.

Defense Update. "Russian Submarine-Launched Ballistic Missiles Tested," July 24, 2009. http://defense-update.com/20090724_russian_sub_test.html.

Department of Defense. *Report to Congress on Arctic Operations and the Northwest Passage*. Washington, DC: Department of Defense, 2011.

Devyatkin, Pavel. "Russia's Arctic Strategy: Aimed at Conflict or Cooperation? (Part I)." Arctic Institute, February 6, 2018. https://www.thearcticinstitute.org/russias-arctic-strategy-aimed-conflict-cooperation-part-one/.

Devyatkin, Pavel. "Russia's Arctic Strategy: Maritime Shipping (Part IV)." Arctic Institute, February 27, 2018. https://www.thearcticinstitute.org/russias-arctic-strategy-maritime-shipping-part-iv/.

Djankov, Simeon. "Why Has Russia Failed to Diversify Exports?" Peterson Institute for International Economics, September 28, 2015. https://piie.com/blogs/trade-investment-policy-watch/why-has-russia-failed-diversify-exports.

Dodds, Klaus. "Flag Planting and Finger Pointing: The Law of the Sea, the Arctic and the Political Geographies of the Outer Continental Shelf." *Political Geography* 29, no. 2 (2010): 63–73. https://doi.org/10.1016/j.polgeo.2010.02.004.

Dunning, Thad. *Crude Democracy: Natural Resource Wealth and Political Regimes.* Cambridge: University Press Cambridge, 2008.

Ebinger, Charles K., and Evie Zambetakis. "The Geopolitics of Arctic Melt." *International Affairs* 85, no. 6 (2009): 1215–32. https://doi.org/10.1111/j.1468-2346.2009.00858.x.

Eckstein, Megan. "Zukunft: Changing Arctic Could Lead to Armed U.S. Icebreakers in Future Fleet." USNI News, May 18, 2017. https://news.usni.org/2017/05/18/zukunft-changing-arctic-environment-could-lead-to-more-armed-icebreakers-in-future-fleet.

Economist. "America Lifts Its Ban on Oil Exports." December 18, 2015a. https://www.economist.com/news/finance-economics/21684531-light-sweet-compromise-puts-end-crude-market-distortions-america-lifts.

Economist. "Can Russia Create a New Silicon Valley?," July 14, 2012. http://www.economist.com/node/21558602.

Economist. "Beyond Petroleum." January 29, 2015b. https://www.economist.com/news/americas/21641288-growth-shifting-oil-producing-west-back-traditional-economic-heartland.

Economist. "In Russia, Privatisation Can Mean Selling One State-Owned Company to Another." October 20, 2016a. http://www.economist.com/news/europe/21709065-government-sells-bashneft-rosneft-and-books-profit-russia-privatisation-can-mean.

Economist. "Milk without the Cow." October 22, 2016b. https://www.economist.com/news/special-report/21708876-political-reform-essential-prerequisite-flourishing-economy-milk-without.

Economist. "Norway's Election: Rich but Worried." September 17, 2009.

Economist. "The Rich Cousin: Oil Makes Norway Different from the Rest of the Region, but Only up to a Point." February 2, 2013.

Eilperin, Juliet. "Commercial Fishing Is Barred in Parts of Arctic." *Washington Post*, February 6, 2009.

Emmerson, Charles. *The Future History of the Arctic.* New York: Public Affairs, 2010.

Eurasia Group. "Opportunities and Challenges for Arctic Oil and Gas Development." Washington, DC: Wilson Center, n.d.

Faull, Solrun F. "The Armed Forces Strengthened in the High North." *Norway Today*, April 3, 2018. http://norwaytoday.info/news/armed-forces-strengthened-high-north/.

Fazal, Tanisha. *State Death: The Politics and Geography of Conquest, Occupation, and Annexation.* Princeton, NJ: Princeton University Press, 2007.

Fearon, James D. "Cooperation, Conflict, and the Costs of Anarchy." *International Organization* 72, no. 3 (2018): 523–59.

Fearon, James D. "Two States, Two Types, Two Actions." *Security Studies* 20, no. 3 (2011): 431–40.

Fedyszyn, Thomas R. "Renaissance of the Russian Navy." *Proceedings* 138, no. 3 (March 2012): 30–35.

Fein, Geoff S. "ICEX 2011 Demonstrates Naval Research Projects," April 7, 2011. https://www.navy.mil/submit/display.asp?story_id=59517.

Findlay, Ronald, and Kevin H. O'Rourke. *Power and Plenty: Trade, War, and the World Economy in the Second Millennium.* The Princeton Economic History of the Western World. Princeton, NJ: Princeton University Press, 2009.

Finkel, Abby L. "Arctic Challenge Exercise Aims to Increase Interoperability." US Department of Defense, May 24, 2017. https://www.defense.gov/Newsroom/News/Article/Article/1191916/arctic-challenge-exercise-aims-to-increase-interoperability/.

Finkel, Michael. "The Cold Patrol." *National Geographic*, January 2012. https://www.nationalgeographic.com/magazine/2012/01/cold-patrol/.

Fordham, Benjamin O. "Economic Interests, Party, and Ideology in Early Cold War Era US Foreign Policy." *International Organization* 52, no. 2 (1998): 359–96.

Fordham, Benjamin O. "Who Wants to Be a Major Power? Explaining the Expansion of Foreign Policy Ambition." *Journal of Peace Research* 48, no. 5 (2011): 587–603. https://doi.org/10.1177/0022343311411959.

Foreign Ministry of the People's Republic of China. 中国坚持通过谈判解决中国与菲律宾在南海的有关争议 [China insists on resolving the South China Sea dispute with the Philippines through negotiations]. Beijing: Foreign Ministry of the People's Republic of China (中华人民共和国外交部). Accessed June 20, 2018. http://www.fmprc.gov.cn/web/ziliao_674904/tytj_674911/zcwj_674915/t1380600.shtml.

Frieden, Jeffry A. "Actors and Preferences in International Relations." In *Strategic Choice and International Relations*, edited by David A. Lake and Bob Powell, 39–76. Princeton, NJ: Princeton University Press, 1999.

Frieden, Jeffry A. "International Investment and Colonial Control: A New Interpretation." *International Organization* 48, no. 4 (1994): 559–93.

Gallman, Robert, and Thomas Weiss. "The Service Industries in the Nineteenth Century." In *Production and Productivity in the Service Industries*, edited by Victor R. Fuchs, 287–352. New York: Columbia University Press, 1969.

Gartzke, Erik. "The Capitalist Peace." *American Journal of Political Science* 51, no. 1 (2007): 166–91.

Gartzke, Erik, and Dominic Rohner. "Prosperous Pacifists: The Effects of Development on Initiators and Targets of Territorial Conflict." IEW Working Papers 500. Institute for Empirical Research in Economics, University of Zurich, Zurich, Switzerland, 2010a.

Gartzke, Erik, and Dominic Rohner. "The Political Economy of Imperialism, Decolonization and Development." *British Journal of Political Science* 41, no. 3 (2011b): 1–32.

Gautier, Donald L., Kenneth J. Bird, Ronald R. Charpentier, Arthur Grantz, David W. Houseknecht, Timothy R. Klett, Thomas E. Moore, et al. "Assessment of Undiscovered Oil and Gas in the Arctic." *Science* 324, no. 5931 (2009): 1175–79. https://doi.org/10.1126/science.1169467.

Gavrilov, Viatcheslav V. "Legal Status of the Northern Sea Route and Legislation of the Russian Federation: A Note." *Ocean Development & International Law* 46, no. 3 (2015): 256–63.

GeoPolitics in the High North. "Danish Arctic Strategy." Accessed July 20, 2016.

Gholz, Eugene. "Globalization, Systems Integration, and the Future of Great Power War." *Security Studies* 16, no. 4 (2007): 615–36. https://doi.org/10.1080/09636410701740908.

Gholz, Eugene, Daryl G. Press, and Harvey M. Sapolsky. "Come Home, America: The Strategy of Restraint in the Face of Temptation." *International Security* 21, no. 4 (1997): 5–48.

Glaser, Bonnie S., and Gregory Poling. "Vanishing Borders in the South China Sea." *Foreign Affairs*, June 5, 2018. https://www.foreignaffairs.com/articles/china/2018-06-05/vanishing-borders-south-china-sea.

Glaser, Charles L. *Rational Theory of International Politics*. Princeton, NJ: Princeton University Press, 2010.

GlobalSecurity.org. "Project 10510 Lider LK-100Ya—Atomic Icebreaker." Accessed August 20, 2017. https://www.globalsecurity.org/military/world/russia/lk-100ya.htm.

Goertz, Gary, Paul F. Diehl, and Alexandru Balas. *The Puzzle of Peace: The Evolution of Peace in the International System*. New York: Oxford University Press, 2016.

Golts, Alexander. "The Arctic: A Clash of Interests or Clash of Ambitions." In *Russia in the Arctic*, edited by Stephen J. Blank. Carlisle, PA: Strategic Studies Institute, 2011.

Gooderham, Paul N., Steen E. Navrbjerg, Karen Modesta Olsen, and Christina Roe Steen. "The Labor Market Regimes of Denmark and Norway—One Nordic Model?" *Journal of Industrial Relations* 57, no. 2 (2015): 166–86. https://doi.org/10.1177/0022185614534103.

Gotkowska, Justyna. *Norway and the Bear: Norwegian Defence Policy—Lessons for the Baltic Sea Region*. Warsaw, Poland: Center for Eastern Studies, 2014.

Government of Canada. "Achievements under Canada's Northern Strategy, 2007–2011," n.d.a. http://publications.gc.ca/collections/collection_2012/aadnc-aandc/R3-150-2011.pdf.

Government of Canada. "Canada First Defence Strategy," n.d.b. Accessed June 21, 2016. https://
    www.canada.ca/en/department-national-defence/corporate/policies-standards/canada-
    first-defence-strategy-complete-document.html.
Government of Canada, Foreign Affairs Trade and Development Canada. "Canada's Arctic
    Foreign Policy." Accessed July 20, 2017. https://www.international.gc.ca/world-monde/
    international_relations-relations_internationales/arctic-arctique/arctic_policy-canada-
    politique_arctique.aspx?lang=eng.
Government of Canada, National Defence. "Canadian Rangers," March 8, 2013. http://www.army-
    armee.forces.gc.ca/en/canadian-rangers/index.page.
Government of Canada, National Defence. "Joint and Integrated CF Operation in Canada's Eastern
    Arctic," August 11, 2006. http://www.forces.gc.ca/en/news/article.page?doc=joint-and-
    integrated-cf-operation-in-canada-s-eastern-arctic/hnocfocm.
Government of Norway. "Norway's Oil History in 5 Minutes." Redaksjonellartikkel. October 9,
    2013. https://www.regjeringen.no/en/topics/energy/oil-and-gas/norways-oil-history-in-5-
    minutes/id440538/.
Graham, Benjamin A.T and Tucker, Jacob R, "International Political Economy Data Resource
    Version 2.0" July 10, 2017.
Gramer, Robbie. "Here's What Russia's Military Build-Up in the Arctic Looks Like." Foreign Policy
    (blog), January 25, 2017. https://foreignpolicy.com/2017/01/25/heres-what-russias-
    military-build-up-in-the-arctic-looks-like-trump-oil-military-high-north-infographic-map/.
Grant, Shelagh D. Polar Imperative: A History of Arctic Sovereignty in North America. Vancouver,
    Canada: Douglas & McIntyre, 2010.
Gray, Christopher, Leif Bergey, and Walter A. Berbrick. "Fleet Arctic Operations Game: Game
    Report." Defense Technical Information Center, 2011. https://www.hsdl.org/
    ?abstract&did=746182.
Green, Douglas. "Caspian Sea Dispute: Where Solutions Jump ahead of Problems." Times of
    Central Asia, June 1, 2017. https://timesca.com/index.php/news/26-opinion-head/
    18120-caspian-sea-dispute-where-solutions-jump-ahead-of-problems.
Groves, Steven. "U.S. Accession to U.N. Convention on the Law of the Sea Unnecessary to
    Develop Oil and Gas Resources." The Heritage Foundation, May 14, 2012. http://www.
    heritage.org/report/us-accession-un-convention-the-law-the-sea-unnecessary-develop-
    oil-and-gas-resources.
Gunn, Andrea. "Sixth Arctic and Offshore Patrol Ship about Readiness, Not Fairness, Experts Say."
    Chronicle Herald, November 6, 2018. https://www.thechronicleherald.ca/news/local/sixth-
    arctic-and-offshore-patrol-ship-about-readiness-not-fairness-experts-say-256850/.
Halpin, Tony. "Russian Bases Stake Claim to Arctic Wealth." The Australian, March 30, 2009.
Harkins, Gina. "50,000 Troops Prep for NATO's Biggest Show of Force since the Cold War." Military.
    com, October 22, 2018. https://www.military.com/daily-news/2018/10/22/50000-troops-
    prep-natos-biggest-show-force-cold-war.html.
Harvard Kennedy School Belfer Center for Science and International Affairs. "Claim in 2018: Russia
    Relies Heavily on Energy Exports for Close to Three-Quarters of Its Export Earnings and over
    Half of Its Budget." Russia Matters, July 2018. www.russiamatters.org.
Hathaway, Oona Anne, and Scott Shapiro. The Internationalists: How a Radical Plan to Outlaw War
    Remade the World. New York: Simon & Schuster, 2017.
Hayes, Guy. "Service Members Support Arctic Care in Rural Alaska," April 27, 2011. https://www.
    af.mil/News/Article-Display/Article/113493/service-members-support-arctic-care-in-
    rural-alaska/.
Hayward, Jonathan. "Canadian Coast Guard May Be Forced to Lease Icebreakers as Aging
    Fleet Increasingly at Risk of Breakdowns." National Post (blog), November 18, 2016.
    http://nationalpost.com/news/canada/canadian-coast-guard-may-be-forced-to-
    lease-icebreakers-as-aging-fleet-increasingly-at-risk-of-breakdowns/wcm/
    4d424729-80b0-4d5f-8de0-7076650571ba.

Headrick, Daniel R. *The Tools of Empire: Technology and European Imperialism in the Nineteenth Century*. Oxford: Oxford University Press, 1981.

Heininen, Lassi, Alexander Sergunin, and Gleb Yarovoy. *Russian Strategies in the Arctic: Avoiding a New Cold War*. Valdai Discussion Club, September 2014. http://www.uarctic.org/media/857300/arctic_eng.pdf.

Hendrix, Cullen S. "Cold War Geopolitics and the Making of the Oil Curse." *Journal of Global Security Studies* 3, no. 1 (2018): 2–22.

Hendrix, Cullen S. "Kicking a Crude Habit: Diversifying away from Oil and Gas in the Twenty-First Century." *International Review of Applied Economics* 33, no. 2 (2019): 188–208.

Henehan, Marie, and John A. Vasquez. "The Changing Probability of Interstate War, 1816–1992: Identifying Peaceful Eras." In *The Waning of Major War: Theories and Debates*, edited by Raimo Väyrynen, 280–99. Contemporary Security Studies Series. London and New York: Routledge, 2006.

Henriksen, Anders, and Jon Rahbek-Clemmensen. "The Greenland Card: Prospects for and Barriers to Danish Arctic Diplomacy in Washington." In *Danish Foreign Policy Yearbook 2017*, 75–98. Copenhagen: Danish Institute for International Studies, 2017.

Heritage Foundation. "Index of Economic Freedom." n.d. Accessed August 2, 2017. http://www.heritage.org/index/visualize.

Hill, Fiona, and Clifford G. Gaddy. *Mr. Putin: Operative in the Kremlin* (new exp. ed.). Washington, DC: Brookings Institution Press, 2015.

Hiltermann, Joost, and Maria Fantappie. "Twilight of the Kurds." *Foreign Policy*, January 16, 2018. https://foreignpolicy.com/2018/01/16/twilight-of-the-kurds-iraq-syria-kurdistan/.

Hirschfeld Davis, Julie. "Obama to Call for More Icebreakers in Arctic as U.S. Seeks Foothold. *New York Times*, September 1, 2015. http://www.nytimes.com/2015/09/02/us/politics/obama-to-call-for-more-icebreakers-in-arctic-as-us-seeks-foothold.html?smprod=nytcore-iphone&smid=nytcore-iphone-share.

Holsti, Kalevi J. *Peace and War: Armed Conflicts and International Order, 1648–1989*. Cambridge: Cambridge University Press, 1991.

Home, Andy. "Will the Real Norilsk Owner Please Stand Up?" Reuters, 2012. http://www.reuters.com/article/2012/12/07/column-home-norilsk-nickel-idUSL5E8N790C20121207.

Homer-Dixon, Thomas F. "Environmental Scarcities and Violent Conflict: Evidence from Cases." *International Security* 19, no. 1 (1994): 5–40.

Hong, Nong. "Emerging Interests of Non-Arctic Countries in the Arctic: A Chinese Perspective." *Polar Journal* 4, no. 2 (2014): 271–86.

Horne, Anders. "Skal rustes for 15 fly." Fremover, June 28, 2012. https://www.fremover.no/lokale_nyheter/article6127882.ece?ns_campaign=article&ns_mchannel=recommend_button&ns_source=facebook&ns_linkname=facebook&ns_fee=0.

Horowitz, Michael C. *The Diffusion of Military Power: Causes and Consequences for International Politics*. Princeton, NJ: Princeton University Press, 2010.

Howard, Roger. *The Arctic Gold Rush: The New Race for Tomorrow's Natural Resources*. New York: Continuum, 2009.

Huebert, Rob. "Canada and the Newly Emerging International Arctic Security Regime." In *Arctic Security in an Age of Climate Change*, edited by James Kraska, 193–217. New York: Cambridge University Press, 2011.

Huebert, Rob. "Canadian Arctic Security Issues: Transformation in the Post–Cold War Era." *International Journal* 54, no. 2 (1999): 203–29.

Huebert, Rob. "The Arctic and the Strategic Defence of North America: Resumption of the 'Long Polar Watch.'" In *North American Strategic Defense in the 21st Century: Security and Sovereignty in an Uncertain World*, edited by Christian Leuprecht, Joel J. Sokolsky, and Thomas Hughes, 174–86. Advanced Sciences and Technologies for Security Applications. Cham, Switzerland: Springer International Publishing, 2018. https://doi.org/10.1007/978-3-319-90978-3_14.

Huebert, Rob. *United States Arctic Policy: The Reluctant Arctic Power.* University of Calgary Publications Series 2, no. 2. Calgary, Canada: University of Calgary, School of Public Policy, 2009.

Huebert, Rob. "The Return of the Vikings." In *Breaking Ice: Renewable Resource and Ocean Management in the Canadian North,* edited by F. Berkes, Robert Huebert, Helen Fast, Micheline Manseau, and Alan Diduck, 319–36. Calgary, Canada: University of Calgary Press, 2005.

Huebert, Rob, Heather Exner-Pirot, Adam Lajeunesse, and Jay Gulledge. *Climate Change and International Security: The Arctic as a Bellwether.* Arlington, VA: Center for Climate and Energy Solutions, 2012.

Humpert, Av Malte. "Shipping Traffic on Northern Sea Route Grows by 40 Percent. High North News, December 19, 2017. http://www.highnorthnews.com/shipping-traffic-on-northern-sea-route-grows-by-40-percent/.

Hutchison, Michael M. "Manufacturing Sector Resiliency to Energy Booms: Empirical Evidence from Norway, the Netherlands, and the United Kingdom." *Oxford Economic Papers* 46, no. 2 (1994): 311–29.

Huth, Paul K. "Territory: Why Are Territorial Disputes between States a Central Cause of International Conflict." In *What Do We Know about War,* edited by John A. Vasquez, 85–110. New York: Rowman & Littlefield, 2000.

Ingimundarson, Valur. "Managing a Contested Region: The Arctic Council and the Politics of Arctic Governance." *Polar Journal* 4, no. 1 (2014): 183–98. https://doi.org/10.1080/2154896X.2014.913918.

Inman, Phillip. "Norway's Sovereign Wealth Fund 'Is Example for Oil-Rich Nations.'" *The Guardian,* September 30, 2013. https://www.theguardian.com/business/2013/sep/30/norway-oil-sovereign-wealth-fund.

Intergovernmental Panel on Climate Change, ed. *Climate Change 2007: The Physical Science Basis. Contribution of Working Group I to the Fourth Assessment Report of the Intergovernmental Panel on Climate Change.* Cambridge, UK: Cambridge University Press, 2007.

International Expert Council on Cooperation in the Arctic. "The Development Strategy of the Arctic Zone of the Russian Federation." April 14, 2013. Accessed July 8, 2017. http://www.iecca.ru/en/legislation/strategies/item/99-the-development-strategy-of-the-arctic-zone-of-the-russian-federation.

Isted, Kathryn. "Sovereignty in the Arctic: An Analysis of the Territorial Disputes and Environmental Policy Considerations." *Transnational Journal of Law and Policy* 18, no. 2 (2009): 343–76.

ITMO.News. "Exploring Innopolis: Russia's Silicon Valley." August 5, 2016. http://news.ifmo.ru/en/archive/news/5887/.

Izundu, Uchenna. "The Race Is on for Greenland's Arctic Oilfields." *Sunday Telegraph,* September 26, 2010. https://www.telegraph.co.uk/finance/newsbysector/energy/oilandgas/8025096/The-race-is-on-for-Greenlands-Arctic-oilfields.html.

Izyumov, Alexei, and John Vahaly. "Old Capital vs. New Investment in Post-Soviet Economies: Conceptual Issues and Estimates." *Comparative Economic Studies* 50, no. 1 (2008): 79–110.

Jakobson, Linda, and Neil Melvin, eds. *The New Arctic Governance.* SIPRI Research Report 25. New York: Oxford University Press, 2016a.

Jensen, Nathan M. *Nation-States and the Multinational Corporation: A Political Economy of Foreign Direct Investment.* Princeton, NJ: Princeton University Press, 2006.

Jensen, Oystein, and Svein Vigeland Rottem. "The Politics of Security and International Law in Norway's Arctic Waters." *Polar Record* 46, no. 1 (2010): 75–83. https://doi.org/10.1017/S0032247409990076.

Johnson, D. Gale. "The Declining Importance of Natural Resources: Lessons from Agricultural Land." *Resource and Energy Economics* 24, no. 1–2 (2002): 157–71.

Jokela, Juha, ed. *Arctic Security Matters.* Paris: EU Institute for Security Studies, 2015.

Jones, Bruce, and Tom Parfitt. "Russia Reasserts Ownership over the North Pole." *Business Insider*, September 28, 2012.

Käpylä, Juha, and Harri Mikkola. *Continental Shelf Claims in the Arctic: Will Legal Procedure Survive the Growing Uncertainty?* Helsinki: Finnish Institute of International Affairs, 2015. http://www.fiia.fi/en/publication/516/continental_shelf_claims_in_the_arctic/.

Karl, Terry Lynn. *The Paradox of Plenty: Oil Booms and Petro-States*. Berkeley: University of California Press, 1997.

Kaysen, Carl. "Is War Obsolete?: A Review Essay." *International Security* 14, no. 4 (1990): 42–64.

Keating, Giles, Micheal O'Sullivan, Anthony Shorrocks, James B. Davies, Rodrigo Lluberas, and Antonios Koutsoukis. *Global Wealth Report 2013*. Zurich, Switzerland: Credit Suisse, 2013.

Keil, Kathrin. "The Arctic: A New Region of Conflict? The Case of Oil and Gas." *Cooperation and Conflict* 49, no. 2 (2013): 162–90. https://doi.org/10.1177/0010836713482555.

Kelly, Mary Louise. "Russia Aims to Profit Big from Arktika, World's Largest Icebreaker Ship." *Weekend Edition Saturday*, NPR.org, June 18, 2016. http://www.npr.org/2016/06/18/482594632/russia-aims-to-profit-big-from-arktika-world-s-largest-icebreaker-ship.

Kennedy, Paul. *The Rise and Fall of the Great Powers: Economic Change and Military Power from 1500 to 2000*. New York: Random House, 1987.

Kinnard, Christophe, Christian M. Zdanowicz, David A. Fisher, Elisabeth Isaksson, Anne de Vernal, and Lonnie G. Thompson. "Reconstructed Changes in Arctic Sea Ice over the Past 1,450 Years." *Nature* 479, no. 7374 (2011): 509–12.

Klare, Michael. *Resource Wars: The New Landscape of Global Conflict*. New York: Henry Holt, 2001.

Klare, Michael. *Rising Powers, Shrinking Planet: The New Geopolitics of Energy*. London: Metropolitan Books, 2008.

Klauss, Nicole. "US Navy Lacks Ability to Operate in Arctic, Games Reveal." *Alaska Dispatch News*, September 29, 2016. https://www.adn.com/alaska-news/article/us-navy-lacks-ability-operate-arctic-games-reveal/2012/04/29/.

Knecht, Sebastian, and Kathrin Keil. "Arctic Geopolitics Revisited: Spatialising Governance in the Circumpolar North." *Polar Journal* 3, no. 1 (2013): 178–203. https://doi.org/10.1080/2154896X.2013.783276.

Konyshev, Valery, and Alexander Sergunin. "Is Russia a Revisionist Military Power in the Arctic?" *Defense & Security Analysis* 30, no. 4 (2014): 323–35. https://doi.org/10.1080/14751798.2014.948276.

Kramer, Andrew E. "Putin Needs Higher Oil Prices to Pay for Campaign Promises." *New York Times*, March 16, 2012.

Kramer, Andrew E., and Stanley Reed. "BP Will Switch Russian Partners through a Deal with Rosneft." *New York Times*, October 22, 2012.

Kramnik, Ilya. "NATO, Russia Stage Arctic War Games." April 25, 2012. https://www.atlanticcouncil.org/blogs/natosource/nato-russia-stage-arctic-war-games/.

Kraska, James, ed. *Arctic Security in an Age of Climate Change*. New York: Cambridge University Press, 2011.

Kraska, James, "The New Arctic Geography and U.S. Strategy." In *Arctic Security in an Age of Climate Change*, edited by James Kraska, 244–66. New York: Cambridge University Press, 2011.

Krasner, Stephen D. *Defending the National Interest: Raw Materials Investments and US Foreign Policy*. Princeton, NJ: Princeton University Press, 1978.

Lackenbauer, P. Whitney. "Polar Race or Polar Saga? Canada and the Circumpolar World." In *Arctic Security in an Age of Climate Change*, edited by James Kraska, 218–43. New York: Cambridge University Press, 2011.

Lackenbauer, P. Whitney, and Ryan Dean. *Canada's Northern Strategy under Prime Minister Stephen Harper: Key Speeches and Documents, 2005–15*. Calgary, Canada: Arctic Institute of North America, 2016.

Lake, David A. "Anarchy, Hierarchy, and the Variety of International Relations." *International Organization* 50, no. 1 (1996): 1–33.

Lake, David A. "Powerful Pacifists: Democratic States and War." *American Political Science Review* 86, no. 1 (1992): 24–37.

Lake, David A. "The Rise, Fall, and Future of the Russian Empire: A Theoretical Interpretation." In *The End of Empire? The Transformation of the USSR in Comparative Perspective*, edited by Karen Dawisha and Bruce Parrott, 30–62. The International Politics of Eurasia 9. Armonk, NY: M. E. Sharpe, 1997.

Lamothe, Dan. "Trump Pledges to Build Coast Guard Icebreakers, but It's Unclear How Different This Plan Is from Obama's." *Washington Post*, May 17, 2017. https://www.washingtonpost. com/news/checkpoint/wp/2017/05/17/trump-pledges-to-build-coast-guard-icebreakers-but-its-unclear-how-different-his-plan-is-than-obamas/?utm_term=.e6da0d6771ce.

Landler, Mark, and Eric Dash. "Drama Behind a \$250 Billion Banking Deal." *New York Times*, October 14, 2008. http://www.nytimes.com/2008/10/15/business/economy/15bailout. html.

Landriault, Mathieu, and Paul Minard. "Does Standing up for Sovereignty Pay Off Politically? Arctic Military Announcements and Governing Party Support in Canada from 2006 to 2014." *International Journal* 71, no. 1 (2016): 41–61.

Lane, Frederic C. *Profits from Power: Readings in Protection Rent and Violence-Controlling Enterprises.* Albany: State University of New York Press, 1979.

Lansberg-Rodríguez, Daniel. "An Oil Strike in No Man's Land." *Foreign Policy*, June 16, 2015. https://foreignpolicy.com/2015/06/16/an-oil-strike-in-no-mans-land/.

Larsen, Erling Røed. "Escaping the Resource Curse and the Dutch Disease?" *American Journal of Economics and Sociology* 65, no. 3 (2006): 605–40. http://onlinelibrary.wiley.com/doi/ 10.1111/j.1536-7150.2006.00476.x/abstract.

Laruelle, Marlene. "Resource, State Reassertion and International Recognition: Locating the Drivers of Russia's Arctic Policy." *Polar Journal* 4, no. 2 (2014): 253–70.

Lasserre, Frederic, Jerome Le Roy, and Richard Garon. "Is There an Arms Race in the Arctic?" *Journal of Military and Strategic Studies* 14, no. 3–4 (2013). http://hdl.handle.net/20.500.11794/860.

Leblanc, Pierre. "Canada Needs More Coast Guard Icebreakers." Arctic Deeply, February 17, 2017. https://www.newsdeeply.com/arctic/community/2017/02/17/canada-needs-more-coast-guard-icebreakers.

Lemke, Douglas. *Regions of War and Peace.* Cambridge: Cambridge University Press, 2002.

Liberman, Peter. *Does Conquest Pay?: The Exploitation of Occupied Industrial Societies.* Princeton, NJ: Princeton University Press, 1996.

Lind, Jennifer, and Daryl G. Press. "Markets or Mercantilism? How China Secures Its Energy Supplies." *International Security* 42, no. 4 (2018): 170–204.

Lindemann, Ole Andreas. "Norwegian Foreign Policy in the High North. International Cooperation and the Relations to Russia." *Forsvaret*, 2009. https://brage.bibsys.no/xmlui/handle/11250/ 99637.

Lindqvist, Andreas. *Danish Defence Intelligence Service: Danger of Military Clashes in the Arctic.* BBC Monitoring International Reports. London: BBC, 2011.

Lippman, Tom. "Saudi Arabian Oil and U.S. Interests." In *Crude Strategy: Rethinking the US Military Commitment to Defend Persian Gulf Oil*, edited by Charles L. Glaser and Rosemary A. Kelanic. Washington D.C: Georgetown University Press, 2016.Accessed April 19, 2017. https://www. academia.edu/26575022/Chapter_4_Saudi_Arabian_Oil_and_U.S._Interests.

Looney, Robert E., and P. C. Frederiksen. "The Evolution and Evaluation of Saudi Arabian Economic Planning." *Journal of South Asian and Middle Eastern Studies* 9, no. 2 (1985): 3–19.

Lunde Saxi, Håkon. *Norwegian and Danish Defence Policy.* Oslo: Norwegian Institute for Defence Studies, 2010.

Lupia, Arthur, Adam Seth Levine, Jesse O. Menning, and Gisela Sin. "Were Bush Tax Cut Supporters 'Simply Ignorant?' A Second Look at Conservatives and Liberals in 'Homer Gets a Tax Cut.'" *Perspectives on Politics* 5, no. 4 (December 2007): 773–84.

Macalister, Terry. "US and Russia Stir up Political Tensions over Arctic." *The Guardian*, July 6, 2011.

Mangersnes, *The Role of the National Joint Headquarters of Norway*. Carlisle, PA: US Army War College, 2012, 1.

Markowitz, Jonathan N., Benjamin A. T. Graham, Suzie Mulesky, and Christopher J. Fariss. "Productive Pacifists: The Rise of Production-Oriented States and Decline of Territorial Conquest." APSA Working Paper, 2019. https://ssrn.com/abstract=3382506.

Markowitz, Jonathan, Christopher Fariss, and R. Blake McMahon. "Producing Goods and Projecting Power: How What You Make Influences What You Take." *Journal of Conflict Resolution* 63, no. 6 (2018): 1368–1402.

Marshall, Monty G., Ted R. Gurr, and Keith Jaggers. *Polity IV Project. Political Regime Charateristics and Transitions, 1800–2015, Dataset Users' Manual*. Vienna, VA: Center for Systemic Peace, 2016.

Marshall, Steve. "Arctic Blocks 'in the Bag' for Rosneft." Upstream, February 4, 2013. https://www.upstreamonline.com/online/arctic-blocks-in-the-bag-for-rosneft/1-1-1148843.

Mattis, Jim. *Summary of the 2018 National Defense Strategy*. Washington, DC: Department of Defense, 2018.

McDonald, Patrick J. "Great Powers, Hierarchy, and Endogenous Regimes: Rethinking the Domestic Causes of Peace." *International Organization* 69, no. 3 (2015): 557–88.

McDonald, Patrick J. *The Invisible Hand of Peace: Capitalism, The War Machine, and International Relations Theory*. New York: Cambridge University Press, 2009.

Mearsheimer, John. *The Tragedy of Great Power Politics*. New York: W. W. Norton & Company, 2001.

Meierding, Emily. "The Real Reason Tensions Are Rising in the South China Sea." Vox, May 24, 2015. https://www.vox.com/2015/5/24/8646571/the-real-reason-tensions-are-rising-in-the-south-china-sea.

Menaldo, Victor. *The Institutions Curse: Natural Resources, Politics, and Development* (Cambridge: Cambridge University Press, 2016).

Merchant, Brian. "Russia Is Swarming the Arctic with Military Drones." Motherboard, September 14, 2015. https://motherboard.vice.com/en_us/article/8qxzd5/russia-is-swarming-the-arctic-with-military-drones.

Micallef, Joseph V. "Polar Politics: The Competition to Control the Arctic Heats Up." *Huffington Post* (blog), September 11, 2016. http://www.huffingtonpost.com/joseph-v-micallef/polar-politics-the-compet_b_11920192.html.

Milne, Richard. "Norway Opens up Record 93 Blocks for Arctic Oil Exploration." *Financial Times*, June 21, 2017. https://www.ft.com/content/a120d578-567e-11e7-9fed-c19e2700005f.

Milne, Richard. "Oil and the Battle for Norway's Soul." *Financial Times*, July 26, 2017. https://www.ft.com/content/c2dad93c-7192-11e7-aca6-c6bd07df1a3c.

Ministry of Foreign Affairs of Denmark. "Greenland and Denmark Present Claims Relating to the Continental Shelf to the United Nations in New York." n.d. Accessed July 5, 2019. http://um.dk/en/news/newsdisplaypage/?newsid=3a2bd941-d477-4df9-8ad7-ef6f15ae9ec8.

Ministry of Security and Service Organization. "Norway's Governments since 1945." Regjeringen. no. n.d. Accessed July 2, 2018. https://www.regjeringen.no/en/the-government/previous-governments/regjeringer-siden-1814/historiske-regjeringer/governments-since-1945/id438715/.

Missile Defense Agency. "Ground-Based Miscourse Defense (GMD) Expanded Capability, Fort Greely Alaska: Proposed Final Environmental Assessment." Department of Defense, February 2018. https://mda.mil/global/documents/pdf/GMD_ECFinalEA13Feb18.pdf.

Moe, Arild, and Elana Wilson Rowe. "Northern Offshore and Oil and Gas Resources." In *Russia and the North*, edited by Elana Wilson Rowe, 107–28. Ottawa, Canada: University of Ottawa, 2009.

Molla, Rani. "Tracking Lobbyist Spending in 2014," *Wall Street Journal* (blog), July 30, 2014. http://blogs.wsj.com/numbers/tracking-lobbyist-spending-so-far-in-2014-1625/.

Morgenthau, Hans J. *Politics among Nations: The Struggle for Power and Peace*. New York: Knopf, 1948.

Mousseau, Michael. "Comparing New Theory with Prior Beliefs: Market Civilization and the Democratic Peace." *Conflict Management and Peace Science* 22, no. 1 (2005): 63–77.

Mullen, M. G. *The National Military Strategy of the United States of America, 2011: Redefining America's Military Leadership*. Washington, DC: Joint Chiefs of Staff, 2011.

Munk School of Global Affairs. "Operation NANOOK." n.d.

Myers, Steven Lee. "Hillary Clinton Takes Seat at Arctic Council." *New York Times, Green* (blog), May 12, 2011. https://green.blogs.nytimes.com/2011/05/12/hillary-clinton-takes-seat-at-arctic-council/.

National Oceanic and Atmospheric Administration. "Arctic Nearly Free of Summer Sea Ice during First Half of 21st Century." *NOAA Research News*, April 12, 2013.

National Public Radio. "Denmark Claims Part of the Arctic, Including the North Pole." December 15, 2014. http://www.npr.org/sections/thetwo-way/2014/12/15/370980109/denmark-claims-part-of-the-arctic-including-the-north-pole.

National Research Council. *National Security Implications of Climate Change for US Naval Forces*. Washington, DC: National Academies Press, 2011.

National Research Council. "The U.S. Coast Guard Icebreaker Fleet." In *Polar Icebreaker Roles and U.S. Future Needs: A Preliminary Assessment*, 16–23. Washington, DC: National Academies Press, 2005. https://doi.org/10.17226/11525.

National Snow & Ice Data Center. "Arctic Sea Ice News Fall 2007." Accessed April 25, 2017. http://nsidc.org/arcticseaicenews/2007/10/589/.

National Snow & Ice Data Center. "Frequently Asked Questions on Arctic Sea Ice." Arctic Sea Ice News and Analysis, n.d. http://nsidc.org/arcticseaicenews/faq/.

NATOSource."Sixteen Nations Participating in Norway's Cold Response Military Exercise This Week." Atlantic Council, March 10th, 2014. https://www.atlanticcouncil.org/blogs/natosource/sixteen-nations-participating-in-norway-s-cold-response-military-exercise-this-week/.

Natural Resources Canada. "10 Key Facts on Canada's Natural Resources." October 2016. https://www.nrcan.gc.ca/sites/www.nrcan.gc.ca/files/files/pdf/10_key_facts_nrcan_2016-access_e.pdf.

Natural Resources Canada. "Additional Statistics on Energy." August 18, 2011. http://www.nrcan.gc.ca/publications/statistics-facts/1239.

Nelsen, Brent F. *The State Offshore: Petroleum, Politics, and State Intervention on the British and Norwegian Continental Shelves*. New York: Praeger, 1991.

Neuman, William. "In Guyana, a Land Dispute with Venezuela Escalates over Oil." *New York Times*, November 18, 2015. https://www.nytimes.com/2015/11/19/world/americas/in-guyana-a-land-dispute-with-venezuela-escalates-over-oil.html?ref=nyt-es&mcid=nyt-es&subid=article.

Newsday. "U.S. Is Phasing out Attack Sub Patrols under Arctic Ice Cat-and-Mouse Game with Russians Is Ending." *Baltimore Sun*, November 16, 1997. http://articles.baltimoresun.com/1997-11-16/news/1997320037_1_subs-arctic-russian.

News in English. "Fighter Jet Base Landed at Ørland." March 2, 2012. http://www.newsinenglish.no/2012/03/02/fighter-jet-base-landed-at-orland/.

New York Times. "Adding Up the Government's Total Bailout Tab." July 24, 2011. Accessed April 13, 2017. http://www.mainstreetforumnc.org/wp-content/uploads/2012/05/Adding-Up-the-Government%E2%80%99s-Total-Bailout-Tab-Interactive-Graphic-NYTimes.pdf.

Nilsen, Thomas. "'Admiral Kuznetsov' Ready for Winter Migration to the South." *Barents Observer*, September 29, 2011. http://barentsobserver.com/en/news/admiral-kuznetsov-ready-winter-migration-south.

Nilsen, Thomas. "Norway Creates New Army Unit on Border to Russia." *Independent Barents Observer*, June 17, 2016. https://thebarentsobserver.com/en/security/2016/06/norway-creates-new-army-unit-border-russia.

Nilsen, Thomas. "Norway Teams up with Germany for New Submarines." *Independent Barents Observer*, February 3, 2017. https://thebarentsobserver.com/en/security/2017/02/norway-teams-germany-new-submarines.

Nilsen, Thomas. "Strong Norwegian Reaction to Rogozin's Svalbard Tour." *Barents Observer*, April 18, 2015. http://barentsobserver.com/en/politics/2015/04/strong-norwegian-reaction-rogozins-svalbard-tour-18-04.

Nilsen, Thomas. "U.S. and Russian Bombers Test Airspace over European Arctic." Eye on the Arctic, February 27, 2019. http://www.rcinet.ca/eye-on-the-arctic/2018/09/24/russia-usa-bombers-barents-norway-sea-airspace-military-mission/.

Norberg, Johan, Fredrik Westerlund, Carolina Vendil Pallin, and Roger Roffey. "Russia's Armed Forces in 2016." In *Russian Military Capability in a Ten-Year Perspective—2016*, edited by Gudrun Persson, 23–66. Stockholm: Swedish Defence Research Agency, 2016.

Nord University, CHNL Information Office. "27 Transit Voyages during the Year 2018." June 14, 2019. http://arctic-lio.com/27-transit-voyages-during-the-year-2018/.

Norges Bank. "Returns." Accessed July 31, 2017. https://www.nbim.no/en/the-fund/return-on-the-fund/.

North, Douglass C., John Joseph Wallis, Steven B. Webb, and Barry R. Weingast. *Limited Access Orders: Rethinking the Problems of Development and Violence*. Stanford, CA: Stanford University, 2011.

Northam, Jackie. "As the Arctic Opens up, the U.S. Is Down to a Single Icebreaker." NPR.org, June 1, 2015. http://www.npr.org/sections/parallels/2015/06/01/411199853/as-the-arctic-opens-up-the-u-s-is-down-to-a-single-icebreaker.

Klinkhammer, Ruth. "Northern Exposure: Promoting Arctic Science News to the Canadian Public." *Arctic* 62, no. 1 (2009): 114–17. www.jstor.org/stable/40513277.

Norwegian Armed Forces. "På Vingene 41 Ganger (English Translation on Wings 41 Times)," n.d.

Norwegian Armed Forces. "Exercise Cold Response 2016." Updated March 4th, 2016. https://forsvaret.no/en/ForsvaretDocuments/Information%20Folder.pdf.

Norwegian Ministry of Defence. *Capable and Sustainable: Long Term Defence Plan*. Oslo: Norwegian Ministry of Defence, 2016. https://www.regjeringen.no/globalassets/departementene/fd/dokumenter/rapporter-og-regelverk/capable-and-sustainable-ltp-english-brochure.pdf.

Norwegian Ministry of Defence. *Capable Force: Strategic Concept for the Norwegian Armed Forces*. Oslo: Norwegian Ministry of Defence, 2009. Accessed August 6, 2017. https://www.regjeringen.no/globalassets/upload/FD/Dokumenter/Capable-force_strategic-concept.pdf.

Norwegian Ministry of Defence. *Norwegian Defence 2008*. Oslo: Norwegian Ministry of Defence, 2008. https://www.regjeringen.no/globalassets/upload/fd/dokumenter/fakta2008_eng.pdf.

Norwegian Ministry of Foreign Affairs. *The High North: Visions and Strategies*. Meld. St. 7 (2011-2012) Report to the Storting (White Paper). Oslo: Norwegian Ministry of Foreign Affairs, 2012.

Norwegian Ministry of Petroleum and Energy. "The Government's Revenues." May 16, 2018. http://www.norskpetroleum.no/en/economy/governments-revenues/.

Norwegian Petroleum Directorate. *Norwegian Continental Shelf* 12, no. 2 (2015). https://www.npd.no/globalassets/1-npd/publikasjoner/norsk-sokkel-en/arcive/norwegian-continental-shelf-no-2-2015.pdf.

Norwegian Petroleum Directorate. *Undiscovered Resources*. n.d.

Nour, Samia Satti Osman Mohamed. "Assessment of the Impacts of Oil: Opportunities and Challenges for Economic Development in Sudan." MERIT Working Paper. United Nations University—Maastricht Economic and Social Research Institute on Innovation and Technology, Maastricht, The Netherlands, 2011. https://econpapers.repec.org/paper/unmunumer/2011006.htm.

Nuclear Threat Initiative. "Russia Nuclear Chronology." July 2010. http://www.nti.org/media/pdfs/russia_nuclear.pdf?_=1316466791.

Obama, Barack. *National Strategy for the Arctic Region*. Washington, DC: Office of the President, May 2013.

Obama, Barack, and Leon E. Panetta. *Sustaining US Global Leadership: Priorities for 21st Century Defense*. Vol. 1. Washington DC: Department of Defense, 2012.

O'Dwyer, Gerard. "Denmark Boosts Resources for Arctic Security." *Defense News*, October 8, 2013.

Office of the Under Secretary of Defense for Policy. *Report to Congress: Department of Defense Arctic Strategy*. Washington, DC: Department of Defense, 2019. https://media.defense.gov/2019/Jun/06/2002141657/-1/-1/1/2019-DOD-ARCTIC-STRATEGY.PDF.

Oliver, Joe. *Natural Resources: Canada's Advantage, Canada's Opportunity*. Vancouver, Canada: Canaccord Genuity Corporation, 2012.

Oluoch, Fred. "South Sudan Risks Losing Oil-Rich Abyei." *The East African (Nairobi)*, February 21, 2017. https://allafrica.com/stories/201702210653.html.

Oreshenkov, Alexander. "Arctic Square of Opportunities." *Russia in Global Affairs* (December 25, 2010). http://eng.globalaffairs.ru/number/Arctic-Square-of-Opportunities-15085.

Orme, John. "The Utility of Force in a World of Scarcity." *International Security* 22, no. 3 (1997): 138–67.

O'Rourke, Ronald. *Changes in the Arctic: Background and Issues for Congress*. Washington, DC: Congressional Research Service, 2013.

O'Rourke, Ronald. *Coast Guard Polar Icebreaker Modernization: Background and Issues for Congress*. Washington, DC: Congressional Research Service, 2012.

O'Rourke, Ronald. *Coast Guard Polar Icebreaker Program: Background and Issues for Congress*. Washington, DC: Congressional Research Service, 2018.

O'Rourke, Ronald. *Coast Guard Polar Icebreaker Modernization: Background, Issues, and Options*. Washington, DC: Congressional Research Service, September 29, 2010.

Ørts Hansen, Carsten, Peter Grønsedt, Christian Lindstrøm Graversen, and Christian Hendriksen. *Arctic Shipping—Commercial Opportunities and Challenges*. Copenhagen, Denmark: CBS Maritime, 2016. Accessed July 18, 2017. https://services-webdav.cbs.dk/doc/CBS.dk/Arctic%20Shipping%20-%20Commercial%20Opportunities%20and%20Challenges.pdf.

Osthagen, Andreas. "Coastguards in Peril: A Study of Arctic Defense Collaboration." *Defense Studies* 15, no. 2 (2015): 143–60. http://dx.doi.org/10.1080/14702436.2015.1035949.

Overland, James E., and Muyin Wang. "When Will the Summer Arctic Be Nearly Sea Ice Free?" *Geophysical Research Letters* 40, no. 10 (2013): 2097–2101. https://doi.org/10.1002/grl.50316.

Owsiak, Andrew P., Paul F. Diehl, and Gary Goertz. "Border Settlement and the Movement toward and from Negative Peace." *Conflict Management and Peace Science* 34, no. 2 (2017): 176–93.

Oxenstierna, Susanne. "Russian Military Expenditure." In *Russian Military Capability in a Ten-Year Perspective—2016*, 133–50. Stockholm: Swedish Defence Research Agency, 2016.

Padrtová, Barbora. "Russian Military Build Up In the Arctic: Strategic Shift in the Balance of Power or Bellicose Rhetoric Only." *Arctic Yearbook* (2014): 1–19.

Palosaari, Teemu, and Frank Möller. "Security and Marginality: Arctic Europe and the Double Engagement." *Journal of the Nordic International Studies* 39, no. 9 (2004): 255–81.

Papp, Robert J., Jr. "Charting the Coast Guard's Course." *Proceedings* 137, no. 3 (2011): 21.

Parfitt, Tom. "Russia Unveils Its Giant New Arctic Base." *The Times*, April 18, 2017. https://www.thetimes.co.uk/article/russia-unveils-its-giant-new-arctic-base-p0qjg3jl6.

Patey, Luke. *The New Kings of Crude: China, India, and the Global Struggle for Oil in Sudan and South Sudan*. London: Hurst, 2014.

Pawlyk, Oriana. "No Additional Marines Bound for Norway as Cold-Weather Training Advances." Military.com, May 14, 2019. https://www.military.com/daily-news/2019/05/14/no-additional-marines-bound-norway-cold-weather-training-advances.html.

Pedersen, Torbjørn. "The Constrained Politics of the Svalbard Offshore Area." *Marine Policy* 32, no. 6 (2008): 913–19. https://doi.org/10.1016/j.marpol.2008.01.006.

Perry, Charles M., and Bobby Andersen. *New Strategic Dynamics in the Arctic Region*. Cambridge, MA: Institute for Foreign Policy Analysis, 2012.

Peters, Michael A. "Three Forms of the Knowledge Economy: Learning, Creativity and Openness." *British Journal of Educational Studies* 58, no. 1 (2010): 67–88.

Petersen, Nikolai. "The Arctic Challenge to Danish Foreign and Security Policy." In *Arctic Security in an Age of Climate Change*, 145–65. New York: Cambridge University Press, 2011.

Petersen, S. Torp. *THETIS Class Patrol Frigate*. Copenhagen: Royal Danish Navy, n.d. Accessed July 5, 2019. http://www.marinehist.dk/orlogsbib/THETIS-class.pdf.

Peterson, Nikolaj. "The Arctic as a New Arena for Danish Foreign Policy: The Ilulissat Initiative and Its Implication." In *Danish Foreign Policy Yearbook 2009*, 35–78. Copenhagen: Danish Institute for International Studies, 2009.

Pettersen, Trude. "Cold 'Cold Response.'" *Barents Observer*, February 24, 2010. Accessed June 13th, 2018. https://barentsobserver.com/en/sections/topics/cold-cold-response?qt-popular_content=0.

Pettersen, Trude. "New Garrison for the Norwegian Border Guards." *Barents Observer*, October 19, 2009. Accessed August 14, 2013. https://barentsobserver.com/en/topics/new-garrison-norwegian-border-guards.

Pettersen, Trude. "New Helicopters Give Better Preparedness in the Arctic." *Barents Observer*, December 11, 2012. http://barentsobserver.com/en/arctic/2012/12/new-helicopters-give-better-preparedness-arctic-11-12.

Pettersen, Trude. "Norway Establishes 'Arctic Battalion.'" *Barents Observer*, March 29, 2012a. http://barentsobserver.com/en/topics/norway-establishes-arctic-battalion.

Pettersen, Trude. "Norway Sends Warship to Svalbard." *Barents Observer*, November 15, 2012b. http://barentsobserver.com/en/security/norway-sends-warship-svalbard-15-11.

Pettersen, Trude. "Russia Re-Opens Arctic Cold War Era Air Base." *Barents Observer*, October 30, 2013. http://barentsobserver.com/en/security/2013/10/russia-re-opens-arctic-cold-war-era-air-base-30-10.

Pettersen, Trude. "Russian Military Instructors Plan to Land on Svalbard." *Barents Observer*, April 7, 2016. https://thebarentsobserver.com/en/security/2016/04/russian-military-instructors-plan-land-svalbard.

Pettersen, Trude. "Stable Russian Air Activity in the North." *Barents Observer*, December 19, 2014. http://barentsobserver.com/en/security/2014/12/stable-russian-air-activity-north-19-12.

Pettersson, Thérése, and Peter Wallensteen. "Armed Conflicts, 1946–2014." *Journal of Peace Research* 52, no. 4 (2015): 536–50.

Pezard, Stephanie, Abbie Tingstad, Kristin Van Abel, and Scott Stephenson. *Maintaining Arctic Cooperation with Russia: Planning for Regional Change in the Far North*. Santa Monica, CA: RAND Corporation, 2017. https://doi.org/10.7249/RR1731.

Pierson, Paul. *Politics in Time: History, Institutions, and Social Analysis*. Princeton, NJ: Princeton University Press, 2011.

Piketty, Thomas. *Capital in the Twenty-First Century*. Cambridge, MA: Harvard University Press, 2014.

Pincus, Rebecca. "'The US Is an Arctic Nation': Policy, Implementation and US Icebreaking Capabilities in a Changing Arctic." *Polar Journal* 3, no. 1 (2013): 149–62.

Pinker, Steven. *The Better Angels of Our Nature: Why Violence Has Declined*. New York: Viking, 2011.

Piontkovsky, Andrei. "Reading Russia: The Dying Mutant." *Journal of Democracy* 20, no. 2 (2009): 52–55. https://doi.org/10.1353/jod.0.0074.

Plouffe, Joël. *U.S. Arctic Foreign Policy in the Era of President Trump: A Preliminary Assessment*. Calgary: Canadian Global Affairs Institute, 2017.

Poast, Paul. "Beyond the 'Sinew of War': The Political Economy of Security as a Subfield." *Annual Review of Political Science* 22, no. 1 (2019): 223–39.

Polar Connection. *A Northern Vision: A Stronger North and a Better Canada*. London: Polar Research & Policy Initiative, 2007. http://polarconnection.org/northern-vision-stronger-north-better-canada-2007/.

Pollack, Kenneth M. *Arabs at War: Military Effectiveness, 1948–1991*. Studies in War, Society, and the Military. Lincoln: University of Nebraska Press, 2002.

Polus, Andrzej, and Wojciech J. Tycholiz. "The Norwegian Model of Oil Extraction and Revenues Management in Uganda." *African Studies Review* 60, no. 3 (2017): 181–201.

Posen, Barry. *Restraint: A New Foundation for U.S. Grand Strategy*. Ithaca, NY: Cornell University Press, 2014.

Posen, Barry R. "Command of the Commons: The Military Foundation of U.S. Hegemony." *International Security* 28, no. 1 (2003): 5–46.

Praprotnik, Tina. "Arctic Offshore Energy Resources: Distribution across International Boundaries and Climatic Impact." Master's thesis, Duke University, 2013. https://dukespace.lib.duke.edu/dspace/bitstream/handle/10161/6855/Praprotnik%20Master%27s%20Project.pdf?sequence=1.

Praprotnik, Tina. "Boundaries and Climatic Impact." Master's thesis, Duke University, 2013. https://dukespace.lib.duke.edu/dspace/bitstream/handle/10161/6855/Praprotnik%20Master%27s%20Project.pdf?sequence=1.

Press, Daryl G. *Calculating Credibility: How Leaders Assess Military Threats*. Ithaca, NY: Cornell University Press, 2005.

Pruyn, Jeroen F. J. "Will the Northern Sea Route Ever Be a Viable Alternative?" *Maritime Policy & Management* 43, no. 6 (2016): 661–75.

Pugliese, David. "Arctic Sovereignty at Risk: Military Warns North's Riches Open to Plunder by Foreign Lands; Threat Rises as Forces' Power Slips." *Ottawa Citizen*, December 7, 2000.

Pugliese, David. "Canadian Forces to Expand Nunavut Training Centre as Russia Plans More Bases in the Arctic." *National Post* (blog), February 23, 2016. http://nationalpost.com/news/canada/canadian-forces-to-expand-nunavut-training-centre-as-russias-plans-more-bases-in-the-arctic/wcm/bfaf4835-78c9-4927-aec5-f9c97048d2cf.

Pugliese, David. "Canada's Special Forces to Get New Vehicles for the Arctic but Army Left Out in the Cold"" *Ottawa Citizen* April 18, 2014. https://o.canada.com/news/national/canadas-special-forces-to-get-new-vehicles-for-the-arctic-but-army-left-out-in-the-cold.

Putin, Vladimir. "Meeting of the Security Council on State Policy in the Arctic." April 22, 2014. http://en.special.kremlin.ru/events/security-council/20845.

Rahbek-Clemmensen, Jon. "'Arctic-Vism' in Practice: The Challenges Facing Denmark's Political–Military Strategy in the High North." *Arctic Yearbook* 2014 (2014): 399–414.

Rahbek-Clemmensen, Jon. "Carving up the Arctic: The Continental Shelf Process between International Law and Geopolitics." *Arctic Yearbook* 2015 (2015): 327–44.

Rahbek-Clemmensen, Jon. "The Arctic Turn—How Did the High North Become a Foreign and Security Policy Priority for Denmark?" In *Greenland and the International Politics of a Changing Arctic: Postcolonial Paradiplomacy between High and Low Politics*. Abingdon, UK: Routledge, 2017.

Rasen, Bjørn. "A Rich Inheritance." Norwegian Petroleum Directorate, November 16, 2011a.

Rasen, Bjørn. "The Oil Industry Must Also Have Two Ideas in Its Head at Once." Norwegian Petroleum Directorate, November 16, 2011b. http://www.npd.no/en/Publications/Norwegian-Continental-Shelf/No2-2015/The-interview/.

Recknagel, Charles. "What Can Norway Teach Other Oil-Rich Countries?" RadioFreeEurope/RadioLiberty, November 27, 2014. Accessed July 30, 2017. https://www.rferl.org/a/what-can-norway-teach-other-oil-rich-countries/26713453.html.

Regehr, Ernie. *Ilulissat and Arctic Amity: Ten Years Later*. Arctic Security Briefing Papers. Vancouver, Canada: Simons Foundation, May 14, 2018. http://www.thesimonsfoundation.ca/sites/default/files/Ilulissat%20and%20Arctic%20Amity-Ten%20Years%20Later%20-%20Arctic%20Security%20Briefing%20Paper%2C%20May%2014%202018.pdf

Reiss, Bob. "Bolstered by Trump, Big Oil Resumes Its 40-Year Quest to Drill in an Arctic Wildlife Refuge." *Fortune*, September 15, 2017. http://fortune.com/2017/09/15/donald-trump-big-oil-alaska-arctic-wildlife-refuge/.

Reterski, Milosz. "Breaking the Ice." *Foreign Affairs*, December 11, 2014. https://www.foreignaffairs. com/articles/united-states/2014-12-11/breaking-ice.

Riddell-Dixon, Elizabeth. *Breaking the Ice: Canada, Sovereignty, and the Arctic Extended Continental Shelf*. Toronto: Dundurn, 2017.

Roberts, Kari. "Jets, Flags, and a New Cold War? Demystifying Russia's Arctic Intentions." *International Journal* 65, no. 4 (2010): 957–76.

Rodgers, W. "War over the Arctic? Global Warming Skeptics Distract Us from Security Risks." *Christian Science Monitor*, March 2, 2010.

Roeder, Philip G. *Red Sunset: The Failure of Soviet Politics*. Princeton, NJ: Princeton University Press, 1993.

Rogozin, Dmitriy. "Third Cable." May 21, 2011. http://news.bbc.co.uk/2/shared/bsp/hi/pdfs/ 12_05_11_wikicables_artic.pdf.

Rosamond, Annika Bergman. *Perspectives on Security in the Arctic Area*. DIIS Report 2011:09. Copenhagen, Denmark: Danish Institute for International Studies, 2011.

Rosecrance, Richard. *The Rise of the Trading State: Commerce and Conquest in the Modern World*. New York: Basic Books, 1986.

Ross, Michael. "The Political Economy of the Resource Curse." *World Politics* 51, no. 2 (1999): 297–332.

Ross, Michael L. "What Do We Know about Economic Diversification in Oil-Producing Countries?" Energy and Economic Growth State-of-Knowledge Paper Series 5.2. Berkeley: University of California Berkeley Center for Effective Global Action, 2017.

Ross, Michael L. "What Do We Know about Natural Resources and Civil War?" *Journal of Peace Research* 41, no. 3 (2004): 337–56.

Ross, Michael L. "What Have We Learned about the Resource Curse?" *Annual Review of Political Science* 18, no. 1 (2015): 239–59.

Rozhnov, Konstantin. "Norway and Russia 'Open up for Business' in the Barents Sea." BBC News, September 15, 2010. http://www.bbc.co.uk/news/business-11299024.

Rubin, Michael. "An Independent Kurdistan Would Be a Failed State." *Newsweek*, July 4, 2017. https://www.newsweek.com/independent-kurdistan-would-be-failed-state-631778.

Ruel, Geneviève King. "The (Arctic) Show Must Go on: Natural Resource Craze and National Identity in Arctic Politics." *International Journal* 66, no. 4 (2011): 825–33.

Russian Security Council. *National Security Strategy of the Russian Federation up to 2020*. Moscow: Russian Security Council, 2009.

Schultz, Kenneth A. "Borders, Conflict, and Trade." *Annual Review of Political Science* 18, no. 1 (2015): 125–45.

Schweller, Randall L. "Bandwagoning for Profit: Bringing the Revisionist State Back in." *International Security* 19, no. 1 (1994): 72–107.

Sea Around US Project. "Exclusive Economic Zones." Pew Charitable Trust, September 24, 2013. http://www.seaaroundus.org

Sergunin, Alexander, and Valery Konyshev. "Russia in Search of Its Arctic Strategy: Between Hard and Soft Power?" *Polar Journal* 4, no. 1 (2014): 69–87. https://doi.org/10.1080/ 2154896X.2014.913930.

Sergunin, Alexander, and Valery Konyshev. *Russia in the Arctic: Hard or Soft Power?* New York: Columbia University Press, 2015.

Sevunts, Levon. "Denmark's New Defence Agreement Renews Focus on Protecting the Baltic." Eye on the Arctic, October 16, 2017. https://www.rcinet.ca/eye-on-the-arctic/2017/10/16/ denmarks-new-defence-agreement-renews-focus-on-protecting-the-baltic/.

Sevunts, Levon. "Ottawa Commits to Complete Fleet Renewal for Canada's Coast Guard." Radio Canada International, May 22, 2019. https://www.rcinet.ca/en/2019/05/22/canadian-coast-guard-fleet-renewal-justin-trudeau/.

Sharp, Greg. "Trudeau and Canada's Arctic Priorities: More of the Same." Arctic Institute, December 6, 2016. https://www.thearcticinstitute.org/trudeau-canadas-arctic-priorities/.

Sharp, Todd L. "The Implications of Ice Melt on Arctic Security." *Defence Studies* 11, no. 2 (2011): 297–322.

Shirk, Susan L. *The Political Logic of Economic Reform in China.* Berkeley: University of California Press, 1993.

Shuster, Simon. "As Russia Stakes a Claim, the Race to Control the Arctic Heats Up." *Time*, July 8, 2011. http://www.time.com/time/world/article/0,8599,2082207,00.html.

Simonsson, Lennart, and Nick Allen. "Russia and Norway Wrestle over Barents Sea." June 14, 2006. http://www.lngplants.com/TurkistanGasNewsletterJune152006.html.

Smolchenko, Anna. "Gref Urges Diversity to Preserve Growth." *Moscow Times*, July 11, 2006.

Snyder, Jack L. *Myths of Empire: Domestic Politics and International Ambition.* Ithaca, NY: Cornell University Press, 1991.

Sokoloff, Kenneth L., and Stanley L. Engerman. "History Lessons: Institutions, Factors Endowments, and Paths of Development in the New World." *Journal of Economic Perspectives* 14, no. 3 (2000): 217–32.

Solingen, Etel. *Regional Orders at Century's Dawn: Global and Domestic Influences on Grand Strategy.* Princeton, NJ: Princeton University Press, 1998.

Solomon, Jesse. "Top 10 Companies Lobbying Washington." CNN Money, October 1, 2014. http://money.cnn.com/2014/10/01/investing/companies-lobbying-10-biggest-spenders/.

Staalesen, Atle. "Expansionist Rogozin Looks to Arctic." *Barents Observer*, April 21, 2015. https://barentsobserver.com/en/arctic/2015/04/expansionist-rogozin-looks-arctic-21-04.

Staalesen, Atle. "More than 300 Russian Paratroopers Have Been on North Pole." *Barents Observer*, January 5, 2017. https://thebarentsobserver.com/en/security/2017/01/more-300-russian-paratroopers-have-been-north-pole.

Staalesen, Atle. "Moscow Boasts Potential, but Arctic Transit Shipments between Europe–Asia Remain Poor." *Barents Observer*, March 2, 2017. https://thebarentsobserver.com/en/arctic/2017/03/moscow-boasts-potential-arctic-transit-shipments-between-europe-asia-remain-poor.

State Council Information Office. *China's Arctic Policy.* Beijing: State Council Information Office, 2018.

Statistics and Models Administration Unit. "Panama Canal Traffic: Fiscal Years 2016 through 2018, Table No. 1." Statistics and Models Administration Unit, of the Panama Canal Authority 2018. http://pancanal.com/eng/op/transit-stats/2018/Table-01.pdf.

Statistics Norway. *Population at Population Censuses in 2001 and 2011 by County and Municipality.* Oslo: Statistics Norway, 2011.

Stavrakis, Peter J. "Russia's Evolution as a Predatory State." In *Russia's Uncertain Economic Future*, edited by John Pearce Hardt, xxii, 481. Armonk, NY: M. E. Sharpe, 2003.

Stolberg, Sheryl Gay. "Bush Calls for End to Ban on Offshore Oil Drilling." *New York Times*, June 19, 2008. https://www.nytimes.com/2008/06/19/washington/19drill.html.

Stroeve, Julienne, Marika M. Holland, Walt Meier, Ted Scambos, and Mark Serreze. "Arctic Sea Ice Decline: Faster than Forecast." *Geophysical Research Letters* 34, no. 9 (2007): L09501.

Struzik, Ed. "Canada's Trudeau Is under Fire for His Record on Green Issues." *Yale Environment 360*. January 19, 2017. Accessed June 20, 2018. https://e360.yale.edu/features/canada_justin_trudeau_environmental_policy_pipelines?utm_source=folwd.com.

Suez Canal Authority. "Suez Canal Authority Navigation Statistics: Yearly Statistics." 2019. https://www.suezcanal.gov.eg/English/Navigation/Pages/NavigationStatistics.aspx.

Systemic Peace. *Polity IV Country Report 2010: Canada.* Vienna, VA: Systemic Peace, 2010. Accessed September 30, 2016. http://www.systemicpeace.org/polity/Canada2010.pdf.

Tammes, Rolf. "Arctic Security and Norway." In *Arctic Security in an Age of Climate Change*, edited by James Kraska, 47–63. New York: Cambridge University Press, 2011.

Tilly, Charles. *Coercion, Capital, and European States, AD, 990–1992.* Malden, MA: Blackwell, 1990.

The Royal House of Norway. "Cold response 2007." The Royal house of Norway, 2007. Accessed June 13th, 2018. https://www.royalcourt.no/nyhet.html?tid=31115&sek=27262.

Tooze, Adam. *The Wages of Destruction: The Making and Breaking of the Nazi Economy.* New York: Viking, 2007.

Transportation Research Board and National Research Council. *Polar Icebreakers in a Changing World: An Assessment of U.S. Needs.* Washington, DC: National Academies Press, 2006. https://doi.org/10.17226/11753.

Traynor, Ian. "Climate Change May Spark Conflict with Russia, EU Told." *The Guardian*, March 10, 2008. http://www.theguardian.com/world/2008/mar/10/eu.climatechange.

Treisman, Daniel. "'Loans for Shares' Revisited." *Post-Soviet Affairs* 26, no. 3 (2013): 207–27.

Trevithick, Joseph. "Russia Watched as American Bombers Showed Off over the Arctic." *Medium* (blog), April 3, 2015. https://medium.com/war-is-boring/russia-watched-as-american-bombers-showed-off-over-the-arctic-8302cebcc8ba.

Truman, Harry S. "Telegram, George Kennan to George Marshall [Long Telegram]." Administration File, Elsey Papers, February 22, 1946.

Tullock, Gordon. "Rent Seeking as a Zero-Sum Game." In *Toward a Theory of the Rent-Seeking Society*, edited by James M. Buchanan, Robert D. Tollison, and Gordon Tullock, 16–38. College Station: Texas A&M University Press, 1980.

United Nations. *World Population Prospects: The 2015 Revision, Key Findings and Advance Tables.* New York: United Nations, Department of Economic and Social Affairs, Population Division, 2015.

Upbin, Bruce. "Meet Frederik Paulsen, the Swedish Pharma Billionaire without Fear." *Forbes*, March 23, 2013. https://www.forbes.com/sites/bruceupbin/2013/03/23/meet-frederik-paulsen-the-swedish-pharma-billionaire-without-fear/#4cb3a5eb57eb.

US Coast Guard. *Arctic Strategic Outlook.* Washington, DC: US Coast Guard, April 2019. https://www.uscg.mil/Portals/0/Images/arctic/Arctic_Strategic_Outlook_APR_2019.pdf.

US Department of Defense. "Secretary of Defense Speech." May 3, 2010. http://archive.defense.gov/Speeches/Speech.aspx?SpeechID=1460.

US Department of Homeland Security. *The Coast Guard's Polar Icebreaker Maintenance, Upgrade, and Acquisition Program.* Washington, DC: US Department of Homeland Security, 2011.

US Energy Information Administration. "South China Sea," February 7, 2013. https://www.eia.gov/beta/international/regions-topics.php?RegionTopicID=SCS.

US Energy Information Administration. "Today in Energy: U.S. Remained World's Largest Producer of Petroleum and Natural Gas Hydrocarbons in 2014." April 7, 2015. https://www.eia.gov/todayinenergy/detail.php?id=20692.

US Geological Survey. "90 Billion Barrels of Oil and 1,670 Trillion Cubic Feet of National Gas Assessed in the Arctic." Podcast, produced by Jessica Robertson, July 23, 2008. https://archive.usgs.gov/archive/sites/www.usgs.gov/newsroom/article.asp-ID=1980.html.

US Geological Survey. "Circum-Arctic Resource Appraisal: Estimates of Undiscovered Oil and Gas North of the Arctic Circle." USGS Fact Sheet 2008-3049. 2008. Accessed July 8, 2017. https://pubs.usgs.gov/fs/2008/3049/fs2008-3049.pdf.

US Government Accountability Office. *Arctic Capabilities: DOD Addressed Many Specified Reporting Elements in Its 2011 Arctic Report but Should Take Steps to Meet Near- and Long-Term Needs.* GAO-12-180. Washington, DC: US Government Accountability Office, 2012. http://www.gao.gov/products/GAO-12-180.

US Government Accountability Office. *Coast Guard: Status of Polar Icebreaking Fleet Capability and Recapitalization Plan.* GAO-17-698R. Washington, DC: US Government Accountability Office, 2017. https://www.gao.gov/products/GAO-17-698R.

US Strategic Command. "Strategic Bombers Participate in POLAR ROAR." August 1, 2016. http://www.usafe.af.mil/News/Article-Display/Article/881697/strategic-bombers-participate-in-polar-roar/.

US Strategic Command Public Affairs. "Strategic Bomber Force Showcases Allied Interoperability During POLAR." August 3, 2016. http://www.stratcom.mil/Media/News/News-Article-

View/Article/983671/strategic-bomber-force-showcases-allied-interoperability-during-polar-roar/.

Vance, Ashlee. "Inside Russia's Creepy, Innovative Internet." Bloomberg, November 30, 2016. http://www.bloomberg.com/features/2016-hello-world-russia/.

Vershinin, Alexander. "Cold Combat: No Fighting in Arctic but Russia to Show Specialized Weapons." *Russia Beyond the Headlines*, April 19, 2017. https://www.rbth.com/defence/2017/04/19/cold-combat-no-fighting-in-arctic-but-russia-to-show-specialized-weapons_746193.

Wall Street Journal. "The Future of Arctic Shipping." October 24, 2018. http://www.wsj.com/graphics/the-future-of-arctic-shipping/.

Walt, Stephen M. *The Origins of Alliances.* Ithaca, NY: Cornell University Press, 1987.

Walt, Vivienne. "U.S. Companies Shut Out as Iraq Auctions Its Oil Fields." *Time*, December 19, 2009. http://content.time.com/time/world/article/0,8599,1948787,00.html.

Wang, Muyin, and James E. Overland. "A Sea Ice Free Summer Arctic within 30 Years?" *Geophysical Research Letters* 36, no. 7 (2009): L07502. https://doi.org/10.1029/2009GL037820.

Wang, Muyin, and James E. Overland. "A Sea Ice Free Summer Arctic within 30 Years: An Update from CMIP5 Models: SUMMER ARCTIC SEA ICE." *Geophysical Research Letters* 39, no. 18 (2012): L18501. https://doi.org/10.1029/2012GL052868.

Weber, Bob. "Stephen Harper's North Pole Bid Caught Bureaucrats by Surprise." CBC/Radio-Canada, November 9, 2014. https://www.cbc.ca/news/politics/stephen-harper-s-north-pole-bid-caught-bureaucrats-by-surprise-1.2829243.

Weigert, Hans W. "Iceland, Greenland and the United States." *Foreign Affairs* (October 1944). https://www.foreignaffairs.com/articles/iceland/1944-10-01/iceland-greenland-and-united-states.

Wezeman, Siemon T. "Military Capabilities in the Arctic." SIPRI Background Paper. Stockholm: Stockholm International Peace Research Institute, 2012.

Wezeman, Siemon T. "Military Capabilities in the Arctic: A New Cold War in the High North?" SIPRI Background Paper. Stockholm: Stockholm International Peace Research Institute, 2016. http://www.css.ethz.ch/content/dam/ethz/special-interest/gess/cis/center-for-securities-studies/resources/docs/SIPRI%20Military-capabilities-in-the-Arctic.pdf.

Wikileaks. "Canada's Conservative Government and Its Arctic Focus." January 21, 2010. https://wikileaks.org/plusd/cables/10OTTAWA29_a.html.

Wikileaks. "Norway, Russia and Georgia; Opportunity to Strengthen Ties to Norway." Public Library of US Diplomacy, September 16, 2008. https://search.wikileaks.org/plusd/cables/08OSLO513_a.html.

Wikileaks. "U.S. Force Reductions in Europe: View from Norway." September 15, 2009. https://search.wikileaks.org/plusd/cables/09OSLO564_a.html.

Wilson, Andrew. *Virtual Politics: Faking Democracy in the Post-Soviet World.* New Haven, CT: Yale University Press, 2005.

Wilson, Ernest J. III, and Adam Segal. "Trends in China's Transition toward a Knowledge Economy." *Asian Survey* 45, no. 6 (2005): 886–906.

Wohlforth, William C. "The Stability of a Unipolar World." *International Security* 24, no. 1 (1999): 5–41.

Woodward, Bob. "Greenspan: Ouster of Hussein Crucial for Oil Security." *Washington Post*, September 17, 2007. http://www.washingtonpost.com/wp-dyn/content/article/2007/09/16/AR2007091601287.html.

World Bank. "Agriculture, Value Added (% of GDP)." Accessed July 15, 2018. https://data.worldbank.org/indicator/NV.AGR.TOTL.ZS?end=2016&start=1988&view=chart.

World Bank. "Doing Business: Measuring Business Regulations. Historical Data Sets and Trends Data." n.d. Accessed July 26, 2017. http://www.doingbusiness.org/Custom-Query.

World Bank. "Employment in Agriculture (% of Total Employment)." http://data.worldbank.org/indicator/SL.AGR.EMPL.ZS?page=2.

World Bank. "Exports of Goods and Services (% of GDP)." Accessed September 16, 2016b. http://data.worldbank.org/indicator/NE.EXP.GNFS.ZS.

World Bank. "Fuel Exports (% of Merchandise Exports)." Accessed June 12, 2019. https://data.worldbank.org/indicator/TX.VAL.FUEL.ZS.UN.

World Bank. "GDP at Market Prices (constant 2010 US$)." Accessed January 11, 2017. http://data.worldbank.org/indicator/NY.GDP.MKTP.KD.

World Bank. "GDP (Current US$) | Data." 2017. https://data.worldbank.org/indicator/NY.GDP.MKTP.CD.

World Bank. "GDP per Capita (Constant 2010 US$)." Accessed January 11, 2017. http://data.worldbank.org/indicator/NY.GDP.PCAP.KD?locations=RU.

World Bank. "GDP per Capita, PPP (Current International $)." 2018. https://data.worldbank.org/indicator/NY.GDP.PCAP.PP.CD?locations=DK-NO.

World Bank. "Research and Development Expenditure (% of GDP)." n.d. http://data.worldbank.org/indicator/GB.XPD.RSDV.GD.ZS.

World Bank. "Total Natural Resources Rents (% of GDP)." World Development Indicators, June 25, 2018. https://data.worldbank.org/indicator/NY.GDP.TOTL.RT.ZS.

World Bank. "Total Natural Resources Rents (% of GDP)." World Development Indicators, June 20, 2019. https://data.worldbank.org/indicator/NY.GDP.TOTL.RT.ZS?locations=US&view=chart.

World Bank. "World Development Indicators." July 1, 2017. Accessed August 15, 2017. http://data.worldbank.org/data-catalog/world-development-indicators.

World Bank Group. *Russia Economic Report: The Long Journey to Recovery*. Washington, DC: World Bank, 2016.

World's 50 Best Restaurants Academy. "About the Academy." Accessed August 1, 2019. https://www.theworlds50best.com/the-academy/about-us.

Yaffa, Joshua. "Putin's Shadow Cabinet and the Bridge to Crimea." *New Yorker*, May 22, 2017. https://www.newyorker.com/magazine/2017/05/29/putins-shadow-cabinet-and-the-bridge-to-crimea.

Yakovlev, Andrei. *What Is Russia Trying to Defend?* BOFIT Policy Brief 2016. Helsinki: Bank of Finland, 2016.

Yergin, Daniel. *The Prize: The Epic Quest for Oil, Money, and Power*. New York: Simon & Schuster, 1992.

Yergin, Daniel. *The Quest: Energy, Security, and the Remaking of the Modern World*. New York: Penguin, 2011.

Yergin, Daniel, and Joseph Stanislaw. *The Commanding Heights: The Battle for the World Economy* (rev. and updated). New York: Simon & Schuster, 2002.

Young, Oran R. "A Peaceful Arctic." *Nature* 478, no. 7368 (2011): 180–81. https://doi.org/10.1038/478180a.

Young, Oran R. "The Future of the Arctic: Cauldron of Conflict or Zone of Peace?" *International Affairs* 87, no. 1 (2011): 185–93.

Zacher, Mark W. "The Territorial Integrity Norm: International Boundaries and the Use of Force." *International Organization* 55, no. 2 (2001): 215–50.

Zagorski, Andrei. "Russia Arctic Governance Policies." In *The New Arctic Governance*, edited by Linda Jakobson and Neil Melvin, 76–97. New York: Oxford University Press, 2016.

Zaller, John R. "Monica Lewinsky's Contribution to Political Science." *PS: Political Science and Politics* 31, no. 2 (1998): 182–9.

Zhang, Feng. "Chinese Thinking on the South China Sea and the Future of Regional Security." *Political Science Quarterly* 132, no. 3 (September 2017): 435–66. https://doi.org/10.1002/polq.12658.

Ziyadzade, Ziyad. "Drilling for Black Gold: The Demarcation for Hydrocarbon Resources in the Caspian Sea." *Chicago Journal of International Law* 16, no. 1 (2015): 312–39.

Zysk, Katarzyna. "Military Aspects of Russia's Arctic Policy: Hard Power and Natural Resources." In *Arctic Security in an Age of Climate Change*, edited by James Kraska, 85–106. New York: Cambridge University Press, 2011.

Zysk, Katarzyna. "Russian Military Power and the Arctic." *EU-Russia Centre Review*, no. 8 (2008): 80–86. http://kms2.isn.ethz.ch/serviceengine/Files/RESSpecNet/99789/ichaptersection_singledocument/F3C8FB3B-0DA9-473A-8814-19CB883B6F11/en/Pages+from+review_viii_final_13_10-9.pdf.

Zysk, Katarzyna, and David Titley. "Signals, Noise, and Swans in Today's Arctic." *SAIS Review of International Affairs* 35, no. 1 (2015): 169–81.

INDEX